NEW MORNING MERCIES

Other Crossway Books by Paul David Tripp

Awe: Why It Matters for Everything We Think, Say, and Do

Come, Let Us Adore Him: A Daily Advent Devotional

Dangerous Calling: Confronting the Unique Challenges of Pastoral Ministry

My Heart Cries Out: Gospel Meditations for Everyday Life

Parenting: 14 Gospel Principles That Can Radically Change Your Family

Redeeming Money: How God Reveals and Reorients Our Hearts

Sex in a Broken World: How Christ Redeems What Sin Distorts

A Shelter in the Time of Storm: Meditations on God and Trouble

Suffering: Gospel Hope When Life Doesn't Make Sense

What Did You Expect? Redeeming the Realities of Marriage

Whiter Than Snow: Meditations on Sin and Mercy

NEW MORNING MERCIES

A Daily Gospel Devotional

PAUL DAVID TRIPP

CROSSWAY®

WHEATON, ILLINOIS

First printing 2014

Reprinted with new cover 2019

Printed in China

All Scripture quotations are from the ESV® Bible (The Holy Bible, English Standard Version®), copyright © 2001 by Crossway. 2011 Text Edition. Used by permission. All rights reserved.

All emphases in Scripture quotations have been added by the author.

Lyrics from the following songs and hymns are cited in the devotions indicated in parentheses:

"Great Is Thy Faithfulness!" by Thomas O. Chisholm (© 1923, renewal 1951, Hope Publishing Co., Carol Stream, IL 60188). (Introduction)

"Joy to the World! The Lord Is Come," by Isaac Watts, 1719. (April 11)

"Not In Me," words and music by Eric Schumacher and David L. Ward, copyright © 2012 by ThousandTongues.org. Used with permission. (September 19)

"Come, Thou Fount of Every Blessing," by Robert Robinson, 1758. (December 6)

"Thou Didst Leave Thy Throne and Thy Kingly Crown," by Emily Elizabeth Steele Elliott, 1864. (December 21)

Hardcover: 978-1-4335-4138-4
Gift Edition: 978-1-4335-5501-5
Trutone Edition: 978-1-4335-6963-0
Christianbook Edition: 978-1-4335-6981-4
ePub ISBN: 978-1-4335-4141-4
PDF ISBN: 978-1-4335-4139-1
Mobipocket ISBN: 978-1-4335-4140-7

Library of Congress Cataloging-in-Publication Data
Tripp, Paul David, 1950-
   New morning mercies : a daily gospel devotional / Paul David Tripp.
      pages cm.
Includes index.
   ISBN 978-1-4335-4138-4 (hc)
   1. Devotional calendars. I. Title.
BV4811.T76   2014
242'.2—dc23   2014005330

Crossway is a publishing ministry of Good News Publishers.

RRDS		28	27	26	25	24	23	22	21
15	14	13	12	11	10	9	8	7	

Ben, you asked to be mentored and you became a substantial contributor. Isn't that just the way our God works?

INTRODUCTION

Each morning, I "tweet" three gospel thoughts. That is, I post three brief thoughts about the Christian faith on the social media site Twitter. My goal is to confront and comfort people with the life-rattling truths of the gospel of Jesus Christ. I want people to see that the grace of the gospel is not so much about changing the religious aspect of their lives, but about everything in life that defines, identifies, and motivates them. I am calling people to see the gospel as a window through which they are to look at everything in life.

By the Lord's grace, these tweets have been well received, and numerous people have encouraged me to use them as the basis for a devotional book, with 365 meditations on the gospel truths expressed in the tweets. The book you are holding in your hands is my response to those requests. Each day's reading opens with one of my gospel tweets, lightly edited, and then a meditation that expands on it.

It is a daunting task to sit down and write 365 devotions. My willingness to attempt such a feat wasn't rooted in my pride in my ability as an author, but in my confidence in the amazing breadth and depth of the gospel of the Lord Jesus Christ. As I began writing, I was excited to do some spiritual spelunking, that is, venturing down into the cavernous depths of the faith that I hold so dear. I did so, not so much as an expert, but as a pilgrim or an explorer. I sat down to write, not thinking that I had the gospel mastered, but that there was evidence in my life that I needed to be further mastered by the very message of grace that sits at the epicenter of everything I do in ministry.

Now, I have to be honest here—I didn't write this devotional just for you. No, I wrote it for myself as well. There is no reality, principle, observation, truth, command, encouragement, exhortation, or rebuke in this devotional that I don't desperately need myself. I'm like you; familiarity causes me not to treasure the gospel of Jesus Christ as I should. As the themes of grace get more and more familiar and common, they don't capture my attention and awe as they once did. When amazing realities of the gospel quit commanding your attention, your awe, and your worship, other things in your life will capture your attention instead. When you quit celebrating grace, you begin to forget how much you need grace, and when you forget how much you need grace, you quit seeking the rescue and strength that only grace can give. This means you begin to see yourself as more righteous, strong, and wise than you actually are, and in so doing, you set yourself up for trouble.

So this devotional is a call for you and me to remember. It's a call to remember the horrible disaster of sin. It's a call to remember Jesus, who stood in our place. It's a call to remember the righteousness that is his gift. It's call to remember the transforming power of the grace you and I couldn't have earned. It's a call to remember the destiny that is guaranteed to all of God's blood-purchased children. It's a call to remember his sovereignty and his glory. It's a call to remember that remembering is spiritual war; even for this we need grace.

The title of this devotional is not only a reference to the way the Bible talks about God's grace (Lam. 3:22–23), but also an allusion to a famous hymn that I think we should sing every day.

"Great is thy faithfulness! Great is thy faithfulness!
Morning by morning new mercies I see:
All I have needed thy hand hath provided—
Great is thy faithfulness, Lord, unto me!

One of the stunning realities of the Christian life is that in a world where everything is in some state of decay, God's mercies never grow old. They never run out. They never are ill timed. They never dry up. They never grow weak. They never get weary. They never fail to meet the need. They never disappoint. They never, ever fail, because they really are new every morning. Formfitted for the challenges, disappointments, sufferings, temptations, and struggles with sin within and without are the mercies of our Lord. Sometimes they are:

Awe-inspiring mercies
Rebuking mercies
Strengthening mercies
Hope-giving mercies
Heart-exposing mercies
Rescuing mercies
Transforming mercies
Forgiving mercies
Provision-making mercies
Uncomfortable mercies
Glory-revealing mercies
Truth-illumining mercies
Courage-giving mercies.

God's mercies don't come in one color; no, they come in every shade of every color of the rainbow of his grace. God's mercies are not the sound of one instrument; no, they sound the note of every instrument of his grace. God's mercy is general; all of his children bask in his mercy. God's mercy is specific; each child receives the mercy that is designed for his or her particular moment of need. God's mercy is predictable; it is the fountain that never stops flowing. God's mercy is unpredictable; it comes to us in surprising forms. God's mercy is a radical theology, but it is more than a theology; it is life to all who believe. God's mercy is ultimate comfort, but it is also a call to a brand-new way of living. God's mercy really does change everything forever, for all upon whom this mercy is bestowed.

So read and remember God's new morning mercies and celebrate your identity as the object of mercy that reaches beyond the ability of the heart to grasp and the words of one author to describe.

JANUARY 1

*Here's the bottom line. The Christian life, the church, our faith are
not about us, they're about him—his plan, his kingdom, his glory.*

It really is the struggle of struggles. It is counterintuitive for us all. It is the thing that makes our lives messy and our relationships conflictual. It is what sidetracks our thoughts and kidnaps our desires. It is the thing below all the other things that you could point to that argues for our need for grace. It is the one battle that one never escapes. It is the one place where ten out of ten of us need rescue. It is the fight that God wages on our behalf to help us to remember that life is simply not about us. It is about God—his plan, his kingdom, and his glory.

This is precisely why the first four words of the Bible may be its most important words: "In the beginning, God . . ." These are four thunderously important words. They really do change everything, from the way that you think about your identity, meaning, and purpose to the way that you approach even the most incidental of human duties. Everything that was created was made by God and for God. All the glories of the created world were designed to point to his glory. The universe is his, designed to function according to his purpose and plan. That includes you and me. We were not made to live independent, self-directed lives. We were not meant to exist according to our own little self-oriented plans, living for our own moments of glory. No, we were created to live for him.

Where is this Godward living meant to find expression? It is meant to be expressed not just in the religious dimension of our lives, but in every aspect of our existence. I love how Paul captures this in 1 Corinthians 10:31: "So, whether you eat or drink, or whatever you do, do all to the glory of God." When Paul thinks of the call to live for the glory of God, he doesn't first think of the big, life-changing, self-consciously spiritual moments of life. No, he thinks of something as mundane and repetitive as eating and drinking. Even the most regular, seemingly unimportant tasks of my life must be shaped and directed by a heartfelt desire for the glory of God. Now, I don't know about you, but in the busyness of life I lose sight of God's existence, let alone his glory!

Let's start the new year by admitting that there is nothing less natural for us than to live for the glory of another. This admission is the doorway not to despair, but to hope. God knew that in your sin you would never live this way, so he sent his Son to live the life you couldn't, to die on your behalf, and to rise again, conquering sin and death. He did this so that you would not only be forgiven for your allegiance to your own glory, but have every grace you need to live for his. When you admit your need for help, you connect yourself to the rescue he has already provided in his Son, Jesus. Reach out for hope by reaching out for the rescue again today.

For further study and encouragement: Psalm 115

JANUARY 2

Your rest is not to be found in figuring your life out, but in trusting the One who has it all figured out for your good and his glory.

We were on our way to the local mall with our two young boys when the three-year-old asked out of the blue, "Daddy, if God made everything, did he make light poles?" I had the thought that all parents have, again and again, as they deal with the endless "why" questions that little ones ask: "How do we get from where we are to where we need to be in this conversation?" Or, "Why does he have to ask me 'why' questions all the time?"

Human beings have a deep desire to know and understand. We spend much of our daily mental time trying to figure things out. We don't live by instinct. We don't leave our lives alone. We are all theologians. We are all philosophers. We are all archaeologists who dig into the mounds of our lives to try to make sense of the civilization that is our story. This God-designed mental motivation is accompanied by wonderful and mysterious analytical gifts. This drive and those gifts set us apart from the rest of creation. They are holy, created by God to draw us to him, so that we can know him and understand ourselves in light of his existence and will.

But sin makes this drive and these gifts dangerous. They tempt us to think that we can find our hearts by figuring it all out. It's the "If only I could understand this or that, then I'd be secure" way of living. But it never works. In your most brilliant moment, you will still be left with mystery in your life; sometimes even painful mystery. We all face things that appear to make little sense and don't seem to serve any good purpose. So rest is never found in the quest to understand it all. No, rest is found in trusting the One who understands it all and rules it all for his glory and our good.

Few passages capture that rest better than Psalm 62:5–7: "For God alone, O my soul, wait in silence, for my hope is from him. He only is my rock and my salvation, my fortress; I shall not be shaken. On God rests my salvation and my glory; my mighty rock, my refuge is God."

In moments when you wish you knew what you can't know, there is rest to be found. There is One who knows. He loves you and rules what you don't understand with your good in mind.

For further study and encouragement: 2 Corinthians 5:1–10

JANUARY 3

If eternity is the plan, then it makes no sense to shrink your living down to the needs and wants of this little moment.

There is no doubt about it—the Bible is a big-picture book that calls us to big-picture living. It stretches the elasticity of your mind as it calls you to think about things before the world began and thousands of years into eternity. The Bible simply does not permit you to live for the moment. It doesn't give you room to shrink your thoughts, desires, words, and actions down to whatever spontaneous thought, emotion, or need grips you at any given time. In a moment, your thoughts can seem more important than they actually are. In a moment, your emotions can seem more reliable than they really are. In a moment, your needs can seem more essential than they truly are. We are meant to live lives that are connected to beginnings and to endings. And we are meant to live this way because all that we do is meant to have connection to the God of beginnings and endings, by whom and for whom we were created.

It's hard to live with eternity in view. Life does shrink to the moment again and again. There are moments when it seems that the most important thing in life is getting through this traffic, winning this argument, or satisfying this sexual desire. There are moments when our happiness and contentment shrink to getting those new shoes or to the steak that is just ten minutes away. There are moments when who we are, who God is, and where this whole thing is going shrink into the background of the thoughts, emotions, and needs of the moment. There are moments when we get lost in the middle of God's story. We lose our minds, we lose our sense of direction, and we lose our remembrance of him.

God reminds us that this is not all there is, that we were created and re-created in Christ Jesus for eternity. He reminds us not to live for the treasures of the moment: "Do not lay up for yourselves treasures on earth, where moth and rust destroy and where thieves break in and steal, but lay up for yourselves treasures in heaven" (Matt. 6:19–20).

Think about this: if God has already granted you a place in eternity, then he has also granted you all the grace you need along the way, or you'd never get there. There is grace for our fickle and easily distracted hearts. There is rescue for our self-absorption and lack of focus. The God of eternity grants you his eternal grace so that you can live with eternity in view.

For further study and encouragement: Luke 12:13–21

JANUARY 4

The best theology will not remove mystery from your life, so rest is found in trusting the One who rules, is all, and knows no mystery.

Her voice quivered that morning as she told me to get home as quickly as I could. My wife, Luella, is a very emotionally stable woman. She isn't easily rocked. I knew what we were facing was serious because it *had* rocked her. I was about six hours away; with my assistant, I made the nervous trip home.

Nicole, our daughter, had started her walk home from work late the previous night, as she had done many nights before. A car driven by a drunk and unlicensed driver careered up on the sidewalk and crushed Nicole against a wall. She had devastating injuries, including eleven breaks of her pelvis and massive internal bleeding. When I finally got to the hospital and walked into Nicole's intensive-care room, I did what any father with a drop of parental blood in him would do. I fell apart. I crawled up on Nicole's bed, not sure if she could hear me, and said, "It's Dad, you're not alone, and God is with you, too."

When I walked into that room, it was as if the whole world went dark. My heart cried, "Why, why, why?" If I could choose, I wouldn't have any of my children go through such a thing. And if I had had to choose one of my children, I wouldn't have chosen Nicole at that moment in her life; she seemed so vulnerable. In an instant, we were cast into life-changing mystery, and our theological non-negotiables didn't take that mystery away. Nicole did recover well, but we lived through four years of travail.

I held onto the thought that our lives were not out of control. We were comforted again and again with the thought that when it came to Nicole's accident, God was neither surprised nor afraid. You see, there is no mystery with God. He is never caught off guard. He never wonders how he is going to deal with the unexpected thing. I love the words of Daniel 2:22: "He knows what is in the darkness, and light dwells with him."

God is with you in your moments of darkness because he will never leave you. But your darkness isn't dark to him. Your mysteries aren't mysterious to him. Your surprises don't surprise him. He understands all the things that confuse you the most. Not only are your mysteries not mysterious to him, but he is in complete charge of all that is mysterious to you and me.

Remember today that there is One who looks at what you see as dark and sees light. And as you remember that, remember, too, that he is the ultimate definition of everything that is wise, good, true, loving, and faithful. He holds both you and your mysteries in his gracious hands, and because he does, you can find rest even when the darkness of mystery has entered your door.

For further study and encouragement: Isaiah 40:12–31

JANUARY 5

*If you obey for a thousand years, you're no more accepted
than when you first believed; your acceptance is based
on Christ's righteousness and not yours.*

The fact is that sin is a bigger disaster than we think it is and grace is more amazing than we seem to be able to grasp that it is. No one who really understands what Scripture has to say about the comprehensive, every-aspect-of-your-personhood-altering nature of sin would ever think that anyone could muster enough motivation and strength to rise to God's standard of perfection. The thought that any fallen human being would be able to perform his or her way into acceptance with God has to be the most insane of all delusions. Yet we all tend to think that we are more righteous than we are, and when we think this, we have taken the first step to embracing the delusion that maybe we're not so bad in God's eyes after all.

This is why the reality check of Romans 3:20 is so important. Paul writes, "For by works of the law no human being will be justified in his sight." If you prayed every moment of your life, you could not pray enough prayers to earn acceptance with God. If you gave every penny of every dollar that you ever earned in every job you ever had, you could not give enough to deserve acceptance with God. If every word you ever spoke was uttered with the purest of conscientious motivations, you would never be able to speak your way into reconciliation with God. If you gave yourself to an unbroken, moment-by-moment life of ministry, you could never minister enough to achieve God's favor. Sin is too big. God's bar is too high. It is beyond the reach of every human being who has ever taken his or her first breath.

This is why God, in love, sent his Son: "God shows his love for us in that while we were still sinners, Christ died for us" (Rom. 5:8). You see, there was and is no other way. There is only one portal to acceptance with God—the righteousness of Christ. His righteousness is given over to our account; sinners are welcomed into the presence of a holy God based on the perfect obedience of another. Christ is our hope, Christ is our rest, Christ is our peace. He perfectly fulfilled God's requirement so that in our sin, weakness, and failure we would never again have to fear God's anger. This is what grace does! So as the children of grace, we obey as a service of worship, not in a desperate attempt to do what is impossible—independently earn God's favor.

For further study and encouragement: Galatians 3:1–14

JANUARY 6

Contentment celebrates grace. The contented heart is satisfied with the Giver and is therefore freed from craving the next gift.

Sin does two very significant things to us all. First, it causes us all to insert ourselves into the center of our worlds, making life all about us. In our self-focus, we are all too motivated by our wants, our needs, and our feelings, and because we are, we tend to be more aware of what we don't have than of the many wonderful blessings that we have been given. But there is more; because we are self-focused, we tend to be scorekeepers, constantly comparing our piles of stuff to the piles of others. It's a life of discontentment and envy. Envy is always selfish.

There is a second thing of equal significance that sin does to us. It causes us to look horizontally for what can only ever be found vertically. So we look to creation for life, hope, peace, rest, contentment, identity, meaning and purpose, inner peace, and motivation to continue. The problem is that nothing in creation can give you these things. Creation was never designed to satisfy your heart. Creation was made to be one big finger pointing you to the One who alone has the ability to satisfy your heart. Many people will get up today and in some way will ask creation to be their savior, that is, to give them what only God is able to give.

"Whom have I in heaven but you? And there is nothing on earth that I desire besides you. My flesh and my heart may fail, but God is the strength of my heart and my portion forever" (Ps. 73:25–26). These are the words of a man who learned the secret to contentment. When you are satisfied with the Giver, because you have found in him the life you were looking for, you are freed from the ravenous quest for satisfaction that is the discouraging existence of so many people. Yes, it is true that your heart will rest only ever when it has found its rest in him.

Here is one of the most beautiful fruits of grace—a heart that is content, more given to worship than demand and more given to the joy of gratitude than the anxiety of want. It is grace and grace alone that can make this kind of peaceful living possible for each of us. Won't you reach out today for that grace?

For further study and encouragement: 1 Timothy 6:6–10

JANUARY 7

Every day you need it. You and I simply can't live without it.
What is it? The indwelling presence of the Holy Spirit.

I don't know where I was when the memo went out. I'm not sure why I missed the discussion. I can't explain why I had this miserable gap in my understanding of the gospel. I can't tell you why this item was missing in my theological outline, but it was, and the fact that it was missing made my Christian life pretty miserable.

Here was my functional theology of my life as a child of God: I knew that by grace I had been granted God's forgiveness and I knew that I had been graced with an all-inclusive pass into eternity, but I thought that between now and then, my job was to just gut it out. It was my responsibility to identify sin, to cut it out of my life, and to give myself to living in a much better, more biblical way. I tried this, trust me; I tried it and found it didn't work. I messed up again and again. It seemed that I failed more times than I succeeded. I became more and more frustrated and discouraged. It felt as if I had been drafted into a game that I had no ability to play by someone who kept perfect score. I can remember the moment in college when it all came to a head. It was six o'clock in the morning, as I was having the devotions that I really didn't want to have, when I finally put my head down on my desk and cried, "I can't do what you're asking me to do!" Then I read the next chapter in my daily Bible reading, and by God's grace it was Romans 8.

I read that chapter over and over, including these words: "For if you live according to the flesh you will die, but if by the Spirit you put to death the deeds of the body, you will live" (v. 13). They were like fireworks going off in my head. God knew that my need as a sinner was so great that it was not enough for him to just forgive me; he had to come and live inside me or I would not be what I had been re-created to be or do what I had been reborn to do.

I need the presence and power of the Holy Spirit living inside me because sin kidnaps the desires of my heart, blinds my eyes, and weakens my knees. My problem is not just the *guilt* of sin; it's the *inability* of sin as well. So God graces his children with the convicting, sight-giving, desire-producing, and strength-affording presence of the Spirit. It can't be said any better than Paul says it at the end of his discussion of the gift of the Spirit: "He gives life to your mortal bodies" (Rom. 8:11, my paraphrase).

For further study and encouragement: Romans 8:1–17

JANUARY 8

God calls you to believe and then works with zeal to craft
you into a person who really does live by faith.

I don't know how much you've thought about this, but faith isn't natural for you and me. Doubt is natural. Fear is natural. Living on the basis of your collected experience is natural. Pushing the current catalog of personal "what-ifs" through your mind before you go to sleep or when you wake up in the morning is natural. Living based on the thinking of your brain and your physical senses is natural. Envying the life of someone else and wondering why it isn't your life is natural. Wishing that you were more sovereign over people, situations, and locations than you will ever be is natural. Manipulating your way into personal control so you can guarantee that you will get what you think you need is natural. Looking horizontally for the peace that you will only ever find vertically is natural. Anxiously wishing for change in things that you have no ability to change is natural. Giving way to despondency, discouragement, depression, or despair is natural. Numbing yourself with busyness, material things, media, food, or some other substance is natural. Lowering your standards to deal with your disappointment is natural. But faith simply isn't natural to us.

So, in grace, God grants us to believe. As Paul says in Ephesians 2:8, faith really is the gift of God. There is no more counterintuitive function to the average, sin-damaged human being than faith in God. Sure, we'll put our faith in a lot of things, but not in a God we cannot see or hear, who makes promises so grand they seem impossible to keep. God gives us the power to first believe, but he doesn't stop there. By grace he works in the situations, locations, and relationships of our everyday lives to craft, hammer, bend, and mold us into people who build life based on the radical belief that he really does exist and he really does reward those who seek him (Heb. 11:6).

Next time you face the unexpected, a moment of difficulty you really don't want to go through, remember that such a moment doesn't picture a God who has forgotten you, but one who is near to you and doing in you a very good thing. He is rescuing you from thinking that you can live the life you were meant to live while relying on the inadequate resources of your wisdom, experience, righteousness, and strength; and he is transforming you into a person who lives a life shaped by radical God-centered faith. He is the ultimate craftsman, and we are his clay. He will not take us off his wheel until his fingers have molded us into those who really do believe and do not doubt.

For further study and encouragement: Mark 6:30–52

JANUARY 9

For the believer, fear is always God-forgetful. If God is sovereign and his rule is complete, wise, righteous, and good, why would you fear?

The words of Hezekiah, king of Judah, ring as true today as they did in the scary moment centuries and centuries ago when they were first spoken. Judah had been invaded by the powerful king of Assyria, Sennacherib. Hezekiah prepared and armed Judah for battle, but that is not all he did. He addressed the people with a more significant issue. He knew that in these moments God's people were often given to fear, and he knew where that fear came from. Often in these moments of challenge the people of God would panic because they were *identity amnesiacs*. They would forget who they were as the children of God and they would forget who God is in all his almighty power and glory. So at this moment, Hezekiah knew that he couldn't just be a good king and a skilled general; he must also be a wise pastor to his people.

As they were preparing for the Assyrian onslaught, Hezekiah didn't want the people of Judah to think that they were left to their battle courage, their war experience, and their skill with weapons. He wanted them to know that they had been amazingly blessed with another ingredient, one that they could not, must not forget. So he said: "Be strong and courageous. Do not be afraid or dismayed before the king of Assyria and all the horde that is with him. . . . With him is an arm of flesh, but with us is the LORD our God, to help us and to fight our battles" (2 Chron. 32:7–8).

There will be a moment when you will ask, "Where is courage to be found to face what I am facing?" Hezekiah gives you your answer: "Look up and remember your God." As God's child, you are never left to battle on your own.

For further study and encouragement: Isaiah 51:12–16

JANUARY 10

*The DNA of joy is thankfulness. Have you noticed that entitled,
complaining people don't happen to be very joyful?*

I wish I always
carried it with me.
I wished it always
shaped the way
I look at life.
I wish it directed
my desires.
I wish it was
the natural inclination of
my heart.
I wish remembering
your boundless grace
would silence
my grumbling.
I wish
my worship of you,
my trust of you,
my rest in you
would drive away
all complaint.
If my heart is ever
going to be freed of
grumbling
and ruled by
gratitude,
I need your grace:
grace to remember,
grace to see,
grace that produces
a heart of humble joy.

For further study and encouragement: Psalm 107

JANUARY 11

*If you have been freed from needing success and acclaim to
feel good about yourself, you know grace has visited you.*

It is an intensely human endeavor. It is the quest we all pursue. We all want to feel good about ourselves. We all want to think that we are okay. It is a fearful and anxious quest from which only grace can free you.

Here's what happens to us all—we seek horizontally for the personal rest that we are to find vertically, and it never works. Looking to others for your inner sense of well-being is pointless. First, you will never be good enough, consistently enough, to get the regular praise of others that you are seeking. You're going to mess up. You're bound to disappoint. You will have a bad day. You'll lose your way. At some point, you'll say or do things that you shouldn't. Add to this the fact that the people around you aren't typically interested in taking on the burden of being your personal messiah. They don't want to live with the responsibility of having your identity in their hands. Looking to people for your inner self-worth never works.

The peace that success gives is unreliable as well. Since you are less than perfect, whatever success you are able to achieve will soon be followed by failure of some kind. Then there is the fact that the buzz of success is short-lived. It isn't long before you're searching for the next success to keep you going. That's why the reality that Jesus has become your righteousness is so precious. His grace has forever freed us from needing to prove our righteousness and our worth. So we remind ourselves every day not to search horizontally for what we've already been given vertically. "And the effect of righteousness will be peace, and the result of righteousness, quietness and trust forever" (Isa. 32:17). That righteousness is found in Christ alone.

For further study and encouragement: 2 Corinthians 6:3–10

JANUARY 12

God calls you to persevere by faith, and then,
with powerful grace, he protects and keeps you.

It is a wonderfully encouraging name for the God you serve, yet it's possible to let it pass through your eyes and into your brain without stopping to celebrate its glory. In Romans 15:5, Paul calls your Lord "the God of endurance." This title really gets at the center of where your hope is to be found. Let me state it plainly: your hope is not to be found in your willingness and ability to endure, but in God's unshakable, enduring commitment to never turn from his work of grace. Your hope is that you have been welcomed into communion with One who will endure no matter what.

Why is this so important to understand? Because your endurance will be spotty at best. There will be moments when you will forget who you are and live as a grace amnesiac. There will be times when you will get discouraged and for a while quit doing the good things God calls you to do. There will be moments, big and small, when you will willingly rebel. You may be thinking, "Not me." But think with me—when you, as a Christian, say something nasty to another person, you don't do it because you're ignorant that it is wrong, but because at that point you don't give a rip about what is wrong.

You see, perfect endurance demands just that, perfection, and since none of us is there yet, we must look outside ourselves for hope. Your hope of enduring is not to be found in your character or strength, but in your Lord's. Because he will ever be faithful, you can bank on the fact that he will give you what you need to be faithful too. Your perseverance rests on him, and he defines what endurance looks like! It is the grace of endurance granted to you by the God of endurance that provides you with everything you need to continue to be what he calls you to be and do what he calls you to do between this moment and the moment when you cross over to the other side. When difficulty exposes the weakness of your resolve and the limits of your strength, you do not have to panic, because he will endure even in those moments when you don't feel able to do so yourself.

For further study and encouragement: 1 Timothy 6:11–16

JANUARY 13

Yes, it is true—God will remain faithful even when you're not, because his faithfulness rests on who he is, not on what you're doing.

Second Timothy 2:13: "If we are faithless, he remains faithful—for he cannot deny himself." This verse pictures a radically different way of living, one not natural to most of us. Most human beings buy into a view of life characterized by the "life is on your shoulders," "you make or break your life," "pay your money and take your choice," or " you have no one to look to or blame but yourself" outlook. In this view, you are the master of your fate. You have little to rely on other than your instincts, your strength, the wisdom that you've collected over the years, your ability to anticipate what is around the corner, your character and maturity, and the natural gifts that you have been given. It is a scary "you against the world" way of living.

But your welcome into God's family turns all of this upside down. God not only forgives your sins and guarantees you a seat in eternity, but welcomes you to a radically new way of living. This new way of living is not just about submitting to God's moral code. No, it is about God covenantally committing himself to be faithful to you forever, unleashing his wisdom, power, and grace for your eternal good. Think about this. The One who created and controls the world, the One who is the ultimate definition of what is loving, true, and good, and the One who alone has the power to finally defeat sin has chosen, because of his grace, to wrap his arms of faithful love and protection around you, and he will not let you go.

You can take your life off your shoulders because God has placed it on his. This doesn't mean that it doesn't matter how you live, but that your security is not found in your faithfulness, but in his. He can be trusted even when you cannot. He will be faithful and good even when you're not. He will do what is right and best even when you don't. And he is faithful to forgive you when convicting grace reveals how unfaithful you have been.

Rather than giving you license to do whatever, this truth should give you motivation to continue. His grace calls you to invest in the one thing that will never come up short, and that one thing is the faithfulness of your Lord.

For further study and encouragement: 1 Corinthians 1:4–9

JANUARY 14

Don't be discouraged today. You can leave your "what-ifs" and
"if-onlys" in the hands of the One who loves you and rules all things.

Even though you're a person of faith who has acquired some degree of biblical literacy and theological knowledge, there's one thing you can be sure of—God will confuse you. Your theology will give you only a limited ability to exegete your experiences. The commands, principles, and case studies of Scripture will take you only so far in your quest to figure out your life. There will be moments when you simply don't understand what is going on. In fact, you will face moments when what the God who has declared himself to be good brings into your life won't seem good. It may even seem bad, very bad.

Now, if your faith is based on your ability to fully understand your past, present, and future, then your moments of confusion will become moments of weakening faith. But the reality is that you are not left with only two options—understand everything and rest in peace or understand little and be tormented by anxiety. There is a third way. It really is the way of true biblical faith. The Bible tells you that real peace is found in resting in the wisdom of the One who holds all of your "what-ifs" and "if-onlys" in his loving hands. Isaiah captures this well with these comforting words: "You keep him in perfect peace whose mind is stayed on you, because he trusts in you" (Isa. 26:3).

Real, sturdy, lasting peace, peace that doesn't rise and fall with circumstances, isn't to be found in picking apart your life until you have understood all of the components. You will never understand it all because God, for your good and his glory, keeps some of it shrouded in mystery. So peace is found only in trust, trust of the One who is in careful control of all the things that tend to rob you of your peace. He knows, he understands, he is in control of what appears to be chaos, he is never surprised, he is never confused, he never worries or loses a night's sleep, he never walks off the job to take a rest, he never gets so busy with one thing that he neglects another, and he never plays favorites.

You need to remind yourself again and again of his wise and loving control, not because that will immediately make your life make sense, but because it will give you rest and peace in those moments that all of us face at one time or another—when life doesn't seem to make any sense.

For further study and encouragement: Luke 12:22–34

JANUARY 15

Unlike human love, which is often fickle and temporary,
God's love never fails, no matter what.

I love Psalm 136. I love all of the psalms, but Psalm 136 blows me away every time I read it. I love the repetition that makes this psalm stand out from all the others. I love the fact that Psalm 136 is a history psalm that, because of its refrain, gets turned into a love poem. I love that it affirms again and again what we desperately need to hear again and again—not once or twice, but twenty-six times! Now, I think that whenever God speaks, you and I should humbly shut up and listen, but I also think that we should pay careful attention to those places where God chooses to repeat himself, and even more so when he repeats himself so many times!

Why does God repeat, over and over through the pen of the psalmist, "for his steadfast love endures forever"? There are two answers to this question.

First, there is no reality more radical and foundational to a biblical worldview and a personal sense of identity than this. What is the biblical story? It's the story of a God of love invading the world in the person of his Son of love to establish his kingdom of love by a radical sacrifice of love, to forgive us in love and draw us into his family of love, and to send us out as ambassadors of the very same love. The entire hope of fallen humanity rests on this one thing—that there is a Savior who is eternally steadfast in redeeming, forgiving, reconciling, transforming, and delivering love. Without this, the Bible is a book of interesting stories and helpful principles, but it is devoid of any power to fix what sin has broken.

The second reason God repeats this refrain is that we have no experience in our lives of this kind of love. You always begin to understand anything that is new to you from the vantage point of your own experience. All the human love we've experienced has been flawed in some way. But not God's; his love is perfect and perfectly steadfast forever. It is the single most stunning reality in the life of a believer. God has placed his love on us and he will never again remove it. There's a reason to continue, no matter how hard life seems and how weak you feel.

For further study and encouragement: Psalm 118

JANUARY 16

*There's not a day without sin rearing its ugly head and not
a day in which God's abundant mercies are not new.*

They really are the two foundation stones of a God-honoring life. They must be held together; neither side can be forsaken. Every day you and I give empirical evidence to the existence of both. Here are these foundation-stone realities: you still have sin living inside you and God is abundant in mercy. You and I must stand on both these stones. Letting go of either casts us into danger. Because I am a sinner, I need mercy, and because God is merciful, I can face the reality of my sin.

The words in Nehemiah 9 describe us all: "They . . . did not obey your commandments, but sinned against your rules" (v. 29). Maybe it's a thoughtless word, a selfish act, a prideful thought, a moment of envy, a flash of lust, a willing act of disobedience, an attitude of vengeance, or a minor moment of thievery; maybe it's wanting your glory more than God's, failing to give grace where grace is needed, bending the truth, giving in to an addiction, or working to make these kinds of things in your life look not as bad as they actually are. In some way, we all give daily proof to the truth that sin still lives inside us. None of us is yet sin-free. We all continue to fail in word, thought, desire, and action. It is humbling but important to admit, because it's only when you admit how deep and comprehensive your problem is that you get excited about the rescue that only God's mercy can supply.

We aren't just left in our sins. Nehemiah 9 continues, "Nevertheless, in your great mercies you did not make an end of them or forsake them, for you are a gracious and merciful God" (v. 31). You can be courageous in admitting your sin precisely because God is richly abundant in his mercy. He comes to you in mercy not because you are good but because you are a sinner, and he knows that because of this condition, you are unable to help yourself. Since sin means that you are a bigger danger to you than anything else in your life and since it is impossible for you to run from you, there is only one hope for you. It is that someone with power, wisdom, and mercy will invade your life, forgive your sins, and progressively deliver you from the hold that sin has had on you. That mercy comes to you in a person, the Lord Jesus Christ, and his mercy is always fresh, uniquely fashioned for the sin struggles of this new day.

For further study and encouragement: Ephesians 2:1–10

JANUARY 17

To think today, when your life doesn't work as planned, that it's out of control is to forget that Jesus reigns for your sake and his glory.

What are you facing today that you wouldn't be facing if you were in control? What are you required to deal with that you really wish you could avoid? Where have your plans dripped like sand through your fingers? Where would you like to take back choices and redo decisions? Where do you tend to look over the fence and wish you had someone else's life? Where do you feel troubled, inadequate, weak, defeated, overwhelmed, alienated, or alone? Where do thoughts of the past tend to flood you with regret, or visions of the future make you a bit afraid? What causes you to wish life was easier or at least a bit more predictable? If you could change a couple of things in your life right now, what would they be? Where does it feel to you as if you're on an amusement park ride that you never intended to be on?

If you're not in one of the moments I've described above, you will be someday, and you are near to someone who is. Life in this fallen world is often very hard. This world and everything in it are not functioning the way God intended. The brokenness of this fallen world will enter your door and somehow alter the trajectory of your life. In those moments, it is tempting to conclude that life is all about surviving the chaos. You feel that you don't have much power, you have been confronted with the fact that there's not much that you control, and you have no idea of what might be lurking around the corner. It all seems impossible and scary.

But this is not where God's Word leaves us. Yes, it does confront us with our smallness, weakness, and lack of control, but it doesn't leave us there. The Bible declares something to us that is the opposite of the way we tend to think. It tells us that the difficulties that we face every day, the seeming chaos that regularly greets us, are not the result of the world being out of control, but the result of the reign of One who is in complete control. Paul says in Ephesians 1:22, "And he [God] put all things under his [Christ's] feet and gave him as head over all things to the church" (the explanations in brackets are mine).

So no matter how it looks to you at street level, your world is not out of control; no, it is under careful rule. As radical as that thought is, it's not radical enough, because it does not do justice to all that Paul says. Paul wants you to know something else. That rule has you in view! Right now, Jesus rules over all things for the sake of his children. This is where peace is to be found.

For further study and encouragement: Acts 17:22–28

JANUARY 18

If you're God's child, you will never again have just you to depend on. No, you've been blessed, right here, right now, with grace.

It's a bigger problem than I think most of us think it is. It's something I have encountered again and again as I have traveled around the world. It's in the lives of singles and the married, the old and the young, men and women, and leaders and followers. It is one of those subtle omissions, the results of which are anything but subtle in the lives of so many. It has the power to leave you feeling frustrated and unable or overwhelmed and discouraged. It causes you to miss the answers that are right in front of your face and to look for answers where they aren't to be found. It has the power to put your Bible on the lower shelves of your life rather than on the top shelf, where it needs to be. It turns you into a passive and somewhat cynical waiter, just hanging around until the good stuff finally happens. It changes the way you think about yourself and the way you make decisions. I'm not sure how we got here, but I am sure that it is terribly important that we find our way out.

What's the problem that I'm fretting about? It's the fact that so many of us have a huge dark hole in the middle of our gospel. Sure, we have a pretty good understanding of the gospel past, the forgiveness that we have received through the sacrifice of Jesus, and a fairly clear understanding of salvation future, the eternity that we will spend with Jesus, but have we really understood well the benefits of the work of Christ in the here and now? The Bible powerfully declares that Jesus didn't just die for your past or your future, but for all the things that you face right here, right now. We need to study, examine, teach, preach, counsel, and encourage one another with the *nowism* of the gospel of Jesus Christ. Listen to the present tense gospel in the words of Galatians 2:20: "I have been crucified with Christ [a statement of historical redemptive fact]. It is no longer I who live, but Christ who lives in me [a statement of present redemptive reality]. And the life I now live in the flesh I live by faith in the Son of God, who loved me and gave himself for me [living in light of the gospel right here, right now]."

What does the gospel say you have been given right here, right now, so that you can be what you've been called to be and do what you've been called to do? The answer is Christ! He is in you. He is with you. He is for you. In him, you really do have everything you need. You simply have not been left to yourself.

For further study and encouragement: Hebrews 12:7–17

JANUARY 19

If you look into the mirror of God's Word and see someone in need of grace, why would you be impatient with others who share that need?

Maybe one of the biggest sins in our relationships with one another is the sin of forgetting. I wish I could say that this is not my problem, but it is. It is so easy to forget how profound your need of grace is, and it is equally easy to forget the amazing grace that has been freely showered upon you. And when you forget the grace that you've been given, it becomes very easy to respond to the people around you with nongrace.

It is very clear that grace toward others isn't best born out of duty. Pretend with me that I plop down on the couch next to my dear wife, Luella, and say these words: "You know, Luella, I have come to the realization that it's my duty to be gracious to you. So I'll tell you what I'm going to do. I'm going to give you grace, not because I really want to, but because I guess it's what I have to do." Do you think that Luella would be encouraged by that statement for a moment? I think not. A joyful life of grace toward others grows best in the soil of gratitude. When I really reflect on who I am, when I take time to consider the grace that I couldn't have earned, achieved, or deserved but which has been lavished on me, and when I remember that that grace came at the cost of the life of another, then I am joyfully motivated to give that grace to others.

For the believer, harsh, critical, impatient, and irritated responses to others are always connected to forgetting or denying who we are and what we have been given in Jesus. It is very clear that no one gives grace better than a person who is deeply convinced of his own need of it and who is cogently aware of the grace he has been, and is being, given.

Because we forget so quickly, because we fall into believing that we are deserving, and because we tend to think that we're more righteous and capable than we actually are, we all need to be given grace right at the very moment when we are called to be a tool of grace in the life of another. The God of grace is working his grace into everyone in the room. First John 4:19 really is true: "We love because he first loved us." Now, that's worth remembering.

For further study and encouragement: Ephesians 3:14–21

JANUARY 20

Where is hope to be found? In five life-altering words:
"I am with you always."

You and I are on a constant quest for hope. We all want a reason to get up in the morning and motivation to continue. Here are some things you have to know about hope:

1. *God hardwired human beings for hope.* We don't live by instinct; we all find our identity, meaning, purpose, and inner sense of well-being in something.
2. *What you place your hope in will set the direction of your life.* Whether you know it or not, your life path is directed by hope. Whether it's hope in a philosophy, a person, a dream, a location, or whatever, your life will be shaped by what you place your hope in.
3. *Hope always includes an* expectation *and an* object. I am hoping for something and hoping that someone or something will deliver it.
4. *Hope, to be hope, has to fix what is broken.* Hope that does not address your needs isn't very hopeful. You place your hope in your mechanic only if he has the ability to fix what's broken on your car.
5. *You always preach to yourself a gospel of some kind of hope.* You're always reaching for hope and preaching to yourself the validity of what you reach for.

But here is the radical truth of the gospel. Hope is not a situation. Hope is not a location. Hope is not a possession. Hope is not an experience. Hope is more than an insight or a truism. Hope is a person, and his name is Jesus! He comes to you and makes a commitment of hope: "And behold, I am with you always, to the end of the age" (Matt. 28:20). Now, there's hope. You have something profoundly deeper to hold on to than the hope that people will be nice to you, that your job will work out, that you will make good choices when tempted, that you'll be smart enough to make good decisions, that you'll be able to avoid poverty or sickness, or that you'll have a good place to live and enough to eat. No, this is eternal and deeply personal hope. It rests in the truth that Jesus has wrapped his powerful arms around you and he will never, ever let you go. If nothing you envisioned ever works out and all the bad things that you've dreaded come your way, you still have hope, because he is with you in power and grace.

For further study and encouragement: Haggai 1:12–15

JANUARY 21

When we ask the present to give us what only eternity can give,
we end up driven, frustrated, discouraged, and ultimately hopeless.

It's a case of modern evangelical schizophrenia. It causes us so much confusion, frustration, and discouragement. It leaves us with unrealistic expectations, naïveté toward temptation, and regular disappointment. It leads us to ask far too much from the people around us and to expect more than we should from the situations and locations in our lives. It makes us search over and over again for what we will not find and spend endless hours wondering why we haven't found it. It even results in some of us beginning to doubt the goodness of God.

"What is this schizophrenia?" you ask. It is the fact that we declare that we believe in forever, yet we live as if this is all there is. This functional contradiction between our belief system and our daily living cannot work. Here's why.

First, you cannot make any sense out of the Christian life without eternity. This is the whole argument of 1 Corinthians 15. If the One you've given your life to doesn't ultimately fix all that sin has broken, so that you can live with him forever without its effects, what is your faith worth?

Second, you and I have been hardwired for eternity. Ecclesiastes 3:11 declares that God has placed eternity in every person's heart. That means everyone hungers for paradise. No one is satisfied with things the way they are. So either you try your hardest to turn your life right here, right now into the paradise it will never be and therefore become driven and disappointed, or you live in this broken world with the rest and peace that comes from knowing that a guaranteed place in paradise is in your future. You're sad that things are as broken as they are, so you work to be an agent of change in God's gracious and powerful hands, but you're not anxious or driven. You know that this world is not stuck and that it hasn't been abandoned by God. You know that God is working his eternal plan. He is moving things toward their final conclusion. You can't see it every day, but you know it's true. In the middle of your sadness there is celebration, because you've read the final chapter and you know how God's grand story is going to end.

So you get up every morning and give yourself to doing the things that God says are good, because you know that if grace has put eternity in your future there's nothing that you could ever do in God's name that is in vain.

For further study and encouragement: 1 Corinthians 15:12–34

JANUARY 22

*You and I don't need to be rescued only from the idols around
us. No, we need to be rescued from our idolatrous hearts.*

I was in Northern India, in one of the high, holy cities of Hinduism. It was my first
time ministering there, so I was on a four-day introduction tour of Hinduism. We
had entered a temple that held the most horrific idol I had ever seen. I had no idea
that things like this existed. It was a huge, maybe 20-foot-high, image of a male
sexual organ. The Hindu pilgrims around me seemed emotional as they entered
the temple. They seemed joyous, grateful that they were there. Many of them laid
down flat on their stomachs before it. They kissed its base. It was one of the darkest
spiritual scenes I had ever seen. Through our translator, we interviewed the members
of a dirt-poor Indian family who had walked for months to get to this holy city, to
this temple of darkness. The scene was so spiritually oppressive that all I wanted to
do was get out of the building.

I found myself trying to get through the busy streets to our vehicle, and as I did
I kept saying to myself, "I thank God I'm not like these people, I thank God I'm not
like these people." Then it hit me—I am! No, my idols aren't the dark idols of formal
religion; they're the subtle idols of my everyday world. They're things that claim the
place in my heart that only God should have. And they are just as vomitous to my
Lord as that idol was to me. At that moment, I confessed to the worship war that
takes place in my heart every day. I cried out for the rescue that only the grace of
the Lord Jesus Christ could provide and I longed for the day when that war would
finally be over.

Worship is not something we do only in formal religious settings once a week.
God designed us to be worshipers. Everything we do is the product of worship. We
are always giving our hearts to something, and if it's not God, it's something God
created. All of this takes place in the little moments of our lives, and for that we
need moment-by-moment grace. That's why John counsels us in 1 John 5:21 to keep
ourselves from idols. There is no greater argument for our need for grace than the
ease with which our hearts fall under the rule of things other than God. But that
grace is yours for the taking. Won't you live in that rescuing grace today by resisting
and running from the idols that challenge God's place in your heart?

For further study and encouragement: Ezekiel 20

JANUARY 23

Hope is not a thing, not a location, not a situation, not an experience. Hope is a person, and his name is Jesus.

If you pay attention and listen carefully to what you and the people around you are saying, you will realize that we are hope obsessed. Day after day, the things we do are fueled by hope. Little third-grader Sally says to her mom as she gets ready for school, "I sure hope the girls at school like me." Mom thinks to herself that day, "I hope our marriage gets better." Teenager Tim says to his buddy, "I got a new job after school; I hope it's decent." Dad worries in the hope that he won't be one of the guys who's caught in the downsizing that his corporation is doing. From hoping that a certain meal will be good to hoping that we will have the moral strength to do the things we should do, our lives are fueled and directed by hope.

What we're all searching for is hope that won't disappoint us, that won't leave us hopeless in the end. And we all want to convince ourselves that what we have placed our hope in will deliver. What are you asking of something when you place your hope in it? You're asking it to give you peace of heart. You're asking it to give your life meaning. You're asking it to give you purpose and direction. You're asking it to give you a reason to continue. You're asking it to help you get through difficulty and disappointment. You're asking it to free you from envy or anxiety. You're asking it to give you joy in the morning and rest at night. Now, that's a lot to ask of anything. That fact confronts you with this reality—if your hope disappoints you, it's because it's the wrong hope.

Romans 5:1–5 talks about a hope that won't disappoint you even in times of suffering. Maybe you're thinking, "Where can I find that hope?" Sturdy hope that does not vanish with the constant changes in situations, locations, and relationships that make up all of our lives—hope that simply will never, ever disappoint us—can be found in only one place. It is not to be found in a certain thing. It is, in fact, a person, Jesus. Whether you have realized it or not, he is what your hoping heart has been searching for, because what you've really been searching for is life, real heart-changing, heart-satisfying life—life to the fullest, life abundant. People can love and respect you, but they can't give you life. Situations can make your life easier, but they can't give you life. Locations can bring some changes to your life, but they can't give you life. Achievements can be temporarily satisfying, but they can't give you life. True lasting hope is never found horizontally. It's only ever found vertically, at the feet of the Messiah, the One who *is* hope. Place your hopeful heart in his hands today.

For further study and encouragement: Colossians 1:15–29

*Your little kingdom of one cannot compete with the glory of the
kingdom of God, which is yours by grace and grace alone.*

One of the sweetest, most encouraging things that Jesus said to his followers is recorded in Luke 12:32: "Fear not, little flock, for it is your Father's good pleasure to
give you the kingdom." You and I are kingdom oriented. We are always in pursuit of
and in service to some kind of kingdom. We are either living in allegiance to the King
of kings, celebrating our welcome into his kingdom of glory and grace, or we are
anointing ourselves as kings and working to set up our own little kingdoms of one.

Here is what is important for us to understand. God didn't give us his grace in
order to make our little claustrophobic kingdoms of one work, but to invite us to a
much, much better kingdom. We think we know what is best for us, but we don't.
We think we are able to rule our own lives, but we aren't. We set our hearts on things
that we think will make us happy, but they won't. We think that we can defend ourselves against temptation, but by ourselves we can't. Every human being is in need
of a king. All human beings need the rescue, forgiveness, justice, mercy, refuge, and
protection that they are unable to give themselves.

The beauty of the work of Christ is not only that in his life, death, and resurrection we are offered forgiveness forever, but that with it we are welcomed into the
kingdom of the universe's most powerful and only perfect king. He blesses us with
what no human kingdom can ever give. He showers us with forgiveness, reconciliation, peace, and hope. He protects us when we don't have the sense to protect ourselves. He rules over all the moments that seem to us to be out of control. He sets
up his kingdom in our hearts, rescuing us from all the other things that would rule
us. And he patiently teaches us that we weren't created to live as kings, anxiously
working to set up our own little kingdoms. He teaches us what it means to rest in
his kingship and to live for his glory. And he encourages us with the truth that his
kingdom will never, ever end.

Are you loading kingly burdens on your shoulders today, trying to build what
you cannot build and forgetting what God has already built for you? Or are you resting in the peace that it is the good pleasure of your Lord to give you his kingdom?

For further study and encouragement: Matthew 6:19–24

JANUARY 25

Theology without love is simply very bad theology.

It was one of those amazing moments teachers are given—moments that you can't plan for and don't know you are going to have. I was teaching the one seminary course that many of the future pastors didn't want to take. It was a course about pastoral care/counseling. My class was filled with prospective pastors who thought that if they preached theologically sound and exegetically accurate sermons, no one who heard them would need counseling. Since I knew that the students in my class didn't really want to be there and weren't really hungry for what I had to offer, I began each semester by telling stories of the messes that some people had made of their lives and how they had looked to me to help them through difficulty and disaster. I would tell these stories until someone in the class would say, "Okay, we get it, we really *will* need what this class has to offer."

In the middle of one of these stories, a student raised his hand and said, "All right, *Professor* Tripp, we know we're going to have these projects in our churches; tell us what to do with them so we can get back to the work of ministry." I was both stunned by what he said and thankful for what it allowed me to say. Here was a man heading for ministry who clearly loved ideas more than he loved people! My poor student was far from the biblical norm, "[Speak] the truth in love" (Eph. 4:15). The call is to do theology in loving community with other people. Truth not spoken in love ceases to be true because it's bent and twisted by other human agendas. I cannot forsake truth for relationships, and I cannot forsake relationships for truth. They need to be held together, because we need to understand truth in community with one another to compensate for our blindness and bias, and we need truth to define for us what kind of community we should live in together.

Finally, we must understand that theology is never an end in itself, but a means to an end, the end that we would progressively become like the One who is the ultimate definition of what love is and what love does. In his grace, he provides everything we need to be a loving community and theologically pure at the same time. To forsake either is not only a failure to love, but bad theology as well. It both compromises God's truth and rejects his call. It is in a community of humble love that we are best positioned to understand all that God has said to us in his Word.

For further study and encouragement: Ephesians 4:1–16

JANUARY 26

Mercy for others will reveal your ongoing need for mercy, driving you to the end of yourself and into the arms of your merciful Savior.

It's simply not natural for us. It's natural to make sure all your needs are met. It's natural to hoard what you have in the fear that at some point you won't have enough. It's natural to carry around with you a long catalog of things you want for yourself. It's natural to be more in tune with your feelings than with the feelings of others. It's natural to want mercy for yourself but justice for others. It's natural to be very aware of the sin of others, yet blind to your own. If we are ever going to be people of mercy, we need bountiful mercy ourselves, because what stands in the way of our being a community of mercy is *us*!

It's impossible for me to think about God's call to us to be his instruments of mercy and not reflect on Jesus's powerful parable in Matthew 18:21–35. Please stop and read it right now. Christ had two reasons for telling this story. The first was to reveal the heart behind Peter's question: "All right, Lord, how many times do I have to forgive?" This question evidenced a heart that lacked mercy. Christ's second reason for telling this story was to reveal our hearts. You see, we're all the unjust servant. We celebrate God's mercy but scream at our children when they mess up. We sing of amazing grace but punish our spouses with silence when they offend us. We praise God for his love but forsake a friendship because someone has been momentarily disloyal. We are thankful that we've been forgiven but say that a person who is suffering the result of his decisions is getting what he deserves. We bask in God's grace but throw the law at others. We're simply not that good at mercy because we tend to see ourselves as more deserving than the poor and needy.

But when God's call of mercy collides with your lack of mercy, you begin to see yourself with accuracy. You begin to confess that you don't have inside you what God requires. You begin to admit to yourself and others that you cannot live up to God's standard, so you begin to cry out for the very thing that you have refused to give to others. And as you begin to remember that God's mercy is your only hope and you meditate on the grandeur of the mercy that has been showered on you, you begin to want to help others experience that same mercy. You see, to the degree that you forget the mercy you've been given, it is easier for you to not give mercy to others. I daily need God's work of mercy in order to do his work of mercy.

For further study and encouragement: Psalm 103

JANUARY 27

*God's call to obey is itself a grace. In this call,
he is actively rescuing you from you.*

We're all slaves; the question is, to whom or to what? Everyone is willing to make sacrifices; the question is, to whom or for what? We all follow sets of rules; the question is, whose and for what? We all give our hearts to something; the question is, to whom or to what? We were never hardwired to be free, if by "freedom" we mean an independent, self-sufficient life. We were created by God to be connected to something vastly bigger than ourselves. We were designed to have our lives organized and directed by an agenda that is bigger than our truncated personal desires and goals. We were carefully built by God to have every aspect of our personhood connected to him and his plans for us, and when we reject him, we don't live autonomously; we replace him with something or someone.

So God in grace doesn't set you free, because he knows you wouldn't be free. You and I would quickly enslave ourselves once again. Because sin still lives in our hearts, we're all slaves going somewhere to happen. And the sad reality is that it doesn't take much to enslave us again to a person or a thing that begins to function as our replacement messiah. So what does grace offer you? The answer is the world's most wonderful, heart-satisfying, life-changing, and hope-producing slavery. The one who is the final definition of love, wisdom, mercy, and power makes us his slaves. He who alone is able to give us life enslaves our hearts to him. His absolute rulership over every area of our lives is not a deadening law but a life-giving grace. He is freeing us from our slavery to what is not true and cannot deliver. He is rescuing us from serving what will never give us life. He is protecting us from seeking hope where hope will never be found. It really is true—his call to obey is a tool of his rescuing grace.

He really does know how short-lived our resolve tends to be. He really understands our wandering eyes and our oft-disloyal hearts. So he commands our allegiance so that we will not serve other masters. Paul says it well in Romans 6:22: "But now that you have been set free from sin and have becomes slaves of God, the fruit you get leads to sanctification and its end, eternal life." God's call to obey doesn't end your life; it is meant to protect the life that only he can give you.

For further study and encouragement: Romans 5:1–11

JANUARY 28

Prayer calls me to abandon the present as my only lens on life and commit to look at life from the perspective of reality.

What is the most needed, yet the most dangerous, prayer you could ever pray? It is the one prayer that takes you beyond the small-picture hopes and dreams that kidnap so much of your prayer. It is all right to pray about your job, marriage, family, finances, house, children, retirement, vacation, investments, church, health, government, and the weather, but it is not enough. This kind of prayer follows the "right now-me" model of prayer. It is about life right here, right now and about what I have come to think that I need right here, right now. Yes, God cares about your present life. He gives you grace for this moment. Right now he is with, for, and in you. But he calls you to view yourself and your life from a perspective that goes far beyond this moment and extends far beyond your ability to diagnose what you truly need.

The one prayer Christ calls us all to pray requires us to let go of our momentary agendas and take up his eternal one. It requires us to surrender our distorted sense of need to his perfect sense of what is best. It is the "forever-you" model of prayer. It requires you to take the long view—to let go of your hold on your life and surrender to the kingship of another. It is captured by a few dangerous words. Why "dangerous"? Because they have the power to turn your life upside down, to make you a very different you than you have been. Here is what we have been called to pray: "Your kingdom come, your will be done, right here, right now in my life as it is in heaven" (see Matt. 6:10). It is only in the context of the surrender of these words that Jesus welcomes you to pray about your right-here, right-now needs.

Here is grace. I don't have to work to be a king and I don't have to carry the burdens of a king because I have been gifted with a King. In his kingdom, I am blessed with every good thing I will ever need, and in my welcome to his kingdom, I am included in something that will never, ever end. So pray that prayer because its dangerous grace is really what you (and I) need. Don't hesitate. Do it now. Why live for what will pass away? Why give your searching heart to what can never satisfy? Why tell yourself that you know what you need, when the One who created you knows better and has promised to deliver?

For further study and encouragement: Luke 22:39–48

JANUARY 29

Today your heart will search for satisfaction. Will you look for it in the creation or in relationship to the Creator?

It was obvious what was happening, but not to him. What he was trying to do would never work. I was his gardener, and I was at the base of his property, near the entrance, when he drove in with yet another new car. I had seen him do this same thing again and again. In fact, he was quickly running out of room. As he hopped out of his expensive new toy, he asked me what I thought. I said, "I don't think its working." He said, "I don't know what you're talking about, it's a brand-new car." I said, "I think what you're trying to do will never work." He said, "I have no idea what you're trying to say to me." I asked, "How many cars is it going to take before you realize that an automobile has no capacity whatsoever to satisfy your heart?" Disappointed, he said, "Boy, you're raining on my parade." I was, and it was a big gospel moment.

The sight-sound-smell-touch-taste created world is amazing and beautiful. There seems to be an endless display of glories for us to discover around each corner. The song of a bird, the smell of a grilling steak, the grandeur of a mountain, the power of the wind, the grace of a deer, the lapping waves of the sea, the beauty of the sunset, and the tenderness of a kiss are all amazing in their own way. But there is one thing you must always remember as you take in creation's multisensory display. Creation does not have the ability to satisfy your heart. Earth simply will never be your savior. When you ask the created thing to do what it was not designed to do, you get short-term fulfillment, so you have to go back again and again. Because you have to go back again and again, rather than leaving you full and satisfied, the created world leaves you fat, addicted, and in debt.

The glories of the created world are meant to be glorious, but they are not meant to be the thing that you look to for life. No, all the glories of the created world together are meant to be one big finger that points you to the God of glory, who made each one of them and is alone able to give you life. Worshiping the creation is never a pathway to life; it leads you in the opposite direction. Today you will give your life to something. Will it be the Creator, whose grace alone can satisfy and transform your heart, or the creation, which was designed to do neither?

For further study and encouragement: Jeremiah 10

JANUARY 30

Face it, your most brilliant act of righteousness wouldn't measure up to God's standard; that's why you've been given the grace of Jesus.

The more you understand the magnitude of God's grace, the more accurate will be your view of the depth of your unrighteousness; and the more you understand the depth of your unrighteousness, the more you will appreciate the magnitude of God's gift of grace. The person who is comfortable in his own righteousness hasn't really understood grace, and the person who is unimpressed by God's grace hasn't really understood his sin. So let's talk about the essentiality of God's grace.

To talk about the essential nature of God's grace means first talking about the disaster of sin. Sin isn't primarily about acts of rebellion. Sin is, first of all, a condition of the heart that results in acts of rebellion. You and I commit sins because we are sinners. The condition of sin, into which every person who has ever lived was born, renders each of us unable to live up to God's standard. Sin leaves us without the desire, will, or ability to do perfectly what God declares is right. Whether it's a situation in which we try and fail or a moment when we rebel and don't care, the playing field is level—we all fall short of God's standard. Read Romans 3. It is a devastating analysis that shows us all to be in a dire and unalterable spiritual condition. We are all unable, we are all guilty, and there is not a thing we can do to help ourselves. None of us is good in God's eyes and none of us can satisfy his requirement. It is an inescapable, humbling, and sad reality.

But God didn't leave us in this sorry, helpless, and hopeless state. He sent his Son to do what we could not do, to die as we should have died, and to rise again, defeating sin and death. He did all this so that we could rest in a righteousness that is not our own, but a righteousness that fully satisfies God's requirement. So, unable as we are, we are not without hope. We can stand before a perfectly holy God, broken, weak, and failing, and be completely unafraid because we stand before him in the righteousness of Jesus Christ. You no longer have to hope and pray that someday you will measure up, because Jesus has measured up on your behalf. How could you hear better news than that?

For further study and encouragement: Galatians 3:15–29

JANUARY 31

If you're God's child, it's no more you against the world than it was David, by himself, against the great warrior Goliath.

I love the story of the Israelite army in the Valley of Elah as they faced the Philistine army (1 Samuel 17). On the first day of the face-off, out came that giant warrior, Goliath, and called for Israel to send out its best man to do battle with him. Remember, these Israelite soldiers were the army of the Most High God, the Lord almighty, who had promised that he would deliver these enemies into their hands. Yet what did the soldiers do in the face of Goliath's challenge? They were immediately filled with fear and withdrew to their tents to commiserate. You can imagine them saying, "What are we going to do; what are we going to do?" This was their response for forty days.

Why didn't these soldiers stand up to Goliath's challenge? Why didn't they fight in the name of the Lord? The answer is clear and unavoidable—they were an army of *identity amnesiacs.* Because they had forgotten who they were, they were filled with fear and drew a fallacious spiritual conclusion. They compared their puny selves to this massive warrior and concluded there was no path to victory.

David showed up to deliver a lunch to his brothers. He wondered why this Philistine was permitted to taunt God's army. He shockingly said that he would go; he would answer this man's challenge. Was he arrogant? Was David delusional? No, he knew who he was. He understood what it means to be a child of the living God. David drew the right spiritual conclusion. It was not little him against this huge warrior. No, it was this puny Philistine warrior against almighty God. Now, who do you think was going to win? David walked into that valley because he had his identity clear and won a victory because he knew what he had been given.

What identity will you assign to yourself today? Will you deal with life based on what you assess you bring to the table or based on who you now are as a child of the King of kings and Lord of lords—the Savior who is always with you in power and grace? Will you live in timidity and fear or in the courage of hope? Will you avoid challenges of faith in fear or move toward them, resting not in your own ability but in the presence, power, and grace of the One who rules all and has become your Father? May God give you grace to remember your identity as his child in those moments when remembering is essential.

For further study and encouragement: Ephesians 1:3–14

FEBRUARY 1

Sure, you'll face difficulty. God is prying open your fingers so you'll let go of your dreams, rest in his comforts, and take up his call.

Think about the words penned by Peter near the beginning of his New Testament letter: "Now for a little while, if necessary, you have been grieved by various trials, so that the tested genuineness of your faith—more precious than gold that perishes though it is tested by fire—may be found to result in praise and glory and honor at the revelation of Jesus Christ" (1 Pet. 1:6–7).

As he opens his letter, Peter gives us a past-present-future summary of God's redemptive plan, but his interest is really in what God is doing right here, right now between Christ's first and second comings. Of all of the words that he could use to describe what God is doing now, he selects these three: *grieved*, *trials*, and *tested*. These are three words that most of us hope would never describe our lives. None of us gets up in the morning and prays, "Lord, if you love me, you will send more suffering my way today." Rather, when we are living in the middle of difficulty, we are tempted to view it as a sign of God's unfaithfulness or inattention.

Peter, however, doesn't see moments of difficulty as objects in the way of God's plan or indications of the failure of God's plan. No, for him they are an important part of God's plan. Rather than being signs of his inattention, they are sure signs of the zeal of his redemptive love. In grace, he leads you where you didn't plan to go in order to produce in you what you couldn't achieve on your own. In these moments, he works to alter the values of your heart so that you let go of your little kingdom of one and give yourself to his kingdom of glory and grace.

God is working right now, but not so much to give us predictable, comfortable, and pleasurable lives. He isn't so much working to transform our circumstances as he is working through hard circumstances to transform you and me. Perhaps in hard moments, when we are tempted to wonder where God's grace is, it is grace that we are getting, but not grace in the form of a soft pillow or a cool drink. Rather, in those moments, we are being blessed with the heart-transforming grace of difficulty because the God who loves us knows that this is exactly the grace we need.

For further study and encouragement: James 1:2–11

FEBRUARY 2

*Today you are not alone against temptation because the One who is
your Savior is also your fortress, your hiding place, and your defense.*

The Bible calls you, as a believer, to live with three realities in view. The first greets you every day. It is the reality that you live in a world that has been dramatically broken by sin and does not function the way God intended. Paul says it very well in Romans 8, noting that the whole world is "groaning" as it waits for redemption. Because the world you live in isn't operating as per God's original design, it presents you with temptations everywhere you live. These temptations play to the sin and weakness that still lives inside you and that is being progressively eradicated by God's transforming grace. You and I must live temptation-aware; to fail to do so is to fail to recognize the fallenness of the world that happens to be the address where we live.

The second reality is that even though we are God's children, we lack the power on our own to fight the spiritual battles in which the world of sin and temptation engages us. As we face our vulnerability and weakness, there are things you and I should pray for regularly. We should pray for purity of desire, wisdom to recognize the enemy's tricks, and strength to fight the battles we can't avoid. All of this comes out of a humble recognition that wrong doesn't always look wrong to us. What God says is dangerous doesn't always seem dangerous. Evil doesn't always appear so evil in our eyes. So we need protection, not just from external temptation but from our own blind eyes and wandering hearts.

Finally, you and I are welcomed as God's children to rest in the reality that in this fallen world that throws temptation at us every day, we are never, ever alone. God is with us. He provides the safety we could never provide for ourselves. He fights on our behalf even when we don't have the sense to resist. He gives us wisdom and strength at those moments when that's exactly what we need. You and I can face the harsh realities of life in this broken world with courage and hope because we do not face them all by ourselves. Immanuel ("God with us") is indeed with us in power, glory, and grace. The words of Zephaniah 3:17 ring with as much hope today as they did generations ago when they were penned: "The LORD your God is in your midst, a mighty one who will save."

For further study and encouragement: 1 Corinthians 10:1–13

FEBRUARY 3

*God's grace not only provides you with what you need, but also
transforms you into what he in wisdom created you to be.*

What is it that you need most? No, it's not that girl or that new car that you've had
your eyes on. It's not that promotion you've worked so hard for or that vacation
you've dreamed of. No, it's not the perseverance to lose the weight you know you
need to lose or the discipline to climb your way out of debt. It's not a closer circle
of friends or a solid church to attend. It's not freedom from physical sickness or
restoration to your estranged family. It's not freedom from addiction, fear, depression, or worry. All of these things are very important in their own way, but they don't
represent your biggest need. There is one thing that every human being desperately
needs, whether he knows it or not. This needs gets to the heart of who you are and
the heart of what God designed you to be and to do.

Your biggest need (and mine) is a fully restored relationship with God. We were
created to live in worshipful community with him. Our lives were meant to be shaped
by love for him. We were hardwired to live for his glory. If you are still living in a
broken relationship to him, you are missing the primary purpose for your existence.
So God in grace made a way, through the life, death, and resurrection of his Son, for
that essential relationship to be fully restored. Through him, we are once again given
access to the Father. Through him, we are restored to God's family.

But God does even more than this. As great as is the miracle that sinners, by
grace, can be restored to God, he knows that there is something else that must be
addressed. Sin not only left us separate from God, it left us damaged too. The damage of sin extends to every aspect of our personhood. So God not only meets our
deepest need; he commits himself to the long-term process of personal heart and
life transformation. He is not satisfied that we have been restored to him; he now
works so that we will become like him. Paul says it this way: "For those whom he
foreknew he also predestined to be conformed to the image of his Son" (Rom. 8:29).

So God has welcomed you into his arms, but he's not satisfied. He will not leave
his work of redemption until every heart of every one of his children has been fully
transformed by his powerful grace. Now that we are *with* him by grace, he works by
the very same grace so that we will be *like* him.

For further study and encouragement: 2 Peter 1:3–11

FEBRUARY 4

Every day you preach to yourself some kind of gospel—a false "I can't do this" gospel or the true "I have all I need in Christ" gospel.

I find myself saying it over and over again. When I do, people often laugh, but I'm really quite serious. No one is more influential in your life than you are because no one talks to you more than you do. It's a fact that you and I are in an endless conversation with ourselves. Most of us have learned that it's best not to move our lips because people will think we're crazy, but we never stop talking to ourselves. In this inner discussion, we're always talking about God, life, others, and ourselves, and the things we say to ourselves are very important because they are formative of the things we desire, choose, say, and do. What have you been saying to you? What have you been saying to you about yourself? What have you been saying to you about God? What have you been saying to you about life, meaning and purpose, right and wrong, true and false, and good and bad?

In Psalm 42, we are invited to eavesdrop on a man's private preaching. Yes, you read it right; like us, the psalmist was always preaching some kind of gospel to himself. We either preach to ourselves a gospel of aloneness, poverty, and inability or the true gospel of God's presence, power, and constant provision. You are preaching to yourself a gospel that produces fear and timidity or one that propels you with courage and hope. You are preaching to yourself of a God who is distant, passive, and uncaring or of a God who is near, caring, and active. You are always preaching to yourself a gospel that causes you to rest in his wisdom or a gospel that produces a bit of panic because it seems as if there are no answers to be found.

Today, when it feels as if no one understands, what gospel will you preach to you? As you face physical sickness, the loss of a job, or the disloyalty of a friend, what message will you bring to you? When you are tempted to give way to despondency or fear, what will you say to you? When life seems hard and unfair, what gospel will you preach to you? When parenting or your marriage seems difficult and overwhelming, what will you share with you? When your dreams elude your grasp, what will you say to you? When you face a disease that you thought you'd never face, what gospel will you preach to you?

It really is true—no one talks to you more than you do. So God in his grace has given you his Word so that you may preach to yourself what is true in those moments when the only one talking to you is you.

For further study and encouragement: Psalm 42

FEBRUARY 5

God will not rest from his redemptive work until he has once and for all presided over the funeral of sin and death.

If someone asked you, "What is God doing right now?" what would you answer? I am afraid that many of us are confused when it comes to the present benefits and activity of Jesus. We get that we have been forgiven and we understand that we have eternity with him in our future, but we're not sure what the agenda is in the here and now. Because we don't understand what God has committed himself to in the present, we are tempted to question his wisdom and doubt his love. Our problem is not that God is inactive or that he has abandoned us, but that we are not on his agenda page. Left with confusion about his plan and carrying with us unrealistic expectations, we get disappointed and a little bit cynical, and we quit running to him for help. It is a bit of a spiritual mess.

The answer to the big question we have proposed is really quite easy and straight-forward. What is God up to right here, right now? Redemption! He is actively working on sin's final defeat and our complete deliverance. He is working out the spoils of the victory that Christ accomplished on the cross of Calvary. Listen to the encouraging words of 1 Corinthians 15:25–26: "For he must reign until he has put all his enemies under his feet. The last enemy to be destroyed is death."

Now, you and I need to understand two things in these words that answer our question. What is God doing? First, he's reigning! No, your world is not out of control. No, the bad guys are not going to win. No, sin will not have the final victory. Because your world is not out of control but under God's careful redemptive control, you can have hope even when it looks to you as if darkness is winning the day.

What is God doing? This passage gives a second answer. He is putting the enemies of his redemptive purpose under his feet. He will crush enemy after enemy until the last enemy, death, is defeated. He will not sit down, he will not rest, he will not relent until sin and death are completely defeated and we are finally and forever delivered. Hope right here, right now doesn't rest in your understanding or strength, but in the sin- and death-defeating rule of the King of kings and Lord of lords. His reign is your present protection and your future hope.

For further study and encouragement: 1 Corinthians 15:50–58

FEBRUARY 6

You don't have to be anxious about the future. A God of grace has invaded your life, and he always completes what he starts.

It's natural; we all do it. We all wonder about what is to come. Some of us think about the future and hope our dreams will come true. Some of us dread the future and pray that we will not have to face the things that we fear. For some of us, the future seems foggy and unknowable. For all of us, it's hard to look into the future and be secure, because the future is simply out of our hands. With all of our consideration, meditation, and planning for what is to come, things never turn out the way we envisioned. There are always unexpected turns in the road. There are potholes and ditches we did not anticipate. There are mountains and valleys we just did not foresee. We find ourselves walking through moments of darkness when we thought we'd be living and walking in the light. It doesn't take long for us to begin to acquiesce to the fact that we don't ever quite know what is around the next corner.

But we don't have to live plagued by the anxiety of the unknown. We don't have to go to sleep wondering what the next day will bring or wake up working our way through all the "what-ifs" we can think of. We don't have to seek some means to figure out what we will never be able to figure out. No, we can have rest when we are confused. We can experience peace in the face of the unknown. We can feel an inner well-being while living in the middle of mystery. Why? Because our peace of heart does not rest on how much we know, how much we have figured out, or how accurately we have been able to predict the future. No, our rest is in the person who holds our individual futures in his wise and gracious hands. We have peace because we know that he will complete the good things that he in grace has initiated in our lives. He is faithful, so he never leaves the work of his hands. He is gracious, so he gives us what we need, not what we deserve. He is wise, so what he does is always best. He is sovereign, so he rules all the situations and locations where we live. He is powerful, so he can do what he pleases, when he pleases.

Paul says it well in Philippians 1:6: "And I am sure of this, that he who began a good work in you will bring it to completion at the day of Jesus Christ." Are you experiencing anxiety because you've forgotten who you are and what you've been given? Are you experiencing the fear that results from trying to know what you'll never know? He knows, he cares, and he will complete the job he's begun.

For further study and encouragement: Romans 8:18–39

FEBRUARY 7

Corporate worship is designed to humble you by pointing out the depth of your need and enthrall you by pointing to the glory of God's provision.

We all do it in our own way. Seldom does a day go by without our doing it again. We even do it in the middle of worship services. But it is a dangerous thing to do. It doesn't lead us anywhere good. We don't like it when other people do it, but we fail to recognize how much we do it ourselves. We all work to convince ourselves that we are better off than we are. We all want to believe that we are not that sinful after all. We compare ourselves to those who seem more sinful than us. We rewrite our history to make ourselves look better than we really are. We evaluate ourselves by looking into mirrors other than the one truly accurate mirror, the mirror of the Word of God. We list our good deeds to ourselves. We argue to ourselves and to others that what looked like sin was not sin at all. It is all a function of the delusional self-righteousness of sin. It involves daily acts of self-atonement. It is us working to convince ourselves that we really don't need the amazing grace of a faithful, loving Savior. At street level, we all tend to back away from the radical message that we all say we believe. It is a shocking denial of sin and a minimizing of the grace that is a sinner's only hope.

God knew that this would be our tendency. He is fully aware of the self-righteousness that still lives inside all of us. God knew that we would convince ourselves that we are okay when we're not okay. So he designed a means for us to be confronted again and again with the depth of our sin and the expansive glory of his provision in the person and work of the Lamb, the Savior, the Redeemer—the Lord Jesus Christ. He ordained that we gather again and again in services of corporate worship and be confronted with our true identity as both sinners and children of grace. You see, when you understand the free gift of God's provision of grace, you aren't afraid to admit to the depth of your sin, and it is only when you have admitted the disaster of your sin that you are excited about the grace of Christ Jesus. Corporate worship really does confront us with the fact that we are worse off than we thought and that God's grace is more amazing than we ever could have imagined. We will continue to need that reminder until our sin is no more and we are with him and like him forever. Corporate worship is not a thankless duty for the religiously committed. No, it's another gift of mercy from a God of glorious grace (see Heb. 10:23–25).

For further study and encouragement: Romans 3:9–20

FEBRUARY 8

*Quit being paralyzed by your past. Grace offers you
life in the present and a guarantee of a future.*

It is a simple fact of nature that once the leaves are off the tree, you cannot put them back again. Once you have uttered words, you cannot rip them out of another's hearing. Once you have acted on a choice, you cannot relive that moment again. Once you have behaved in a certain way at a certain time, you cannot ask for a redo. You and I just don't have the option of reliving our past to try to do better any more than we have the power to glue the leaves back on the tree and make them live once again. What's done is done and cannot be redone.

But we all wish we could live certain moments and certain decisions over again. If you're at all humble and able to look back on your past with a degree of accuracy, you experience regret. None of us has always desired the right thing. None of us has always made the best decision. None of us has always been humble, kind, and loving. We haven't always jumped to serve and forgive. None of us has always spoken the truth. None of us has been free of anger, envy, or vengeance. None of us has walked through life with unblemished nobility. None of us. So all of us have reason for remorse and regret. All of us are left with the sadness of what has been done and can't be undone.

That's why all of us should daily celebrate the grace that frees us from the regret of the past. This freedom is not the freedom of retraction or denial. It's not the freedom of rewriting our history. No, it's the freedom of forgiving and transforming grace. This grace welcomes me to live with hope in the present because it frees me to leave my past behind. All of what I look back on and would like to redo has been fully covered by the blood of Jesus. I no longer need to carry the burden of the past on my shoulders, so I am free to fully give myself to what God has called me to in the here and now. "But one thing I do: forgetting what lies behind and straining forward to what lies ahead, I press on toward the goal for the prize of the upward call of God in Christ Jesus" (Phil. 3:13–14).

Are you paralyzed by your past? Are you living under the dark shroud of the "if-onlys"? Does your past influence your present more than God's past, present, and future grace? Have you received and are you living out of the forgiveness that is yours because of the life, death, and resurrection of Jesus?

For further study and encouragement: Jeremiah 29:1–14

FEBRUARY 9

*Today you will celebrate that grace has made you part of God's great
plan or mourn the places where you aren't getting your own way.*

He may have been the hardest person I ever counseled. He was self-assured and
controlling. He argued for the rightfulness of everything he had ever done. He acted
like the victim when in fact he was the victimizer. He had crushed his marriage and
alienated his children. He loved himself and had a wonderful plan for his life. It was
his will in his way at his time. He made everyone a slave to his plan or he drove them
out of his life. He made incredible sacrifices to get what he wanted but chafed against
the sacrifices God called him to make. But in a moment of grace I will never forget,
he quit fighting, controlling, and defending. He asked me to stop talking and said:
"Paul, I get it. I have been so busy being God that I have had little time or interest in
serving God." It was one of the most accurate moments of self-diagnosis I had ever
experienced. He was right. No sooner had the words come out of his mouth than he
began to weep like I had never seen a man weep. His body shook with grief as grace
began its work of freeing him from his bondage to himself.

But my friend was not unique. If you're a parent, you know that your children
are collections of self-sovereignty. All a child really wants is his own way. He doesn't
want to be told what to eat, what to wear, when to go to bed, how to steward his
possessions, or how to treat others. He wants to be in the center of his own little
world and to write his own set of rules. And he is surprised that you have the audac-
ity to tell him what to do. But it isn't just children. Sin causes this self-sovereignty
to live in all of us. We tend to want more control than we are wise enough or strong
enough to handle. We want people to follow our way and stay out of our way. But
when we wish for these things, we are forgetting who we are, who God is, and what
grace has blessed us with. We are always either mourning the fact that we aren't
getting our way or celebrating that grace welcomes us to a new and better way. We
are either frustrated that we lack control or resting in the One who is "head over all
things to the church" (Eph. 1:22). I think there is probably a mix of mourning and
celebration in all of us.

What will it be for you today? Will you give way to the frustration that you are
not getting your way or celebrate the grace that has included you in the most wonderful plan that was ever conceived?

For further study and encouragement: Psalm 73

FEBRUARY 10

There's not a day that you won't need it; there's not a situation that won't demand it. What is it? The power of Jesus.

I knew there was only one way to help him. It was the only way because he didn't want my help. He was only four years old and had already begun to deny his weaknesses. He desperately wanted to be independently strong and wise, but he wasn't. He wanted to believe that he didn't need the wise words and strong arms of a parent, but he did. He wanted to believe that he knew more than he did and had more ability than he had. So he fought my parenting care once again. Then it hit me—he needed to experience his weakness so that he would run for my care. So I walked away. No, not because I was mad at him and walking away was the best way to punish him. I walked away because I loved him and it was the best way to get him to seek and esteem that love. I knew what would happen. I knew he could not do what he was fighting so hard to do independently. I knew that at some point he would give up, admit his weakness to himself, and seek my help.

About a half hour later, I heard the pitter-patter of his little feet on the hallway floor. He peeked around the corner and said, "I can't do it." I said, "What do you want Daddy to do?" And he said words that were good for his heart to say: "I need your help."

You and I weren't created for independent living. We were created to be dependent on God. Add to this the fact that sin leaves us broken and weak. We all need strength beyond our own and power that we'll never independently possess. So God, in grace, grants us power in the person of the Holy Spirit, who lives inside each of his children. We simply are no longer left to the resources of our own strength (see Eph. 3:20–21). To remind us of who we are, what we need, and what we've been given, God will walk down the hallway and let us experience our weakness once again so that we will seek and celebrate the strength that is only ever found in him. When he does this, it is not an act of divine anger but a response of tender parental grace—the kind of grace you and I will continue to need until grace has finished its work.

For further study and encouragement: 2 Corinthians 12:1–10

FEBRUARY 11

Grace works to free you from your eternity amnesia so that you will be willing and able to live with the purifying hope of what is to come.

You and I don't always live what we say we believe. There is often a disconnect between our confessional theology and our street-level functional theology. There is often a separation between, on the one hand, the doctrines we say we have embraced and, on the other hand, the choices we make and the anxieties that we feel. One of the places where this disconnect exists for many of us is the biblical teaching about eternity. We say we believe in the hereafter. We say that this moment in time is not all there is. We say that we are hardwired for forever. But often we live with the compulsion, anxiety, and drivenness of *eternity amnesiacs*. We get so focused on the opportunities, responsibilities, needs, and desires of the here and now that we lose sight of what is to come.

The fact is that you cannot make sense out of life unless you look at it from the vantage point of eternity. If all God's grace gives us is a little better here and now, if it doesn't finally fix all that sin had broken, then perhaps we have believed in vain: "If in Christ we have hope in this life only, we are of all people most to be pitied" (1 Cor. 15:19). There has to be more to God's plan than this world of sin, sickness, sorrow, and death. There has to be more than the temporary pleasures of this physical world. Yes, there is more, and when you live like there's more to come, you live in a radically different way.

When you forget eternity, you tend to lose sight of what's important. When you lose sight of what's truly important, you live for what is temporary, and your heart seeks for satisfaction where it cannot be found. Looking for satisfaction where it cannot be found leaves you spiritually empty and potentially hopeless. Meanwhile, you are dealing with all the difficulties of this fallen world with little hope that things will ever be different. Living as an eternity amnesiac just doesn't work. It leaves you either hoping that now will be the paradise it will never be or hopeless that what is broken will ever be fixed. So it's important to fix your eyes on what God has promised will surely come. Let the values of eternity be the values that shape your living today, and keep telling yourself that the difficulties of today will someday completely pass away. Belief in eternity can clarify your values and renew your hope. Pray that God, by his grace, will help you remember forever right here, right now.

For further study and encouragement: 2 Corinthians 4:7–18

FEBRUARY 12

Faith isn't natural for us. Doubt is, fear is, and pride is, but faith in the words and works of another isn't, and for that there's grace.

God hasn't just forgiven you—praise him that he has—but he has also called you to a brand-new way of living. He has called you to live by faith. Now, here's the rub. Faith is not normal for us. Faith is frankly a counterintuitive way for us to live. Doubt is quite natural for us. Wondering what God is doing is natural. It's normal to think your life is harder than that of others. Envying the life of someone else is natural. Wishing life were easier and that you had more control is natural. It's typical for you and me to try to figure out the future. Worry is natural. Fear is natural. Wanting to give up is natural. It's natural to wonder if all of your good habits make a difference in the end. It's normal to be occasionally haunted by the question of whether what you have staked your life on is really true. But faith isn't natural.

This means that faith isn't something you can work up inside yourself. Faith comes to you as God's gift of grace: "For by grace you have been saved through faith. And this is not your own doing; it is the gift of God" (Eph. 2:8). Not only is your salvation a gift of God, but the faith to embrace it is his gift as well. But here is what you need to understand: God not only gives you the grace to believe for your salvation, but he also works to enable you to live by faith. If you are living by faith, you know that you have been visited by powerful transforming grace, because that way of living just isn't normal for you and me. If your way of living is no longer based on what your eyes can see and your mind can understand, but on God's presence, promises, principles, and provisions, it is because God has crafted faith in you.

Could it be that all of those things that come your way that confuse you and that you never would've chosen for yourself are God's tools to build your faith? By progressive transforming grace, he is enabling you to live the brand-new life he calls all of his children to live—the Godward life for which you were created. You don't have to hide in guilt when weak faith gets you off the path, because your hope in life isn't your faithfulness, but his. You can run in weakness and once again seek his strength. And you can know that in zealous grace he will not leave his craftwork until faith fully rules your heart unchallenged. He always gives freely what we need in order to do what he has called us to do.

For further study and encouragement: Hebrews 11

FEBRUARY 13

Tear up your list and throw it away—what God has planned for you is better than anything you've dreamed of for yourself.

It is the big delusion,
the height of arrogance,
the seductive trap,
the big, dark danger.
It leads nowhere
good.
It's destiny is
death.
It sat at the center of the
disaster in the garden.
It propelled the sad
rebellion of Adam and Eve.
It tempts us all
again and again in
situation after situation,
location after location,
relationship after relationship.
We fall into thinking
what multitudes of our
lost forefathers thought.
We buy into this one fateful
thought,
that perhaps we're smarter than
God,
that maybe our way is better than
his way.
Only grace can deliver
the deluded from the
danger that they are
to themselves.

For further study and encouragement: Psalm 14

FEBRUARY 14

God's grace will expose what you want to hide,
not to shame you, but to forgive and deliver you.

"It's a sad way to live," I thought as I listened to him recount the events of the night before. He worked next to me on the long packing table that kept our hands busy eight hours a day. But our mouths were free to talk, and talk we did. He was being unfaithful to his wife. He thought he was in charge, he thought he was free, but he wasn't. He told of taking his girlfriend to a certain restaurant in the small community where he lived, only to see his wife's car parked outside. He told of going to another place but having to make sure the coast was clear before they left so they wouldn't get caught. I said to him: "You think you're free, but you're not free. You have to hide. You have to worry about being caught. You have to lurk around in the darkness." I then said: "You think I'm bound, but I'm the one who's free. When I go out with my wife, I never have to worry about where we're going. I never have to fear being caught. I can boldly live in the light."

Sin turns all of us into citizens of the night. Sin causes all of us to be committed to low-light living. We hide, we deny, we cover, we lie, we excuse, we shift the blame, we rationalize, we defend, and we explain away. These are all acts of darkness by people who fear exposure.

What is the movement of grace? It is to shine light on what once lived in darkness. "And this is the judgment: the light has come into the world, and people loved the darkness rather than the light because their deeds were evil. For everyone who does wicked things hates the light and does not come to the light, lest his works should be exposed" (John 3:19–20). Grace shatters our darkness. Grace explodes on us with penetrating, heart-exposing light. Grace illumines our dank hallways and our dark corners. The Son of grace shines the light of his grace into the darkest recesses of our hearts, not as an act of vengeance or punishment, but as a move of forgiving, transforming, and delivering grace. He dispels our self-inflicted darkness because he knows that we cannot grieve what we do not see, we cannot confess what we have not grieved, and we cannot turn from what we haven't confessed.

The light has come. Run to the light; it is not to be feared. Yes, it is the light of exposure, but what will be exposed has already been covered by the blood of the One who exposes it.

For further study and encouragement: John 1:1–18

FEBRUARY 15

We will never get the freedom and long-term satisfaction we thought self-rule would bring. Ignoring God is never a pathway to blessing.

There are two lies that tempt each of us somehow, some way. They are the lies that fueled the disastrous choice of Adam and Eve in that moment of temptation in the garden. Yes, it is true, these lies have as much power today as they did then. The first is the lie of *autonomy*. This lie says that you are an independent human being with the right to live as you wish. Now, if you're a parent, you know that your children fall into embracing that lie. That's why they don't hunger for more of your correction and don't esteem your authority. From day one, our children want to believe that their lives belong to them and that they are the only authority that they need. But we *don't* belong to ourselves. If God created us—and he did—then we belong to him. I am a painter by avocation, and when I finish a painting, it belongs to me precisely because I made it. The painting is not autonomous. In the same way, human autonomy is a lie.

The second lie is the lie of *self-sufficiency*, which tells me that I have everything I need within myself to be what I was created to be and to do what I was designed to do. The fact is that God is the only self-sufficient being in the universe. We were created for dependency, first on God and then on one another in loving community. We need to be taught, encouraged, warned, strengthened, forgiven, healed, restored, counseled, loved, rebuked, and delivered—all things we cannot provide for ourselves. Human self-sufficiency is a lie.

So Jesus calls us to reject the lie and come to him. Under his yoke is the only place where true freedom can be found. He says: "Come to me, all who labor and are heavy laden, and I will give you rest. Take my yoke upon you, and learn from me, for I am gentle and lowly in heart, and you will find rest for your souls. For my yoke is easy, and my burden is light" (Matt. 11:28–30). There is freedom to be found, but not in empty promises of autonomy and self-sufficiency. True freedom is only ever found when grace ties your heart to Christ. Freed from trying to be what you can't be and to do what you were not designed to do, you are now free to carry the light burdens of forgiveness-giving and life-restoring grace.

For further study and encouragement: Genesis 3

FEBRUARY 16

In Christ, you have everything you need to live in peace
with God and the people he has placed in your life.

Grace produces what you and I desperately need but have no power to produce on our own—vertical and horizontal peace. Jesus really is the Prince of Peace! Sin alienates us from God and one another. Sin makes us the enemies of God and casts us into constant conflict with other people. Sin cuts us off from the two communities of love that we were created to live in—loving and worshipful community with God and loving community with others. Sin makes us better fighters than lovers. Sin is antisocial; it is fundamentally destructive to the relationships that are to shape our lives. We desperately need peace, but it often seems as if there is no peace to be found. This is why Isaiah's Old Testament prophecy of a Prince of Peace who was to come was so important, so exciting, and so encouraging (Isa. 9:6). The world was groaning, burdened and broken by vertical and horizontal conflict. The world and the people in it could not fix themselves. Peace seemed to be a distant and delusional hope. But then came the words of Isaiah.

God had a solution. It would not be a negotiation. It would not be a call to action. It would not be a strategy for peace. No, God's solution would come in the gift of his Son. He would bring the peace that eluded our grasp. He would live the life we could not live, fulfilling God's requirement. He would bear our punishment, satisfying God's anger. He would rise from the grave, defeating sin and death. He would do it all so that we could experience what we could never have achieved, earned, or deserved—peace with God. And peace with God is the only road to lasting peace with one another. It is only when the peace of God rules my heart that I can know real peace with you.

This is the good news of the gospel. Peace came. Peace lived. Peace died. Peace rose again. Peace reigns on your behalf. Peace indwells you by the Spirit. Peace graces you with everything you need. Peace convicts, forgives, and delivers you. Peace will finish his work in you. Peace will welcome you into glory, where Peace will live with you in peace and righteousness forever. Peace isn't a faded dream. No, Peace is real. Peace is a person, and his name is Jesus.

For further study and encouragement: Ephesians 2:11–22

FEBRUARY 17

Don't fear your weaknesses—God supplies all the strength you need.
Be afraid of those moments when you think you're independently strong.

Admit it, you don't like being weak. It's not fun being the last one chosen to play on the team. It's embarrassing to be asked a question you can't answer. It's frustrating not to be able to figure out the directions for assembling the furniture you just bought. It's mortifying to forget that important appointment or the name of a good friend. It's humbling to fail at a task, to drop the ball, or to make a promise and not be able to keep it. We don't like getting lost or forgetting a phone number. We all hate those moments when we feel unqualified or unprepared. We don't like being confused or not knowing. We covet the muscles and the brains of others. We all hate being afraid and wish we had more courage. In the face of heroes, we feel anything but. In the face of the accomplishments of others, we wonder if we have done much that's worthwhile. We don't like facing the truth that we're all weak in our own ways. It is the universal condition of humanity.

In a world where you are on your own, where you have to find your own way and independently build your life, weakness is a thing to be feared. In a world where all you have in the end is your thinking, your drive, your performance, and your achievements, weakness is a thing to be regretted. In a world where you have no one to turn to for strength and few who accept you when you don't have it, weakness is a thing to be avoided. But here is what you need to understand. Weakness is not the big danger to be avoided. What you need to avoid is your delusions of strength. Those assessments of independent strength are much more dangerous.

Are you confused? The fact is that we are all weak. We're weak in wisdom, weak in strength, and weak in righteousness. Sin has left us weak of heart and hands. It has left us feeble and lame in many ways. But God's grace makes weakness a thing to be feared no longer. The God of grace who calls you to himself and calls you to live for him blesses you with all the strength you need to do what he's called you to do. The way to enter into that strength is to admit how little strength you actually have. Grace frees me from being devastated that I can no longer trust me because grace connects me to One who is worthy of my trust and who will always deliver what I need. "Some trust in chariots and some in horses, but we trust in the name of the Lord our God. They collapse and fall, but we rise and stand upright" (Ps. 20:7–8).

For further study and encouragement: Psalm 27

FEBRUARY 18

Today you'll look to find rest by trying to understand your life, or you'll rest in the One who understands everything, including your life.

Yes, it's true, we're all theologians, scientists, archaeologists, and philosophers. We're created by God to be meaning makers. We never leave our lives alone. We pick through them all the time, trying to make sense out of the civilization that they comprise. We do forensic investigations of our past, we leaf through the layers of our present, and we try our best to figure out the future. Made in the image of God, we live our lives based not on the facts of our experiences, but on our unique interpretations of those facts. That's why the little girl asks that seemingly endless list of "why" questions; she has an inner drive to know. That's why the teenager seems a bit lost; he is trying to figure his life out. That's why the bride is a bit nervous before her wedding; she is wondering what the future will bring. That's why the old man gazes off into the distance; he is recounting what once was.

It's not wrong to think and think hard. It's not a sin to want to understand life. It's not bad to embark on a quest to know, but you'd better not be looking for peace of heart. God created you with the ability to think and the desire for life to make sense. These traits were given to you so that you could come to know God and understand what he's communicated to you. But it is important to remember that rest is never to be found in trying to figure it all out, because you never will. There will always be mystery in your life. God will always surprise you with what he brings your way. You will always be confronted with the unplanned and the unexpected. All of this is because you don't rule your own life and you don't write your own story. And the One who does rule and write doesn't tell you everything about your life and his plan. No, he tells you the things you need to know to live as you were designed to live, and then he graces you with his presence and his power.

Because he controls the details of your life, he is always near; at any moment, you can reach out and touch him (see Acts 17:26–27). Rest is only ever found in trusting the One who has everything figured out for your good and his glory. Because he is wise, gracious, faithful, and powerful, he is worthy of your trust and is alone able to give your heart rest.

For further study and encouragement: Psalm 139

FEBRUARY 19

When hardship comes your way, will you tell yourself it's a tool of God's grace and a sign of his love, or will you give in to doubting his goodness?

If you are not on God's redemptive agenda page, you will end up doubting his goodness. One of the most important questions you could ask is: "What is God doing in the here and now?" The follow-up question is also important: "How should I respond to it?" It is nearly impossible to think about life properly and to live appropriately if you are fundamentally confused about what God is doing. If someone were to ask you the first of those two questions, how would you respond? Are you tracking with God's agenda? Are you after what God's after? Are you living in a way that is consistent with what God is doing? Do you struggle with questions of God's love, faithfulness, wisdom, and goodness? Do you ever envy the life of another? Do you sometimes feel alone? Do you fall into thinking that no one understands what you're going through? Are you ever plagued by doubts as to whether Christianity is true after all? If you aren't struggling with these things, are you near someone who is?

Here's the bottom line. Right here, right now, God isn't so much working to deliver to you your personal definition of happiness. He's not committed to give you a predictable schedule, happy relationships, or comfortable surroundings. He hasn't promised you a successful career, a nice place to live, and a community of people who appreciate you. What he has promised you is *himself*, and what he brings to you is the zeal of his transforming grace. No, he's not first working on your happiness; he's committed to your holiness. That doesn't mean he is offering you less than you've hoped for, but much, much more. In grace, he is intent on delivering you from your greatest, deepest, and most long-term problem: sin. He offers you gifts of grace that transcend the moment, that literally are of eternal value. He has not unleashed his power in your life only to deliver to you things that quickly pass away and that have no capacity at all to satisfy your heart.

This means that often when you are tempted to think that God is loving you less because your life is hard, he is actually loving you more. The hardships that you are facing are the tool of his exposing, forgiving, liberating, and transforming grace. These hard moments aren't in your life because God is distant and uncaring, but rather because he loves you so fully. These moments become moments of faith and not doubt when by grace you begin to value what God says is truly valuable. Do you value what God values?

For further study and encouragement: James 1:12–18

FEBRUARY 20

Today you'll face things bigger than you, but you needn't be afraid because none is bigger than the One who rules them all for your sake.

You might not know it, you might not be aware as you're doing it, but you are always measuring your potential. The toddler who is just beginning to walk stands with wobbling legs and holds on to his mommy's knee as he measures his potential to walk across the room to daddy without falling on his face. The teenager walks up to his first job with clammy hands and a rapidly beating heart as he measures his potential to get through the day without being fired. The bride has a nauseous stomach two hours before her wedding as she measures her potential to live successfully in the most important human relationship she will ever have. The senior citizen sits nervously in her doctor's office as she measures her potential to deal with the physical hardships of old age. The widower stands at the edge of his wife's grave with tears in his eyes as he measures his potential to live without her. We are all constantly measuring our potential to do what is before us.

Now, the typical way to measure your potential is to compare the size of the problem to your natural gifts and your track record so far. No, it's not irrational to measure your potential this way, but for the believer in Christ Jesus, it simply isn't enough. By grace, God doesn't leave you on your own. He doesn't leave you with the tool box of your own strength, righteousness, and wisdom. No, he invades you with his presence, power, wisdom, and grace. Paul captures this reality with these life-altering words: "It is no longer I who live, but Christ who lives in me" (Gal. 2:20). He's obviously not saying that he's dead, because if he was, he wouldn't be writing those words. No, he's reminding you and me of a very significant spiritual reality. Here it is: if you are God's child, the life force that energizes your thoughts, desires, words, and actions is no longer you; it's Christ! God didn't just forgive you. No, he has come to live inside of you so you will have the power to desire and do what he calls you to do. And not only does he live inside of you, he rules all the situations, locations, and relationships that are out of your control. He is not only your indwelling Savior, he is your reigning King. He does in you what you could not do for yourself and he does outside of you what you have no power or authority to do. And he does all of this with your redemptive good in mind. Since this is true, why would you give way to fear?

For further study and encouragement: Psalm 95

FEBRUARY 21

Today you will fight temptation, but not alone, because a
Warrior Spirit lives inside of you and fights on your behalf.

I did it for my children again and again. Often they were unaware that I had done it. I did it in moments when they didn't have the sense to do it for themselves. I did it with commitment and joy because I knew what the world that surrounded them was like and I knew the vulnerability of their hearts. What is this thing that I was committed to as a father? I did everything I could do to protect my children from evil.

I knew that they would minimize or forget two very important realities. First, they didn't understand or would soon forget that they had been born into a dramatically broken world that is not functioning as God intended. They would forget that they woke up every day to a fallen world where real evil still exists. They often didn't seem to understand that this meant they would face temptation of various kinds every single day of their lives. Their eyes would see things that God, in his original plan, never intended them to see. Their ears would hear things that they should not hear. The alluring, deceitful, and seductive pleasures of sin would be held before them again and again.

Second, they also tended to minimize or forget the sin inside of them. They didn't seem to understand that the biggest danger to them was not the evil outside of them but the sin that still lurked with power in their hearts. This meant that they didn't understand how vulnerable they were to the seductive voices of sin that would greet them every day. And when you forget how temptable you are, you don't take precautions for your protection. So I knew that I had to work not only to protect my children from the evil in their environment, but also and more importantly to protect them from themselves.

God knows that we all are a lot like my children. We, too, minimize the fallenness of our world and the power of remaining sin, and when we do, we do not guard ourselves from temptation as we should. Isn't it good to know that God in grace has placed his Warrior Spirit inside of us? He battles on our behalf even in those moments when we don't have the sense to battle for ourselves (see Gal. 5:16–26).

Isn't it good to know that while we still live in a broken world and still have sin inside of us, God constantly battles on our behalf? Now, that's grace!

For further study and encouragement: Isaiah 42

FEBRUARY 22

Envy denies grace. The assumption of envy is that we deserve what another has been given, when, in fact, you and I deserve nothing.

Envy is self-focused and self-righteous. It inserts you into the center of your world. It makes it all about you. It tells you that you deserve what you don't deserve. Envy is expectant and demanding. Envy tells you that you are someone you aren't and you are entitled to what is not rightfully yours. Envy cannot celebrate the blessing of another because it tells you that you are more deserving. Envy tells you that you have earned what you could never earn. The world of envy no more mixes with the world of grace than oil does with water. Envy forgets who you are, forgets who God is, and is confused about what life is all about.

Yet, having said all of that, the fact is that all of us struggle with envy somehow, some way, and at some time. We're jealous that the person next to us has achieved the financial success that we have never enjoyed. We wish our marriage was as happy as that of our friends at church. We wonder why we've been saddled with the job we have when that other guy has such a fulfilling career. We're envious of the other person's small group, which seems to be such a loving community. We wish that we could eat as much as that person does and still stay as slim as she is. The tall guy wishes he wasn't so tall and the short guy would love to look down on people for a change. The curly-haired person covets straight hair and the straight-haired person envies the curls. The nerd envies the jock and the jock wishes he could get better grades. Envy is universal because sin is.

Envy has its roots in the selfishness of sin (see 2 Cor. 5:14–15). Envy is self-focused; because it's self-focused, it's entitled; because it's entitled, it's demanding; because it's demanding, it tends to judge the goodness of God by whether he has delivered what you feel entitled to; and because it judges God on that basis, it leads you to question his goodness. Because you question God's goodness, you won't run to him for help. Envy is a spiritual disaster.

Grace reminds you that you deserve nothing, but it does not stop there—it confronts you with the truth that God is gloriously loving, gracious, and kind, that he lavishes on us things we could have never earned. Grace also reminds us that God is wise and he never gets a wrong address—he gives each of us exactly what he knows we need.

For further study and encouragement: James 3:13–18

FEBRUARY 23

Why do we say we place our hope in the cross of the Lord Jesus Christ and yet practically ask the law to do what only grace can accomplish?

It's done every day in Christian homes around the world. Well-meaning parents, zealous to see their children doing what is right, ask the law to do in the lives of their children what only grace can accomplish. They think that if they have the right set of rules, the right threat of punishment, and consistent enforcement, their children will be okay. In ways these parents fail to understand, they have reduced parenting to being a law-giver, a prosecutor, a jury, and a jailer. They think that their job is to do anything they can to shape, control, and regulate the behavior of their children. And in their zeal to control behavior, they look to the tools of threat ("I'll make you afraid enough that you'll never do this again."), manipulation ("I'll find something you really want and tell you that I'll give it to you if you obey."), and guilt ("I'll make you feel so bad, so ashamed, that you'll decide to not do this again.").

This way of thinking denies two significant things that the Bible tells us. The first is that before sin is a matter of behavior, it is always a matter of the heart. We sin because we are sinners. For example, anger is always an issue of the heart before it is an act of physical aggression. This is important to recognize because no human being has the power to change the heart of another human being. The second is that if threats, manipulation, and guilt could create lasting change in the life of another person, Jesus would not have had to come. So this way of thinking denies the gospel that we say we hold dear. It really does ask the law to do what only God in amazing grace is able to accomplish. If you deny the gospel at street level, you will attempt to create by human means what only God can create by powerful grace, and it will never lead you anywhere good.

Thankfully, God hasn't left us to our own power to change. He meets us with transforming grace and calls us to be tools of that grace in his redemptive hands. He lifts the burden of change off our shoulders and never calls us to do what only he can do. So we expose our children to God's law and faithfully exercise authority while we seek to be tools of heart change in the hands of a God whose grace is greater than all of the sin we're grappling with.

For further study and encouragement: Romans 5:12–21

FEBRUARY 24

Admit it, we're all still a bit of a mess; that's why we need God's grace today as much as we needed it the first day we believed.

You and I need to say it to ourselves again and again. We need to look in the mirror and make the confession as part of our morning routine. Here's what we all need to say: "I am not a grace graduate."

It is so tempting to mount arguments for your own righteousness:

- "That really wasn't lust. I'm just a man who enjoys beauty."
- "That really wasn't gossip. It was just a very detailed, very personal prayer request."
- "I wasn't angry at my kids. I was just acting as one of God's prophets. 'Thus says the Lord . . .'"
- "I'm not on an ugly quest for personal power. No, I'm just exercising God-given leadership gifts."
- "I'm not coldhearted and stingy. I'm just trying to be a good steward of what God has given me."
- "I wasn't being proud. I just thought someone needed to take control of the conversation."
- "It wasn't really a lie. It was just a different way of recounting the facts."

We all tend to want to think we are more righteous than we actually are. We don't like to think of ourselves as still desperately in need of God's rescuing grace. And we surely don't want to face the fact that what we need to be rescued from is us! When you argue for your own righteousness, working hard to deny the empirical evidence of your sin, then you fail to seek the amazing grace that is your only hope. Grace is only ever attractive to sinners. The riches of God's goodness are only ever sought by the poor. The spiritual healing of the Great Physician is only ever esteemed by those who acknowledge that they still suffer from the spiritual disease of sin. It's a tragedy when we praise God for his grace on Sunday and deny our need for that grace the rest of the week. Face the fact today that you'll never outgrow your need for grace, no matter how much you learn and how much you mature, until you are on the other side and your struggle is over because sin is no more (see Phil. 3:12–16). The way to begin to celebrate the grace that God so freely gives you every day is by admitting how much you need it.

For further study and encouragement: Psalm 32

FEBRUARY 25

You're going to hunger for some success in life. May you hunger
for the complete success of the gospel in your heart.

You and I don't live by instinct. We are value-oriented, goal-oriented, purpose-oriented, and importance-oriented human beings. We are constantly rating everything in our lives. We all have things that are important to us and things that are not, things that mean a lot to us and things that mean very little. We willingly make sacrifices for one thing and refuse to sacrifice for another. We grieve the loss of one thing and celebrate the loss of another. We love what another person hates and we see as a treasure something that another person thinks is trash. We look at something and see beauty while the person next to us sees no beauty in it at all. Some things are so important to us that they shape the decisions that we make and the actions that we take. Some things command the allegiance of our hearts, while other things barely get our attention.

In the center of this value system is our definition of success. No rational human being wants to be a failure. No one wants to think that he has wasted his life. No one wants to think that in the end she will look back and realize that she invested in things that just didn't matter. Everyone wants to think that his or her life is or will be successful. But what is success? Is it judged by the size of your house, the prominence of your friends, the success of your career, the power of your position, the size of the pile of your possessions, the perfection of your physical beauty, the breadth of your knowledge, or the list of your achievements? The problem with all of these things is that they quickly pass away, and because they do, if you have lived for these things, you will eventually come up empty.

Contrast that view of success with the success of God's work in and through you. God offers you things of supreme value (his forgiveness, his presence, welcome into his kingdom, a clean conscience, and a pure heart). These things will never pass away. They are the eternally valuable gifts of divine grace. This leaves you with this question: "What do I really want in life: the success of God's agenda of grace or the fulfillment of my catalog of desires?" At the end of the day, what do you long for: for God's grace to do its work or for more of the stuff that this physical created world has to offer? Be honest. What kind of success are you hooking your heart to and how is it shaping the decisions you make and the actions you take?

For further study and encouragement: Matthew 6:25–34

FEBRUARY 26

Your life is not good because it is easy or predictable,
but because the I Am has invaded your existence by his grace.

It is a very instructive vignette in the life of Jesus and his disciples, recorded for us in Mark 6:45–52. Jesus has sent his disciples across the Sea of Galilee to Bethsaida. They have encountered an impossible headwind and angry seas. If you look at the time clues in the larger passage, you can see they have been rowing for about eight hours. They are in a situation that seems impossible, exhausting, frustrating, and potentially dangerous. They are far beyond their strength and ability. As you read the passage, you have to ask yourself why Jesus would ever want his disciples in this kind of difficulty. It's clear that they're not in this mess because they've been disobedient, arrogant, or unwise, but because they have obeyed Jesus.

Jesus sees that his disciples are in this exhausting and dangerous situation, and he sets out and begins to walk across the sea. Yes, you read it right: he walks across the sea. Now, the moment he begins to take this walk, you are confronted with two things. The first is the fact that Jesus of Nazareth is the Lord God almighty, because no other human being could do what he is doing. But there is a second important thing to observe. The minute he begins to take the walk, you know what he has in mind. If all Jesus wants to do is relieve the difficulty, he wouldn't have to take the walk. All he would need to do is say a prayer from the shore and the wind would cease. He takes the walk because he is not after the difficulty. He is after the men in the middle of the difficulty. He is working to change everything they think about themselves and about their lives. Standing next to the boat as the wind still blows and the waves still crash, he says: "It is I. Do not be afraid." He is actually taking one of the names of God. He is saying the "I am" is with them, the God of Abraham, Isaac, and Jacob, the One on whom all the covenant promises rest. It is impossible for them to be alone because their existence has been invaded by the grace and glory of the I am.

Why did Jesus send his disciples into that storm? He did it for the same reason he sometimes sends you into storms—because he knows that sometimes you need the storm in order to be able to see the glory. For the believer, peace is not to be found in ease of life. Real peace is only ever found in the presence, power, and grace of the Savior, the King, the Lamb, the I am. That peace is yours even when the storms of life take you beyond your natural ability, wisdom, and strength. You can live with hope and courage in the middle of what once would have produced discouragement and fear because you know you are never alone. The I am inhabits all situations, relationships, and locations by his grace. He is in you. He is with you. He is for you. He is your hope.

For further study and encouragement: 1 Samuel 17

FEBRUARY 27

You've been born into a world of authority, and it is not you.
Disobedience dethrones God and enthrones you in your heart.

You could argue that the most important words in all of the Bible are the first four words, "In the beginning, God . . ." Those words are meant to change the way you think about yourself, life, God, and everything else. God was on site before you were. The earth and everything in it is an expression of his design and his purpose. Because he is the Creator of all things, all things belong to him. God created you. That means you belong to him. You and I were carefully designed for his purpose. We did not make ourselves. We did not rise out of the primordial ooze, the result of impersonal forces. We are the direct product of God's creative power and will.

Now, think about this. When I make something, it belongs to me precisely because I made it. The Bible says, "The earth is the LORD's and the fullness thereof, the world and those who dwell therein" (Ps. 24:1). This means there is no such thing as human autonomy. To deny this is to tell myself that my life belongs to me for my use for the purpose of my happiness. This is not only about denying God's existence and authority, but it also is about denying my own humanity. All human beings were created to live with a life-shaping God consciousness and a willing submission to God's authority.

This means that you and I will never be at the center of life, because God is. It will never be about us, because it is about him. It is never about our will and our way, because it is about his. We will never be the ultimate authority in our lives, because he is. To deny this is to deny reality and give yourself to the most dangerous of all delusions. To deny this is like denying the existence of the sun. If you did that, the people around you would think you were crazy. Sin makes us just that crazy. We deny the evidence that is all around us of God's existence and authority. We tell ourselves that we are the only authority that we need. We write our own moral rules. We tell ourselves that we know what is best for us. We willingly step over God's wise and protective boundaries. We run after what God says is wrong and we chafe against what he declares is right. We deny him as King and set ourselves up as the kings of our little worlds. We forget his glory and live for the glory of our own pleasure, power, comfort, and ease.

This is why grace is essential. It takes powerful rescuing grace to transform me from a self-rule junky into a person who willingly and joyfully submits to the plan and purpose of another. It requires powerful mercy for me to become a person who surrenders self-appointed authority to the authority of God. It takes grace for me to acknowledge that there is a King and that he is not me. It takes God's rescuing hand for me to forsake the purpose of my kingdom and take up the purpose of his. Jesus submitted himself to the Father's will even to death so that you and I would have the grace we need to do the same.

For further study and encouragement: Psalm 19

FEBRUARY 28

Love that calls wrong right and right wrong simply
isn't love. Real love rebukes and forgives.

There are an awful lot of things that we call love that don't really rise to the level of what love is and what love does. Being willing to tolerate things that are wrong in the eyes of God may create a comfortable surface peace, but it isn't what love does. Being willing to live inside of a circle of evil and not make waves may cause people to like me, but it isn't love. Saying, "It's okay—don't worry about it," to a person who did something wrong is not really loving. Maintaining peace at any cost isn't love. Remaining silent when I should speak up isn't love. Being unwilling to step into tense moments with you because there is wrong between us that needs to be exposed and discussed isn't love. Asking you to tolerate whatever I do or say because you say you love me is a fundamental misunderstanding of what love is and what love does. Much of what we think love is simply isn't love after all.

Real, biblical, self-sacrificing, God-honoring love never compromises what God says is right and true. Truth and love are inextricably bound together. Love that compromises truth simply isn't love. Truth without love ceases to be truth because it gets bent and twisted by other human agendas. If love wants and works for what is best for you, then love is committed to being part of what God says is best in your life. So, I am committed to being God's tool for what he says is best in your life, even if that means we have to go through tense and difficult moments to get there. I think often we opt for silence, willingly avoiding issues and letting wrong things go on unchecked, not because we love the other person, but because we love ourselves and just don't want to go through the hassle of dealing with something that God says is clearly wrong. We are unwilling to make the hard personal sacrifices that are the call of real love. Now, I'm not talking about being self-righteous, judgmental, critical, and condemning. No, I'm taking about choosing not to ignore wrong, but dealing with wrong with the same grace that you have been given by God. Grace never calls wrong right. If wrong were right, grace wouldn't be necessary. If sin weren't evil and wrong, Jesus would never have had to come.

The cross of Jesus Christ is the only model you need of what love does in the face of wrong. Love doesn't call wrong right. Love doesn't ignore wrong and hope it goes away. Love doesn't turn its back on you because you are wrong. Love doesn't mock you. Love doesn't mean I turn the tables and work to make you hurt in the same way you have hurt me. Love doesn't go passive and stay silent in the face of wrong. Loves moves toward you *because* you are wrong and need to be rescued from you. In moving toward you, love is willing to make sacrifices and endure hardships so that you may be made right again and be reconciled to God and others. God graces us with this kind of love so that we may be tools of this love in the lives of others.

For further study and encouragement: 1 Corinthians 13:4–13

FEBRUARY 29

*Do you need anything more than the cruel cross of Jesus Christ
to convince you of how deep your need for grace is?*

Think about it—God was so sure of the depth and expansiveness of your sin, of your inability to grasp how desperate your condition is (and, even if you were able, your complete inability to free yourself from it), that he was willing to harness the forces of nature and to carefully control the events of human history so that at a certain point Jesus would come to live the life you could not live, die the death that you should have died, and rise again, conquering death. Why did God go to this elaborate and sacrificial extent? There is only one answer to the question. God the Father planned it, God the Son was willing to do it, and God the Holy Spirit applied this work to your heart and mine because there just was no other way.

Sin is every human being's core disease. It is completely beyond the power of any human being to escape it. It separates you from God, for whom you were created. It damages every aspect of your personhood. It makes it impossible for you to be what God created you to be and to do what God designed you to do. It robs you of inner contentment and peace, and it puts you at war with other human beings. It renders you blind, weak, self-oriented, and rebellious. It reduces all of us to fools, and ultimately it leads to death. Sin is an unmitigated, almost incalculable disaster. You can run from a certain situation, you can get yourself out of a relationship, and you can move to another location and choose not to go back again. But you and I have no ability whatsoever to escape from the hold that sin has on us. It is the moral Vise-Grip that has held the heart of every person who has ever lived.

There are few passages that capture the disaster of sin and what it does to people made in God's image better than Genesis 6:5–6: "The LORD saw that the wickedness of man was great in the earth, and that every intention of the thoughts of his heart was only evil continually. And the LORD regretted that he had made man on the earth, and it grieved him to his heart." Note two things from this passage. First, the effect of sin on people was deep, heart deep. Sin is not just a matter of bad behavior. It is a condition of the heart. That's why you cannot free yourself from it. Second, the effects of sin on you and me are comprehensive. Note the words "every intention" coupled with the words "only evil continually."

But the passage tells us more. God was not satisfied leaving us in the disaster of sin. The disease that infected the heart of every human being produced sorrow in his heart. But his sorrow was not just the sorrow of remorse or the sorrow of judgment; it was the sorrow of grace. The words of Genesis 6:8—"But Noah found favor in the eyes of the LORD"—tell you that Genesis 6 is not the end of the story. God would not just punish sin; he would raise up a nation out of which his Son would come to live and die to deliver us from it. The cross of his Son stands as a lasting reminder of just how desperate our need is for the grace that that cross represents.

For further study and encouragement: 1 Peter 3:18–22

MARCH 1

Mercy means I am so deeply grateful for the forgiveness I have received that I cannot help offering you the same.

We all do it, probably every day. We have no idea that we're doing it, yet it has a huge impact on the way we view ourselves and the way we respond to others. It is one of the reasons there is so much relational trouble even in the house of God. What is this thing that we all tend to do that causes so much harm? We all forget. In the busyness and self-centeredness of our lives, we sadly forget how much our lives have been blessed by and radically redirected by mercy. The fact that God has blessed us with his favor when we deserved his wrath fades from our memories like a song whose lyrics we once knew but now cannot recall. The reality that on every morning brand-new mercy greets us is not the thing that grips our minds as we frenetically prepare for our day. When we lay our exhausted heads down at the end of the day for much-needed sleep, we often fail to look back on the many mercies that dripped from God's hands onto our little lives. We don't often take time to sit and meditate on what our lives would've been like if the mercy of the Redeemer had not been written into our personal stories. Sadly, we all tend to be way too mercy-forgetful.

Mercy-forgetfulness is dangerous, because it shapes the way you think about yourself and others. When you remember mercy, you also remember that you simply did nothing whatsoever to earn that with which mercy has blessed you. When you remember mercy, you are humble, thankful, and tender. When you remember mercy, complaining gives way to gratitude and self-focused desire gives way to worship. But when you forget mercy, you proudly tell yourself that what you have is what you've achieved. When you forget mercy, you take credit for what only mercy could produce. When you forget mercy, you name yourself as righteous and deserving, and you live an entitled and demanding life.

When you forget mercy and think you're deserving, you find it all too easy not to extend mercy to others. Proudly, you think that you're getting what you deserve and that they are, too. Your proud heart is not tender, so it is not easily moved by the sorry plight of others. You forget that you are more like than unlike your needy brother, failing to acknowledge that neither of you stands before God as deserving. Humility is the soil in which mercy for others grows. Gratitude for mercy given is what motivates mercy extended. Paul says, "Be kind to one another, tenderhearted, forgiving one another, as God in Christ forgave you" (Eph. 4:32).

For further study and encouragement: Luke 6:27–36; Matthew 18:21–35

MARCH 2

Waiting on God doesn't mean sitting around and hoping. Waiting means believing he will do what he's promised and then acting with confidence.

Waiting on God is not at all like the meaningless waiting that you do at the dentist's office. You know, he's overbooked, so you're still sitting there more than an hour past your scheduled appointment. You're a man, but you're now reading *Family Circle* magazine. You've begun to read the article titled "The 7 Best Chicken Recipes in the World." When you're a man and you're getting ready to tear a chicken recipe out of *Family Circle* magazine because the recipe sounds so good, you know that you have been waiting too long!

But waiting on God is not like that. Waiting on God is an active life based on confidence in his presence and promises, not a passive existence haunted by occasional doubt. Waiting on God isn't internal torment that results in paralysis. No, waiting on God is internal rest that results in courageous action.

Waiting is your calling. Waiting is your blessing. Every one of God's children has been chosen to wait, because every one of God's children lives between the "already" and the "not yet." Already this world has been broken by sin, but not yet has it been made new again. Already Jesus has come, but not yet has he returned to take you home with him forever. Already your sin has been forgiven, but not yet have you been fully delivered from it. Already Jesus reigns, but not yet has his final kingdom come. Already sin has been defeated, but not yet has it been completely destroyed. Already the Holy Spirit has been given, but not yet have you been perfectly formed into the likeness of Jesus. Already God has given you his Word, but not yet has it totally transformed your life. Already you have been given grace, but not yet has that grace finished its work. You see, we're all called to wait because we all live right smack dab in the middle of God's grand redemptive story. We all wait for the final end of the work that God has begun in and for us.

We don't just wait—we wait in hope. And what does hope in God look like? It is a confident expectation of a guaranteed result. We wait believing that what God has begun he will complete, so we live with confidence and courage. We get up every morning and act upon what is to come, and because what is to come is sure, we know that our labor in God's name is never in vain. So we wait and act. We wait and work. We wait and fight. We wait and conquer. We wait and proclaim. We wait and run. We wait and sacrifice. We wait and give. We wait and worship. Waiting on God is an action based on confident assurance of grace to come.

For further study and encouragement: Romans 4

MARCH 3

Prayer is abandoning my reliance on me and running toward the rest that can be found only when I rely on the power of God.

Prayer abandons independence. Prayer forsakes any thought that you can make it on your own. Prayer affirms dependency. Prayer acknowledges weakness. Prayer renounces assessments of capability. Prayer embraces the reality of failure. Prayer tells you that you are not at the center. Prayer calls you to abandon your plans for the wiser plans of another. Prayer flows from a deep personal sense of need and runs toward God's abundant grace.

Because of what prayer really is, prayer is not natural for us. It's not natural for us to embrace our sin, weakness, and failure. It's not natural for us to be comfortable depending on the mercy of another. It's not natural for us to surrender our hopes and dreams to the better vision of another. It's not natural for us to surrender our wisdom and control to someone greater than us. It's not natural for us to think that we need grace. On the other hand, it's natural for us to think that our righteousness, wisdom, strength, and work are enough. As a result, many of our prayers are the religious pronouncements of self-righteous people, the long wish lists of entitled people, or the impatient demands of people who are wondering what in the world God is doing. So many of our prayers aren't prayers at all (see Luke 18:9–14).

Here is the bottom line. We need to be met by God's grace if, in true humility, we are ever going to be able to abandon our self-reliance and pray for grace. It is only by grace that we will ever acknowledge our need for grace and worship God for the grace he has so willingly lavished on us. Since prayer is fundamentally counterintuitive, we need grace to rescue us from our self-oriented religious meanderings so that, with humble hearts, we may acknowledge God as the Redeemer-King and cast ourselves on his gracious care. Prayer always forsakes the kingdom of self for the kingdom of God, and for that we all need forgiving, rescuing, and transforming grace. This is just the kind of grace for which true prayer leads us to cry out.

For further study and encouragement: Luke 11:1–13

MARCH 4

If you don't acknowledge sin, you won't value grace.
If you don't value grace, you won't seek the
forgiveness and rescue it provides.

I will make this confession,
although it hurts to do so:
I am a very skilled
self-swindler.
I am very good at playing
monkey games with my
morality.
All too often, I argue for
righteousness that simply
is not there.
It's too easy for me
to convince myself that
the wrong
that I have done is not
so wrong after all.
And as I work to minimize
the gravity of my condition,
I in turn devalue
the grace
that is my only hope of
rescue,
transformation,
deliverance.
Lord,
please crush my heart with
the guilt of my sin
so that you may fill it once again
with the glory of your
redeeming grace.

For further study and encouragement: Psalm 38

MARCH 5

*If you're God's child, you can rest assured today that both your
standing before God and his rule on your behalf are sure and secure.*

There are two things in life you simply don't have to worry about anymore, two big concerns that you just don't have to carry. Every day, you and I carry important life concerns. No, I'm not talking about being crushed with worry, but rather about taking important things seriously. It's right to be concerned about your finances. It's important to carry the concern that your marriage would be all that God means it to be. It's good to focus much concern on the welfare and development of your children. It's vital to take your church and your relationship to the body of Christ seriously. It would be silly not to see your physical health as an important concern. It is responsible to carry these concerns. It would be unwise not to consider all of these things as important and worthy of your attention.

But you do not have to carry the two most significant and important things in your life as concerns. You do not have to burden yourself with worry about these things. You do not have to plague yourself with the thought that though these things are yours today, they may not be yours tomorrow. You can wake up morning after morning after morning with a smile on your face put there by the knowledge that the most important things in your life are simply never, ever at risk. It is one of the sweet gifts of God's grace that you can rest assured that these things that now define you and your life are yours forever. You can lose your house, your job, your family, your friendships, your health, and your church, but you will not lose these things. You can face disappointment and loss, but these things will remain. You can suffer the pain of defeat, but these things will still be yours. You can lose it all, but nothing can take life from you, because what defines life is simply not for the taking.

There aren't two things in all of life more important than these—that grace has purchased for you a place in God's family and that, because you are in his family, God rules over all things for your good. You could never have earned these two unshakable realities. They are only ever yours by grace. It is because of grace that you have a forever place in God's family. It is because of grace that your life is under the careful administration of the King of kings himself. It is because of grace that on your darkest day, you are still loved and accepted. It is because of grace that when nothing in life makes sense, your life is still under his control. There is much for you to be concerned about, but not these two things. His love will never fail, and his rule on your behalf is eternal.

For further study and encouragement: Romans 8:31–39

MARCH 6

Since your standing with God is based not on your righteousness but on Christ's, in moments of failure, you can run to him and not from him.

It's what we all are. We're all failures. Own it; it will be good for you. There is not a day in any of our lives when we don't lay down empirical evidence that we are failures. Maybe it's in an unkind word, an ugly thought, or an ungodly desire. Maybe it's in a moment of selfish envy or unbridled greed. Maybe it's in a moment of pride, when we have to be the center of attention or steal some of God's glory. Perhaps it's in acts of gluttony or in the desires of lust. Maybe it's in an instance when our hearts are cold and lack sympathy for the poor or the suffering. Maybe it shows itself when we are jealous of the beauty or power of another. Perhaps it's revealed when we surrender our hearts once again to some earthbound idol. Perhaps it shows itself when we take what is not ours to take or fail to give what we have been called to give. Somehow, some way, we all do it every day—we fall short of God's righteous standard. We all fail to be what he has created and called us to be.

Now, when confronted with your failure—and you will be if you're at all humble and honest—you have only three choices. You can commit to be an evidence denier, working to convince yourself that you're okay when you're really not okay. You can comfort yourself with plausible arguments for your righteousness, giving ease to your conscience. Or, in the face of your failure, you can wallow in guilt and shame, beating yourself up because you did not do better and working hard to hide your failure from God and others. Or, in the brokenness and grief of conviction, you can run not away from God but to him. You can run into the light of his holy presence utterly unafraid, filled with the confidence that although he is righteous and you are not, he will not turn you away. You can do this because your standing with him has never been based on your righteous performance, but on the perfect obedience of your Savior. Because you are in him, you are counted by God as righteous and therefore accepted into his holy presence forever and ever and ever.

Yes, you are called to live a holy life, but your way of living has not been and never will be the basis of your standing with God. You can bow at his feet and confess your sins, knowing that you will receive grace and not punishment, because righteous Jesus took the full brunt of your penalty so that you would never, ever bear it. Ephesians 3:12 reminds us that in Christ we can have boldness and confidence through our faith in him. So when you fail again today, where will you run?

For further study and encouragement: Hebrews 4:14–16

MARCH 7

It's the heart that's the problem. People, locations, and situations don't cause me to sin; they're where the sin of my heart gets revealed.

If you ask the little boy why he hit his sister, he won't tell you it was because of the sin that's in his heart. No, he'll say, "She was bothering me." If you ask the teenager why he came in so late, he won't willingly take responsibility. He'll tell you a long story of how there was an accident on the freeway, then a long train he had to wait for, and then a water main break that flooded the street he normally drives on. If you ask the father why he is so angry all the time, he won't tell you it's because of the selfishness and impatience in his heart. No, he'll say it's because of his kids; they just drive him crazy. If you ask the single person why she's so moody and discontent, she won't say it's because of the jealousy that resides in her heart. She'll point to all the ways that life has been hard. If you ask the old man why he is so mean, he won't tell you it's because of the bitterness that has captured his heart. No, he'll talk about all the times in his life when he didn't get what he knew he deserved. Sometimes I think it's the one biblical truth that no one believes. When we do something wrong, we all tend to point outside ourselves for the cause: "This traffic makes me so angry"; "She gets me so upset"; or "My boss pulls the worst out of me."

It's a comfortable, street-level heresy. It feels good to think that your biggest problems in life exist outside you and not inside you, but the problem is that it simply is not true. Jesus devastated the self-atoning perspective on human behavior in the Sermon on the Mount: "You have heard that it was said to those of old, 'You shall not murder. . . .' But I say to you that everyone who is angry with his brother will be liable to judgment. . . . You have heard that it was said, 'You shall not commit adultery.' But I say to you that everyone who looks at a woman with lustful intent has already committed adultery with her in his heart" (Matt. 5:21–22, 27–28). Sin is a matter of the heart before it is ever an issue of our behavior. This means that your and my biggest problem in life exists inside us and not outside us. It's the evil inside me that connects me to the evil outside me. So I must confess that I am my greatest problem. And if I confess this, I am saying that I don't so much need to be rescued from people, locations, and situations. I am in desperate need of the grace that is alone able to rescue me from me. I can escape situations and relationships, but I have no power to escape me. This is exactly why David prayed in Psalm 51 that God would create a clean heart in him. God's grace is grace for the heart, and that is very good news.

For further study and encouragement: James 4:1–10

MARCH 8

Yes, your life is messy and hard, but that's not a failure of the plan; it is the plan. It's God working to complete what he's begun in you.

It is so very different from the way we normally think about grace. It's not the way we tend to think about God's love. It doesn't seem wise and good to us. It causes us to question God's faithfulness and love. It's just not what we thought we signed on for when we placed our trust in Jesus Christ. It's not a typical definition of the good life, and it causes us to think at times that God isn't paying attention and that the bad guys are winning.

You are tempted to think that because you're God's child, your life should be easier, more predictable, and definitely more comfortable. But that's not what the Bible teaches. Instead, it reveals that struggles are part of God's plan for you. This means that if you're God's child, you must never allow yourself to think that the hard things you are now going through are failures of God's character, promises, power, or plan. You must not allow yourself to think that God has turned his back on you. You must not let yourself begin to buy into the possibility that God is not as trustworthy as you thought him to be. You must not let yourself do any of these things, because when you begin to doubt God's goodness, you quit going to him for help. You see, you don't run for help to those characters you have come to doubt.

God has chosen to let you live in this fallen world because he plans to employ the difficulties of it to continue and complete his work in you. This means that those moments of difficulty are not an interruption of his plan or the failure of his plan, but rather an important part of his plan. I think there are times for many of us when we cry out for God's grace and we get it—but not the grace that we're looking for. We want the grace of relief or release. We get those in little pieces, but largely they are yet to come. What we all really need right now is the grace of transformation. God's grace is not always pleasant. It often comes in the form of something we never would have chosen to go through if we were controlling the joystick.

We all need to teach and encourage one another with the theology of uncomfortable grace, because on this side of eternity, God's grace often comes to us in uncomfortable forms. It may not be what you and I want, but it is precisely what we need. God is faithful; he will use the brokenness of the world that is your present address to complete the loving work of personal transformation that he has begun. Now, that's grace!

For *further study and encouragement:* Psalm 66

MARCH 9

God questions us, "Why spend money on what's not bread and labor for what doesn't satisfy?" Sadly, many of us do that day after day.

It's another one of those things that we all tend to do. We all tend to look for life in all the wrong places. We all tend to look for life horizontally when the reality is that we will only ever find life vertically. Somehow, some way, we all tend to look to the created world to give us life. We all carry around with us our personal catalog of "if-onlys." "If only I was married, then I'd be happy." "If only I could snag that job, then I'd be satisfied." "If only we could buy that house, I don't think I'd want another thing." "If only my marriage was better, then I'd be okay." "If only my children would turn out right, then I'd been content." "If only I could achieve _____, I wouldn't want anything more." "If only our finances were more stable, then I wouldn't complain anymore." Whatever sits on the other side of your "if-only" is where you are looking for life, peace, joy, hope, and lasting contentment of heart. The problem is that you continue to spend money on what won't fill you and to work too hard to get what won't ever satisfy you. It is a big, disastrous spiritual mess that leaves you fat, addicted, in debt, and with a still unsatisfied heart. Why? Because earth will never be your savior. This physical, created world, with all of its sights, sounds, locations, experiences, and relationships, has no capacity to make your heart content. This physical world was designed by God to be one big finger that points you to the only place where your heart will find satisfaction and rest. Your heart will rest only when it finds its rest in God, and God alone.

So Jesus says: "Sell your possessions, and give to the needy. Provide yourselves with moneybags that do not grow old, with a treasure in the heavens that does not fail, where no thief approaches and no moth destroys" (Luke 12:33). What will you hook your heart to today in the hope that it will give you life? Where will you look for peace and rest of heart? What will you reach for to give you hope, courage, and a reason to continue? Where will you look in creation to try to get what only the Creator can give you? What bread will you buy today that will never fill your spiritual stomach?

Why would you frantically look to creation to give you what you already have been given in Christ? Why would you ask this broken world to be your savior when Jesus has come as your Savior to supply in his grace everything that you need?

For further study and encouragement: Isaiah 55

MARCH 10

The stuff outside you, no matter how troubling, is not as dangerous as the mess inside you, and for that you have the grace of Jesus.

Listen to the words of Jesus:

> And he called the people to him again and said to them, "Hear me, all of you, and understand: There is nothing outside a person that by going into him can defile him, but the things that come out of a person are what defile him." And when he had entered the house and left the people, his disciples asked him about the parable. And he said to them, "Then are you also without understanding? Do you not see that whatever goes into a person from outside cannot defile him, since it enters not his heart but his stomach, and is expelled?" (Thus he declared all foods clean.) And he said, "What comes out of a person is what defiles him. For from within, out of the heart of man, come evil thoughts, sexual immorality, theft, murder, adultery, coveting, wickedness, deceit, sensuality, envy, slander, pride, foolishness. All these evil things come from within, and they defile a person." (Mark 7:14–23)

Jesus is making a very powerful point. You don't defeat the disaster of sin by separating yourself from sinful people, places, or experiences. Now, that may be a very good thing to do, but it will never eradicate your sin problem. If you could defeat sin by separating yourself from its external manifestations, Jesus would never have needed to come. Look, we're not the medieval monastics, who thought that the way to defeat sin was to separate oneself from the sinful world behind big walls. We know that those monks replicated all the evils that were present in the world they sought to escape. You know what the big mistake of the monasteries was? It's an easy answer—they let people in. When people walked inside the walls, they brought their sinful hearts with them, and because of that, they re-created all the things they were seeking to escape.

In his words, Jesus calls us to humbly admit that the biggest danger to each of us is not the sin that lurks outside us, but the iniquity that still resides in our hearts. Once you admit this, you begin to get excited about God's grace in Jesus Christ. If your biggest problem lives outside of you, you don't really need grace, you just need situational or relational change. I understand why many people who call themselves Christians are not excited about grace. If you think your environment is your problem, you won't esteem grace, but once you admit that you're your biggest problem, you will celebrate the grace that rescues you from you.

For further study and encouragement: Romans 3:21–31

MARCH 11

*Of course you haven't been fulfilled in this world. It's a
sign that you have been designed for a world to come.*

It is an item on each of our theological outlines, but we don't actually live as though
we believe it. We all say that we believe that this is not all there is. We say we really
do believe that there is life after this one ends. Our formal theology contains the fact
of a new heaven and a new earth to come. But we tend to live with the anxiety and
drivenness that come when we believe that all we have is this moment.

Here's the real-life, street-level issue: if you don't keep the eyes of your heart
focused on the paradise that is to come, you will try to turn this poor fallen world
into the paradise it will never be. In the heart of every living person is the longing
for paradise. The cry of a toddler who has just fallen down is a cry for paradise. The
tears of the school-age child who has been rejected on the playground are tears of
one reaching out for paradise. The pain of aloneness that a person without friends or
family feels is the pain of one longing for paradise. The hurt the couple feels as their
marriage dissolves is the hurt of those crying out for paradise. The sadness that the
old man feels as his body weakens is the sadness of one who longs for paradise. We
all have this longing, even when we are not aware of it, because it was placed there
by our Creator. He has placed eternity in each one of our hearts (Eccl. 3:11). Our
cries are more than cries of pain; they are also cries of longing for more and better
than we will ever experience in this fallen world.

When you forget this, you work very hard to try to turn this moment into the
paradise it will never be. Your marriage will not be a paradise. Your job will not be
the paradise you long for. Your friendships will not be the paradise your heart craves.
The world around you will not function like paradise. Your children will not deliver
paradise to you. Even your church will not live up to the standard of paradise. If
you're God's child, paradise has been guaranteed for you, but it will not be right
here, right now. All the things that disappoint you now are to remind you that this is
not all there is and to cause you to long for the paradise that is to come. The dreams
that die remind you that this is not paradise. The flowers that wilt remind you that
this is not paradise. The sin that captivates you should remind you that this is not
paradise. The diseases that infect you are to remind you that this is not paradise.
Live in hope because paradise is surely coming, and stop asking this fallen world to
be the paradise it will never be.

For further study and encouragement: 2 Corinthians 4

MARCH 12

*If you mourn the fallenness of your world rather than curse
its difficulties, you know that grace has visited you.*

Life in this terribly broken world *is* hard. You are constantly dealing with the frustration of this world not operating the way God intended. You are always facing the unexpected. Almost daily you are required to deal with something you wouldn't have chosen for your life, but it's there because of the location where we live. Life right here, right now is like living in a disheveled house that has begun to fall down on its own foundation. It is still a house, but it doesn't function as it was meant to. The doors constantly get stuck shut. The plumbing only occasionally works properly. You are never sure what's going to happen when you plug an appliance in, and it seems that the roof leaks even when it's not raining. So it is with the world that you and I live in. It really is a broken-down house.

Now, there are really only two responses we can have to the brokenness that complicates all of our lives: *cursing* or *mourning.* Let's be honest. Cursing is the more natural response. We curse the fact that we have to deal with flawed people. We curse the fact that we have to deal with things that don't work right. We curse the fact that we have to deal with pollution and disease. We curse the fact that promises get broken, relationships shatter, and dreams die. We curse the realities of pain and suffering. We curse the fact that this broken-down world has been assigned to be the address where we live. It all makes us irritated, impatient, bitter, angry, and discontent. Yes, it's right not to like these things. It's natural to find them frustrating, because as Paul says in Romans 8, the whole world groans as it waits for redemption. But cursing is the wrong response. We curse what we have to deal with because it makes our lives harder than we want them to be. Cursing is all about our comfort, our pleasure, our ease. Cursing is fundamentally self-centered.

Mourning is the much better response. Mourning embraces the tragedy of the fall. Mourning acknowledges that the world is not the way God meant it to be. Mourning cries out for God's redeeming, restoring hand. Mourning acknowledges the suffering of others. Mourning is about something bigger than the fact that life is hard. Mourning grieves what sin has done to the cosmos and longs for the Redeemer to come and make his broken world new again. Mourning, then, is a response that is prompted by grace.

This side of eternity in this broken world, cursing is the default language of the kingdom of self, but mourning is the default language of the kingdom of God. Which language will you speak today?

For further study and encouragement: Genesis 1–3

MARCH 13

You don't have to worry about whether your world is under control.
God rules. You just have to learn to trust him when his rule isn't evident.

I looked everywhere. I looked high and low. There wasn't a drawer, a cabinet, or a dark closet I didn't tear apart in my search. I even went out to the car twice to make sure I hadn't left it there. The file contained important papers, and I had lost it somewhere. It was so frustrating. And after all my searching, it was just as lost as when I had begun. That night it hit me that my lost file was a picture of how little control I have over my own life. I do not even have sovereignty over my little world to guarantee that I will never lose important things. It can be a bit scary to consider. You and I have very little power and control over the most significant things in our lives. You and I don't know what's going to happen next. We don't have a clue what will be on our plates next week or next month. We have little control over the principal people in our lives, little power over the situations in which we live, and almost no control over the locations of our lives.

Honestly facing your lack of sovereignty over your own life produces either anxiety or relief. Anxiety is God-forgetting. It is the result of thinking that life is on your shoulders, that it is your job to figure it all out and keep things in order. It's worrisome to think that your job in life is to work yourself into enough control over people, locations, and situations that you can rest assured that you will get what you think you need and accomplish what you think you need to accomplish. If you fall into this way of thinking, your life will be burdened with worry and your heart will be filled with dread.

But there is a much better way. It is God-remembering. It rests in the relief that although it may not look like it, your life is under the careful control of One who defines wisdom, power, and love. In all of those moments when life is out of *your* control, it is not out of *his* control: "For his dominion is an everlasting dominion, and his kingdom endures from generation to generation; . . . and he does according to his will among the host of heaven and among the inhabitants of the earth; and none can stay his hand or say to him, 'What have you done?'" (Dan. 4:34–35).

You see, rest is not to be found in your control but in God's absolute rule over everything. You will never be in a situation, location, or relationship that is not under his control.

For further study and encouragement: Psalm 97

MARCH 14

Corporate worship is designed to once again clear up our confusion as to what is truly important in life.

Here's what we all need to understand. This side of eternity, it's very hard for us to keep what God says is important as important in our hearts. For all of us, things rise to levels of importance far beyond their true importance and begin to command the thoughts, motives, desires, choices, and allegiance of our hearts. As human beings made in the likeness of God, we don't live by instinct. No, we are value-oriented, goal-oriented, purpose-oriented, and importance-oriented beings. We are always living in the quest for something. We are always in pursuit of some vision, some desire, or some dream. Every day we all name things as important, and when we do, we work to have those things in our lives. You could argue that everything we do and say is our attempt to get what is important to us from the situations, relationships, and locations in which we live.

What I am describing is a huge spiritual battle that is fought on the turf of your heart. You see, whatever important thing rules your heart also shapes your words and behavior. The fact of the matter is that we all lose sight of what is truly important. Winning an argument becomes too important for us. A beautiful house rises in importance beyond its true worth. Getting that next promotion becomes too important. Having a comfortable and predictable life takes on too much value. Being liked by other people becomes more important to us than the favor of God. Physical beauty and pleasure take on too much value in our hearts. A cool car, a great steak, nice clothes, or the last bowl of cereal from the box rises in value far beyond its true significance. We all need to be reminded again and again of what God has declared are the most important things in life.

So in grace, God has designed us to regularly gather together and remember the things that are worth living for. Corporate worship reminds us of his power, glory, and grace. It reminds us of the depth of our spiritual needs. It reminds us of the eternity that is to come. It reminds us of salvation past, present, and future. And as it reminds us of these things, it clears up our values confusion once again, rescuing us from our wandering and often-fickle hearts, and pointing us to the One who rightly commands our allegiance and in grace gives us every important thing that we would ever need.

For further study and encouragement: Hebrews 10:19–25

MARCH 15

Any time you question God's wisdom or step over his boundaries,
you are telling yourself that you are smarter than God.

It is one of those "put-you-in-your-place responses." God is speaking to Job and drawing the Creator/creature line of distinction in bold strokes. It is a stunning description of God's majesty and Job's smallness. These are words we should read again and again:

Then the LORD answered Job out
of the whirlwind and said:

"Who is this that darkens counsel by
    words without knowledge?
Dress for action like a man;
    I will question you, and you
      make it known to me.

"Where were you when I laid the
    foundation of the earth?
    Tell me, if you have
      understanding.
Who determined its measurements—
    surely you know!
Or who stretched the line
    upon it?

On what were its bases sunk,
    or who laid its cornerstone,
when the morning stars sang together
    and all the sons of God shouted
      for joy?

"Or who shut in the sea with doors
    when it burst out from the womb,
when I made clouds its garment
    and thick darkness its swaddling
      band,
and prescribed limits for it
    and set bars and doors,
and said, 'Thus far shall you come,
    and no farther,
    and here shall your proud waves
      be stayed?'" (Job 38:1–11)

Turn to your Bible and continue reading through chapter 40. Let your heart take in the grandeur of God's wisdom and power. Let your soul rest in jaw-dropping awe of his majesty. Then remember your own smallness and frailty. Let yourself be humbled by how little you know and how few things you are able to do. Begin to embrace the utterly laughable irrationality of ever thinking that in any situation, location, or relationship it would ever be possible for you to be smarter than God. Laugh at the delusion of your own grandeur. Mock the illusion of your own glory. And in humble gratitude for grace that humbles, bow down and worship.

After you have bowed down and worshiped, get up and serve this One of awesome glory. Refuse to question his will. Refuse to let yourself think that his boundaries are ill placed. Be thankful his majesty is your protection, his glory is your motivation, his grace is your help, and his wisdom is your direction. He is infinitely smarter than you and me in our most brilliant moments.

For further study and encouragement: Job 38:1–42:46

MARCH 16

Discontent is good if it makes you long for home, but bad if it makes you doubt the One who prepares a place for you in his home.

Answer me when I call, O God of my righteousness!
    You have given me relief when I was in distress.
    Be gracious to me and hear my prayer!

O men, how long shall my honor be turned into shame?
    How long will you love vain words and seek after lies? *Selah*
But know that the LORD has set apart the godly for himself;
    the LORD hears when I call to him.

Be angry, and do not sin;
    ponder in your own hearts on your beds, and be silent. *Selah*
Offer right sacrifices,
    and put your trust in the LORD.

There are many who say, "Who will show us some good?
    Lift up the light of your face upon us, O LORD!"
You have put more joy in my heart
    than they have when their grain and wine abound.

In peace I will both lie down and sleep;
    for you alone, O LORD, make me dwell in safety. (Psalm 4)

These words were penned by David in one of the most heartbreaking moments of his life. He's hiding out in a cave with a band of faithful men because his son is out to take his throne. In a monarchy, the only way to securely take a throne is by ending the life of the person who is on the throne. Imagine where your thoughts would go, where your emotions would be, and where your heart would run to in a situation like this. Is David content? Of course not. It appears that little good can come out of this moment in his life. Yet in his grief and discontent, he knows remarkable peace. He even talks about his heart being filled with joy! Why? Because at the deepest of levels, neither his peace nor his joy is based on the circumstances, but on the God who rules the circumstances. If David's security is in God and God alone, then he has as much security in that cave as he does in the palace, because it is the Lord alone who makes him dwell in safety. There is no doubt in David's words.

What will it be for you today—the discontent of doubt and fear or the contentment of peace and rest? It is only grace that can deliver us from fear and give our hearts rest even when we're in the cave once again.

For further study and encouragement: Micah 7

MARCH 17

If you put too many things in your need category, you will end up frustrated with life, hurt by others, and doubting God's goodness.

It really is one of the sloppiest words used in human culture. If *need* means "essential for life," then the vast majority of the things we say that we need we don't actually need. You know this if you have children or are around children. Let's say you're a parent and you have taken your child to the mall (which is your first mistake). As you're walking through the mall, your child sees the sneaker store and immediately makes a left-hand turn. Now, with nose pressed against the window of the store, he says, "Mom, I neeeeeeed those sneakers." You look down at his feet, which are encased in perfectly good shoes, and you say: "No, I'm not getting you those sneakers. You already have perfectly good shoes." Now, when you say this, your child does not think: "What a wise mother I have been blessed with. She has seen through my distorted sense of need, has recognized selfish desire, and has lovingly rescued me from me." No, your child lashes out against you: "You always say 'no' to me. I don't know why I have to have the one mom who hates sneakers." Then your child refuses to relate to you for the rest of the time that you are in the mall.

When you tell yourself that something is a need, three things follow. First, you feel entitled to the thing, because, after all, it is a need. Second, because it is a need, you feel it's your right to demand it. And third, you then judge the love of another person by his or her willingness to deliver the thing. This not only happens in our relationships with one another, but more important, it happens in our relationship with God. When you name something as a need and God doesn't deliver it, you begin to doubt his goodness. What is deadly about this is that you simply don't run for help to someone whose character you've come to doubt.

In Matthew 6:32, Jesus reminds us that we have a heavenly Father who knows exactly what we need. There is comfort and confrontation in Jesus's words. The confrontation is this: the reason Jesus reminds us that we have a Father who has a clear understanding of our true needs is because we don't have such an understanding. We constantly get needs and wants confused, and when we do, we are tempted to question the love of our heavenly Father. The comfort is that, by grace, we have been made to be the children of the wisest, most loving Father that the universe has ever known. He is never, ever confused. He knows our every need because he created us. We can rest in the grace that has made us his children, knowing that our place in his family guarantees that we will have what we need.

For further study and encouragement: Psalm 145

MARCH 18

Facing disappointment and failure? Don't be surprised—you're still
flawed and your world is still fallen. For this, there's grace.

If you fail to take seriously what the Bible says about who we are and about the nature of the world we live in, you will live with unrealistic expectations, you'll be naive when it comes to temptation, and you'll find yourself regularly surprised and disappointed. Let's examine what the Bible says about us and our world in this period of time between the "already" and the "not yet".

Although God's work of redemption has begun, you and I still live in a world that is terribly broken and simply does not function in the beautiful way that God intended when he put it together. No passage captures the current brokenness of our world better than Romans 8. Paul employs three provocative phrases to capture this brokenness: "subjected to futility" (v. 20), "bondage to decay" (v. 21), and "in the pains of childbirth" (v. 22). There is a constant futility to life in a fallen world. Things just don't work right, and no matter how hard you try, you can't escape the frustration of a world that's not operating properly. There is death and decay all around us. People die. Things die. Dreams die. Relationships die. Physical creation dies. Then there are times when the suffering is severe, just like the acute pain of childbirth. Under the weight of all this brokenness, Paul says that this world is "groaning together" (v. 22). Scripture calls you to be aware of the environment in which you live.

The Bible also has clear and humbling things to say about you and me. John says, "If we say we have no sin, we deceive ourselves, and the truth is not in us" (1 John 1:8). Yes, the power of sin has been broken, but the presence of sin still remains inside us and is being progressively eradicated by God's delivering grace. So every day we all give empirical evidence that we are sinners. We all still carry around inside us the darkness of iniquity, transgression, and sin. We have not yet fully escaped the dire danger that is us.

Now, if you fail to take seriously what the Bible has to say about the world in which you live and you fail to take seriously what the Bible has to say about what still lives inside you, you won't seek the forgiving, rescuing, protecting, transforming, and delivering grace that is your only hope. That grace alone has the power to protect you from the evil outside you and to deliver you from the evil that lives inside you.

In a real way, things are worse than you ever thought they could be, but God's grace is greater than you could ever have imagined it would be. Biblical faith lives at the intersection of shocking honesty and glorious hope.

For further study and encouragement: Genesis 6:1–8

MARCH 19

Faith is about measuring your potential, not on the basis of your natural gifts and experience, but in the surety of God's presence and promises.

It is almost a humorous story. It's found in Judges 6:11–18:

> Now the angel of the LORD came and sat under the terebinth at Ophrah, which belonged to Joash the Abiezrite, while his son Gideon was beating out wheat in the winepress to hide it from the Midianites. And the angel of the LORD appeared to him and said to him, "The LORD is with you, O mighty man of valor." And Gideon said to him, "Please, sir, if the LORD is with us, why then has all this happened to us? And where are all his wonderful deeds that our fathers recounted to us, saying, 'Did not the LORD bring us up from Egypt?' But now the LORD has forsaken us and given us into the hand of Midian." And the LORD turned to him and said, "Go in this might of yours and save Israel from the hand of Midian; do not I send you?" And he said to him, "Please, Lord, how can I save Israel? Behold, my clan is the weakest in Manasseh, and I am the least in my father's house." And the LORD said to him, "But I will be with you, and you shall strike the Midianites as one man." And he said to him, "If now I have found favor in your eyes, then show me a sign that it is you who speak with me. Please do not depart from here until I come to you and bring out my present and set it before you." And he said, "I will stay till you return."

God approaches Gideon to call him to lead Israel in a very important battle and calls him a "mighty man of valor." Where does he find this "mighty man"? He finds him threshing wheat in a winepress. He's doing something indoors that you normally do outdoors because he is afraid of the very people whom God is going to call him to attack! God calls him a mighty man not because of Gideon's natural strength and courage, but because of what Gideon will be able to do in the power that God will give him. We know this is true because God begins his statement with these words: "The LORD is with you." Poor fearful Gideon even questions that.

Then Gideon essentially says: "God, you must have the wrong address. I'm the least son of the most inconsequential tribe in all of Israel. How in the world do you expect me to save Israel?" As this statement reveals, Gideon both misunderstands who he is and who God is. If you fail to remember who God is in his power, glory, and grace, and you forget who you are as a child in his family, you will always mismeasure your potential to do what God has called you to do. You will measure your capability based on your natural gifts and the size of whatever it is that God has chosen you to face. Thankfully, since God is with you, you have been blessed with wisdom and power beyond your own that give you potential you would not have on your own.

For further study and encouragement: 1 Corinthians 1:26–31

MARCH 20

Christ's sacrifice satisfied the Father's anger so that, as his child,
you will receive his discipline but need not fear his wrath.

It is the bottom line of your acceptance with God. It is the foundational reason why grace is your only hope. *Jesus fully and completely satisfied the Father's anger so that you and I will never, ever again face the penalty for our sin.* You do not have to live in fear of God's anger. On your very worst, most rebellious, and most faithless day, you can run into the holy presence of your heavenly Father and he will not turn you away. Your acceptance has not been, nor will it ever be, based on your performance. You have not been welcomed into an eternal relationship with God because you have kept the law, but because Jesus did. If you obey God for a thousand years, you will not have earned more of his acceptance than you were granted the very first moment you believed. Here's how radical the gospel of grace really is—you do not have to be something before God because Jesus accomplished everything on your behalf.

Since you are God's child and he loves you dearly, he disciplines you. But in the face of his loving discipline, a very important distinction needs to be made. His discipline is not punishment for your sin, because all of your punishment has been borne by your Savior, Jesus. Rather than being punitive, his fatherly discipline is transformative. It is designed to change your heart. It is one of the tools God uses to propel and ultimately to complete his agenda of grace. His discipline is not teaching you what to do to earn your place as one of his children; his careful, loving discipline actually proves that you *are* one of his children:

> It is for discipline that you have to endure. God is treating you as sons. For what son is there whom his father does not discipline? If you are left without discipline, in which all have participated, then you are illegitimate children and not sons. Besides this, we have had earthly fathers who disciplined us and we respected them. Shall we not much more be subject to the Father of spirits and live? For they disciplined us for a short time as it seemed best to them, but he disciplines us for our good, that we may share his holiness. For the moment all discipline seems painful rather than pleasant, but later it yields the peaceful fruit of righteousness to those who have been trained by it. (Heb. 12:7–11)

So God's discipline is an instrument of his grace. It is a continuation of his work of personal heart-and-life transformation. God's discipline is not him turning his angry back on us. It is God turning his face of grace toward us once again, and he will continue to do this until his grace has finished its work.

For further study and encouragement: Job 5:17–27

MARCH 21

No need to be paralyzed by regret, because your slate has been wiped clean by God's amazing forgiving grace.

Let yourself bask today in the comfort of these passages:

And you, who were once alienated and hostile in mind, doing evil deeds, he has now reconciled in his body of flesh by his death, in order to present you holy and blameless and above reproach before him. (Col. 1:21–22)

For if while we were enemies we were reconciled to God by the death of his Son, much more, now that we are reconciled, shall we be saved by his life. (Rom. 5:10)

Christ redeemed us from the curse of the law by becoming a curse for us—for it is written, "Cursed is everyone who is hanged on a tree"—so that in Christ Jesus the blessing of Abraham might come to the Gentiles. (Gal. 3:13–14)

For by grace you have been saved through faith. And this is not your own doing; it is the gift of God, not a result of works, so that no one may boast. (Eph. 2:8–9)

And you, who were dead in your trespasses and the uncircumcision of your flesh, God made alive together with him, having forgiven us all our trespasses, by canceling the record of debt that stood against us with its legal demands. This he set aside, nailing it to the cross. (Col. 2:13–14)

There is therefore now no condemnation for those who are in Christ Jesus. For the law of the Spirit of life has set you free in Christ Jesus from the law of sin and death. (Rom. 8:1–2)

Therefore, since we have been justified by faith, we have peace with God through our Lord Jesus Christ. Through him we have also obtained access by faith into this grace in which we stand, and we rejoice in hope of the glory of God. (Rom. 5:1–2)

In this is love, not that we have loved God but that he loved us and sent his Son to be the propitiation for our sins. (1 John 4:10)

The message is clear! It is most clearly stated by that comfort-stimulating passage from Colossians 2, quoted above. Let your mind embrace the comfort of these words, comfort that is nowhere else to be found: "[God has canceled] the record of debt that stood against us with its legal demands. This he set aside, nailing it to the cross."

If God has willingly canceled whatever regret causes you to hold on to, you are free to let it go as well. You are free to quit punishing yourself for debts that God has already canceled. Now, that's freedom!

For further study and encouragement: Colossians 2

MARCH 22

Obedience is freedom. Better to follow the Master's plan than to do what you weren't wired to do—master yourself.

It is true that the thing that you and I most need to be rescued from is us! The greatest danger that we face is the danger that we are to ourselves. Who we think we are is a delusion and what we all tend to want is a disaster. Put together, they lead to only one place—death.

If you're a parent, you see it in your children. It didn't take long for you to realize that you are parenting a little self-sovereign, who thinks at the deepest level that he needs no authority in his life but himself. Even if he cannot yet walk or speak, he rejects your wisdom and rebels against your authority. He has no idea what is good or bad to eat, but he fights your every effort to put into his mouth something that he has decided he doesn't want. As he grows, he has little ability to comprehend the danger of the electric wall outlet, but he tries to stick his fingers in it precisely because you have instructed him not to. He wants to exercise complete control over his sleep, diet, and activities. He believes it is his right to rule his life, so he fights your attempts to bring him under submission to your loving authority.

Not only does your little one resist your attempts to bring him under your authority, he tries to exercise authority over you. He is quick to tell you what to do and does not fail to let you know when you have done something that he does not like. He celebrates you when you submit to his desires and finds ways to punish you when you fail to submit to his demands.

Now, here's what you have to understand: when you're at the end of a very long parenting day, when your children seemed to conspire together to be particularly rebellious, and you're sitting on your bed exhausted and frustrated, you need to remember that you are more like your children than unlike them. We all want to rule our worlds. Each of us has times when we see authority as something that ends freedom rather than gives it. Each of us wants God to sign the bottom of our personal wish list, and if he does, we celebrate his goodness. But if he doesn't, we begin to wonder if it's worth following him at all. Like our children, each of us is on a quest to be and to do what we were not designed by our Creator to be or to do.

So grace comes to decimate our delusions of self-sufficiency. Grace works to destroy our dangerous hope for autonomy. Grace helps to make us reach out for what we really need and submit to the wisdom of the Giver. Yes, it's true, grace rescues us from us.

For further study and encouragement: Psalm 119:1–88

Because God rules all the places where you live, he is able to deliver
his promises to you in the very circumstances where they are needed.

I don't know whether you have ever thought of this before, but God's promises are only as good as the extent of his sovereignty. He can deliver what you need only in the places where he rules. If his rule is not firm and unchanging, his promises are not either. I think that many of us fail to make this connection, and when we do, we allow ourselves to celebrate his promises while subtly resisting his rule. He is your sovereign Savior. If he were not sovereign, you would have no guarantee that he could exercise the authority necessary to be your Savior.

Think for a moment about the flow of biblical history. Think of the many generations of people that existed between the fall of Adam and Eve and the birth of Jesus Christ. Think of the myriad situations and locations in that span of time. Think of all the human governments that rose and fell. Think of all the decisions, great and small, that people made. Think of the constant life-and-death cycle of the physical creation. Now consider this—in order for Jesus to be born as was promised, to live as was necessary, and to die and rise on our behalf as he said he would, God had to exercise absolute rule over the forces of nature and complete control over the events of human history so that, at just the right moment, Jesus would be born, live, die, and rise again for our redemption.

Without the rule of the Almighty, there would've been no prophets predicting the birth of the Messiah, no angels announcing it to the shepherds, and no Mary wondering about the babe in the manger. There would've been no miracles in Palestine. There would've been no perfectly obedient Son of Man. There would've been no unjust trial and cruel cross. There would've been no disciples to pass the life-giving gospel down to us, no Scripture, no church, and no hope of eternal life.

If you are going to reach for the life-giving promises of the gospel, you must also celebrate the absolute rule of the One who, because of his rule, is able to deliver those promises to you. Hope is not found just in the beauty of those promises, but in the incalculable power and authority of the One who has made them. There is no hope in the promises of one who has little power over the situations and locations where they must be delivered. But you can have hope because your Lord has complete rule over all the places where you will need his promises to become your reality.

For further study and encouragement: Jeremiah 32:16–27

MARCH 24

Only the gargantuan glory of God can rescue you from all the miniglories of creation that regularly seduce and kidnap your heart.

Imagine that I decided to take my family to Walt Disney World in about a year's time. And imagine that I sat down at the computer with my children and showed them the multifaceted sight-and-sound glories of Disney. Imagine further that through the year, as the children lost sight of what was to come and complained about the sacrifices we were having to make, I took them back to the Disney Web site over and over again to remind them of the unparalleled entertainment glories that are only ever found there. Imagine now that we finally load ourselves in the car and begin the long trip to this glorious place. Imagine our children getting impatient and wondering how long it will be before we are actually at Disney. And imagine that after many long hours of travel, we are coursing our way down the highway in Florida and we see a sign that says, "Walt Disney World 120 miles." Now, imagine that I park beside this sign, and we have our vacation there. You would think that I have lost my mind. Yet millions of people do that every day. Confused? Permit me to explain.

There is one thing that you know for sure—the sign is not the thing. The sign was created to point you to the thing. It cannot give you what the thing can deliver. The sign can only point you to where the thing can be found. The sign pointing to Walt Disney World will not ever give you what Walt Disney World can. So it is with the physical glories of creation.

Here's what you need to understand: only two types of glory exist—*sign* glory and *ultimate* glory. Sign glory is all the wondrous display of sights, sounds, colors, textures, tastes, smells, and experiences of the physical world that God created. These glories were not designed to satisfy your heart. They were not made to give you contentment, peace, meaning, and purpose. They have no capacity to give you life. Earth will never be your savior. Rather, all of creation was designed to be one big sign that points you to the One of ultimate glory who alone has the power to give you life and to satisfy your heart. God alone is able to give you life. He alone is able to give rest to your searching heart. He designed his world to point to him, not to replace him (see Psalm 19).

Where will you look for life today? Will you live like the father having his vacation next to the sign along the highway or will you run to where the sign points? It really is true that your heart will only ever be satisfied when it finds its satisfaction in him.

For further study and encouragement: Joel 2:21–27

MARCH 25

We are often quick to anger and slow to love, but God is not like us. He's slow to anger and abounding in love.

You know the scene. You've rushed to the grocery store to get a few critical items your family needs. Your plan is to get in and out as quickly as is humanly possible. You sprint down the aisles and grab your stuff, then run to the checkout lines, only to discover that the self-serve lanes are closed for repair and only one clerk is working. Just as you reach her lane, a woman pulls in front of you with a cart of 150 items. You can feel your chest tighten. It's not enough that she slowly reexamines every item as she puts it on the belt, but after emptying her cart she pulls out 120 coupons that have to be cross-checked with the corresponding grocery items. You're beginning to get angry. Finally her quest to save every last penny is over, but then she discovers that she has to pay. It's as if it's a fresh concept to her. Until this point, she has made no move toward her purse, which is about the size of a camping tent for six. As she begins to pull makeup, cookies, and small children out of her purse, you bellow, "Come on, are you kidding me?" As everyone at the front of the store turns to look at you, you realize you said it louder than you planned.

Examine the moment with me. You are livid at this woman, but she didn't purposefully delay you. You are seething, but you have lost only ten minutes out of your day. You're incensed, but the whole thing is ridiculously minor. You're mad because your anger is close to the surface. You're irritated because anger is more natural to you than patient love. You have not loved the woman in front of you well because you were so busy focusing on yourself that you had little energy left to respond lovingly toward her.

Isn't it comforting to know that God is the polar opposite of what I have just described? He who has the right to be angry with us and the power to do whatever his anger desires is in fact slow to anger. The Bible doesn't tell you that he abounds in anger, but it is quick to reassure you that he is abounding in love. Be thankful today that God is not like us, because if he were, you and I would be damned. Be thankful that he is incredibly patient and eternally kind. Be thankful that he is tender, gentle, and gracious. Be thankful that he does not treat you as your sins deserve. Be thankful that because of the work of Jesus, he will respond to you with lovingkindness even on your worst day. "The Lord is slow to anger and abounding in steadfast love, forgiving iniquity and transgression" (Num. 14:18).

For further study and encouragement: Psalm 104

MARCH 26

Today you'll encounter things that will confuse you, but rest
assured the One who rules all those things is not confused.

We really don't know much. Every day we are all greeted with mysteries. None of us can predict for sure where our personal stories are going. We are all confused about what happens to us, to those close to us, and in the world in which we live. As much as we try to make sense of our lives, there are things that we simply aren't able to understand. Here's what all of this means—you and I will never find inner peace and rest by trying to figure it all out. Peace is found in resting in the wisdom and grace of the One who has it all figured out and rules it all for his glory and our good.

When our children were very young, when I would refuse to let them do something, they didn't understand why, so they would begin to protest. I would then get down on my knees so we could be face to face, and then I would talk with them. The conversation would go like this:

"Do you know that your daddy loves you?"

"Yes, I know my daddy loves me."

"Is your daddy mean and bad to you?"

"No, you don't like to be mean."

"Is your daddy a horrible, bad daddy?"

"No."

"Then listen to what daddy is going to say. I would like to tell you why I had to say 'no' to what you wanted to do, but I can't. If I explained it to you, you wouldn't understand anyway, so here's what you need to do. You need to walk down the hallway and say to yourself, 'I don't know why daddy said no to me, but I know my daddy loves me and I'm going to trust my daddy.' I really do love you."

"I love you too."

There is so much that we don't understand. There is so much that we are incapable of understanding. So rest is found in trusting the Father. He is not confused, and he surely does have your best interest in mind. Yes, he will ask you to do hard things and he will bring difficult things your way, but he is worthy of your trust and he loves you dearly. Today your heavenly Father reaches down to you and says: "I know you don't understand all that you face, but remember, I love you. Trust me and you will find peace that can be found no other way."

For further study and encouragement: Isaiah 40

MARCH 27

Get up and face life with courage because, as God's child, you have not been left to the limits of your own strength and wisdom.

Galatians 2:20 captures who you are as a child of God and what you have been given so well:

1. **A statement of redemptive-historical fact.** "*I have been crucified with Christ.*" What Paul is saying here is hugely important. On the cross of Calvary, Jesus didn't purchase general savability. He didn't die to make salvation possible. No, Jesus took names to the cross. He specifically and effectively died for you and me. His death was just as effective for us as if we had died ourselves. Because he died as our representative, his death satisfied God's anger against us, so that we face it no more.

2. **A statement of present redemptive reality.** "*It is no longer I who live, but Christ who lives in me.*" This is radical and hard to grasp, but important to consider. You and I died with Christ so that he could live within us now. Paul's not talking about physical life here, but spiritual. The power that now animates, motivates, and propels your spiritual life is not you, but Christ! By grace, he makes you the place where he dwells. This means you are never in a situation, location, or relationship by yourself. He is always with you. And because he is always with you, you are never left to the limited resources of your own wisdom, strength, and righteousness (see Eph. 3:20–21).

3. **The life-shaping result.** "*The life I now live in the flesh I live by faith in the Son of God, who loved me and gave himself for me.*" I place my faith in the fact of his death for me and his life within me, and I live on that basis. I live with peace, hope, and courage, but not because I understand all that is going on inside me or around me. It is because I have not only been forgiven, but I have been blessed with resources beyond my imagination because the King of kings and the Lord of lords, the Creator-Savior, now lives inside me. I don't understand much, but of this I am sure—he is with me, he is in me, and he is for me. I cannot allow myself to think that I am poor when his presence makes me rich. I cannot tell myself that I am unable when he empowers me by grace. Here's the bottom line—I am comfortable with not knowing, because he knows and he is with me forever.

For further study and encouragement: Habakkuk 3:17–19

MARCH 28

*You were hardwired for love, so everything you decide, desire, think,
say, and do is an expression of love for someone or something.*

The counsel of John is clear and just as important today as when he penned the
words:

> Do not love the world or the things in the world. If anyone loves the world, the
> love of the Father is not in him. For all that is in the world—the desires of the
> flesh and the desires of the eyes and pride of life—is not from the Father but is
> from the world. And the world is passing away along with its desires, but whoever
> does the will of God abides forever. (1 John 2:15–17)

You are a lover; we all are. We love. It's what human beings do every moment of
every day, in every location, and in every situation. You are never not loving. It's in
the very fiber of your being. It's the way God carefully constructed you. Why did he
hardwire you to love? Why is this such an essential part of who you are? God created you with this capacity so that you would have what you need to live in a deeply
loving, heart-controlling, motivation-producing, worship-initiating, joy-stimulating
relationship with him. Your capacity to love was created for him. Your desire to love
was meant to draw you to him. Your heart was designed to long for love, and that
longing was meant to find its final and complete fulfillment in him.

Here is the tragedy. Sin causes us all, in some way, to turn our backs on the love
of God and give the principal love of our hearts to someone or something else. We
seek to have our hearts fulfilled by love for something other than God. We love the
creation more than the Creator. We love other people more than we love God. We
love ourselves so much that we have little energy left to love the One who is love. We
run from thing to thing, hoping our hearts will be content in love. We're all spiritually promiscuous, running from lover to lover, giving the loyalty of our hearts to
things other than God. We're all spiritual adulterers, giving away what by the design
of creation belongs to God and God alone. The Bible is the story of a love drama
that looked as if it would end in tragedy—but then Jesus came.

You see, God, who is love, sent the Son of his love to make the ultimate sacrifice
of love so that we would become people who love him as we have never loved him
before. In love, he showers us with love that does not quit even on our most unloving
day. And by grace, he transforms our hearts so that increasingly we are able to keep
creation in its proper place and keep the ultimate love of our hearts for him and him
alone. Now celebrate the gift of that rescuing love!

For further study and encouragement: Deuteronomy 6–8

MARCH 29

*Living in this present broken world is designed by God
to produce longing, readiness, and hope in me.*

It's not natural for us to think about our lives in this way, but the difficulties we all face in this broken world are not in the way of God's plan. No, they are part of it. The fallen world that is your address is not your address because he didn't think through his redemptive plan very well. You are living where you're living and facing what you're facing because that's exactly how God wanted it to be. The hardships that we all face between the "already" and the "not yet" are not a sign of the failure of God's redeeming work, but rather a very important tool of it.

What we are all going through right here, right now is a massive, progressive process of values clarification and heart protection. God is daily employing the brokenness of this present world to clarify your values. Why do you need this? You need it because you struggle in this life to remember what is truly important, that is, what God says is important. You and I place much more importance on things than they truly possess, and when we do so, these things begin to claim our heart allegiance. So God ordains for us to experience that physical things get old and break. The people in our lives fail us. Relationships sour and become painful. Our physical bodies weaken. Flowers die and food spoils. All of this is meant to teach us that these things are beautiful and enjoyable, but they cannot give us what we all long for—life.

In this world that is groaning, God is protecting our hearts. He is protecting us from us. Our hearts can be so fickle. We can worship God one day, only to turn and give the worship of our hearts to something else the next. So, in love, God lets pieces of the creation die in our hands so that increasingly we are freed from asking earth to give us what only he can give. He works through loss to protect us from giving our allegiance to things that will never, ever deliver what our hearts seek. This is all designed to deepen our love and worship of him. It is all crafted to propel the joy that we have in him. And in so doing, he is preparing us for that moment when we will be freed from this present travail and give all of our being to the worship of him forever and ever.

Your Lord knows that even as his child your heart is still prone to wander, so in tender, patient grace he keeps you in a world that teaches you that he alone is worthy of the deepest, most worshipful allegiance of your heart.

For further study and encouragement: 1 Peter 1:3–12

MARCH 30

*If you are God's child, you're either giving in to sin or giving way
to the operation of rescuing grace, but your heart's never neutral.*

One of the beautiful results of God's redeeming grace in your life and mine is that the hearts of stone have been taken out of us and replaced with hearts of flesh. Think of the word picture here. If I had a stone in my hands and I pressed it with all of my might, what do you think would happen? Well, if you could see the size of my arms, you would immediately know the answer to the question. I could press that stone with all of the strength that I have and nothing whatsoever would happen. Stone is not malleable. It exists in a fixed shape. Before your conversion, you had that kind of heart. It was resistant to change. But that is not true any longer. Grace has given you a fleshy heart, one that is moldable by transforming grace.

Now, this means that when you sin, desiring, thinking, saying, or doing what is wrong in God's eyes, your conscience bothers you. What we're talking about here is the convicting ministry of the Holy Spirit. When your conscience bothers you, you have only two choices. You can gladly confess that what you've done is sin and place yourself once again under the justifying mercies of Christ, or you can erect some system of self-justification that makes what God says is wrong acceptable to your conscience. We are all so good at doing this. We are good at pointing to something or someone who justifies what we have done. We are all very good at systems of self-atonement that essentially argue for our righteousness.

What is deadly about this is that when you convince yourself that you are righteous, you quit seeking the grace that is your only hope in life or death. "If we say we have no sin, we deceive ourselves, and the truth is not in us. If we confess our sins, he is faithful and just to forgive us our sins and to cleanse us from all unrighteousness" (1 John 1:8–9).

The fact of the matter is that none of us are grace graduates, including the man who is writing this devotion. We are all in daily and desperate need of forgiving, rescuing, transforming, and delivering grace. When you resist humble acknowledgment of your sin, you resist the ever-present Redeemer who is making that sin known to you. He does this not to humiliate or punish you, but because he loves you so much that he will not turn from his work of grace in your heart until that work has accomplished all that Jesus died to give you. There is little room for neutrality here. Today you will resist grace or you will humbly run to grace. May the latter be your choice.

For further study and encouragement: Galatians 6:1–10

MARCH 31

The cross is evidence that in the hands of the Redeemer, moments of apparent defeat become wonderful moments of grace and victory.

At the center of a biblical worldview is this radical recognition—the most horrible thing that ever happened was the most wonderful thing that ever happened. Consider the cross of Jesus Christ. Could it be possible for something to happen that was more terrible than this? Could any injustice be greater? Could any loss be more painful? Could any suffering be worse? The only man who ever lived a life that was perfect in every way possible, who gave his life for the sake of many, and who willingly suffered from birth to death in loyalty to his calling was cruelly and publicly murdered in the most vicious of ways. How could it happen that the Son of Man could die? How could it be that men could capture and torture the Messiah? Was this not the end of everything good, true, and beautiful? If this could happen, is there any hope for the world?

Well, the answer is yes. There is hope! The cross was not the end of the story! In God's righteous and wise plan, this dark and disastrous moment was ordained to be the moment that would fix all the dark and disastrous things that sin had done to the world. This moment of death was at the same time a moment of life. This hopeless moment was the moment when eternal hope was given. This terrible moment of injustice was at the very same time a moment of amazing grace. This moment of extreme suffering guaranteed that suffering would end one day, once and for all. This moment of sadness welcomed us to eternal joy of heart and life. The capture and death of Christ purchased for us life and freedom. The very worst thing that could happen was at the very same time the very best thing that could happen. Only God is able to do such a thing.

The same God who planned that the worst thing would be the best thing is your Father. He rules over every moment in your life, and in powerful grace he is able to do for you just what he did in redemptive history. He takes the disasters in your life and makes them tools of redemption. He takes your failure and employs it as a tool of grace. He uses the "death" of the fallen world to motivate you to reach out for life. The hardest things in your life become the sweetest tools of grace in his wise and loving hands.

So be careful how you make sense of your life. What looks like a disaster may in fact be grace. What looks like the end may be the beginning. What looks hopeless may be God's instrument to give you real and lasting hope. Your Father is committed to taking what seems so bad and turning it into something that is very, very good.

For further study and encouragement: Acts 2:14–36

APRIL 1

Worshiping with other believers helps you view all of life from the vantage point of the resurrection of the Lord Jesus Christ.

It's not just the most important miracle ever. It's not just the most astounding event in the life of the Messiah. It's not just an essential item in your theological outline. It's not just the reason for the most important celebratory season of the church. It's not just your hope for the future. No, the resurrection is all that and more. It is also meant to be the window through which you view all of life. Second Corinthians 4:13–15 captures this truth very well: "[We know] that he who raised the Lord Jesus will raise us also with Jesus and bring us with you into his presence. For it is all for your sake, so that as grace extends to more and more people it may increase thanksgiving, to the glory of God." But what does it look like to look at life through the window of the resurrection? As I assess my life right here, right now, what about the resurrection must I remember? Let me suggest five things.

1. *The resurrection of Jesus guarantees your resurrection too.* Life is not a constantly repeating cycle of the same old same old. No, under God's rule this world is marching toward a conclusion. Your life is being carried to a glorious end. There will be a moment when God will raise you out of this broken world, and sin and suffering will be no more.
2. *The resurrection tells you what Jesus is now doing.* Jesus now reigns. First Corinthians 15 says that he will continue to reign until the final enemy is under his feet. You see, your world is not out of control, but under the careful control of One who is still doing his sin-defeating work.
3. *The resurrection promises you all the grace you need between Jesus's resurrection and yours.* If your end has already been guaranteed, then all the grace you need along the way has been guaranteed as well, or you would never make it to your appointed end. Future grace always carries with it the promise of present grace.
4. *The resurrection of Jesus motivates you to do what is right, no matter what you are facing.* The resurrection tells you that God will win. His truth will reign. His plan will be accomplished. Sin will be defeated. Righteousness will overcome evil. This means that everything you do in God's name is worth it, no matter what the cost.
5. *The resurrection tells you that you always have reason for thanks.* Quite apart from anything you have earned, you have been welcomed into the most exciting story ever and have been granted a future of joy and peace forever.

No matter what happens today, look at life through this window.

For further study and encouragement: 1 Corinthians 15:1–11

APRIL 2

Prayer is abandoning my addiction to other glories and delighting in the one glory that is truly glorious—the glory of God.

Sadly, prayer for many of us has been shrunk to an agenda that is little bigger than asking God for stuff. It has become that spiritual place where we ask God to sign our personal wish lists. For many, it is little more than a repeated cycle of requesting, followed by waiting to see if God, in fact, comes through. If he does, we celebrate his faithfulness and love; but if he doesn't, we not only wonder if he cares, we are also tempted to wonder if he's there. In this way, prayer often amounts to shopping at the Trinitarian department store for things that you have told yourself you need with the hope that they will be free.

But consider the Lord's Prayer for a moment. It doesn't look anything like what I've just described. This prayer is a prayer of worship and surrender. It recognizes, at the deepest level, the war that still goes on in my heart between the kingdom of self and the kingdom of God. It faces the fact that I can be so blind to the glory of God, and as I am, I become captured by the small glories of the created world. It does more surrendering and celebrating than it does asking. And the asking that it does is in the context not of self-glory wishing, but rather in the context of submission and worship.

How does this prayer begin? It begins by reminding you of the most astounding reality of your life. It begins with a celebration of grace: "Our Father in heaven . . ." (Matt. 6:9a). You and I must never stop celebrating this reality. God, the Creator, King, Savior, and Lord, exercised his power and grace so that people like us would become his children. What's next? "Hallowed be your name" (v. 9b). Here I surrender myself to the agenda of agendas. It is the reason the world was made. It is why you and I were created. It was all brought into being so that God would get the glory that he is due. Here I let go of all the other glories that may lay claim to my wandering heart. Here I find my motivation for all that I do. Here I cry out for rescuing grace for my disloyal heart.

Then this model prayer hits its bottom line. The next words contain a comfort and a call: "Your kingdom come, your will be done, on earth as it is in heaven" (v. 10). The comfort is that the Father, in redeeming love, has graciously chosen to give us his kingdom. He blesses us with his rule, which is always wise, loving, faithful, true, gracious, and good, and in so doing, rescues us from our little kingdoms of one. The call is to let go of our Vise-Grip hold on our Lilliputian kingdoms and give ourselves to his kingdom of glory and grace. It is only when our hearts have been protected by the worship and celebration of these requests that we are able to properly pray what comes next.

For further study and encouragement: Matthew 6:5–15

APRIL 3

Obedience never ends freedom; it is the evidence that true freedom has entered your life and liberated your heart.

I have been liberated,
set free,
and given new life,
new hope,
new motivation,
and new peace
of heart and mind.
No, I have not been freed
from the authority of
another.
I have not been freed
to walk my own way,
to write my own rules,
or to do what I choose.
No, I have been given
the best of freedoms.
I have been freed,
not from God's rule,
but from my bondage
to me.
Following,
obeying,
serving,
submitting to God
is the thing I was created to do,
so it is the place where
true freedom is to be found.
Rebellion never gives life.
Self-rule never brings freedom.
So grace has worked to rescue
me from me,
so that I can know the true freedom
of serving him.

For further study and encouragement: Psalm 116

APRIL 4

Human beings, who were created to live in awe of God, are in grave danger when familiarity causes them to be bored with God.

Familiarity is a beautiful thing. It's wonderful to be familiar with a beautiful piece of music. It means you've been blessed to hear it over and over again. It's a blessing to be familiar with roses because it means you have the privilege of having bushes nearby that you lay your eyes on every day. But the blessing of blessings is to be familiar with the ways, the character, the presence, and the promises of God. That means that grace has bridged the separation between you and God, and has drawn you into close communion with him. It also means that the Spirit of God has opened your eyes, heart, and mind to the things of God, so that what was once foolishness to you now brings you hope, comfort, and joy.

Yes, familiarity *is* a wonderful thing, but it can also be a very dangerous thing. Here is the scary dynamic of familiarity—the more you are near something and the more familiar it becomes, the less you actually see and appreciate that thing in the way you once did. When you first bought your house, perhaps you were blown away by the grand, majestic two-hundred-year-old tree that stood regally in the backyard. But something has happened as the years have gone by. You don't really see that tree anymore. It doesn't blow you away anymore, and the only time you talk about it is when you complain that you have to rake the piles of leaves it annually drops. Familiarity can be a dangerous thing.

Now, here's the vertical connection. Every human being was designed by God to have his hopes, dreams, choices, words, actions, desires, and motivations shaped by a jaw-dropping, heart-controlling, life-shaping awe of God. The stunning reality of God's existence and his grandeur and glory were meant to be at the center of human consciousness. We were all meant to live with a God awareness and, because of that awareness, to live in a Godward way. Awe of God was designed to be the principal motivation for everything we would ever do. But something happens to us as we are drawn into a close relationship with God and are blessed to live close to his secret things. Familiarity causes us to lose our awe of God. What once stunned us doesn't anymore. What produced worship in our hearts doesn't anymore. What caused us to act with hope and courage doesn't anymore. What caused us to say no to sin and yes to righteousness doesn't anymore. I am afraid that many of us have lost our awe of God and we don't even know it.

Is there evidence in your life that you are awe deficient? Cry out for eyes to see once again, for a heart ripped by awe once again. And be thankful for the grace that assures you that you will be heard and answered.

For further study and encouragement: Isaiah 6

APRIL 5

Rejoice, the Lord who has redeemed you is worthy of your love and worship.

You should enjoy food because it is God's gift, but if you love it, you'll end up fat and unhealthy. You should be thankful for the money that God provides, but if you love it, you will find yourself a workaholic or in debt. Surely you should celebrate the pleasures and comforts that God puts in your life, but if you love them, you will soon be addicted.

Here is the spiritual reality that you need to know, understand, and live in light of—*if you love the gifts and not the Giver, your heart will never be satisfied, but if you love the Giver, your heart will be content and you will be able to enjoy his gifts while keeping them in their proper place.* Beneath this reality are even deeper spiritual realities. The first is that you need to understand that you were created to love. You don't just love, you are a lover. Every human being's life is a quest to find something to love and a quest to be loved. This means that you are always surrendering the affections of your heart to something. Whatever commands the love of your heart also shapes the direction of your life. But there is more to be said. You were also created to worship. You don't just occasionally worship in moments of intentional and formal religious activity; you are a worshiper. You are always looking for something to which you can attach your identity, your hopes and dreams, and your inner peace. Whatever controls the worship of your heart controls your choices, words, emotions, and actions.

Now, because you are a sinner, it is very tempting to give the love and worship that you were meant to give to God and God alone to something in the creation (see Rom. 1:22–25). You take the affection, submission, and service of your heart that was meant to be reserved for the Creator and you place it on some created thing. We all do this in some way. So the desire for good possessions is not wrong, but it must not rule your heart. The hunger for comfort and ease is not ungodly in itself, but it must not rule your heart. The desire for the love of another person is not wrong, but it must not rule your heart. *A desire for even a good thing becomes a bad thing when that desire becomes a ruling thing.* Good things never result when love for and worship of the Creator are replaced by love for and worship of created things.

So what does grace do? Grace works to rescue you from you by progressively breaking your bondage to the created world and turning the deepest affection of your heart toward God. God alone is worthy of your worship. God alone is able to satisfy and bring peace to your heart. This work of rescue is not yet complete in any of us. Yes, by grace we love the world less than we once did and we surely love God more than before, but our hearts are still torn and our loyalties at points are still confused. But we need not fret, because grace will win and bring final rest to our worship and our love.

For further study and encouragement: 1 John 2:1–17

APRIL 6

Don't be discouraged at the spiritual war you're called to fight every day.
The Lord almighty is with you and wars on your behalf.

Between the "already" and the "not yet," life is war. It can be exhausting, frustrating, and discouraging. We all go through moments when we wish life could just be easier. We wonder why parenting has to be such a continual spiritual battle. We all wish our marriages could be free of war. We all would love it if there were no conflicts at our jobs or in our churches. But we all wake up to a war-torn world every day. It is the sad legacy of a world that has been broken by sin and is constantly under the attack of the enemy.

The way the apostle Paul ends his letter to the Ephesian church is interesting and instructive. Having laid out the truths of the gospel of Jesus Christ and having detailed their implications for our street-level living, he ends by talking about spiritual warfare:

> Finally, be strong in the Lord and in the strength of his might. Put on the whole armor of God, that you may be able to stand against the schemes of the devil. For we do not wrestle against flesh and blood, but against the rulers, against the authorities, against the cosmic powers over this present darkness, against the spiritual forces of evil in the heavenly places. Therefore take up the whole armor of God, that you may be able to withstand in the evil day, and having done all, to stand firm. Stand therefore, having fastened on the belt of truth, and having put on the breastplate of righteousness, and, as shoes for your feet, having put on the readiness given by the gospel of peace. In all circumstances take up the shield of faith, with which you can extinguish all the flaming darts of the evil one; and take the helmet of salvation, and the sword of the Spirit, which is the word of God, praying at all times in the Spirit, with all prayer and supplication. To that end keep alert with all perseverance, making supplication for all the saints, and also for me, that words may be given to me in opening my mouth boldly to proclaim the mystery of the gospel, for which I am an ambassador in chains, that I may declare it boldly, as I ought to speak. (Eph. 6:10–20)

When you get to this final part of Paul's letter, it's tempting to think that he has entirely changed the subject. No longer, it seems, is he talking about everyday Christianity. But that's exactly what he's talking about. He is saying to the Ephesian believers, "You know all that I've said about marriage, parenting, communication, anger, the church, and so on—it's all one big spiritual war." Paul is reminding you that at street level, practical, daily Christianity is war. There really is moral right and wrong. There really is an enemy. There really is seductive and deceptive temptation. You really are spiritually vulnerable. But he says more. He reminds you that by grace you have been properly armed for the battle. The question is, will you use the implements of battle that the cross of Jesus Christ has provided for you?

For further study and encouragement: 1 Peter 5:6–11

APRIL 7

Corporate worship is designed to confront you with a view of life that has at its center a dead man's cross and a living man's empty tomb.

There are two themes that I have repeated in writing and speaking again and again. I will repeat them here:

1. *Human beings made in the image of God do not live life based on the facts of their experience, but based on their interpretation of the facts.* Whether you know it or not, you have been designed by God to be a meaning maker. You are a rational human being (even if you don't always show it), and you have a constant desire for life to make sense. So you are constantly thinking and constantly interpreting. You don't actually respond to what is going on around you; you respond to the sense you have made of what is going on around you. This means that there is always some kind of interpretive grid that you are carrying around with you that helps you to make sense out of your life. Everybody believes something. Everybody assumes that certain things are true. Everybody brings some system of "wisdom" to their lives to help them to explain and understand.

2. *No one is more influential in your life than you are, because no one talks to you more than you do.* We never stop talking to ourselves. We are in a constant conversation with ourselves about God, others, ourselves, meaning and purpose, identity, and such. The things you say to you about you, God, and life are profoundly important because they form and shape the way you then respond to the things that God has put on your plate. You see, you are always preaching to yourself some kind of worldview, some kind of "gospel," if you will. The question is, in your private moment-by-moment conversation, what are you saying to you?

Paul argues very powerfully that the "dead man's cross, live man's empty tomb" gospel of the Lord Jesus Christ, which the world sees as utter foolishness, is in fact the wisest of wisdom. It is the only way to make sense out of life. It is the only lens through which you can see life accurately. It is the only kind of wisdom that really does give a final and reliable answer to the fundamental questions of life that every person asks. And at the center of this message of wisdom is not a set of ideas but a person who, in his life and death, offers you not only answers, but every grace you need to be what you were created to be and to do what you have been called to do.

For further study and encouragement: 1 Corinthians 1:18–25

APRIL 8

God uses the picture of physical food to point to universal spiritual hunger. Life is all about what we look to to fill us.

"Come, everyone who thirsts,
come to the waters;
and he who has no money,
come, buy and eat!
Come, buy wine and milk
without money and without
price.
Why do you spend your money for
that which is not bread,
and your labor for that which
does not satisfy?
Listen diligently to me, and eat what
is good,
and delight yourselves in rich
food.
Incline your ear, and come to me;
hear, that your soul may live;
and I will make with you an
everlasting covenant,
my steadfast, sure love for David.
Behold, I made him a witness to the
peoples,
a leader and commander for the
peoples.
Behold, you shall call a nation that
you do not know,
and a nation that did not know
you shall run to you,
because of the Lord your God, and
of the Holy One of Israel,
for he has glorified you.

"Seek the Lord while he may be
found;
call upon him while he is near;
let the wicked forsake his way,
and the unrighteous man his
thoughts;
let him return to the Lord, that he
may have compassion on
him,
and to our God, for he will
abundantly pardon."
(Isa. 55:1–7)

They are beautiful words of invitation and grace. And they are spoken in a language that we can all understand. We all know what it's like to be hungry, and we all know what it's like to consume a meal that just doesn't satisfy. The Bible uses this powerful food metaphor because its authors were zealous to alert you to the fact that there is a deeper hunger within you than the physical hunger with which you are so familiar. Yes, your body hungers to be filled, but your soul hungers even more. This is true for all of us, and because it is, every person who has ever lived has worked to satisfy the hunger of his soul in some way. The important thing to know is that there are only two banquet tables from which you can eat: the costly, unsatisfying table of the physical world or the soul-satisfying table of the Lord of abundant mercy and grace. God's question for you today is this: "Why do you spend your money for that which is not bread, and your labor for that which does not satisfy?" It is a question worth considering.

For further study and encouragement: John 6

APRIL 9

Don't be discouraged today. Yes, you're aware of your weaknesses and failures, but for each of them there's forgiving, transforming grace.

When you read it, it doesn't seem right. It seems that you've entered some topsy-turvy, inside-out universe. But Paul is both serious and dead right in what he says:

> So to keep me from becoming conceited because of the surpassing greatness of the revelations, a thorn was given me in the flesh, a messenger of Satan to harass me, to keep me from becoming conceited. Three times I pleaded with the Lord about this, that it should leave me. But he said to me, "My grace is sufficient for you, for my power is made perfect in weakness." Therefore I will boast all the more gladly of my weaknesses, so that the power of Christ may rest upon me. For the sake of Christ, then, I am content with weaknesses, insults, hardships, persecutions, and calamities. For when I am weak, then I am strong. (2 Cor. 12:7–10)

Fasten your seat belts; here we go. God chooses for you to be weak to protect you from you and to cause you to value the strength that only he can give. In this way, the weaknesses that he sends your way are not impediments to the good life. They are not in the way of his loving plan. They are not signs of his lack of care. They are not indicators of the failure of his promises. They do not expose gaps in the theology that we hold dear. They are not indications that the Bible contradicts itself when it says that God will meet all of your needs. No, these weaknesses are tools of his zealous and amazing grace. They protect you from the arrogance of self-reliance that tempts us all. They keep you from thinking that you're capable of what you're not. They remind you that you are needy and were created to be dependent on One greater than you. They cause you to do what all of us in some way resist doing—humbly run to God for the help that only he can give.

So your weaknesses are not the big danger that you should fear. What you should really fear are your delusions of strength. When you tell yourself that you are strong, you quit being excited about God's rescuing, transforming, and empowering grace. Paul actually celebrated his weaknesses, because as he did, the power of God rested upon him. He didn't live a fearful, discouraged, and envious life; he was content because he knew weakness is the doorway to real power, power that only God can and willingly does supply.

For further study and encouragement: Ephesians 6:10–20

APRIL 10

Faith in Christ is not just about knowing the truths
of the gospel, but about living them as well.

It is vital to know that faith is not just an action of your brain; it's an investment of your life. Faith is not just something you think; it's something you live. Hear these words from Hebrews 11:

> Now faith is the assurance of things hoped for, the conviction of things not seen. For by it the people of old received their commendation. By faith we understand that the universe was created by the word of God, so that what is seen was not made out of things that are visible.
>
> By faith Abel offered to God a more acceptable sacrifice than Cain, through which he was commended as righteous, God commending him by accepting his gifts. And through his faith, though he died, he still speaks. By faith Enoch was taken up so that he should not see death, and he was not found, because God had taken him. Now before he was taken he was commended as having pleased God. And without faith it is impossible to please him, for whoever would draw near to God must believe that he exists and that he rewards those who seek him. By faith Noah, being warned by God concerning events as yet unseen, in reverent fear constructed an ark for the saving of his household. By this he condemned the world and became an heir of the righteousness that comes by faith. (vv. 1–7)

What is faith? Verse 6 is very helpful. Biblical faith has this foundation—you must believe that God exists. This is the watershed, the great divide. There are only two types of people in this world—those who believe that the most important fact that a human being could ever consider and give assent to is the existence of God, and those who either casually or philosophically deny his existence. But intellectual commitment to God's existence is not all that faith is about; faith means you live as though you believe in God's existence, or as though you believe, as the writer says, "he rewards those who seek him."

Faith is a deep-seated belief in the existence of God that radically alters the way you live your life. Now, here's the rub. Faith isn't natural for us. Biblical faith is counterintuitive and countercultural. So we even need God's grace to have faith to believe in the existence of the One whose grace we so desperately need. And the grace is yours for the asking again today.

For further study and encouragement: James 2:14–26

APRIL 11

God will not rest from his redemptive work until every
aspect of his creation has been made new again.

It was written in 1719 by the great hymn writer Isaac Watts. He wrote it as a part of his *Psalm of David Imitated* and never intended it to be a Christmas carol. But "Joy to the World" has become one of the most beloved carols ever written. With all of its powerful lyrics, the third verse of this hymn is particularly profound and encouraging:

> No more let sins and sorrows grow,
> Nor thorns infest the ground;
> He comes to make his blessings flow
> Far as the curse is found,
> Far as the curse is found,
> Far as, far as the curse is found.

What was the mission of Jesus? What is the promise of the bloody cross and the empty tomb? What is the ultimate goal of the reigning King Christ? What is the scope of the work of redemption? What in the world is God working on? What does the final chapter of the grand redemptive story look like? The words of this great old hymn capture it with accuracy and power. Jesus really did come "to make his blessings flow." That is true to say, but not enough to say. You must add, "far as the curse is found." You see, Jesus didn't simply come to rescue disembodied souls. Yes, he saves our souls from eternal damnation, and for that we should be eternally grateful. But he also came to unleash his powerful restoring grace as far as the furthest effect of sin. He came to restore every single thing that sin has broken. He came to fix it all! His redemptive mission is as complete as sin's destruction is comprehensive.

I love the words of Revelation 21:5, and so should you: "Behold, I am making all things new." Are you tired of the futility and frustration of this broken world? Are you exhausted by sin, suffering, and death? Are you burdened with the pain that lives inside you and outside you? At times, do you wonder if anyone knows, if anyone understands, and if anyone cares? Then the words of this great hymn and this encouraging passage from the final book of the Bible are for you. Your Redeemer knows. Your Redeemer understands. Your Redeemer cares. His grace has been unleashed and its work will not be done until every last sin-broken thing has been fully and completely made new again. Be encouraged, your Redeemer is at work!

For further study and encouragement: Psalm 98

APRIL 12

If God is your Father, the Son is your Savior, and the Spirit is your indwelling Helper, you have hope no matter what you're facing.

Who in the world do you think you are? I'm serious. Who do you think you are? You and I are always assigning to ourselves some kind of identity. And the things that you and I do are shaped by the identity that we have given ourselves. So it's important to acknowledge that God has not just forgiven you (and that is a wonderful thing), but he has also given you a brand-new identity. If you're God's child, you are now a son or daughter of the King of kings and the Lord of lords. You are in the family of the Savior, who is your friend and brother. You are the temple where the Spirit of God now lives. Yes, it really is true—you've been given a radically new identity.

The problem, sadly, is that many of us live in a constant, or at least a rather regular, state of *identity amnesia*. We forget who we are, and when we do, we begin to give way to doubt, fear, and timidity. Identity amnesia makes you feel poor when in fact you are rich. It makes you feel foolish when in fact you are in a personal relationship with the One who is wisdom. It makes you feel unable when in fact you have been blessed with strength. It makes you feel alone when in fact, since the Spirit lives inside of you, it is impossible for you to be alone. You feel unloved when in fact, as a child of the heavenly Father, you have been graced with eternal love. You feel like you don't measure up when in fact the Savior measured up on your behalf. Identity amnesia sucks the life out of your Christianity in the right here, right now moment in which all of us live.

If you've forgotten who you are in Christ, what are you left with? You're left with *Christless Christianity*, which is little more than a system of theology and rules. And you know that if all you needed was theology and rules, Jesus wouldn't have had to come. All God would have needed to do was drop the Bible down on you and walk away. But he didn't walk away; he invaded your life as Father, Savior, and Helper. By grace, he made you a part of his family. By grace, he made you the place where he lives. And he did all this so that you not only would receive his forgiveness, but so that you would have everything you need for life and godliness.

So if you're his child, ward off the fear that knocks on your door by remembering who God is and who you've become as his chosen child. And don't just celebrate his grace; let it reshape the way you live today and the tomorrows that follow.

For further study and encouragement: 1 John 3:1–10

APRIL 13

God's story has a beginning and an end that never ends, and
if you're God's child, his story is now your biography. Wow!

You're probably like me—you like a good story. Whether it's a TV drama, a box-office hit movie, or a million-seller novel, we tend to line up for the good story. Or maybe you're sitting in a restaurant or around a campfire, and your friends begin to tell stories. Each one seems better than the one before. It begins to feel a bit like a contest. It seems as if people are trying to "outstory" one another. So you begin to thumb through your mental catalog of personal stories to see if you are carrying one that may just win the day. Or maybe someone tells you a fantastic story and you can't wait for the opportunity to retell it to someone else. Yep, we all love a good story.

Now, most great stories are great because, through myriad characters, relationships, situations, and locations, they march you to an incredible ending. When someone is talking to you about a great movie he just saw or a great book he just read, he often says, "And you will just not believe the ending!" But the best story ever conceived, written, and acted out in real life is the best story precisely because it has no ending. The one story you need to know, understand, and give your heart to is hopeful, encouraging, and life-transforming because it offers you the two wonderful things that no other story can offer you. First, it offers you a place in the story, a place that was planned for you long before the story was written. But it also offers you something that is hard for the human brain to grasp and the human imagination to envision. It offers you life that never, ever ends.

We are all so used to death that we sadly think of it as a normal part of life. Things die, people die, end of story. But that's not the end of this story. God's amazing story of redemption, which is written for you on the pages of your Bible, is radically different because in this story, death dies. Yes, you read it right. The main character of God's story (which is your story if you're his child) comes to earth and defeats sin and death, and because he does, he offers us the one thing that no other character in no other story can offer us—real life now and eternal life to come.

Quite apart from anything you have ever achieved, earned, or deserved as God's child, you have been welcomed into the best story ever by grace and grace alone. And thankfully, this story that is your story has an end that never ends.

For further study and encouragement: John 5:19–24

APRIL 14

*You can rest in God's care. If he freely offered up
his Son for you, will he forget you now?*

It is the irrefutable and comforting logic of redemption, so powerfully captured by Paul in Romans 8:31–39:

> What then shall we say to these things? If God is for us, who can be against us? He who did not spare his own Son but gave him up for us all, how will he not also with him graciously give us all things? Who shall bring any charge against God's elect? It is God who justifies. Who is to condemn? Christ Jesus is the one who died—more than that, who was raised—who is at the right hand of God, who indeed is interceding for us. Who shall separate us from the love of Christ? Shall tribulation, or distress, or persecution, or famine, or nakedness, or danger, or sword? As it is written,
>
> > "For your sake we are being killed all the day long;
> > we are regarded as sheep to be slaughtered."
>
> No, in all these things we are more than conquerors through him who loved us. For I am sure that neither death nor life, nor angels nor rulers, nor things present nor things to come, nor powers, nor height nor depth, nor anything else in all creation, will be able to separate us from the love of God in Christ Jesus our Lord.

Now, it simply defies redemptive logic to allow yourself at any moment in your life to think that God would go to the extent that he has gone to provide you with salvation and then lose you along the way. If he controlled nature and history so that at the right time Jesus came to live, die, and rise again on your behalf; if he worked by grace to expose you to the truth and gave you the heart to believe; and if he now works to bring the events of the universe to a final glorious conclusion, does it make any sense to think that he would fail to provide you with everything you need between your conversion and your final resurrection?

Paul is arguing that God's gift of and sacrifice of his Son is your guarantee that he will grace you with every good thing you need until you are finally free of this broken world and with him forever in eternity. You do not have to wonder about God's presence or his care. You do not have to fear that he will leave you on your own. You do not have to wonder if he will be there for you in your moment of need. When you give way to these fears, you commit an act of gospel irrationality. If he gave you Jesus, he will give you along with him everything you need.

For further study and encouragement: Philippians 4:10–20

APRIL 15

*Since my need for spiritual help is so great, the Bible teaches
that I need the daily intervention of the body of Christ.*

It really is true—your walk with God is a community project. The isolated, separated, loner, Jesus-and-me religion that often marks modern church culture is not the religion that is described in the New Testament. Many of us live virtually unknown, and many of the people whom we think we know we don't actually know. Many of us live in endless networks of terminally casual relationships, in which conversations seldom go deeper than weather, food, politics, the coolest movie that's out, or the latest cute thing your child did. Most of what we call fellowship never really rises to the level of the humble self-disclosure and mutual ministry that make fellowship actually redemptively worthwhile. Most of what we call fellowship is little different from what happens at the pub down the street. We should just call it "pubship" and tell people that they don't have to worry, there will be little fellowship at the church dinner.

Hebrews 3:12–13 addresses the essentiality of community to the work that God has done and is continuing to do in you and me: "Take care, brothers, lest there be in any of you an evil, unbelieving heart, leading you to fall away from the living God. But exhort one another every day, as long as it is called 'today,' that none of you may be hardened by the deceitfulness of sin."

Why do I need the daily intervention of the body of Christ? The answer is as simple as it is humbling. I need this daily ministry because I am a blind man. As much as I would like to think that I see and know myself well, it just isn't true. Because sin blinds me to me, as long as there is still sin inside me there will be pockets of blindness in my view of me. It's actually more serious than what I have just described, because whereas every physically blind person knows that he is blind, spiritually blind people are blind to their blindness; they actually think that they see, when in fact they don't.

What about you? Have you embraced your daily need for the help of the body of Christ? Who knows you? Whom have you invited to intrude into your private space to function for you as an instrument of seeing? Do you have a name in mind right now? When someone who knows you points out a sin, a weakness, or a failure, are you thankful? Or do you feel your chest tighten and your ears get red as you silently prepare yourself to rise to your own defense? Are you skilled at giving nonanswers to personal questions, or do you run toward the daily help that God has provided? That help is not something to be afraid of or shy away from, because it is a tool of God's forgiving, rescuing, transforming, and delivering grace.

For further study and encouragement: 1 Corinthians 12

APRIL 16

What could comfort you more than these words: "I came that they may have life and have it abundantly" (John 10:10)?

Everybody searches for life somewhere. God has placed this quest in each of our hearts. It is there to drive us to him. It is there because we were made for him. But sadly, in their lifelong quest for life, most people ignore God. In their God amnesia, they look for life where it cannot be found, and because they do, they always come up empty.

It's important to realize that you can search for life in only two places. Either you have found life to the fullest vertically or you are shopping for it horizontally. This is a major piece of what Paul is writing about in Romans 1:25 when he says: "They exchanged the truth about God for a lie and worshiped and served the creature rather than the Creator, who is blessed forever! Amen." What is that lie? It is the lie that was first told in the garden of Eden—the false promise that life, heart-satisfying life, could be found somewhere outside the Creator. It is the lie of lies, the cruelest lie ever told. If you believe it, it will not only leave you empty and discouraged, but it will set your life on a course of destruction.

The physical, created world is full of engaging and entertaining delights, but it is important to understand that nothing in the physical world can give you the life that your heart longs for. The delights of the physical world were carefully crafted to point to the One who alone is able to give your heart eternal delight. God alone is able to bring the deepest of joy and contentment to your heart. He alone is able to give you a reason for getting up in the morning and a purpose for living. He alone can infuse your heart with hope, no matter what is going on around you. So in amazing grace, he welcomes you to surrender all your hopes and dreams to him. In love, he beckons you to follow.

Again today, he promises you life. It's what he came to live, die, and rise again to give you. That empty tomb not only means he has conquered death, but it tells you he has life in his hands, the kind of life all human beings were designed to long for whether they know it or not. You can't find or earn that life on your own. It is yours only by means of the work of another.

Could it be today that you will fretfully search horizontally for what you have already been given in Christ? Will you try to drink from an empty well when you have already been given thirst-quenching living water?

For further study and encouragement: John 4:1–26

APRIL 17

*Faith means you take God at his word, you never let yourself think
that you're smarter than him, and you live inside his boundaries.*

Faith so completely takes God at his word that it is willing to do what he says and
stay inside his boundaries. Faith is a response of your heart to God that completely
alters the way you live your life. You don't just think by faith; you live by faith.

Now, it is important to face two implications of real, living faith. First, faith is
simply never natural for us. We aren't born with faith in God. We don't come out of
the womb ready to acknowledge his existence, worship him for his glory, and submit
to his rules. We tend to live by sight, by personal experience, by collective research,
or by good old intuition, but faith isn't natural. It's natural to give yourself to won-
derment about mysteries in your life you'll never solve. It's natural to imagine where
you'll be in ten or twenty years. It's natural to wonder why someone else's life has
turned out so very different from yours. It's natural to panic at moments, wondering
if God really does exist and, if he does, if he hears your prayers. But putting your
entire existence in the hands of One whom you cannot see, touch, or hear is far from
natural. This is why faith is only ever a gift of divine grace. You and I have all the
power in the world to doubt and no independent power at all to believe. So if you
are living by faith, don't proudly pat yourself on the back as if you did something
great. No, raise your eyes and your hands toward heaven and thank God for gifting
you with the desire and ability to believe.

Second, participating in formal Christianity is a part of a life of faith, but it does
not define the life of faith. Just because you participate in the scheduled programs
of your church doesn't mean you're a person of faith. You can praise God for his
wisdom in that service on Sunday but be breaking his law on Tuesday because, at
street level, you really do think you're smarter than him. You can sing in thanks for
his grace on Sunday and resist the work of that grace the rest of the week. It's so
easy to swindle yourself into believing that you're living by faith when you're really
not. So look into the mirror of Hebrews 11 and examine your faith. You don't need
to do that fearfully, anxious at what you'll see. You don't need to deny the reality
of your spiritual struggle or act as if you're something that you're not. You don't
have to fear exposure, because your struggle of faith has been more than adequately
addressed by the grace of the cross of the Lord Jesus. Run to him and confess the
off-and-on-again faith of your heart. He will not turn you away.

For further study and encouragement: Luke 7:1–17

APRIL 18

You have no reason for fear when you answer God's call; you have every reason to be afraid when you put your life in your own hands.

The Bible is dotted with story after story of people who were called by God at certain times and for certain purposes, but who were scared to death to answer his call. Moses did everything he could to get out of going back to Egypt, confronting Pharaoh, and leading the children of Israel out. He was terrified to answer God's call even after God did miracles to convince him of his presence and power (Exodus 3–4). Gideon also argued with God, sure that it had to be a divine mistake for him to be called as the one who would lead Israel to a decisive victory against the Midianites (Judges 6). God had to assure Joshua that he need not be afraid to lead Israel across the Jordan into the Land of Promise (Joshua 1). The people of Israel rebelled against the Lord and refused to go into Canaan because they were afraid of being destroyed by the Amorites (Deuteronomy 1). The soldiers of Israel stayed afraid in their tents when confronted by the giant warrior Goliath (1 Samuel 17). Peter was afraid to identify himself as a disciple of Jesus, and with anxious curses denied his Lord (Matthew 26).

Each moment of fear, each act of refusal, was an act of spiritual irrationality. Each fearful person had been invited to be part of the massive history- and globe-spanning work of the kingdom of God. The One who called them created the world and holds it together by his will. He has power over all things spiritual and physical. He rules every situation, location, and relationship in which his call is to be followed. He is amazing in his wisdom, abundant in his grace, and boundless in his love. He is saving, forgiving, transforming, and delivering. What he says is always best and what he requires is always good. When he calls, he goes with you. What he calls you to do, he empowers by his grace. When he guides, he protects. He stands with power and faithfulness behind every one of his promises. He has never failed to deliver anything that he has promised. There is simply no risk in answering the call of the King of kings.

What is incredibly dangerous is how quickly we forget God and how fast our allegiance to our own purposes and plans develops. We convince ourselves that we are wiser, stronger, and more righteous than we really are, and therefore we step into danger. Only grace can work to remind us that faith in God is a resting place and trust in self is a minefield. It is grace and grace alone that empowers us to follow and to rest.

For further study and encouragement: Isaiah 31:1

APRIL 19

It is grace to not be paralyzed by regret. The cross teaches that
you are not stuck, not cursed to pay forever for your past.

He sat before me with his head in his hands and kept saying over and over again: "I just wish I could have it all back. I just wish I could press a button and do it all over again. I wish I knew then what I know now. I wish I could try again, but I can't." He must have said this or something similar to this ten times. He was incredibly distraught and regretful, and yet in the best spiritual condition he had ever been in. I really did feel his pain and I was very happy that he felt it too, because I knew that what he was experiencing was the pain of grace.

He was a hard, driven, and demanding man who kept moving forward no matter what and never looked back. He didn't care what trail of destruction he left behind him. He was successful. He knew it and wanted everyone else to know it too. He had loved his work more than his family, and in the process, he had lost both. It was all gone—family, job, and wealth. He had played the game by himself and for himself, and had lost in a big way. But now his eyes were open, and the scene broke his heart. Bankrupt and alone, he looked back with grief at every arrogant moment. It was painful, but it was grace. God was making his eyes see so that he would never go back there again.

It's a grace to regret. Grace allows you to face your sin, to own it and not shift the blame. But it is also grace that forgives what has been exposed. Grace forces you to feel the pain of your regrets, but never asks you to pay for them, because the price has already been paid by Jesus. Colossians 2:14 talks about how "the record of debt that stood against us" has been canceled by the sacrifice of Jesus. You can look back, but with your burden lifted by forgiving grace. It is good to look back and celebrate the rescue of grace. It is good to mourn the sins of the past. It is not good to be paralyzed by them. Grace lives at the intersection between clarity of sight and hope for the future. And that grace is yours for the taking. You don't have to rewrite your past, making yourself look more righteous than you ever really were. You can stare the truth in the face because of what Jesus has done for you. You can own what needs to be owned and confess what needs to be confessed, and then move on to live in a new and better way. The same grace that forgives your past empowers you to live in a new way in the future.

So look backward and look forward. God's grace enables you to do both, celebrating forgiveness for the past and embracing power for a new and better future. Only God's grace gifts you with peace with your past and hope for your future.

For further study and encouragement: Philippians 3:12–21

APRIL 20

*Grace doesn't make it okay for you to live for you. No, grace frees
you to experience the joy of living for One greater than you.*

It is universally true that what seems to us to be freedom isn't really freedom after
all. When Adam and Eve stepped outside of God's boundaries, they didn't step into
freedom. They stepped into toil, temptation, suffering, sin, and bondage. Denying
God's existence, desiring his place, ignoring his rules, and determining to make it on
your own might seem like pathways to freedom, but they never, ever are.

You and I weren't designed to live independently. We weren't meant to live in our
own strength. We weren't created to rely on our own wisdom. We weren't given the
ability to write our own moral codes. We weren't put together with the independent
knowledge of how to live, how to steward the physical world, or how to properly
relate to one another. We were not created to live *by* ourselves or *for* ourselves, and
to attempt to do so never leads anywhere good.

So as God blesses us and changes us with his grace, the result isn't a greater ability to live an independent life; the opposite is true. Grace doesn't free us to live for us.
The purpose of God's grace is not to make your little kingdom of one work better.
The purpose of God's grace is to free you from your slavery to you so that you can
live for a much, much better kingdom: "And he died for all, that those who live might
no longer live for themselves but for him who for their sake died and was raised"
(2 Cor. 5:15). True freedom is never found in putting yourself at the center, with
your choices and behavior shaped by your allegiance to you. Real freedom is only
ever found when God's grace liberates you to live for One infinitely greater than you.

It contradicts our normal thinking, but the doorway to freedom is submission.
When I acknowledge that I am a danger to myself and submit to the authority, wisdom, and grace of God, I am not killing any hope I have for freedom. The opposite
is true. Humble admission of need and humble submission to God open me up to the
freest of lives. I was created to live in worshipful and obedient dependency on God,
and when grace restores me to that place, it also gives me back my freedom. It may
seem constricting that the train always has to ride on those tracks, but try driving it
in a meadow and all motion stops. So grace puts you back on the tracks again and
gives you the freedom of forward motion, which you can have no other way.

For further study and encouragement: Romans 6:1–14

APRIL 21

You obey not to get God's attention, but because you have been
the object of his attention since before the world began.

Your obedience is never to be done in the hope that you will get something, but rather in recognition of what you have already been given. Carefully read the following words from Ephesians 1:

> Blessed be the God and Father of our Lord Jesus Christ, who has blessed us in Christ with every spiritual blessing in the heavenly places, even as he chose us in him before the foundation of the world, that we should be holy and blameless before him. In love he predestined us for adoption as sons through Jesus Christ, according to the purpose of his will, to the praise of his glorious grace, with which he has blessed us in the Beloved. In him we have redemption through his blood, the forgiveness of our trespasses, according to the riches of his grace, which he lavished upon us, in all wisdom and insight making known to us the mystery of his will, according to his purpose, which he set forth in Christ as a plan for the fullness of time, to unite all things in him, things in heaven and things on earth.
>
> In him we have obtained an inheritance, having been predestined according to the purpose of him who works all things according to the counsel of his will, so that we who were the first to hope in Christ might be to the praise of his glory. In him you also, when you heard the word of truth, the gospel of your salvation, and believed in him, were sealed with the promised Holy Spirit, who is the guarantee of our inheritance until we acquire possession of it, to the praise of his glory. (vv. 3–14)

So here's the humbling and comforting truth of the gospel. Your obedience doesn't initiate anything. Your obedience and mine only occur because God initiated a redemptive process that resulted in our forgiveness and transformation. We don't obey to get his favor; we obey because his favor has fallen on us and transformed our hearts, giving us the willingness and power to obey. God's work of rescue and forgiveness didn't begin just before you first believed. It didn't begin just before you were born. It began before the world was born. He placed his grace on you and wrote your story in such a way that at a certain point in time you would hear the truths of the gospel of Jesus Christ and believe. His love for you is never a result of your character; it is a clear demonstration of his. He granted you and me what we never could have deserved; our new life is his choice, his gift.

This means that if you obey him for a thousand years, you will have no more of his favor than when you first believed. Now, that truly is grace!

For further study and encouragement: Romans 9:1–18

APRIL 22

If God intended for all the days of your life to be easy, they would be.
No, in grace, he intends for your days to be his tools of refinement.

I am deeply persuaded that many of us struggle with questions of God's goodness, faithfulness, and love, not because he has been unfaithful to any promise in any way, but because we simply are not on his agenda page. Our agenda, our definition of what a good God should give us, is a life that is comfortable, pleasurable, and predictable; one in which there's lots of human affirmation and an absence of suffering. But consider God's agenda, as it's revealed in the following passages:

> Count it all joy, my brothers, when you meet trials of various kinds, for you know that the testing of your faith produces steadfastness. And let steadfastness have its full effect, that you may be perfect and complete, lacking in nothing. (James 1:2–4)

> In this you rejoice, though now for a little while, if necessary, you have been grieved by various trials, so that the tested genuineness of your faith—more precious than gold that perishes though it is tested by fire—may be found to result in praise and glory and honor at the revelation of Jesus Christ. (1 Pet. 1:6–7)

> Therefore, since we have been justified by faith, we have peace with God through our Lord Jesus Christ. Through him we have also obtained access by faith into this grace in which we stand, and we rejoice in hope of the glory of God. Not only that, but we rejoice in our sufferings, knowing that suffering produces endurance, and endurance produces character, and character produces hope, and hope does not put us to shame, because God's love has been poured into our hearts through the Holy Spirit who has been given to us. (Rom. 5:1–5)

> But whatever gain I had, I counted as loss for the sake of Christ. Indeed, I count everything as loss because of the surpassing worth of knowing Christ Jesus my Lord. For his sake I have suffered the loss of all things and count them as rubbish, in order that I may gain Christ and be found in him, not having a righteousness of my own that comes from the law, but that which comes through faith in Christ, the righteousness from God that depends on faith. (Phil. 3:7–9)

The message is consistent throughout all of these passages. God is not working to deliver to you your personal definition of happiness. If you're on that agenda page, you are going to be disappointed with God and you are going to wonder if he loves you. God is after something better—your holiness, that is, the final completion of his redemptive work in you. The difficulties you face are not in the way of God's plan, they do not show the failure of God's plan, and they are not signs he has turned his back on you. No, those tough moments are a sure sign of the zeal of his redemptive love.

For further study and encouragement: 1 Peter 4:12–19

APRIL 23

As God's child, there's never a moment when you're not under God's care, never a time when you're not the object of his love.

The big question is not, does God care for me? The Bible declares he does over and over again. It tells us that God's eyes are on the righteous and his ears are open to their prayers (Ps. 34:15). It says that he is with us wherever we go (Gen. 28:15). The Bible welcomes us to bring our cares to God because he cares for us (1 Pet. 5:7). It tells us that he will never leave us or forsake us (Heb. 13:5). The message is clear and consistent—God cares for his own. If you are God's child, you are never outside the scope of his constant care. The Bible is also clear and consistent when it talks of the unshakability of God's love. His love is eternal. From the verse-by-verse refrain of Psalm 136, "for his steadfast love endures forever," to Paul's declaration in Romans 8 that nothing can separate us from the "love of God in Christ Jesus our Lord" (v. 39), the message is undebatable—God will never turn from the love he has lavished on us.

So if you're God's child, you're wasting your spiritual time and energy worrying about God's love. You're not spending your time well if you're trying to unpack little moments in your life to see if they are an indication of whether he loves you. It's not wise to compare your life to another person's, wondering what the evidence tells you about who God cares for the most. It is tempting to do all of these things, particularly when life is hard, when unpredictable and difficult things have entered your door. But questioning God's love never goes anywhere good. When you are tempted to do so, you need to run to his Word for peace and reassurance. You'll never establish personal peace by picking apart little moments and trying to look into the mysteries of life. The Bible was given to give you peace in those moments when it's hard to figure out what in the world God is doing.

Something else needs to be said. If the big question isn't whether God cares, then maybe the real question, one that is more practical to us all, is, will I recognize God's care when it comes? Perhaps our problem is our definition and expectation of God's care. You see, God's care comes in a variety of packages. His care is not always a cool drink and a soft pillow. God's care is not always relief from circumstances, release from trouble. There are many moments in our lives when the very thing that causes us to wonder about God's care *is* his care. He knows that trouble will reveal our hearts or display his glory. Often trouble is a tool of care in the hands of the One who knows best what we need. He cares; therefore, make sure your definition of his care is not too narrow.

For further study and encouragement: Psalm 8

APRIL 24

*Since God writes your story, he knows what you're facing
and exactly what grace you'll need to live his way.*

Admit it: your life hasn't worked out according to your plan. Last month didn't work out according to your plan. Today won't work out according to your plan. All of this is true because you aren't the author of your story. You don't need to read a mystery novel; your life is a mystery to you. You and I don't have a clue what is around the next corner, let alone where we will be and what we will be doing a decade from now. But even though there is very little that we know for sure about our lives and we experience constant surprises along the way, we need not give way to panic. Yes, our lives are out of our control, but that doesn't mean they are out of control. No, our lives are under the careful administration of the One who had the wisdom and power to be the great Author of it all.

Since God is the Author of every detail of your story, since he writes into your story every situation, location, and relationship, then he knows exactly what you're facing and precisely what grace you need to face it in the way he has planned. You could say it this way: his sovereign control is the guarantee that you will have everything that he has promised you. His sovereign control means he knows what you need because he has planned for you everything that you're now facing. But more needs to be said. His sovereignty is your surety because he can guarantee the delivery of his promises only in the location where he rules. Because he rules over all things at all times (since he wrote the story that includes it all), he can guarantee that you and I will have what he has promised us in the places and at the times they are needed.

Paul says it this way: "And he made from one man every nation of mankind to live on all the face of the earth, having determined allotted periods and the boundaries of their dwelling place, that they should seek God, and perhaps feel their way toward him and find him. Yet he is actually not far from each one of us" (Acts 17:26–27). Paul doesn't think of God as an "out-there and distant sovereign." He reminds us that because God is involved with every detail of our lives, he is near. He is so near that at any moment we can reach out and touch him. This means that every grace that you and I will ever need is near and available to us as well. So reach out today. The Author is near and he has grace in his hands.

For further study and encouragement: 1 Peter 1:13–25

APRIL 25

*Today you will spend solitary moments of conversation with yourself,
either listing your complaints or counting your blessings.*

Think with me for a moment. Do you live a life of blessing or complaint? It is so easy to grumble. It is so easy to find fault. It is so easy to be discontent. It is so easy to find things that are less than you want them to be. It is so easy to be irritated and impatient. It is so easy to groan and moan about the difficulties of life. It is so easy to be dissatisfied.

Why are these things so easy? Well, they're easy because sin still causes us to make it all about us. Because sin really is selfishness at its core, we all still tend to shrink our worlds down to the small confines of our wants, our needs, and our feelings. We then tend to judge the good of our lives by how much of what we want we are able to actually have. At street level, it is tempting to live a God-forgetful, me-istic existence. If you put yourself in the center of your world, you will find plenty of things to complain about.

It is also true that you live in a fallen world where people and things are not functioning the way God intended. This world really is terribly broken. Life here really is hard. You face all kinds of difficulties, big and small. People disappoint you. They make your life hard. Obstacles appear in your way. In some way, the fallenness of your world enters your door every day. Combine the hardships of life in this fallen world with the self-centeredness of sin and you have a recipe for disaster, or at least a miserable life of discontent.

The Bible does not see grumbling and complaining as little things. In Deuteronomy 1, Moses recounts how the people of Israel "murmured" (grumbled) about their lives, and embedded in that murmuring were questions about the goodness and wisdom of God. God's assessment was that by their grumbling the people had rebelled against him; they had shown they were unwilling to do what he had called and enabled them to do. The joy or complaint of your heart always shapes your willingness to trust God and to do his will.

Complaining forgets God's grace. It ignores his presence. It fails to see the beauty of his promises. It allows the display of his splendor in creation to go unnoticed. It questions his goodness, faithfulness, and love. It wonders if he is there and if he cares. If you believe in God and his control over everything that exists, then you have to accept that all of your grumbling is ultimately grumbling against him. Yes, it is so easy to complain. It is so easy to forget the daily blessings that fall down on each of us. Our readiness to complain is another argument for the forgiving and rescuing grace that Jesus, without complaint, willingly died to give us.

For further study and encouragement: Deuteronomy 1

*If you have quit being defensive and are now willingly and humbly
approachable, you know that transforming grace has visited you.*

It started in the garden of Eden, and we have been committed to it ever since. We all point the finger of blame and we all work to convince ourselves that the party to blame is not us. Adam pointed his finger at Eve, and Eve pointed her finger at the Serpent; neither one of them accepted blame. Yes, it is true: there have been generations and generations of finger pointers ever since.

You see, when you've done something wrong, it's not natural to look inside yourself for the cause. Sin makes us all shockingly self-righteous. It makes us all committed self-excusers. Somehow, some way, we all buy into the delusion that our biggest problems live outside us, not inside us. We all have very active inner lawyers, who rise to our defense in the face of any accusation of wrong. We are all very skilled at presenting the logic of the argument that what we have done says more about the flawed people and dysfunctional things around us than it does about us. When our consciences bother us because of the faithful convicting ministry of the Holy Spirit, we are all tempted to dodge blame by locating the cause elsewhere. We all tend to be much more concerned about the sin of others than we are about our own, but, John says, "If we say we have no sin, we deceive ourselves, and the truth is not in us" (1 John 1:8).

Because accepting blame is not natural, it takes rescuing, transforming grace to produce a humble, willing, broken, self-examining, help-seeking heart. Only divine grace can soften a person's heart. Only grace can help your eyes to see what you need to see. Only grace can decimate your defenses and lead you to confess. Only grace can cause you to quit pointing your finger and to run to your Redeemer for his forgiveness and delivering power. Only grace can enable you to forsake your own righteousness and find your hope and rest in the righteousness of another. Only grace can make you more grieved over your sin than about the sins of others. Only grace can make you accept your need for grace. Only grace can cause you and me to abandon our confidence in our own performance and place our confidence in the perfectly acceptable righteousness of Jesus Christ. Only grace can cause us to put our hope in the only place where hope can be found—in God and God alone. Every moment of defensiveness argues how much the grace is still needed.

For further study and encouragement: 1 John 1:5–10

APRIL 27

Your hope is not in your ability to love God, but in his unrelenting and unshakable love for you.

There is nothing that argues more for our desperate need for grace than the two greatest commandments: that we love God and love other people (Matt. 22:34–40). The call to love exposes how dark and depraved our hearts really are. Let's be honest here. It doesn't take much for us to be irritated with other people. It doesn't take much for us to become impatient. Little interruptions, disagreements, and obstacles can cause us to well up with anger. We are easily dismissive of others. It's too easy for us to be prejudiced and judgmental. It's far too simple for us to be racist and xenophobic. In a variety of ways, we look down on others, failing to see them with eyes of compassion and hearts of mercy. It's so easy for us to judge others as foolish, lazy, or otherwise incompetent. I know I'm not the only one who struggles with these things. I think if we were willing to look at our hearts in the mirror of the Word of God, we would be shocked at how unnatural love is for us.

But if horizontal love is hard for us, vertical love is even harder. The connection between the two is cogently made in 1 John 4:20: "If anyone says, 'I love God,' and hates his brother, he is a liar; for he who does not love his brother whom he has seen cannot love God whom he has not seen." Wow! There it is. If I have such a struggle loving the people around me, how great and deep must be my struggle to love God? It's one thing to acknowledge God's existence; it's one thing to mentally assent to the truths of his Word; and it's one thing to participate in the formal ministry of his church. But it is an entirely different thing to have every aspect of my life shaped and moved by love for him.

Yes, the power of sin has been broken by the work of Jesus, but the presence of sin still remains and is being progressively eradicated. So there is still sin in our hearts. That means our hearts are still fickle, we still rebel and want our own way, we still forget God and his glory, we still write our own rules, we still love our kingdoms more than we love his, we still demand what we don't deserve, and we still question God's goodness when we don't get our own way. We all fall into doing these things because we just do not love God as we should. We tend to love ourselves and we tend to love the world, but very often the love of the Father simply is not in us.

So your hope in life and death is never to be found in the degree of your love for God. It is only ever found in the magnitude of his love for you. This love is yours as a gift of his grace even on those days where your heart has run after other lovers. That's just how beautiful and faithful his love for you really is.

For further study and encouragement: 1 John 4:10–21

APRIL 28

*Today the true love of your heart will be revealed by
what you grieve and what you celebrate.*

Our lives are shaped by grief and celebration. This isn't true only for the grand, significant moments of our lives; there are ways in which every day of your life and mine is marked by moments of grief and celebration. Daily we are sad, mad, upset, or disappointed by something, and every day we are excited, happy, joyful, pumped, or thankful for something. It's at the intersection between sadness and celebration that the true love of our hearts is exposed.

Think with me—when you look back on a good week, what are the things that excited you, satisfied you, or otherwise made you so happy that you name it as a good week? When you are happy with a relationship in your life, what are you considering that gives you joy? Be honest as you read this—what is it that brings joy and satisfaction to your heart? Or look at the other side. When you're really disappointed with life, what is it that discourages you? When you are envious of the life of another, what produces that envy? When you have lost your motivation to get up in the morning and face your day, what specifically has robbed you of your motivation? I plead with you to take time to let these questions function as a window to your heart.

Here's the bottom-line question: How much of your joy, celebration, grief, or anger in the last several weeks had anything whatsoever to do with the kingdom of God? Even when I type these words, I am convicted myself. I'm convicted by how much of my joy is connected to getting my own way, to people and things not being in my way, or to actually getting some physical thing I've set my heart on.

Yet, by grace, that is not always true. There are times when my heart grasps the magnitude of God's grace, and I celebrate. There are times when I am captured by the work of God's kingdom. There are moments when I do find joy in serving others. There are times when I am deeply content in the worship of God. I wish I could say that these things were always true of me, but they are not.

So take time today to examine your heart. Take time to exegete your grief or unpack your joy, because if you do, you will see that there *is* evidence of God's transforming grace at work, but there is also evidence of the need for that grace to do more. Yes, you have been and are being rescued, but your grief and celebration tell you that the war for your heart still rages on and, like me, you need for grace to continue to do its rescuing and transforming work every day.

For further study and encouragement: Colossians 1:2–14

APRIL 29

Today you will be tempted to buy into the delusion that you're smarter than God, that your way is better than his.

It is one of the functional contradictions of sin. Even though sin somehow, some way reduces us all to fools, at the very same time it also convinces us that we are smarter than God. While we name ourselves as wise, we look at things that God does or things that he calls us to do as utterly foolish. How many people have said, "How could you ever worship a God who would _____?" How many people have wondered, "If God really loved me, why would he _____?" How many people have said, "I don't see what's so wrong with a little _____"? How many have asked, "Is _____ really that bad?" We really do have the ability to convince ourselves that we know what's best and that we really don't need wisdom greater than our own. I am convinced that most of us do this far more often than we think. We minimize the danger of what God calls dangerous, we question the need for the boundaries that God has set for us, and, in the face of our own sin, we argue that it's not so bad after all. Every day in some situation or relationship, we are tempted to think that we are smarter than God.

Without the rescue of God's grace, we are all wise fools heading for danger we simply don't see. So we eat more than we should while denying the physical, empirical evidence of our foolishness. We spend ourselves into hopeless debt and are surprised when we can no longer pay our bills. We live selfishly and judgmentally in relationships and then wonder why so much tension and distance exist between us. That's why Paul says, "For the foolishness of God is wiser than men, and the weakness of God is stronger than men" (1 Cor. 1:25). Paul is saying that if it were possible for God to be foolish, his most foolish moment would be infinitely wiser than our wisest moment. How humbling!

So where are you tempted to tell yourself that you're wiser than God? Where do you argue that your plan for you is better than his? Where do you lay out the logic to yourself that it makes sense to step over one of his boundaries? Where are you tempted to name sin as something less than sin? Where do you tell yourself that you don't really need grace? What do you call wise that God says is foolish, or foolish that God says is wise? Where do you, like Adam and Eve, accept the illogic that there may be a better way in life than God's way? Where do you take life into your own hands so that you can have it your way? Confess the utter foolishness of ever thinking that you're smarter than God, and run to his wisdom. Pray once more that the One who is the definition of what is wise would by grace make you wise, that is, a person who loves God's wisdom more than you love your own.

For further study and encouragement: Job 40

APRIL 30

Prayer is abandoning hope of independent capability and believing that in Christ you're given everything you need for life and godliness.

Prayer is an act of worship. Prayer is an act of submission. Prayer is an act of obedience. But prayer is also an act of admission. Every instance of prayer is a confession in which I own my condition and embrace my need. Prayer that doesn't do this may be a religious recitation of some sort, but it ceases to be prayer. In prayer, I confess once again that I won't ever be what I'm supposed to be and do what I am supposed to do without the forgiving, empowering, and delivering grace of the One to whom I am praying. Prayer decimates my independent self-surety; it puts my utter dependency before my eyes and calls me to cry out for the help that I am so often tempted to deny I need.

No passage gets at this more clearly than Christ's parable of the Pharisee and the tax collector in Luke 18:9–14:

> He also told this parable to some who trusted in themselves that they were righteous, and treated others with contempt: "Two men went up into the temple to pray, one a Pharisee and the other a tax collector. The Pharisee, standing by himself, prayed thus: 'God, I thank you that I am not like other men, extortioners, unjust, adulterers, or even like this tax collector. I fast twice a week; I give tithes of all that I get.' But the tax collector, standing far off, would not even lift up his eyes to heaven, but beat his breast, saying, 'God, be merciful to me, a sinner!' I tell you, this man went down to his house justified, rather than the other. For everyone who exalts himself will be humbled, but the one who humbles himself will be exalted."

The tax collector prayed the prayer that should be on the lips of every one of us every time we pray. The mercy for which he cried is the mercy that each of us constantly needs. To reduce prayer to a grocery list of things that you want and think you need not only demeans prayer, but it also demeans the sacrifice of love that the One to whom you are praying made so that you and your prayers would be received. The heart of true prayer is vertical confession, not horizontal desire.

The Pharisee's prayer was not a prayer at all. He basically raised his head to heaven and said: "Here I am, God. I'm as righteous as I need to be, so I don't really need your help at the moment." He was revolted by the thought that he might be as sinful and needy as the low-life tax collector who stood not far from him. Self-righteousness crushes prayer, reducing it to an empty religious recitation spoken by one who sees himself as a grace graduate. Run to Jesus in your poverty and weakness, and know that he is never revolted when you do, but always greets you with arms of grace.

For further study and encouragement: James 5:13–16

MAY 1

Jesus commands you to take up your cross and follow him,
and then he gives you the strength to carry the load.

Pay careful attention to these words from 2 Thessalonians 2:16–17, because they offer you a very pointed and practical summary of the work of the gospel on your life: "Now may our Lord Jesus Christ himself, and God our Father, who loved us and gave us eternal comfort and good hope through grace, comfort your hearts and establish them in every good work and word." If someone were to ask you what in the world God is doing in your life right here, right now, what would you answer? I am persuaded that one of the primary reasons many of us struggle with moments of disappointment with God is that we misunderstand what God is doing. Paul really summarizes the work of God in pointing us to two essential pieces of God's redemptive agenda.

First, God has been and is exercising his grace to bring real comfort to our hearts. What is that comfort? It's not that he will make sure that our hopes and dreams are realized, that all our bills are promptly paid, that the people around us like us, or that we escape suffering. His comfort is more foundational and redemptive. Here it is: despite our sin, you and I have been welcomed into an eternal relationship with the Lord almighty because Jesus fully met all the requirements of God that we failed to meet. We no longer have to fear God's wrath. We no longer have to measure up in order to achieve his acceptance. We no longer have to hide in guilt or shame. We are God's forever and ever. He will never turn his back on us. He will never angrily throw our sin in our faces. He will never withdraw his presence and his promises, no matter how messed up we continue to be, because our standing with him is not based on our performance, but on the perfect record of his Son. But that is only one piece of God's agenda.

Yes, we should celebrate our eternal *reconciliation* ("eternal comfort and good hope") to God, but we should also recognize that there is a second part to his work. It is *transformation* ("establish them in every good work and word"). There is no more comforting message than the one preached from the cross of Jesus Christ, and there are no more powerful promises of transformation than those found in the grace of that cross. By grace, God is actively working real vertical comfort into our hearts so that we will not seek comfort horizontally, and by grace he is transforming our hearts so that in our work and our words we will progressively live as he chose us to live. God's comfort doesn't mean that the way we live our lives makes no difference, and the fact that God lays claim to our daily living in no way removes the eternal comfort of his reconciling grace. We are his by grace and we are being changed by grace—all because of his reconciling and transforming zeal. Today, bask in the comfort he gives and respond to his gracious call.

For further study and encouragement: 2 Corinthians 5:14–21

MAY 2

True, humble, joyful, and perseverant love is not born out of raw duty, but out of worshipful gratitude. We love because he first loved us.

As I wrote the character qualities of real love, "true, humble, joyful, and perseverant," that you see in the statement above, my heart was filled with the sadness of conviction. I thought, "My love often fails to be true." No, I don't mean *true* as contrasted with *fake*. I'm not thinking here of hypocritical "I'm going to act like I love you even though I don't" love. *True* here means "straight," like the kind of arrow a marksman makes sure to pull out of his quiver. He wants a completely straight arrow so that when it leaves the bow, it won't veer off in the wrong direction. *True* here means consistent, reliable, and not apt to go in some unloving direction. Sadly, there is still inconsistency in my love. When someone disagrees with me, when someone gets in the way of my plan, when I am forced into an unexpected wait, or when someone gets what I think I deserve, it is very tempting for me to respond in a less-than-loving way.

The second word, *humble*, explains why I respond as I do. I still lack humility. I still tend to make life about my plan, my feelings, my desires, and my expectations. I am still tempted to assess the "good" of a day by whether it pleased me versus whether I pleased God and was loving toward others. I still am tempted to live as if I own my life and still fail to remember that I was bought with a price. And all of this causes love to be burdensome rather than *joyful*, the third descriptive word. It really is true that when you're living for you, the call to love others is always a burden for you.

The final word points us to the highest and hardest standard of love: *perseverant*. Love that isn't faithful is love that has little value. Love that changes with the wind is not really love at all. It is a fickle and momentary put-on that does more damage than it does good. That is why God's faithful, eternal love is such a huge and motivating comfort.

The question then is, "Where in the world am I going to get this kind of love?" Well, it never comes from picking yourself up and telling yourself that you're going to do better. If you had the power for this kind of self-reformation, the cross of Jesus Christ would not have been necessary. The only way I can escape the self-focused bondage of my love for me and actually begin to love others is for forgiving, liberating, empowering, and eternal love to be placed in me. The more I am thankful for that love, the more I find joy in giving it to others. God's love, willingly given, provides the only hope that I can have love in my heart that I joyfully give as well.

For further study and encouragement: 2 Corinthians 9

MAY 3

*God's care for you is secure because it does not
depend on your faithfulness, but on his.*

"Now may the God of peace himself sanctify you completely, and may your whole spirit and soul and body be kept blameless at the coming of our Lord Jesus Christ. He who calls you is faithful; he will surely do it" (1 Thess. 5:23–24). You and I live between the "already" and the "not yet." Already God has set his plan of grace in motion. Already the prophets have spoken. Already Jesus has come. Already he has suffered and died. Already he has risen in victory from the tomb. Already the Spirit has come. Already the Word has been given. But not yet is God's work in the world finished. Not yet is his work in our hearts done. Not yet is the last enemy under his feet. Not yet is he ready to say: "Beloved, all things are now ready. Enter into my final kingdom."

We are right smack dab in the middle of the world's most important incomplete process—sanctification. None of us is yet what grace makes it possible for us to be. The battle with sin and temptation still goes on. The war for what will effectively and functionally rule our hearts still rages. We are not yet even near being blameless in and of ourselves. No, the reality is that between the already and the not yet of God's transforming process, we are all a bit of a mess. We still fall into temptation. We still give way to wrong thoughts and desires. We still say things that we should never say. We still behave in ways that expose the sin that is still in our hearts. So there is simply no way our personal security can be found in ourselves. Peace is not found in the degree of our faithfulness to God, but in the utterly unshakable nature of his faithfulness to the commitment of grace he has made to us.

He never regrets his promises. He never grows bored or weary. He doesn't get mad with us and debate with himself as to whether he should walk away. He never lounges through a lazy, self-centered day. He never withdraws his commitment to us because he has his eye on another. He never makes a promise he doesn't intend to keep. His love isn't a passing fancy. He never threatens to withdraw his love in order to get his own way. He never keeps a record of wrongs against us so that he can use it to get something from us that he wants. He is never disloyal behind our backs. He is completely faithful in the fullest sense of what that means. And here's what is important to understand. His faithfulness is not a demonstration of how well you're doing; no, it's a revelation of how completely holy, righteous, kind, and good he is. He remains faithful even on your most unfaithful day.

For further study and encouragement: Psalm 89

MAY 4

"Our father in heaven . . ." (Matt. 6:9a).
There is no situation or location where I am ever alone,
because my heavenly Father is always with me.

It is such an astounding reality that it is almost impossible for us to comprehend the full meaning of it. It assaults the way we so often think about our identity. It confronts our discouragements and fears. It exposes our self-oriented neediness and our addiction to the acceptance of others. It is the only place where we can find security that stays, that doesn't ride that scary roller-coaster of ever-changing people and situations. It is one of the most amazing, life-altering gifts of the grace of the Lord Jesus Christ. It is a deeply personal, heart-satisfying recognition that we must carry with us wherever we go.

The opening line of Jesus's model prayer for his disciples (Matt. 6:9–13) teaches this unspeakably marvelous truth: *if you're God's child, you have a Father in heaven!* Stop for a moment and let that sink in. What a glorious and encouraging way Christ instructs us to begin our prayers. We are to begin with the most shocking and encouraging of all things that our minds could ever consider. That being who has such incomparable wisdom and power that he was able to design and create everything that exists—that being is our Father. That deity who has been able, by the exercise of supreme authority, to control every event of history; to have his will done in every location; and to completely control every life of every person who has ever lived—that deity is our Father. That One who in magnificent love put the plan of redemption in motion, so that at the right moment his Son came to live, die, and rise again so that we would have new and eternal life—that One is our Father. That King who won't ever leave the work of his hands till everything he has purposed to do in us and in the world that he created has been fully done—that King is our Father. That God who never needed a teacher or a counselor, who knows the stars by name, and who can hold the waters of the universe in the palm of his hand—that God is our Father.

You could do nothing more important than to wake up every morning of your life and remind yourself that the One who created and controls everything that exists has been made, by grace, to be your Father. He thinks of you with pure and faithful fatherly love. He acts toward you with the giving, providing, instructing, patient, and forgiving love of a perfect father. He is always with you. His hand is always upon you. He never stops watching you. His heart is always for you. He is always at work accomplishing his plans for you and through you. He lifts your burdens and lightens your load. He is your God, your Savior, your Friend—your Father. Nothing can ever be the same again because you now live in the Father's house, where glorious grace decorates every room.

For further study and encouragement: Psalm 105

MAY 5

"Hallowed be your name . . ." (Matt. 6:9b). In the little moments of daily life, I must live for a greater honor and glory than my own.

I remember the lecture well. It came with force and clarity at the end of my junior year of high school. My dad called me into the room and said, "Sit down; I want to talk to you for a moment." I thought, "I wonder what I've done?" I hadn't done anything wrong. My dad was just preparing me for the next phase of my life. He told me that my job was to get up every day and look for a job until I had found one. Then he said: "Remember, as you're out there, you carry the name of this family with you. What you do that is good will reflect on this family, and the bad things that you do will reflect on this family as well." It was a crushing burden for me. I thought, "I'm only sixteen years old, and I have to carry the burden of the reputation of this family on my shoulders?"

In case you wonder, this is not what the second statement in our Lord's model prayer is about. It is not about you and me carrying on our shoulders the crushing burden of the reputation of God. No fallen human being on his most brilliantly godly day could successfully carry such a burden. No, this statement frames everything that prayer is about, and in so doing it reveals how precious the grace of Jesus is. Prayer is about something vastly bigger and more beautiful than laying before God your personal wish list for the day, because your life is meant to be about something bigger than that as well. Prayer is, in itself, a recognition that something exists in the world that is greater and more glorious than you. Prayer is meant to remind you that your little world, filled with your little plans, is not ultimate. Prayer teaches you that there is a greater glory than any glory that you could ever want for yourself. Prayer is meant to help you remember that the deepest, most important motivation for every person who has ever taken a breath is the awe of God.

This deep and abiding recognition of the grandeur and glory of God is meant to shape and direct everything in my life. Everything that I do and every request that I make of God is to be done in recognition that everything that exists, including me, was made for his glory. This reality rips a hole in my heart and exposes what is there. I don't really want to live for a greater glory. What I really want is for the people, places, and things in my life to serve the glory of my comfort and satisfaction. Submitting my life to the holy name of God reminds me that I need to pray for something else—grace. Without rescuing grace, I will continue to live as a glory thief, and so will you. Thankfully, that grace is ours in Jesus our Lord.

For further study and encouragement: Isaiah 48:1–11

MAY 6

"Your kingdom come . . ." (Matt. 6:10a). I must remember that God didn't give me grace for my kingdom to work, but to capture me for a better kingdom.

It was one of the sweetest, most precious things Jesus said to his disciples. Remember, they were all really focused on "the kingdom." Not that they were concerned about the honor of the King or the success of his kingdom; no, what obsessed them was their place in that kingdom. For them, the kingdom was about personal power, prominence, and position. Do you remember the incident recorded in Mark 9:30–37?

> They went on from there and passed through Galilee. And he did not want anyone to know, for he was teaching his disciples, saying to them, "The Son of Man is going to be delivered into the hands of men, and they will kill him. And when he is killed, after three days he will rise." But they did not understand the saying, and were afraid to ask him.
>
> And they came to Capernaum. And when he was in the house he asked them, "What were you discussing on the way?" But they kept silent, for on the way they had argued with one another about who was the greatest. And he sat down and called the twelve. And he said to them, "If anyone would be first, he must be last of all and servant of all." And he took a child and put him in the midst of them, and taking him in his arms, he said to them, "Whoever receives one such child in my name receives me, and whoever receives me, receives not me but him who sent me."

Right after Jesus told them that he was going to be captured and killed, they didn't say: "Lord, no, no, you can't let this happen. What will we do without you?" They weren't filled with remorse. No, they began fighting with one another about which one of them was the greatest. This is what sin does to all of us. It causes us all to be little self-sovereigns and self-appointed mini-kings. What we really want is for *our* kingdoms to come and our will to be done right here, right now in our jobs and families. We love being in control. We love getting our own way. We love being indulged and served. We live for being right. We have a wonderful plan for the people in our lives. It is humbling to admit, but we are more like the disciples than unlike them.

So it was a moment of beautiful grace when Jesus looked at these self-oriented disciples and said, "Fear not, little flock, for it is your Father's good pleasure to give you the kingdom" (Luke 12:32). He was saying: "Don't you understand? I didn't come to exercise my power to make your little kingdoms work, but to welcome you, by grace, to a much better kingdom than you could ever quest for on your own." No matter how counterintuitive it is, it really is true that real life is found only when his kingdom comes and his will is done, and that is exactly what grace welcomes you to.

For further study and encouragement: Matthew 13:44–50

MAY 7

"Your will be done . . ." (Matt. 6:10b). The good life is not found in the success of my will, but in the submission of all things to God's will.

It was a 1950s television program unlike anything that would be broadcast today. Even its title is politically incorrect in today's culture (despite this, its episodes are still being aired). *Father Knows Best* was the says-it-all title of this iconic TV series. Maybe today the program would be called *Everyone but Father Knows Best.*

Perhaps *Father Knows Best* is not such a bad title for this section of the Lord's Prayer. Here's what we all need to keep in mind at all times: the One who rules over this world is the ultimate definition of everything that is good, wise, right, loving, faithful, and true. Hope in life is never about doing whatever you need to do to get your way. Hope in life is not found in expending all your resources, time, energy, and gifts to realize your personal dreams. Hope in life is not found in working yourself into as much control as possible over the people and situations in your life. In a word, hope is not found in your will being done.

Hope is found in only one place—in the wise and faithful rule of your Father in heaven. With his "before origin to beyond destiny" perspective, he really does know what is best for you and for everything he created. Prayer is never about asking God to submit his awesome power to your will and plan; prayer is an act of personal submission to the always-right will of God.

Now, here's the problem—we all go through times in our lives when we slide into thinking that we're smarter than God, that is, that what we want for ourselves is better than what he wants for us. We chafe against what he has put on our plates. We rebel against how he has told us to live in his Word. We wonder why our lives seem harder than those of the people next to us. We wonder why breaking one of God's little laws to make things better is such a bad thing.

So cry out for grace. The war between God's will and your will has not yet ended. The desire for God to exercise his power to deliver your personal dreams is not yet gone. The temptation to think that you know better still has the power to capture you. Reach out for the help your Savior died to give you. Ask him again to rescue you from you. Pray for the sense of heart to know that there is no safer place to be than in submission to the will of your Father in heaven. And have the courage this morning to look toward heaven and say, "Your kingdom come, your will be done right here, right now in my life as it is in heaven." And thank God that he cared for you so much that he exercised his will for your welfare and salvation. When you're joyfully willing to submit to the will of this One, you know grace has taken residence in your heart.

For further study and encouragement: Isaiah 26

MAY 8

"Give us this day our daily bread . . ." (Matt. 6:11). I am not independent or self-sufficient, but dependent on the goodness of God for my needs.

It was a very important, street-level warning, and it was given at just the right time:

> And you shall remember the whole way that the LORD your God has led you these forty years in the wilderness, that he might humble you, testing you to know what was in your heart, whether you would keep his commandments or not. And he humbled you and let you hunger and fed you with manna, which you did not know, nor did your fathers know, that he might make you know that man does not live by bread alone, but man lives by every word that comes from the mouth of the LORD. Your clothing did not wear out on you and your foot did not swell these forty years. Know then in your heart that, as a man disciplines his son, the LORD your God disciplines you. So you shall keep the commandments of the LORD your God by walking in his ways and by fearing him. For the LORD your God is bringing you into a good land, a land of brooks of water, of fountains and springs, flowing out in the valleys and hills, a land of wheat and barley, of vines and fig trees and pomegranates, a land of olive trees and honey, a land in which you will eat bread without scarcity, in which you will lack nothing, a land whose stones are iron, and out of whose hills you can dig copper. And you shall eat and be full, and you shall bless the LORD your God for the good land he has given you.
> Take care lest you forget the LORD your God by not keeping his commandments and his rules and his statutes, which I command you today. (Deut. 8:2–11)

The children of Israel were entering the Promised Land, where abundant resources would be available to them and they would face the temptation of affluence. What is that? It is the temptation we all face, when things are going well and supplies are many, to forget our utter dependence on the power, goodness, and faithfulness of God for everything in life. The prayer for daily bread reminds me that I am dependent on God for even the most mundane needs of my life. Only he has the power to control all the conditions, situations, locations, events, and people that need to be controlled in order for me to have the things that I need to have in order to live my life.

Independency is a delusion. Even the most ardent atheist is dependent on God for his life and breath. No one is able to get what he needs for his physical existence on his own. No one lives a self-sufficient life. No one can say, "Look how successfully I have been able to care for me without any outside assistance." No one! It really is true that "Every good and every perfect gift is from above" (James 1:17). So look up and give thanks. There really is a great and loving Supplier.

For further study and encouragement: 1 Kings 17

MAY 9

"Forgive us . . . as we also have forgiven . . ." (Matt. 6:12). I must always re-member the grace I am daily given and extend that grace to the people in my life.

It is really true that one of the greatest sins in our relationships is the sin of forgetful-ness. Consider the following parable of Jesus:

> Therefore the kingdom of heaven may be compared to a king who wished to settle accounts with his servants. When he began to settle, one was brought to him who owed him ten thousand talents. And since he could not pay, his master ordered him to be sold, with his wife and children and all that he had, and pay-ment to be made. So the servant fell on his knees, imploring him, "Have patience with me, and I will pay you everything." And out of pity for him, the master of that servant released him and forgave him the debt. But when that same servant went out, he found one of his fellow servants who owed him a hundred denarii, and seizing him, he began to choke him, saying, "Pay what you owe." So his fellow servant fell down and pleaded with him, "Have patience with me, and I will pay you." He refused and went and put him in prison until he should pay the debt. When his fellow servants saw what had taken place, they were greatly distressed, and they went and reported to their master all that had taken place. Then his master summoned him and said to him, "You wicked servant! I forgave you all that debt because you pleaded with me. And should not you have had mercy on your fellow servant, as I had mercy on you?" (Matt. 18:23–33)

We can all be so forgetful. We can all fail to remember the magnificence of the love and mercy that has been showered down on us. We can all forget that we never could have earned or deserved the best things in our lives; they are only ours by means of grace. Here's the problem: to the degree that you forget the grace that you have been given, to that same degree it is easier for you not to extend grace to others. To the extent that you forget how much you've been forgiven, to that same extent it is easier for you not to forgive the people in your life. If you fail to carry around with you a heart of gratitude for the love you've been so freely given, it is easy for you not to love others as you should.

It is and always has been true that no one gives grace better than a person who is deeply persuaded that he needs it himself and that it has been graciously supplied by a God of tender mercy. He gives what we never could have earned; why, then, do we turn and refuse to give until others have measured up to whatever standard we hold them to? The call to forgive immediately exposes our need for forgiveness. The call to give grace reveals how much we need grace. The call to forgive is at the very same time a call to remember and to be thankful. When you remember how far you fall short, you are tenderhearted toward others who fall short, and you want for them the same grace that is your only hope. May God give us the grace to remember and the willingness to give to others what we have been given.

For further study and encouragement: Ephesians 4:25–32

MAY 10

"Lead us not into temptation . . ." (Matt. 6:13a).
I rest assured that I am loved by a holy God.
His will for me is always right, good, and true.

"But why, Dad, why can't I? All the others kids are doing it. I just don't understand why you have to say no all the time. I don't get why this is such a big deal. Can't I do it just this one time?" I can't tell you how many times we had this conversation. Sometimes it was a quick plea, thankfully followed by submission. At other times it disintegrated into a major, volume-raised debate. But each time it was an instructive reminder.

It's a sad but obvious fact—sinners don't like boundaries. Sinners tend not to esteem rules. Sinners don't like to be told what to do. Sinners don't tend to love authority. Sinners tend to want to author their own moral codes. So you can't even pray this prayer, "Lead us not into temptation," unless grace has visited you. Only powerful, rescuing grace can take you from "Let me do what I want to do" to "Guard me against the temptation to do what you know is best for me not to do." If you're a parent or can honestly reflect on your childhood, you know that one of the biggest and most important battles children have with their parents is the battle of authority. The same is true of our relationship with God. You don't have to read any further than the third chapter of the Bible to see that battle break out and alter the entire course of human history.

In this request, there are three recognitions that only grace can produce. The first recognition is that there is One of ultimate authority who rules over this world and knows what is best. In this recognition is the acknowledgment that I am never ultimate, that even if I am the most powerful human being on earth, I am still a person under authority. The second recognition is that the One who is the ultimate authority has clearly communicated to me how I should live. There is a God-originated, God-communicated set of boundaries that I have been designed to live within. Real life is found inside these boundaries, not in discovering and experiencing what's outside of them. The third recognition is that on this side of eternity, I live in a world of moment-by-moment temptation. The world I live in does not operate as God intended, and because it doesn't, it whispers seductive lies into my ears every day. It works to deceive me into thinking that what is ugly in God's eyes is really beautiful and that what God has said is wrong is really all right after all. So pray that these three recognitions will rule your heart today—that you'll remember God's authority, that you'll love his law, and that you'll have the desire and strength to resist temptation. There is ample grace for all of these things!

For further study and encouragement: Psalm 93

MAY 11

"But deliver us from evil . . ." (Matt. 6:13b).
I admit that it's the evil inside me that hooks me to
the evil outside me, and I seek grace's rescue.

If Billy pushes Suzy, causing her to fall and hit her head, and you come into the room and ask Billy why he did it, he won't talk about himself. He'll talk about what Suzy did or how he tripped over the toys in the room, but he won't say: "I've got sin in my heart that makes me selfish, so I push others when they get in my way. Please pray for me, Mom." You won't hear that because, even though Billy is only five years old, he has already bought into the heresy that his biggest problems in life exist outside him, not inside him. He wants to believe that the big dangers are all "out there."

Like Billy, we are all very skilled at explaining away our wrong behavior by pointing to the situations, locations, events, and people in our lives. We work very hard to convince ourselves that the problem cannot be us. We take ourselves off the hook by saying:

- "She misunderstood me."
- "I was busy."
- "I really didn't mean it that way."
- "I wasn't feeling well."
- "It's just my personality."
- "Sorry, I just forgot."
- "I must not have heard you."
- "He talked me into it."
- "You don't know how difficult he is to live with."
- "I just ran out of time."
- "I'm sorry—other things just got in the way."

We are all very good at swindling ourselves into thinking that what God says is wrong isn't so wrong after all, or that our words and behavior tell us more about the situations and people in our lives than they do about us. We resist the truth that it is only ever the evil inside us that magnetizes us to the evil outside us.

When grace has made you able to pray "deliver us from evil," you are admitting that the evil that is the greatest danger to you is the evil inside you. You are admitting that you can escape the evil in a certain location, you can avoid an evil situation, and you can run from an evil person, but you cannot run from yourself. Only grace has the power to rescue you from you and to deliver you from the most threatening evil of all—the evil that still resides in your heart. Cry out for that grace.

For further study and encouragement: Psalm 14

MAY 12

You were hardwired to live for God, so even though you
may not be aware of it, every good thing or bad
thing you do today has verticality to it.

In the physical realm, you were hardwired to breathe. You do it constantly, even though you are most often unaware of it. You are always inhaling oxygen and exhaling carbon dioxide. You don't have the option of saying, "I'm tired of breathing, I think I'll just stop." You don't have the option of denying that you are a breather. You were hardwired to breathe. It is an inescapable part of your physicality.

In the same way, you were made for relationship with God. This means that everything you do and say, every choice you make, and every decision that shapes your life is somehow, some way done in reference to God. You may ignore his existence, you may think theologically that there is no God, but you cannot escape that you were crafted in his image and connected to him by means of creation. This means that all your life is spiritual. Religion is not just an aspect of your being; you and I are by nature religious beings. We all come from God, we all exist through God, and all that we do is meant to be done for him.

Now, to help us retain our recognition of the inescapable verticality of our existence—that is, to help us remember his existence and our place as his creatures—God has done something wonderful for us. He purposefully created the physical world in such a way that it points to his existence and his character. God *is* the environment in which we live. I like to think of it this way: you can't get up in the morning without bumping into God. The psalmist writes: "The heavens declare the glory of God, and the sky above declares his handiwork. Day after day pours out speech, and night to night reveals knowledge. There is no speech, nor are there words, whose voice is not heard" (Ps. 19:1–3). And Paul says: "For his invisible attributes, namely, his eternal power and divine nature, have been clearly perceived, ever since the creation of the world, in the things that have been made. So they are without excuse" (Rom. 1:20).

The radical truth of the existence of God isn't just preached to us on Sunday; it's preached every day through the beauty of the sunset, the power of the storm, the inexhaustible wings of the hummingbird, the hugeness of the mountain, the whisper of the breeze, the smell of the sizzling steak, the beauty of the petal of a rose, and so on. The power and clarity of creation's message leaves no human being with an excuse. You have to work to deny God's existence because it is so readily visible everywhere you look. God did this because he is a God of grace. He did this so that we would run to him and not from him. He did this so that we would recognize our position as his creatures and bow to his glory. He did this so that we would live in recognition of him.

For further study and encouragement: Romans 1:18–25

MAY 13

*You have not been left to secure your own future, because God in grace
has secured an end to your story more glorious than you can grasp.*

You and I absolutely need our lives to be shaped and reshaped by these words:

> Blessed be the God and Father of our Lord Jesus Christ! According to his great
> mercy, he has caused us to be born again to a living hope through the resurrection
> of Jesus Christ from the dead, to an inheritance that is imperishable, undefiled,
> and unfading, kept in heaven for you, who by God's power are being guarded
> through faith for a salvation ready to be revealed in the last time. (1 Pet. 1:3–5)

One of the most common human fears is fear of the future. We all ask, "What
will happen if . . . ?" or "What will happen next?" or "What is down the road?" Embedded in all of this is the hope that we will be secure and things will be all right in
the future. It is not insane to wonder about the future. It is not a sin to be concerned
about what is to come. It is not wrong to plan for the future. In fact, you and I should
live with the future in view every day of our lives. In some ways, everything that we
think, desire, decide, do, and say should be shaped by what is to come. But there is
a huge difference between worrying about what you have no power over and resting
in what God has revealed about his future plans for you.

Peace and hope are never to be found in your efforts to figure out the future.
God's secret will is called his secret will precisely because it is secret! No, real hope
is found in living inside the implications of what it means that God holds your future
in his wise, powerful, and gracious hands. Peter says, "Don't ever let yourself forget
that Jesus has purchased a future for you that is better than anything you could have
dreamed of or planned for yourself." If you remember that you have this wonderful
future ahead of you, you won't live as if this moment is all you have and you will be
free of the anxiety of fearing that somehow this moment will pass you by. I love the
qualifying words that Peter uses to describe our inheritance as the children of God:
"imperishable, undefiled, and unfading." Together they mean that this inheritance
is protected and untouchable; nothing will be allowed to happen that would damage
it in any way. It is absolutely secure.

But Peter says more. He says that not only is God keeping your inheritance, he's
keeping you. He's not only protecting what is to come, he's protecting you, so that
when what is to come has come, you will be there to receive it and enjoy it forever
and ever. So remember today that no matter how hard your story is right here, right
now, it is guaranteed for you as God's child that it will end better than anything you
can now imagine, and that glory will never end!

For further study and encouragement: 1 Thessalonians 4:13–5:11

MAY 14

Never forget that what God required, you couldn't do.
Christ did it for you. His grace is your hope.

In some way, it is true of us all. We want to swindle ourselves into thinking that we are righteous enough to be accepted in the eyes of God. Maybe for you it is:

- "Look at how much I give to charity."
- "Look at how hospitable I am."
- "Look at the level of my theological knowledge."
- "Look at how often I share the gospel with others."
- "Look at what a good marriage I have."
- "Look how successful my business is."
- "Look at how I've resisted pornography or adultery."
- "Look at the fact that I homeschool my children."
- "Look at how I never curse or swear."
- "Look at how many short-term mission trips I've been on."
- "Look at how consistent my personal devotions are."
- "Look at my willingness to lead a small group."

You and I tend to want to point to anything we can to prove that we are not lawbreakers, but law keepers. Yet the whole argument of the Bible is that if we were able to keep the law with perfection and consistency, Jesus would not have had to come. The sad reality is that alone, none of us is righteous. None of us measures up. None of us has any power whatsoever to keep the law so consistently as to achieve acceptance by a completely holy God. So it was essential that Jesus would come and live in a way that none of us could ever live, to die the death that we all deserve to die, and to rise, defeating sin and death. Hope is never to be found in your performance, no matter what actions you are able to point to. Sin is your infection, and without the grace of the Lord Jesus Christ, it is also your demise. It is inescapable and morally debilitating, and it will lead to your death.

So abandon hope in your own righteousness. Abandon the delusion that somehow you can measure up. Run to the place where hope can be found and throw yourself again today on the grace of Jesus. He did what you could never do so that you would be welcomed into the arms of a righteous God and be fully accepted even though, in reality, you are anything but righteous. How can God accept you and not compromise his own righteousness? He can do this because Christ's righteousness has been credited to your moral account. Now, that's amazing grace!

For further study and encouragement: Hebrews 2:10–18

MAY 15

Corporate worship is designed to alert you to the war for control
of your heart and to the help that is found only in Jesus.

One of the reasons God has called us to gather together regularly is that we are so forgetful. We forget who God is and endeavor to live based on our own merit and strength. We forget who we are and the empirical evidence that we lay down every day of our desperate need for redeeming grace. We forget how broken is the world in which we live, so we live with unrealistic expectations and naïveté toward temptation. We forget how magnificent our resources are in Christ, how complete his provision is, and how precious it is that he is always near. We forget how wise, encouraging, protective, and freeing God's Word is. We forget our need for the body of Christ; that our spiritual life is meant to be a group project. We forget that we have not only been blessed to be recipients of God's grace, but have been called to be tools of that grace in the lives of others. We forget that there really is an enemy who prowls around to devour us spiritually. We forget that life can never be found in the physical creation. We forget that we have been created to live for a glory that is bigger than our own and for a kingdom that is greater than what we would construct on our own. Yes, we need to gather again and again, and through worship, preaching, and mutual fellowship, to remember what we would otherwise forget.

One of the things we forget is that the major, big-deal war in our lives is not a war with things outside us; it's the war that still rages inside us. In every situation, location, and relationship in our lives, there is a war for control of our hearts. This is the war of wars because we were made by God to live out of our hearts. This means that what rules our hearts shapes our words and actions. So the big war is not any of the smaller wars we have with other people, debt, material possessions, sex, and so on. No, the war is more foundational than all of these. It is captured by 2 Corinthians 5:15: "He died for all, that those who live might no longer live for themselves but for him who for their sake died and was raised." Will we live for ourselves, reducing life down to the small confines of our wants, feelings, needs, demands, expectations, and so on, or will we live for God? It all sounds so theological, but it is very practical. Every day you attach the hopes and dreams of your heart, your satisfaction, and your joy to something. Every day you look to something to give you life. Every day you give yourself to something in the hope that it will give you peace and joy. Every day you attach your identity to something, and there are only two places to look. You are either looking for life in the creation and are on your way to crushing disappointment, or you are looking to the Creator and are on your way to lasting peace of heart. Corporate worship is designed to remind you again and again where life can be found so that you can quit searching horizontally for what you have already been given in Jesus.

For further study and encouragement: James 4:13–5:6

MAY 16

We are guilty. The cross purchased our forgiveness. We are unable. The Spirit gives us power. We are foolish. God's Word provides wisdom.

What did I bring
to your salvation table?
I had
no righteousness to offer,
no strength to give,
no wisdom to present.
There was
nothing
that I could deliver
that would commend me
to you.
I crawled broken
to your table,
weighed down and crippled by
my sin,
my guilt,
my weakness,
my foolishness,
my pride,
my shame.
I had no right
to be with you,
but you picked me up
and placed me there.
You fed me
the life-giving nutrients
of grace
with your
nail-scarred hands.
And I haven't left your
table of mercy since.

For further study and encouragement: Romans 8:18–30

MAY 17

*The grand delusion of every act of sin is that we can be
disloyal to God and everything will work out in the end.*

We all do it sometimes and in some ways. In little and not so little moments of disloyalty to God, we work to excuse ourselves and convince ourselves that it will all be
okay in the end. In private moments of moral self-conversation, we say:

- "I can handle this; it will be okay."
- "I'll only do it this once."
- "I really didn't have much of a choice."
- "It's not really such a big deal."
- "Other people do it all the time."
- "It's not really clearly forbidden by the Bible."
- "What else could I do?"
- "I just chose the lesser of two evils."
- "God is good; he'll forgive me."
- "It's not like I do this all the time."
- "Doesn't God want me to be happy?"

Each statement is designed to relieve the burden of conviction. Each is meant to
mask the reality that we have chosen to be disloyal to God, rebellious to his authority, and resistant to his call. Each is meant to cover the true allegiance of our hearts.
Each is designed to enable us to feel okay about what God clearly says is not okay.
Each is meant to make sin look not so sinful after all. Each is meant to ease our fear
that sin really is destructive and that it really does lead to death.

There are moments when we are all tempted to give in to the delusional logic of
Adam and Eve in the garden of Eden (see Genesis 3). In the mundane moments of
our daily lives, we buy into the fallacy that we can step over God's loving and wise
moral boundaries without consequences. In myriad little moments, we're morally
disloyal to the One who is our wisdom, righteousness, and hope. And what's important about this is that the character of a life isn't set in three or four big moments of
life, but in ten thousand little, virtually unnoticed moments. These acts of disloyalty
expose the war that still rages for the rulership of our hearts and the depth of our
ongoing need for rescuing and forgiving grace. Isn't it good to know that that grace
is ours in Christ Jesus?

For further study and encouragement: Romans 6:15–23

MAY 18

Change is not found in defending our righteousness,
but in admitting our weakness and crying for help.

I wish I could say that this is not my struggle. I wish I could say that I've fully accepted the reality of my spiritual battle. I wish I could say that I am always thankful for the help God provides. I wish I could say that I am always open and approachable. I wish I could say all of these things, but sadly, I can't. When I'm approached about a wrong I've committed, I don't tend to say to the other person: "Thank you so much for confronting me. I know that I suffer from spiritual blindness and don't see myself accurately. Please keep rebuking me; I know it's a visible sign of God's love." No, there are two things that tend to be more natural for me as I feel my ears redden and my chest tighten. I first activate my internal defense system and mount arguments in my mind against the charge. Perhaps I was misunderstood. Maybe this is an invalid judgment of my motives. Perhaps what this person thought I did, I just didn't do. Then I work to erect arguments for my righteousness. I list all of the good, but maybe unnoticed, things I am doing. I work to convince myself and the person confronting me that I am righteous. In these two actions, not only am I negating empirical evidence of the sin that still resides in my heart, but I am also defending righteousness that doesn't exist.

Here's the sad part: in doing both of these things, I'm devaluing the grace that is my only hope in life and death. To whatever extent I am able to convince myself that my sin isn't really sin—that is, that my little wrongs do not really rise to the level of what Jesus died for—I am not really that excited about grace. Why? Because I have convinced myself that I don't really need the rescue and forgiveness that grace offers. And to the degree that I am able to work myself into believing that I am righteous, I have less esteem for the perfect righteousness of Christ, which is the only righteousness with which I can stand before God.

So I may have a crisp and clear theology of grace and I may be able to point to passages in God's Word that clearly preach that grace, but where the rubber meets the road in everyday life, self-righteousness stands in the way of that grace having functional and transformative value in my life. My defensiveness in the face of the confrontation of the body of Christ and the convicting ministry of the Holy Spirit stands as a practical denial of what I say I believe. It keeps me supporting what I should flee from and stops me from running to the place where help is only ever found.

What about you? Have you really abandoned your righteousness? Does that make you run toward the grace of Jesus? Or will you defend today what Jesus died to destroy? Perhaps before you start confessing your sin you should first confess your righteousness.

For further study and encouragement: Luke 18:9–14

MAY 19

*If your heart isn't ruled by God's honor and your life by God's plan,
you may seem religious, but what you're living isn't biblical faith.*

I want to use marriage as a case study for the principle stated above. None of us has lived in a marriage that is completely free of conflict and tension. None of us has been able to escape moments of irritation and impatience. We all have had nasty arguments or extended moments of silence. We all have been disappointed in our marriages in some way. (If you're single, apply everything I've said to the relationships in your life.) Now, you just have to ask, "What is all that tension and conflict about?" If you were to read the average Christian marriage book, you would be led to conclude that all of the fights and quarrels are about the inescapable horizontal issues within every marriage. So the conclusion is that if you are smart enough to discuss gender differences, personality differences, role expectations, finances, sex, parenting, diet, and so on, you will be able to avoid most of those conflicts.

On the surface, it sounds right, but it isn't what the Bible says. Consider the following provocative passage:

> What causes quarrels and what causes fights among you? Is it not this, that your passions are at war within you? You desire and do not have, so you murder. You covet and cannot obtain, so you fight and quarrel. You do not have, because you do not ask. You ask and do not receive, because you ask wrongly, to spend it on your passions. You adulterous people! Do you not know that friendship with the world is enmity with God? Therefore whoever wishes to be a friend of the world makes himself an enemy of God. Or do you suppose it is to no purpose that the Scripture says, "He yearns jealously over the spirit that he has made to dwell in us"? But he gives more grace. Therefore it says, "God opposes the proud, but gives grace to the humble." Submit yourselves therefore to God. Resist the devil, and he will flee from you. Draw near to God, and he will draw near to you. Cleanse your hands, you sinners, and purify your hearts, you double-minded. Be wretched and mourn and weep. Let your laughter be turned to mourning and your joy to gloom. Humble yourselves before the Lord, and he will exalt you. (James 4:1–10)

Notice how James explains why we have so many fights and quarrels. He doesn't say, "They come from those difficult people you live with" or "They are the result of the practical issues that you're forced to deal with." No, he says they come from the "passions" that wage war in our hearts. In this context, *passion* means a powerful, ruling desire. I fight with you because I have a heart problem. Rather than my heart being ruled by God and motivated by God's honor, my heart is ruled by my wants, my needs, and my feelings. If it is, I am always in some kind of conflict with you. Furthermore, James tells us that human conflict is rooted in spiritual adultery. When we put ourselves where God alone belongs, conflict always results. It is all just another argument for the essentiality of God's grace in Jesus.

For further study and encouragement: Isaiah 29 (especially v. 13)

MAY 20

It's never hopeless and you're never helpless if Immanuel
has invaded your life with his glory and grace.

It is a remarkable story, recorded for our insight, remembrance, and encouragement. It's a window on what every believer needs and has been given by God's grace:

> Now Jericho was shut up inside and outside because of the people of Israel. None went out, and none came in. And the LORD said to Joshua, "See, I have given Jericho into your hand, with its king and mighty men of valor. You shall march around the city, all the men of war going around the city once. Thus shall you do for six days. Seven priests shall bear seven trumpets of rams' horns before the ark. On the seventh day you shall march around the city seven times, and the priests shall blow the trumpets. And when they make a long blast with the ram's horn, when you hear the sound of the trumpet, then all the people shall shout with a great shout, and the wall of the city will fall down flat, and the people shall go up, everyone straight before him." So Joshua the son of Nun called the priests and said to them, "Take up the ark of the covenant and let seven priests bear seven trumpets of rams' horns before the ark of the LORD." And he said to the people, "Go forward. March around the city and let the armed men pass on before the ark of the LORD." (Josh. 6:1–7)

The children of Israel had entered the Promised Land, but lest they forget who they were and what they had been given, God put a trial in front of them that would powerfully demonstrate his glory and grace, which he was willing to exercise for their salvation. There was no way that this ragtag group of pilgrims would ever be able to defeat the fortified city of Jericho, but that was precisely the point. So God asked them to march around the city one time a day for six days, and then, on the seventh day, to parade around it seven times. Now, from a human perspective, what God was proposing was military suicide. God was teaching Israel that they must no longer look at life from the vantage point of human wisdom and strength because they were now the children of the Lord almighty. Their world of weakness and limits had been invaded by One of awesome grace and glory. As they walked around Jericho, God was confronting Israel with their inability, vulnerability, and dependency, and comforting them with the reality that he would be with them wherever they went and whatever they faced. They would face no enemies on their own. They would carry no needs by themselves. They would not have to bear the burden or carry their destiny in their own hands. Grace and glory had come to them in the presence of the Lord, and in the power of the Lord the walls would come down.

If you're God's child, you too must remember who you are and what you've been given. It is never you against the world, because your life has been invaded by the grace and glory of Immanuel. Say no to fear and live with the hope and courage that come only when you remember that the Lord is near.

For further study and encouragement: Hebrews 13:1–6

MAY 21

The gift of eternal life guarantees that I have been and will be forgiven,
and that every broken thing inside me will be completely repaired.

It really is location, location, location. If you're going to live with peace of heart and with hope and courage, you have to know your place in the work of God. There are two markers of that work that really do locate you, tell you what God is doing, and inform you as to how you should live right here, right now. As I have said before, you live between the "already" and the "not yet."

First, it is vital for you and me to always remember that we live in the "already" of *complete forgiveness*. Forgiveness is not a "hope it will be" thing. It's an "accomplished and done" thing. You do not have to hope that you will be forgiven. You do not have to be concerned that the process of forgiveness will somehow fail. Why? Because your complete and final forgiveness was accomplished on the cross of Jesus Christ. The perfect sacrifice of the completely righteous Lamb fully satisfied the holy requirements of God and left you righteous and without penalty in his sight. So you never have to worry that you will be so bad that God will reject you. You never have to hide your sin. You never have to do things to win God's favor. You never have to cower in shame. You never have to rationalize, excuse, defend, or shift the blame. You never have to pretend that you are better than you are. You never have to present arguments for your righteousness. You never have to fear being known or exposed. You never have to compare the size of your sin to the size of another's. You never have to parade your righteousness so it can be seen by others. You never have to wonder if God's going to get exhausted with how often you mess up. All of these are acts of gospel irrationality because you have been completely forgiven.

On the other end, it is essential to understand the "not yet" of your *final repair*. Yes, you have been fully forgiven, but you have not yet been completely rebuilt into all that grace will make you. Sin still remains, the war for your heart still rages, the world around you is still broken, spiritual danger still lurks, and you have not yet been fully re-formed into the image of the Lord Jesus Christ. The cross of Jesus guarantees that all of these broken things will be fixed, but they are not fixed yet.

So as I bask in the complete forgiveness that I have been given and enjoy freedom from the anxiety that I will not measure up, I cannot live unwisely. One danger (sin) still lives inside me and another (temptation) still lurks outside me, so I am still a person in daily and desperate need of grace. Forgiveness is complete. Final restoration is yet to come. Knowing you live in between the two is the key to a restful and wise Christian life.

For further study and encouragement: 2 Peter 3:1–13

MAY 22

No need to wonder what you have to do to get God's acceptance.
Jesus purchased your acceptance on the cross.

The cross of Jesus Christ took the "acceptance with God" issue off the table for every one of his blood-purchased children. Now, you just can't get any better news than that! On the cross, the worst thing that could ever happen became the best thing that could ever happen. Let me explain.

The cruelest aspect of the suffering of Christ was not the human mockery, the slaps and thorns, the whip, or the nails. No, the most horrible moment for Jesus on the cross is recorded in Matthew 27:45–46: "Now from the sixth hour there was darkness over all the land until the ninth hour. And about the ninth hour Jesus cried out with a loud voice, saying, 'Eli, Eli, lema sabachthani?' that is, 'My God, my God, why have you forsaken me?'" Those words of utter grief echo back through the centuries to another horrible moment. It was the moment when the sinful rebellion of Adam and Eve separated them from the God who had created them to know, enjoy, and commune with him forever. It was a moment of horror when God drove them out of the garden and far away from his presence. The deepest need of all humanity from that point on was that somehow, some way communion with God would be restored. But thousands of years went by, each year being stained with the reality of that separation. There was no way people could be what they were meant to be and do what they had been intended to do while they were separated from God.

So Jesus was willing to come and live the life we could not live and die the death that we deserved, but that's not all he was willing to do. He willingly endured the Father's rejection so that we would know his acceptance. What could be more horrible than this separation between the Father and the Son? Yet, this unthinkably awful separation, by sovereign grace, met our deepest need. In Christ's rejection came our acceptance. In Christ's moment of horror we were given eternal hope. Because he was willing to endure the terrible pain of the Father's rejection, you and I will never, ever again see the back of God's head.

Your acceptance before God has been purchased and doesn't need to be purchased again. As God's child, there is nothing that you can do to get more of God's acceptance and there is nothing you can do that would cause him to take your acceptance away. Your acceptance with God is just as secure on your very worst day as it is on your very best day, because it was purchased once and for all by your suffering Savior, the Lord Jesus Christ.

For further study and encouragement: Matthew 27:32–54

MAY 23

You can gaze over the fence and covet another person's
life or tell yourself that God has blessed you in ways
you never could have earned.

Do you ever battle with envy? Have you ever wondered why someone else's life seems easier than yours? Have you ever struggled to celebrate the blessings of someone else who had what you thought you needed? Have you ever wished you could just switch lives with someone? Perhaps there are ways in which envy haunts us all, so it's worth examining the heart of envy.

What things prepare the heart for envy?

1. *Envy is forgetful.* In concentrating on what we don't have that we think we should have, we fail to keep in mind the huge catalog of blessings that are ours simply because God has chosen to place his bountiful love on us. This forgetfulness causes us to do more comparing and complaining than praising and resting.
2. *Envy misunderstands blessing.* So often envy is fueled by misunderstanding what God's care looks like. It is not always the care of provision, relief, or release. Sometimes God's blessing comes in the form of trials that are his means of giving us things we could get no other way.
3. *Envy is selfish.* Envy tends to put us in the center of our own worlds. It tends to make everything about our comfort and ease, our wants, needs, and feelings, and not about the plan and the glory of the God we serve.
4. *Envy is self-righteous.* Envy has an "I deserve _____ more than they do" posture to it. It forgets that we all deserve immediate and eternal punishment, and that any good thing we have is an undeserved gift of God's amazing grace.
5. *Envy is shortsighted.* Envy has a right here, right now aspect to it that overlooks the fact that this moment is not all there is. Envy cannot see that this moment isn't meant to be a destination, but a preparation for a final destination that will be beautiful beyond our wildest imagination.
6. *Envy questions God's wisdom.* When you and I envy, we tend to buy into the thought that we are smarter than God. In envy, we tend to think we know more and better, and if our hands were on the joystick, we would be handling things a different way.
7. *Envy is impatient.* Envy doesn't like to wait. Envy complains quickly and tires easily. Envy doesn't just cry for blessings; it cries for blessings *now*.

What is devastating about envy is that it questions God's goodness, and when you do that, you quit running to him for help. So cry out for rescue—that God would give you a thankful, humble, and patient heart. His transforming grace is your only defense against envy.

For further study and encouragement: Psalm 34

MAY 24

We don't seek satisfaction, hoping that God will deliver it.
No, we seek God, and the result is satisfaction of heart.

It is one of the big ironies of the heart. If you give your heart to seeking satisfaction, satisfaction will be the one thing you'll never find. Your heart will never be satisfied in things. No, your heart will be satisfied only in the Giver of the things. If you seek happiness, happiness will elude you.

I have had many wives say to me in marriage counseling, "All I ever wanted was a husband who would make me happy." Think about the dynamics that this expectation introduces into a relationship. Obviously any woman who makes this statement has some definition of what happiness looks like; she has a marital dream, and she is loading her dream on the shoulders of her husband. Who is this man? Well, he's a flawed human being, living in a fallen world, so it is unlikely that he will ever deliver the dream for which she is looking.

Whenever you name something in creation as the thing that will satisfy you, you are asking that thing to be your personal savior. This means that, in a very practical, street-level way, you are looking horizontally for what will only ever be yours vertically. In other words, you are asking something in creation to do for you what only God can do. Now, the physical, created world was designed to be glorious, and it is. It is a sight-sound-touch-taste-feel symphony of multifaceted physical glories, but these glories cannot satisfy your heart. If you ask them to, your heart will be empty, and you will be frustrated and discouraged. No, the earthly glories that God created are to be like signposts that point us to the one glory that will ever satisfy our hearts.

So here's the bottom line. If you seek satisfaction, satisfaction will escape your grasp. But if you seek God, rest in his presence and grace, and put your heart in his most capable hands, he will satisfy your heart as nothing else can. You were made for him. Your heart was designed to be controlled by worship of him. Your inner security is meant to come from rest in him. Your sense of well-being is intended to come from a reliance on his wisdom, power, and love.

The reality is this—God is the peace that you're looking for. He is the satisfaction that your heart seeks. He is the rest that you crave, the joy you long for, and the comfort your heart desires. All those things that you and I say we need we don't really need. All those things that we think will bring us contentment and joy will fail to deliver. What we need in life is him, and by grace, he is with us, in us, and for us. Our hearts can rest because, by grace, we have been given everything we could ever need, in him.

For further study and encouragement: Psalm 107

MAY 25

What could motivate you more, as you face your weakness,
than these words: "My power is made perfect in weakness"?

I don't know about you, but I tend to not like being weak. I don't enjoy physical or spiritual weakness. I want to be right, strong, able, and in control. I don't want to feel like I'm not up to a challenge. I don't want to be confused or unready. I don't want to feel unqualified for the task at hand. I don't want to be the one who is keeping things from getting done or is holding others back. I don't like it when it seems that there are things I should know that I don't know. I don't want to look back at situations with regret, wishing that I had had a stronger resolve and the power to follow through. I don't want to stare failure in the face. I don't want to let myself or others down. I want to have a track record that I am proud of. I don't find weakness to be very comfortable.

I guess what I'm saying is that I don't want to be who I am or face who I am. And I suspect you're a lot like me. We all dream of independent strength and ability. We all crave independent knowledge and wisdom. We all want righteousness of our own. But the fact is that not only were we not created to be independent, but also sin has ravaged us and left us even weaker and more needy. The theologians call it *total depravity*. It doesn't mean that we are as bad as we could be, but that sin has done its cruel work on every aspect of our personhood. So independent strength is a delusion. This means that your weakness is not the great danger to you that you think it is. Rather, the great danger is your delusion of strength, because if you think you're strong, then you don't seek the help that you desperately need from the One who is the ultimate source of strength of every kind.

This is why Paul says: "But he said to me, 'My grace is sufficient for you, my power is made perfect in weakness.' Therefore, I will boast all the more gladly of my weaknesses, so that the power of Christ may rest on me" (2 Cor. 12:9). You see, knowledge of personal weakness is a blessing from God. If you understand this, it means that, by grace, he has delivered you from bondage to the delusion of your independent ability to be what he created you to be and to do what he calls you to do. So now you are free to seek the real strength that you need, strength that is found only in his capable and gracious hands. The delusional assessment of independent strength locks you out of the place where true strength is found. The hopelessness of weakness is the only door to the hope of real strength. Grace exposes how deep your need really is, then takes you by the hand to where lasting strength can be found. So you can boast in what most people fear because you have been and are being saved by grace.

For further study and encouragement: Jeremiah 9:23–24

MAY 26

Faith is living in light of what God has said, resting in what he has done, and entrusting the future to his care.

It is an incredible story, a clear case study in what faith is and does:

> By faith Abraham, when he was tested, offered up Isaac, and he who had received the promises was in the act of offering up his only son, of whom it was said, "Through Isaac shall your offspring be named." He considered that God was able even to raise him from the dead, from which, figuratively speaking, he did receive him back. (Heb. 11:17–19)

God had promised Abraham that his descendants would be like the stars in the sky and that through his descendants all the nations of the earth would be blessed. But Abraham and his wife, Sarah, didn't have any children, let alone a clue about how he would pass down the promise to the next generation. They waited and waited. Decade piled up on decade, but no son came. Abraham was an old man, and Sarah was decades beyond her childbearing years. Then, in a miracle of God's faithfulness, a son, Isaac, was born. There must have been some kind of celebration that day! God was true to his promises. He did have the power to deliver. He would keep his covenant. Blessing would come to this sin-broken world. It seemed like the end of a beautiful story.

Then God came to Abraham and told him to sacrifice the promised son! It made no sense whatsoever. All God's promises of faithfulness and all the hopes of his covenant rested on this boy. If Abraham killed him, it would all be over. If Isaac died, nothing that had happened for decades would make any sense. You can imagine Abraham saying: "God, ask anything of me, but not this; please, not this. You promised me a son. I waited in faith, and now you want me to kill him. God, I just don't understand." We don't know all the emotions that were inside Abraham, but there is little hint of angst and anger in his reactions. Abraham immediately began to prepare to do what God had called him to do. We know that grace had visited and transformed the heart of this man, or he would not have been able to react as he did.

It's clear that Abraham did not know why God was asking him to do what he had asked, and it is clear that he did not know what God was going to do. Abraham reasoned that maybe God would resurrect Isaac after the sacrifice, but that was not what God was intending. This is where this passage exposes what faith is about. Abraham wasn't relying on what he could see or understand. No, he was at rest because he acted on the firm platform of God's commands, as well as his presence, promises, faithfulness, and power. Faith believes that God really does exist and that he rewards those who seek him. But faith isn't natural for us; it is ours only as a gift of God's grace. Seek that grace again today.

For further study and encouragement: Genesis 22

MAY 27

*Don't give way to fear today. The Lord almighty is your Savior, and
he is with you in whatever you're facing and wherever you go.*

The apostle Paul is in Athens, waiting to make connections with fellow travelers, and
is so moved by what he sees and hears there that he can't resist injecting God into the
conversation. Listen to his words:

> So Paul, standing in the midst of the Areopagus, said: "Men of Athens, I per-
> ceive that in every way you are very religious. For as I passed along and observed
> the objects of your worship, I found also an altar with this inscription, 'To the
> unknown god.' What therefore you worship as unknown, this I proclaim to you.
> The God who made the world and everything in it, being Lord of heaven and
> earth, does not live in temples made by man, nor is he served by human hands, as
> though he needed anything, since he himself gives to all mankind life and breath
> and everything. And he made from one man every nation of mankind to live on
> all the face of the earth, having determined allotted periods and the boundaries
> of their dwelling place, that they should seek God, and perhaps feel their way
> toward him and find him. Yet he is actually not far from each one of us, for
>
> "'In him we live and move and have our being';
>
> as even some of your own poets have said,
>
> "'For we are indeed his offspring.'" (Acts 17:22–28)

There are two things that should calm our fears. The first is the incredible truth
that Paul speaks to the Athenians. Paul announces that the God who is in control of
everything that exists, even down to the exact address where we live, has decided to
rule his world so that he is so near to all of us that any moment we could reach out
and touch him. God is always near and always reachable.

But more needs to be said. Yes, it is true that as Sovereign, God is near in power
and rule, but it must also be said that as Savior, he is near in presence and grace.
As Sovereign, he rules over all the situations, locations, and relationships that may
cause me fear, but as Savior, he is rescuing, empowering, and transforming me by
grace. Because God is my Sovereign, my life is never out of control, and because he
is my Savior, he blesses me with everything I need to live in the middle of things that
are beyond my control. He is a sovereign Savior, which means I don't need to fear,
because he is with me and he provides everything I need for the places where his plan
leads me. He rules, and he graces me with everything I need to live inside his rule
with peace, hope, and courage. Why, then, should I fear?

For further study and encouragement: Isaiah 41:1–20

MAY 28

Today you'll work to deny your sin or you'll receive the Spirit's conviction as grace and run to Christ for rescue and forgiveness.

The words are direct and humbling, and they are written to believers:

> This is the message we have heard from him and proclaim to you, that God is light, and in him is no darkness at all. If we say we have fellowship with him while we walk in darkness, we lie and do not practice the truth. But if we walk in the light, as he is in the light, we have fellowship with one another, and the blood of Jesus his Son cleanses us from all sin. If we say we have no sin, we deceive ourselves, and the truth is not in us. If we confess our sins, he is faithful and just to forgive us our sins and to cleanse us from all unrighteousness. If we say we have not sinned, we make him a liar, and his word is not in us. (1 John 1:5–10)

Let's examine the logic of this passage:

1. *Sin is a big deal.* Grace has brought us into personal communion with a God who is holy in every way. He dwells in eternal light. The darkness of our sin is what separates us from him. The whole movement of history from the time of the fall announces to us that God takes sin so seriously that he wrote the story of history so that his Son would come and, through his life and death, deal with sin and bridge the gap between God and the creatures made in his image. You cannot be serious about your relationship with God and not take sin seriously.
2. *Because sin is a big deal, the cleansing blood of Jesus is our only hope.* Jesus came and lived and died because there was no other way to deal with sin. It is so powerful, destructive, and comprehensive in its effects in us that there is no way we could have ever escaped it or defeated it on our own. Sin required the radical rescue of the shed-blood grace of the Savior.
3. *Denying remaining sin is the height of self-deception.* You and I lay down so much daily empirical evidence of our struggle with sin that it takes a deep commitment to denial for us to convince ourselves that we are, in fact, okay. Every time we excuse, minimize, rationalize, or point the finger of blame, we are participating in that system of denial.
4. *God is always faithful to the promises of the cross of Jesus.* Your Savior loves to forgive. He really is slow to anger and abounding in steadfast love!
5. *Denying sin makes a liar out of God and denies the message of his Word.* Here's the bottom line—either God, in his Word, is true when he says that you have a problem you can't solve or you're right that you're not so bad after all. It can't be both ways.

So why deny today what grace has so completely forgiven and covered?

For further study and encouragement: 1 Timothy 1:12–17

MAY 29

Grace frees you from the dissatisfying claustrophobia of your
individualism to enjoy the fulfilling freedom of loving and serving God.

Individualism is not freedom; it is bondage. Living for yourself is not liberty; it is a self-imposed prison. Doing what you want to do, when you want to do it, and how you want to do it has never been the good life; it never leads to anything good. Making up your own rules and following your own paths leads to disaster. God calls you to himself and commands you to follow him so that, by grace, he may free you from you. In calling you to obedience, God is not robbing you of liberty, but is leading you to the only place where liberty can be found.

To understand this, you must look at life from the vantage point of creation and the fall into sin. As Creator, God designed you to live a dependent life. You were built for a life of loving, worshipful dependency and obedience. You and I just don't have the power and wisdom we would need to live an independent existence. To try to live life completely independent of God is like trying to drive a beautiful boat down a superhighway. That boat is a wonderful creation, loaded with amazing design details, but it was not built to run on a hard surface. If you try to run it on land, you will destroy the boat and you will go nowhere fast.

The entrance of sin into the world and into our hearts teaches us that we were not hardwired for independence. It also complicated things. The fall made us all a danger to ourselves. Because of the sin in us, we think bad things, we desire bad things, we are attracted to bad things, and we choose bad things—and we are blind to much of this going on inside of ourselves. So not only do we need God's presence and his wisdom to guide and protect us, but we also need his grace to rescue us.

The doctrines of creation and the fall drive us to conclude that living for ourselves—that is, working to independently rule our own little worlds—can never work. Life is only ever found when we put ourselves in the hands of our Creator and cast ourselves on his amazing grace. An honest look at how you were put together by the Creator and at what sin did to you destroys any confidence you have in your ability to make it on your own and drives you to the cross of the Lord Jesus Christ.

It really is true that individualism is a delusion, that joyful submission is the good life, and that Jesus alone is able to transport you from one to the other. If you find more joy in serving God than yourself, you know that grace has entered your door, because only grace has the power to rescue you from you.

For further study and encouragement: John 8:31–38

MAY 30

No need to carry the burden of ownership of your life today.
You've been bought with a price, so you don't belong to you anymore.

You and I have been freed from carrying the burden of all the regrets of the past, of our needs in the present, and of all the unanswered questions of the future. We have been freed from living with the anxiety that comes from thinking that we have no greater resources than we can provide for ourselves. You and I have been freed from the stress of thinking that we have to figure it all out on our own. We have been freed from worrying about needing to control things that are actually beyond our control. You and I don't need to wring our hands wondering what is coming unexpectedly down the road. We don't have to fear that we won't have enough or that we'll come up short. You and I don't have to panic at the thought that, in the end, we will fail and be left alone. We have been freed from the burden of finding our own way and writing our own rules. As God's children, we simply do not have to carry any of these burdens. Why? Read on.

You don't have to worry about these things for one simple, transformative reason—you don't belong to you anymore! You have been bought with a price, so your life is now under new ownership and new management. The God who now owns you is committed to keep you and care for you. He is committed to supply everything you need. The God who owns you is in personal and careful control of every situation, location, and circumstance of your life. He covers your past with his grace; he protects, provides for, and empowers you in the present; and he holds every aspect of your future in his sovereign and gracious hands.

Yes, because you were purchased at the price of his blood, you don't belong to you anymore. But that is a good thing. The One who now owns you is a wiser and more powerful manager of your life than you ever would have been. He cares for you with magnificent grace, incalculable wisdom, and limitless power. Being owned by him means you are in the best of hands. It means you're no longer burdened by living for you. A new owner has taken control of your life, and this new owner is more capable than anyone or anything you could give your life to.

So when you get up tomorrow, remind yourself of who you are and what you have become. God's grace has welcomed you to rest and peace because that grace has placed your life under new and capable management. The One who is Creator, Savior, and King has taken ownership. What could be better than that?

For further study and encouragement: 1 Corinthians 7:21–23

MAY 31

Corporate worship rescues us again and again by reminding us that there is only one glory worth giving our lives to—the glory of God.

Life really is all about what glory attracts your eyes and captures your heart. This is true because, as human beings, we're all glory junkies. We all live for glory in some way. We love the glory of that trophy fish attacking the lure or of those stunning red platform shoes. We like experiencing the glory of a brand-new house or running the fastest mile we have ever run. We love watching mind-bending feats of danger or glorious artistic achievements. We can't get enough of the beauty of the tiger's coat or the multihued stripes of the sunset. One bite of chocolate glory is not enough for us and one promotion doesn't satisfy our hearts. The beautiful watch, the cool car, the best taco, the well-designed golf course, the perfectly appointed kitchen, and the stunning piece of music all get our attention and leave us wanting more.

But these glories were created and placed in our lives for a purpose. All of the glories of the physical created world serve this one purpose—to remind us of and point us to the glory of God. We were never meant to live for earthbound glory. We were never meant to seek peace and satisfaction of heart here. We were never meant to offer the desires and allegiance of our hearts to what God made. The physical world *is* wonderfully glorious, but it was never meant to be our stopping point any more than the sign that points to something is meant to be the end of the journey.

Here's what you and I need to remember about signs. The sign is not the thing; the sign points you to the thing. The same can be said of physical creation. It is not the thing that you were made to live for. It was made to point you to the thing you were made to live for, and that thing is God and God alone. How sad it is when a person looks for what can't be found in something that cannot deliver! But many, many people do this every day. They look to created glory to find what cannot be found there.

Yes, God has filled your life with glories of many kinds. There is never a day when you aren't greeted by those glories. But it is vital to remember that the glories that surround you every day in the world that God made are not meant to be your stopping point, because you were created to live for a greater, more glorious glory— the glory of God. Thankfully, you have corporate worship, the regular gathering of the people of God for worship, to remind you of this truth. Worship helps you see once more that it is only when you live for God that your heart finds the peace, satisfaction, and security that it seeks. And it is only God's glory that has the power to rescue you from all the earthbound glories that so easily capture your heart.

For further study and encouragement: Ecclesiastes 2:1–11

JUNE 1

*God's care comes in many forms. He cares enough to
break your bones in order to capture your heart.*

I wish your care was always easy, predictable, safe—
a cool drink
a soft pillow—
but you are too wise,
too loving,
too committed to your work of
transforming grace.
So your gracious care comes to me
in uncomfortable forms:
the redeeming care of
disappointment,
the unexpected
trial,
suffering, loss.
These things don't tell me you're
cold-hearted,
absent,
uninvolved.
No, each is a sign of
zealous grace,
redeeming love.
I struggle to grasp how much you
care,
so I struggle to rest in that
care.
You care enough to give me what I
need,
not what I want.
You care enough to break my bones
in order
to recapture my heart.

For further study and encouragement: Psalm 51 (especially v. 8)

JUNE 2

It never works to ask people to do for you what only God can do. It never works to wait for God to do what he has clearly called you to do.

Here's the principle (which surely is easier to write out than it is to live): you can't look horizontally for what you will get only vertically, and you can't wait vertically for what you have been called to do horizontally. We all get these two confused again and again. Many a wife believes it is her husband's duty to bring her happiness. Such a woman is actually acting as if it's okay to put her inner sense of well-being in the hands of another human being. The person next to you is never a safe source of your happiness because that person is flawed and will inevitably fail you in some way. Only God is ever a safe keeper of the security, peace, and rest of your soul. Here is the bottom line—earth will never be your savior. Earth was created to point you to the One who alone is able to give peace and rest to your searching heart. Yet today many people say they believe in God, but they shop horizontally for what can be found only vertically.

On the other hand, there are many people who give in to the temptation to do the opposite. They wait for God to do for them what he has clearly called and empowered them to do. I've heard many people who were dealing with fractured relationships say to me, "I'm just waiting for the Lord to reconcile our relationship." It sounds spiritual, but it is simply wrong. If you have something against your brother, if there is conflict between you, the Bible tells you to get up, go, and be reconciled to him. When it came time for Israel to enter the Promised Land, God was going to part the waters of the Jordan River, but he commanded the priests to step into it. God was going to defeat Jericho, but he called his children to walk around it. God promises to provide, but he calls us to labor, pray, and give. God alone has the power to save, but he calls us to witness, testify, proclaim, teach, live, and preach. You see, God not only determines outcomes, but he rules over the means by which those outcomes are realized.

So the life of faith is all about rest and work. We rest in God's presence and constant care (vertical), and we toil with our hands, busy at the work we have been commanded to do (horizontal). We rest in our work and work in our rest. At times, we work because we believe that God who is at work calls us to work. At others times, we rest from our work because we believe that the work that needs to be done only God can do. So rest and work and work and rest. It is the rhythm of the life of faith.

For further study and encouragement: Matthew 19:16–30

JUNE 3

It would be amazing if a God of awesome glory recognized our existence, but for him to welcome us into his family is grace beyond amazing!

It is just so incredible, so counterintuitive, and so beyond anything else in our experience that it is very hard for us to wrap our brains around its majesty. There is no human being so creative and imaginative as to be able to pen such a story. You can read the story in Scripture and still not be blown away by its glory because you just don't have categories to understand its depth and breadth. In fact, it takes what this story is about for you to fully understand what this story is about. Only the gift of divine grace is able to help you grasp even a portion of the wonder of divine grace. The expansiveness of God's initiative of grace is so beautiful and transformational that it is the reason John Newton chose the best qualifying word, *amazing*, when he penned his famous hymn about that grace.

Think about it. No human being ever kept God's law (except Jesus). No one has ever given God the honor due his name. No one has lived the life of worship that is the duty and calling of everyone who has ever taken a breath. All people have not only rebelled against God, but they have written their own sets of self-oriented rules. Everyone not only has failed to worship God, but also has worshiped false gods. Every human being not only has failed to recognize the centrality of God in all things, but also has inserted himself or herself in God's position. Everyone not only occasionally breaks one or another of God's laws, but we all, in some way, have broken all of his laws. Not only do we misuse God's creation, but we put it in God's place and give it the worship that belongs to him.

So in the face of the depth and heinous character of all of our rebellion against God and his glory, it would be amazing if we were not exterminated. It would be an act of wondrous grace for God to recognize that we exist. But he has done so much, much more than this. By means of the life, death, and resurrection of his Son, he has made a way for us to be welcomed into an intimate familial relationship with him. He literally adopts us into his family so that, quite apart from anything we could have ever deserved, we are given the full range of rights and privileges of his children. And not only are we granted those things in the here and now, but we are blessed with them forever and ever. Along with this, he has promised us the final end of all the sin, sickness, sorrow, and suffering that our rebellion brought down on this world. So grace lets you have it all—everything, that is, that you need. Grace makes the King of kings your Father and his Savior Son your brother. Now, that really is beyond amazing. Pray for eyes to see it and a heart to embrace it, and then let your soul soar.

For further study and encouragement: Ephesians 1:15–23

JUNE 4

It's only in the mirror of God's Word that you see yourself accurately,
and only in his grace that you find help for what you see.

I saw it again and again in counseling. Maybe it was a husband and wife, an angry teenager, a single person who had lost her way, or a pastor who had gotten himself into trouble. For all of the vast differences in the situations and struggles, they shared a common theme. All of these people thought they knew themselves, but they didn't. They all thought that they saw themselves with accuracy, but they didn't. They all wanted me to agree with the assessments they had made of themselves, but I couldn't. They all suffered from the same disease, but they denied it. It didn't take long for me to realize that I was experiencing firsthand a universal human condition that the Bible talks about. It's called spiritual blindness.

Sin blinds, and because it does, the sin inside me keeps me from seeing me with clarity. Sin is self-excusing and self-aggrandizing. Sin is self-righteous and other-blaming. Sin is self-atoning; it easily rationalizes away my wrongs. Sin allows me to feel all right about what God says is very wrong. The personal sight system that God wired into every human being has been terribly broken by sin. We just do not know ourselves well, and we just don't see ourselves with the clarity necessary to assess who we are and how well we are doing. We all suffer from spiritual blindness. But that is not all. We all also suffer from the fact that we live most of the time blind to our blindness. We don't see ourselves with clarity, but we think we do, and we don't know ourselves with accuracy, but we are convinced we do. This is why we all tend to be offended when someone points out a sin, weakness, or failure. At the moment when we hear such an assessment, we struggle with the fact that what that person has said about us is so fundamentally different from the view of ourselves that we have been carrying around.

So we all need help. It comes to us in the gift of God's Word. Empowered by the convicting ministry of the Holy Spirit, it is the universe's most accurate mirror. Stand in front of it and you will see yourself as you really are. The diagnostic accuracy of the Bible is perfect. And because its diagnosis of your true condition, your true need, is always accurate, the Word of God is able to offer the only reliable cure for your condition. An effective cure is always attached to an accurate diagnosis. And here's the good news. You don't need to be afraid of all the dark things you don't see in yourself but which Scripture reveals about you, because all of those dark things have been covered by and defeated by the powerful grace that is yours in the life, death, and resurrection of Jesus.

For further study and encouragement: Hebrews 3:12–13

JUNE 5

*God's grace is active, rescuing, transformative grace. You celebrate this
by being as serious about your need as the God of this grace is.*

It is a good question to ask yourself, one that is worth not answering quickly. How
serious are you about the sin that was the reason for the most costly sacrifice ever
made? Consider God's seriousness, as pictured for us in the drama in the garden of
Eden. Study the following words carefully:

The LORD God said to the serpent,

"Because you have done this,
　cursed are you above all livestock
　and above all beasts of the field;
on your belly you shall go,
　and dust you shall eat
　all the days of your life.
I will put enmity between you and
　the woman,
　and between your offspring and
　her offspring;
he shall bruise your head,
　and you shall bruise his heel."

To the woman he said,

"I will surely multiply your pain in
　childbearing;
　in pain you shall bring forth
　children.
Your desire shall be for your husband,
　and he shall rule over you."

And to Adam he said,

"Because you have listened to the
　voice of your wife
　and have eaten of the tree
of which I commanded you,
　'You shall not eat of it,'
cursed is the ground because of you;
　in pain you shall eat of it all the
　days of your life;
thorns and thistles it shall bring forth
　for you;
　and you shall eat the plants of
　the field.
By the sweat of your face
　you shall eat bread,
till you return to the ground,
　for out of it you were taken;
for you are dust,
　and to dust you shall return."
(Gen. 3:14–19)

God took sin so seriously that he did two things when the first transgression oc-
curred—he immediately meted out punishment and he immediately set in motion
his plan of rescue and redemption. Both demonstrate God's seriousness about what
we all too easily deny or minimize.

For further study and encouragement: Exodus 34:1–9

JUNE 6

Every human being places his hope in something, and every human being asks that hope to deliver something. Where have you placed your hope?

We've all been hardwired for hope. We all project our lives out into the future to imagine things as we would like them to be. We all carry around with us personal hopes and dreams. We all surrender our hearts to some kind of expectation. We all silently wish that things could be different than they are. We all hope in something and we all hope for something. So much of how we look at life and how we live our lives is connected to the things in which we place the fundamental hopes of our lives.

Hope always has three elements—an assessment, an object, and an expectation. First, hope looks around and assesses that something or someone could be better than it is; that that something or someone is somehow broken. If things were as perfect as they could be, you wouldn't need to hope. Second, hope always has an object. It is the thing that you bank your hope on. You ask the object of your hope to fix what is broken or to deliver what is desired or needed. Third, hope has an expectation. This is what you ask the object of your hope to give you, what you hope the object of your hope will deliver.

Now, there are really only two places to look for foundational life hope, that is, basic meaning and purpose, motivation to continue, a sense of well-being, and that knowledge that you've hooked yourself to what life is really all about. You can search for hope horizontally in the situations, experiences, physical possessions, locations, and relationships of everyday life. There are two problems with looking horizontally. First, all of these things suffer from some degree of brokenness. They are part of the problem, and because they are, they are unable to deliver what you're seeking. Also, these things were never made to be the source of your hope, but to be fingers that point you to where your hope can be found.

Paul says it all in Romans 5:5 when he tells us that hope in God will never put us to shame. It will never embarrass us by failing to deliver. In those words, Paul tells us where hope can be found. It is found only vertically. Only when God is your hope is your hope sure and secure. Only he is able to give you the life that your heart seeks. Only he is able to give your soul the rest that it needs. Only he can deliver the internal peace that is the hunger of every human being. It's only when grace has hooked you to him that you are connected to what life is really all about. In his brief words, Paul confronts us with this thought—if your hope disappoints you, it's because it's the wrong hope! Today, what carries your hope?

For further study and encouragement: Job 1

JUNE 7

*Are you experiencing the schizophrenia of having eternity hardwired
into your heart but living as if this moment is all there is?*

It is sad how many people constantly live in the schizophrenic craziness of eternity amnesia. We were created to live in a forever relationship with a forever God forever. We were designed to live based on a long view of life. We were made to live with one eye on now and one eye on eternity. You and I simply cannot live as we were put together to live without forever. But so many people try. They put all their hopes and dreams in the right here, right now situations, locations, possessions, positions, and people of their daily lives. They load moment after moment with undeliverable expectations. They ask people to be what people this side of eternity will never be. They demand that a seriously broken world deliver what it could never deliver even if it were not broken. They fail to recognize that at the bottom of all of this drivenness and insanity is an expectation that now can be the paradise it will never be.

It's wonderful for you to have a good marriage, but it will never be a paradise. It's great to have a good relationship with your children, but they will never deliver paradise to you. That beautiful house that began decaying from the moment it was built will not be your paradise. Those still-flawed people around you will not offer you paradise-like relationships. In forgetting who you are, forgetting how you were designed to live, forgetting who God is, and forgetting what is to come, you make yourself and those around you crazy.

Your eternity amnesia makes you unrealistically expectant, vulnerable to temptation, all too driven, dependent on people and things that will only disappoint you, and sadly susceptible to doubting the goodness of God. Recognizing the eternity that is to come allows you to be realistic without being hopeless, and hopeful when things around you don't encourage much hope.

The evidence is clear—there just has to be more to life than this. This broken, sin-scarred mess can't be all there is. And Scripture is clear—this is not paradise, and it won't be. Rather, this moment is a time of preparation for the paradise that is to come, where everything that sin has broken will be fully restored to what God originally intended it to be.

Is there schizophrenia in your living? Do you make your hunger for paradise a form of insanity by coupling it with forgetfulness about what is to come? Do you load paradise-like expectations into fallen-world moments? Does your eternity amnesia tempt you to question the goodness of God? Pray for grace to remember God and the unending end he has written into the story of all who put their trust in him. Long-view living is wise living. Long-view living is Godward living. Long-view living is hopeful living. Long-view living will make you thankful for grace.

For further study and encouragement: Ecclesiastes 3

JUNE 8

Corporate worship is designed to confront you with the glory of the grace of Jesus so you won't look for life, help, and hope elsewhere.

As I sat in the balcony with my wife Luella, I remembered how important and wonderful corporate worship is. It was Tenth Presbyterian Church's Spring Choral Worship Service. It featured the original compositions and hymn arrangements of Robert Elmore. We were reminded in song of the miserable condition in which sin left us and our world, and of the glorious rescue of redeeming grace. Each piece was so full of the gospel that I felt as if my heart could not contain anything more. I was thinking of the words of Psalm 89:1: "I will sing of the steadfast love of the LORD, forever; with my mouth I will make known your faithfulness to all generations." I thought we could sing and sing and sing and never exhaust the stunning redemptive themes of the gospel of the Lord Jesus Christ.

Finally, after a lavish gospel meal, the crescendo anthem came. It was such a beautiful celebration of the glory of the gospel that when we came to the last two lines, I quit singing and began to repeat over and over again: "Amen! Amen! Amen!" Corporate worship had performed its work in my heart once again.

Very honestly, I hadn't come to the service with a celebratory heart. I had grumbled my way into the room. It had been a long ministry weekend. I wouldn't have gone to that Sunday evening service if Luella hadn't begged me to. I really didn't want to be there. But in the middle of it all, something captured my heart—glory. The glory of the grace of Jesus suddenly loomed larger than the exhaustion of my body or the weariness of my mind. My cold heart was enlivened by the fire of the gospel of the grace of the Lord Jesus Christ. The talents of the musicians and the voices of the congregation reminded me once again of who I was and what I had been given in the grace of the cross of Jesus. Once again, this grumbler became a celebrant. Once again, the gathering of God's people for worship had done its job.

God ordained for us to gather for worship because he knows us and the weaknesses of our fickle, grumbling, and easily distracted hearts. He knows how soon we forget the depth of our need as sinners and the expansiveness of his provisions in Jesus Christ. He knows that little lies can deceive us and little obstacles can discourage us. He knows that self-righteousness still has the power to delude us. So in grace he calls us to gather and consider glory once again, to be excited once again, and to be rescued once again. It's not only that corporate worship reminds us of God's grace. Corporate worship is itself a gift of grace. Run with celebration to its rescue any time it is available to you.

For further study and encouragement: Psalm 122

JUNE 9

For sin, forgiveness; for weakness, strength; for foolishness, wisdom;
for bondage, deliverance—such is the way of the grace of Jesus.

I love Colossians 2 (stop now and read verses 1–15). Maybe I love it so much because Luella, my wife, is the owner and director of a large private art gallery. You might be thinking, "Well, that's a strange comment, Paul." Permit me to explain. Colossians 2:1–15 is like a gallery of God's grace.

At the beginning of each month, artwork is delivered to Luella's gallery for the next show. The paintings come wrapped protectively or boxed in crates, and it is exciting for Luella to open them and to begin to experience the art that will give life to the gallery over the next month. After she has unpacked all the artwork, Luella goes through the process of arranging and rearranging it until each piece is where it needs to be to be displayed with the most power. The next day, a team of hangers comes into the gallery to help Luella actually affix the paintings to the walls. The final step is for each painting to be properly lit. Every month, it seems that the gallery actually changes shape with the new work. Once it's lit, I like to come down to the gallery in the evening and see the work in all its splendor. Often Luella and I stand across the street at night, look into the huge gallery windows, and take in the beauty. Then Luella does something that bothers me every time. She gets her briefcase and hits the light switch, plunging the gallery into darkness. I always think, "No, no, these paintings should never be in the dark."

If you're God's child, you are a gallery of his glorious grace. The walls of your heart have been festooned with the gorgeous artwork of redemption: wisdom for the foolishness of sin, power for the weakness of sin, forgiveness for the guilt of sin, and deliverance from the bondage of sin. Grace means that beautiful things are being done for you and happening within you. Yet I have this concern—for many believers, the artwork is there, but the lights are out in the gallery. These believers simply don't see or fully understand the stunning beauty of what they have been given in the grace of the Lord Jesus Christ. And because they don't see or understand that grace, they neither celebrate it nor live in light of its majesty. So they give way to weakness when power is at their disposal. They give way to foolishness when they have been personally connected to the One who is wisdom. They hide in guilt when they have been fully forgiven. They surrender to addiction when they have been given freeing grace. Their hearts have been decorated with the artwork of grace, but the lights are out in the gallery. How sad! What about you? Are the lights on, and has that radically changed the way you live?

For further study and encouragement: Galatians 5:16–26

JUNE 10

If you are in Christ, you've been chosen to transcend the borders of your own glory, to reach out toward a greater glory—the glory of God.

They were glory-confused, and because they were, they were also glory thieves. They desperately needed a life-changing glory display, and did they ever get one!

> And after six days Jesus took with him Peter and James, and John his brother, and led them up a high mountain by themselves. And he was transfigured before them, and his face shone like the sun, and his clothes became white as light. And behold, there appeared to them Moses and Elijah, talking with him. And Peter said to Jesus, "Lord, it is good that we are here. If you wish, I will make three tents here, one for you and one for Moses and one for Elijah." He was still speaking when, behold, a bright cloud overshadowed them, and a voice from the cloud said, "This is my beloved Son, with whom I am well pleased; listen to him." When the disciples heard this, they fell on their faces and were terrified. But Jesus came and touched them, saying, "Rise, and have no fear." And when they lifted up their eyes, they saw no one but Jesus only. (Matt. 17:1–8)

In order to rescue his disciples from their bondage to their own glory and their addiction to all the shadow glories of the created world, it was necessary for Jesus to reveal a greater, more transcendent glory. So in one of the most incredible scenes in all of the biblical story, Jesus pulled back the curtain and showed them his glory as the one and only Son of the Most High God. It was a jaw-slackening, heart-stopping, mind-blowing display of divine glory. If they had any sense at all, it would put holy awe—holy terror—in their hearts. Enough of the small glories they had been living for, enough of the small-minded plans they had made for their lives, and enough of their lack of recognition of what they had been called to—Christ's transfiguration was designed to be for them a moment of life-changing transformation. They were being rescued from earthly glory by true glory so that they could take this glory around the world to whoever would listen and hear. There were no thoughts of the petty concerns of life in this moment; no thoughts of personal dreams; no thoughts of personal power.

Here is what life is all about. At its center is a God of awesome glory—glorious in power, wisdom, faithfulness, love, and grace. Here is what everyone needs—rescue by this glory. Here is what everyone was created for—to live for this glory. Here is grace—that God would choose to splash his eternal glory down on inglorious, unthankful, rebellious, and self-oriented people such as us. The fact that Jesus revealed his glory to the disciples wasn't based on the beauty of their character. No, the opposite was true; it was based on the glory of his character. He reveals his glory to us because if he doesn't, there is simply no hope for us. Without this rescue, we surrender our hearts to bondage, to a thick catalog of other glories. This moment is a moment of gorgeous grace, just the grace you and I need.

For further study and encouragement: Luke 9:23–36

JUNE 11

No amount of guilt or shame can do what grace is able to do—
make us people who delight in the Father's will.

You will never understand your struggle with sin unless you grasp that, at its very bottom, sin is a heart problem. It's not first a problem of bad behavior, although it always goes there. It's not first an external temptation problem, although it causes us to give in to temptation's draw. It's not first a location or situation problem, although it expresses itself there. Sin is a matter of the heart. Let me explain what this means.

The Bible uses many terms for the inner, spiritual, thoughtful, desiring, motivational you, but all those terms are gathered together and summarized by one big collective term: *heart*. It is one of the most often used terms in the Bible. In fact, I am persuaded that you cannot understand the transforming message of the Bible unless you understand this term. Here's a definition to carry with you as you read your Bible: the heart is the *causal core of your personhood*. It's the seat of your thoughts, emotions, desires, and motivations. It is the worship center of your self. The heart is the reason you do the things you do and say the things you say. You and I literally live out of our hearts.

Sin lives in our hearts, and because it does, it corrupts our thoughts, desires, choices, and motivations. We were created to be servants of God, but sin makes us lovers of self. We were made to worship the Creator, but sin causes us to worship the creation. We were designed to live for God's glory, but sin causes us to make life all about our own glory. And unless these things change in our hearts, our behavior won't change at all, or if it does change, it won't change for very long. No amount of commitment to self-reformation will change your heart. No amount of work to alter bad habits will change your heart. No amount of beating yourself up with guilt and shame will change your heart. No running from certain situations, locations, and relationships has the power to change your heart. You can't run from sin because you cannot run from you. The most outrageous acts of penance in the world are powerless to do what needs to be done—radically transform your heart.

So you and I are left with only one final option. It is the only choice that makes sense; everything else is insanity. And we need to do this again and again until we don't need to do it anymore. We need to run to the grace of Jesus. Run for forgiveness. Run for power. Run for transformation. Run for deliverance. Run! Run! Run! Don't ever stop running to grace until Jesus has taken you home to a place where you need to run no more.

For further study and encouragement: Mark 7:1–23

JUNE 12

Prayer is abandoning your place in the center of your world and daily surrendering that place to God alone as an act of heartfelt worship.

Prayer is much more than bringing to God your list of wants, desires, and needs. It is a radical act of worship that reminds you of who you are, who God is, and what life is all about. Prayer is surrender:

1. *Prayer is surrender to the reality that there is someone more ultimate than you.* It's natural for each of us to shrink our field of hopes, dreams, and daily concerns down to the small turf of our personal wants, needs, and feelings. Prayer is surrender to the worldview of the first four words of the Bible, "In the beginning, God . . . ," and as such, it puts us in our rightful place.

2. *Prayer is surrender to the reality that life isn't just about you.* If prayer wouldn't be prayer if it did not acknowledge God's existence, then prayer defines us as well. We simply aren't the creators, kings, or owners of our lives. We belong to God for his purpose and his glory. Prayer is letting go of personal autonomy and bowing in reverence to God.

3. *Prayer is surrender to the reality that you need help.* Prayer means humbly confessing that not only are we not autonomous, we are also not self-sufficient. Prayer reminds us that we were not designed to live independent lives. We cannot be what we were made to be or do what we have been called to do without the personal, gracious, and continuous intervention of the One who made us.

4. *Prayer is surrender to the reality that there is wisdom greater than ours.* Prayer confronts us with the fact that we are not as smart as we tend to think we are. It reminds us that there is so much we don't know or understand. It tells us that life is not found in our limited understanding, but in surrendering our lives to the care of the One whose understanding spans from before origin to beyond destiny and includes everything in between.

5. *Prayer is surrender of your right to live as you choose.* Prayer is bowing the knee to the reality that you and I do not have any natural right at all to do what we want to do with our lives. We have been created to live inside God's boundaries.

6. *Prayer is surrender of your hopes to God's grace.* Prayer is remembering that there is no hope in life and death that does not result from the grace of God. I give up my hopes in me and place my hopes in him.

So close your eyes, bow your head, and surrender—and be thankful for the grace that meets you as you do.

For *further study and encouragement: Psalm 63*

JUNE 13

If you hook the hope of your heart to the people around you, you will always be disappointed. No one is able to be your personal messiah.

You should be thankful for the people whom God places in your life. You should love them dearly. You should treat them with honor and respect. You should do all you can to maintain the unity and peace of your relationships with them. You should be willing to give to and serve them. You should be open to them as they speak into your life. You should recognize that you were designed to live in loving community with others like them. But you cannot look to them to provide for you what only God can provide.

There are many, many Christian relationships that are hurtful, painful, and marked by conflict and disappointment because the people in those relationships are placing a burden on those relationships that no human relationship can bear.

- No person can be the source of your identity.
- No one can be the basis of your happiness.
- No individual can give you a reason to get up in the morning and continue.
- No loved one can be the carrier of your hope.
- No one is able to change you from the inside out.
- No human being can alter your past.
- No person is able to atone for your wrongs.
- No one can give your heart peace and rest.

Asking another human being to do those things is like requiring him to be the fourth member of the Trinity and then judging him when he falls short. It simply cannot and will not work. You see, it is vital to remember that human love is a wonderful thing, but you will only ever find life—real, heart-changing, soul-satisfying life—in a vertical relationship. You should enjoy human love, but you should look to God for your spiritual vitality and strength. You should commit to long-term, loving, mutually serving relationships, but you must remember that only God can save you, change you, and deliver you from you. You should be willing to make sacrifices of love for others, but you should place your hope only in the once-for-all sacrifice of the Lord Jesus Christ.

Could it be that the disappointment you experience in your relationships is the product of unrealistic and unattainable expectations? Could it be that you have unwittingly put people in God's place? Could it be that you ask the person next to you to do for you what only God can do? There is but one Savior, and he is yours forever. You don't need to put that burden on the person next to you.

For further study and encouragement: 2 Timothy 4:9–18

JUNE 14

One of sin's greatest rebellions is our repeated refusal to listen and submit to the wisdom of God revealed on every page of his Word.

As I listened to them argue, blame, and graphically recount one another's wrongs, all colored with hurt and anger, a sad thought gripped me. The vast majority of what they needed to hear in order for their relationship to be what God intended for it to be was clearly written in the Bible that they both said they believed. Their marriage was the sad casualty of their street-level unwillingness to listen to God's wisdom and seek the grace he offered to live with one another in light of it.

Consider one passage loaded with essential relational wisdom: "[Live together] with all humility and gentleness, with patience, bearing with one another in love, eager to maintain the unity of the Spirit in the bond of peace" (Eph. 4:2–3). Think about these wise guidelines for relationships:

1. *"with all humility . . . "* Pride always destroys a relationship. It causes you to feel more entitled and to be more demanding than serving and giving. It drives you to insist on control. It makes you have to be right. It forces others to submit to your lordship. Pride is an anti-relational way of having a relationship. Humility is the godly way.
2. *"and gentleness . . . "* Treating a person with gentleness makes him or her want to move near you. Responding with gentleness teaches another person that he or she is safe in your care. It is an essential relational bond.
3. *"with patience . . . "* You cannot have a healthy communion with another flawed human being without being willing to wait. If you demand to have things your way and in your time, you are so busy loving yourself that you have little time left to love the other person.
4. *"bearing with one another in love . . . "* Love requires that you be willing to be forbearing, that is, willing to suffer. Why? Because you are in a relationship with a less-than-perfect person, living together in a fallen world. Both you and that person often fail.
5. *"eager to maintain the unity of the Spirit . . . "* Love means unity is more important to you than being right, having your way, and getting what you want. Love rejoices in the fact that God's Spirit in both of you gives you a wonderful platform for unity.
6. *"in the bond of peace."* Love means committing to make peace, not war.

There simply are no more-important relational commitments that you could cite. The husband and wife I mentioned above held this wisdom in their hands, but did not listen. Do you?

For further study and encouragement: Psalm 119:89–176

JUNE 15

Confession is a grace. Only grace can convince you to abandon your righteousness and run to the merciful arms of the Lord.

Confession is not natural for us. It's natural for us to think of ourselves as more righteous than we are. It's natural to blame our wrongs on others. It's natural to say our behavior was caused by some difficult circumstance we were in. It's natural to exercise our inner lawyers and defend ourselves when we're confronted with a sin, weakness, or failure. It's natural to turn the tables when being confronted and tell our accusers that they are surely bigger sinners than we are. It's natural to see ourselves more as law keepers than as lawbreakers. It's natural to point to our biblical literacy or theological knowledge as proof of our spiritual maturity. It's natural to be more concerned about the sin of others than our own. It's natural to be more critical of the attitudes and behavior of others than our own. It's natural for you and me to be blind to the depth of our spiritual need.

Because this sturdy system of self-righteousness is natural for every sinner, it is unnatural for us to be clear-sighted, humble, self-examining, and ready to confess. Blind eyes and a self-satisfied, self-congratulatory heart stand in the way of the broken heart of confession. We don't grieve our sin because we don't see it. It is ironic that we tend to see the righteousness we don't have and we fail to see the sin that stains every day of our lives.

Here's how confession works. You cannot *confess* what you haven't *grieved*, you can't *grieve* what you do not *see*, and you cannot *repent of* what you have not *confessed*. So one of the most important operations of God's grace is to give us eyes to see our sin and hearts that are willing to confess it. If your eyes are open and you see yourself with accuracy, and if your heart is humbly willing to admit to what your eyes see, you know that glorious, rescuing, forgiving, and transforming grace has visited you. Why? Because what you're doing is simply not natural for sinners. In the face of their sin, Adam blamed Eve, Eve blamed the Serpent, and both of them hid, but neither stepped forward and made willing and heartfelt confession.

So cry out today for eyes to see, that is, for accurate personal insight. Cry out for the defenses of your heart to come down. Ask God to defeat your fear of being exposed, of being known. Cry for the grace to be willing to stop, look, listen, receive, grieve, confess, and turn. Stand with courage and hope before the searching and exposing mirror of the Word of God, and be unafraid. Stand naked before God and know that all that is exposed has been fully and completely covered by the shed blood of your Savior. Because of him, you don't need to be afraid of your unrighteousness; no, it is your delusions of righteousness that are the grave danger.

For further study and encouragement: Acts 3:11–26

JUNE 16

*I still need to be rescued from me because as long as sin remains,
I'll be drawn to desire, think, say, and do what God names as evil.*

Maybe it's because it happens in little moments that we are able to look at it without concern. What am I talking about? Our struggle with sin. It happens in the little moments of life, so it is easy to see what is a very serious thing as not such a big deal. Let me explain. You and I don't live only in big moments. We probably make only a couple of big, life-altering decisions our whole lives. Not many of our biographies will find their way into the history books. Years after we die, as our descendants gather for reunions, they will struggle to remember even the big events of our lives. We all live in little, unnoticed, unremarkable, mundane moments of life, and because we do, it's very easy to back away from the seriousness of our struggle with sin that is constantly being revealed in those little moments.

The little moments of your life are profoundly important precisely because they're little moments that happen to be the address where you live. Think about it this way. The character of any person's life is not shaped by two or three grand, big moments of life. A person's character is formed in ten thousand little, mundane moments of everyday life. It's the character that is formed in those little moments of life that determines how you think and respond in the few big moments of life that you encounter.

So those "little sins" are not so little after all:

- the nasty retort
- the "me first" pride
- the flash of lust at the mall
- the anger at someone who got in your way
- those little bitter thoughts
- your addiction to little pleasures
- the impatience with a loved one

Sure, they all happen in little moments that go by so quickly you may fail to notice them, but they depict a deeply needy heart. They remind you and me that we have not risen above our need for rescuing grace. They tell us that what we have found in Christ we still desperately need. They call us to be aware and to be serious; the war for our hearts is not over. Our need for a conquering Savior has not ended. These little moments actually point the finger at something that is huge—our struggle with sin and our need for the grace that can be found only in our Savior, the King, the Lamb, the Lord Jesus Christ.

For further study and encouragement: Romans 7:14–25

JUNE 17

Through difficult relationships and circumstances, God works to expose your heart so you will seek the grace that can be found only in him.

Where does your mind go, where does your heart run, when difficulty enters your door? None of us likes to suffer. None of us enjoys dealing with the unexpected. We all like our plans to work and our dreams to come true. We all want a life that is comfortable and predictable. The normal person simply doesn't esteem the spiritual value of hardship. Because of this, it tends to be difficult for us to stay on God's agenda page. If our goal for our lives is temporal personal happiness, whatever our definition of that may be, then we're going to live in a street-level agenda conflict with our Savior, no matter what our confessional theology may be.

Many Christians live right there. They say they believe in the truths of Scripture, they say they have placed their trust in the Messiah, but they live in an unspoken state of disappointment, irritation, impatience, or frustration with God. This state is often characterized by this classic question: "If God loves me, then why would he _____?" Let's unpack the question.

First, there is no "if" to the love of God. As the psalmist says, "his steadfast love endures forever!" (Ps. 118:1). His love is never fickle. It never grows weary. It will never run out. This means it is never up for question. Second, consider the content of the question. Rather than asking, "What good and wise thing is the God who loves me doing in what doesn't seem good and wise?" the question immediately expresses doubt about the character of God. The answer to this kind of question never leads you anywhere spiritually good.

Here's the bottom line: you and I struggle with the faithfulness of God, not because he has been unfaithful, but because we have. You may be thinking, "Paul, what are you talking about?" From day one, God has clearly communicated his zeal to us. It is his purpose that, by the means of rescuing, forgiving, transforming grace, we would be brought into relationship with him, and in the context of that relationship, be fully molded into the image of his Son. He has never promised us that he will deliver to us our personal definition of the good life. Rather, he has promised that he will use all the tools at his disposal to complete the work of redemption that he has begun in our hearts and lives. He has not been unfaithful. He has kept every one of his promises. He will do what he said.

Our problem is that we tend to be unfaithful to his holy agenda and get kidnapped by our plans for us and our dreams for our lives. The trials in our lives exist not because he has forgotten us, but because he remembers us and is changing us by his grace. When you remember that, you can have joy in the middle of what is uncomfortable.

For further study and encouragement: 2 Corinthians 4:7–18

JUNE 18

The temporary pleasures of this present world are meant to
point you to the lasting pleasures of knowing God.

The story didn't end the way the crowd thought it would:

> When they found him on the other side of the sea, they said to him, "Rabbi, when did you come here?" Jesus answered them, "Truly, truly, I say to you, you are seeking me, not because you saw signs, but because you ate your fill of the loaves. Do not work for the food that perishes, but for the food that endures to eternal life, which the Son of Man will give to you. For on him God the Father has set his seal." . . . Jesus said to them, "I am the bread of life; whoever comes to me shall not hunger, and whoever believes in me shall never thirst. . . . I am the bread of life. Your fathers ate the manna in the wilderness, and they died. This is the bread that comes down from heaven, so that one may eat of it and not die. I am the living bread that came down from heaven. If anyone eats of this bread, he will live forever. And the bread that I will give for the life of the world is my flesh." (John 6:25–27, 35, 48–51)

Jesus has just fed a large crowd of people with a little boy's lunch. The crowd is amazed at his power and excited about his ability to provide for them physically. They think that this is just the kind of king they want. But Jesus is having none of it. To the surprise of the crowd, he runs and hides. When the crowd finally catches up with him, they confess their confusion at his response, and Jesus essentially says: "I came to earth not just to be your physical provider, but to meet your deepest spiritual needs. Every good physical thing I give you is meant to point you to the spiritual provision that you need and that I will make for you in my life, death, and resurrection." Every physical blessing is designed by God to be a sign that points you to the spiritual blessings that are found only in surrendering your heart to him.

This leaves us all with questions: What do we really want out of life? What do we really want from God? Do we really esteem his work of grace? Do we really admit how much we need his moment-by-moment rescue? Do we value his forgiveness? Do we really care to be transformed? Are we concerned about the character of our hearts and the condition of our souls? Do we have any interest in being holy as he is holy? All these questions boil down to one question: Do we value God's grace, or would we rather have comfortable lives—nice houses, cars, vacations, cuisine, and friends?

What gift could Jesus offer you that would make you want to make him your King? Humbly meditate on this question today. Could it be that you want him to be your King for all the wrong reasons? If your answer is yes, don't run and hide from him, because there's grace for that too!

For further study and encouragement: Titus 2:11–14

JUNE 19

Grace has the power to do what nothing else can do—rescue you from you, and in so doing, restore you to what you were created to be.

They're the two essential parts of redemption, *rescue* and *restoration*, and you and I can't do either one for ourselves. But it's hard to admit that we have a problem that we cannot solve. We like to convince ourselves that our anger tells us more about the flawed people we live near than it tells us about ourselves. We like to think that our impatience is more about the poor planning or character of the people we have to deal with every day. We like to think that our sin can be blamed on the temptations of the fallen world around us. When we do or say what is wrong, we tend to point to a boss, a spouse, one of our children, a friend, a difficult situation, a busy day, the fact that we aren't feeling well, bad parents, some injustice, or a long catalog of other excuses. But the Bible is quite clear. We all suffer from the same terminal disease. None of us has escaped it. It's not caused by the people or situations around us. We brought this destroyer into the world with us. David says it this way: "Behold, I was brought forth in iniquity, and in sin did my mother conceive me" (Ps. 51:5).

You and I can try as we might to fool ourselves. We can work as we might to shrink from responsibility. We can develop skill at pointing the finger of blame to things around us. But there is simply no denying the harsh reality of the Bible's hard-to-accept message—we are our own biggest problem. We are the thing with which we need help. There is no greater danger than the danger we are to ourselves. We need help, help that we cannot give ourselves. We need help that is deeper than education, socialization, politics, or changes of relationship or location. If left on our own, we are doomed, "having no hope and without God in the world" (Eph. 2:12).

But the hope-infused story of Scripture is that we have not been left on our own. God has controlled the events of the world as part of his unstoppable agenda of *rescue* and *restoration*. He sent his holy Son to enter the world and suffer because of sin's mess. He sent him to live the perfect life that we would never live, to sacrifice himself on account of our sin, and to defeat the death that is sin's doom. It is an agenda of awesome grace extended to lost, rebellious, and self-excusing people, who even need that grace to understand how much they need that grace. This grace had to include rescue because we could not escape ourselves, and it had to include restoration because we had no power to transform ourselves into what he created and redeemed us to be. So today confess your need. Denying it never leads anywhere good. Thank God for the rescue and restoration that is your hope. And determine to look honestly into the mirror of God's Word so you will continue to remember how much you need what he has freely given.

For further study and encouragement: Jeremiah 17:5–8

JUNE 20

If you're God's, to tell yourself you can't do what you've been called to do is to preach private heresy. You've been enabled by grace.

We just never stop talking
to ourselves.
We never stop preaching
some kind of gospel
to ourselves.
It's a gospel of
aloneness,
partiality,
poverty,
inability—
of functional hopelessness—
or
it's the true gospel of
Jesus Christ,
a gospel of
hope,
mercy,
forgiveness,
rescue,
love,
transformation;
of never being alone,
of never being without help;
of One who is near,
of One who cares;
of a beautiful forever
awash in victory.
We're always listening
to
what we're preaching.

Today, what kind of gospel will you preach to you, and what effect will it have on how you live?

For further study and encouragement: Psalm 33

JUNE 21

No, you don't know what you'll face today, but your sovereign Savior does, and his mercies are new and formfitted for what you will face.

They are gloriously comforting words, the kinds of words that need to live fresh in the minds of all of God's children this side of eternity. Listen to Hebrews 4:14–16:

> Since then we have a great high priest who has passed through the heavens, Jesus, the Son of God, let us hold fast our confession. For we do not have a high priest who is unable to sympathize with our weaknesses, but one who in every respect has been tempted as we are, yet without sin. Let us then with confidence draw near to the throne of grace, that we may receive mercy and find grace to help in time of need.

Consider the hope that is built into these words:

1. *We have a High Priest.* If all this passage said were this, it would be amazing. The fact that Jesus sits now at the Father's right hand and makes constant intercession for us is a redemptive miracle worthy of eternal celebration.
2. *Our High Priest sympathizes with our weaknesses.* But there is more. This High Priest is uniquely able to be touched by the weakness of our human condition. He is not cold or indifferent to our struggles in any way.
3. *We run to One who has been through what we've been through and more.* It is comforting to remember that this One is so easily touched by our struggles because he walked in our shoes. He willingly faced all that we face and more. He faced higher and deeper pressures than we do, but he never broke, whereas we all give in somewhere along the way.
4. *We can go to this One with confidence.* The result of all of this is that in our struggles with weakness within and temptation without, we have someone we can turn to with complete confidence and sure hope. He really does hold in his hands everything that we need.
5. *We can expect mercy that is formfitted for our particular needs.* Because of his grace, what can we expect? On the basis of his faithful presence and his reliable promises, we can expect mercies exactly right for what we are now facing, and nothing less.

When you struggle and are confronted with your weakness, say to yourself, "For this I have a reliable and understanding High Priest."

For further study and encouragement: Hebrews 1

JUNE 22

What you worship is not best shown on Sunday morning, but demonstrated by your words and behavior the rest of the week.

The word *worship* is widely misunderstood. Most people who hear the word *worship* immediately think of some kind of corporate, formal religious activity. Perhaps what comes to mind is a gathering of pilgrims to lay candles at the feet of Buddha; the singing of a hymn with a thousand fellow believers; or a gathering of a small group on a Wednesday night. In other words, for most people, *worship* is a word that summarizes the outward spiritual activity of their lives. But the Bible employs this word in a fundamentally different way.

The Bible portrays us not just as people who occasionally worship, but *as* worshipers. It's not just that we have a religious aspect to our living. No, this worship thing is much more foundational than that. We have been designed by God to be worshipers. This means that worship is first our identity before it ever becomes our activity. The worship inclination or motivation that resides in all our hearts was placed there to draw us to God, the One to whom we were made to give our worship. There is no such thing as a non-worshiping human being. The only thing that divides human beings is what or whom they worship.

What is it, then, that we're talking about when we say that we are all worshipers? Well, this means that we all attach our identity, our hopes and dreams, our inner sense of well-being, and our meaning and purpose to something. We all give the functional control of our hearts to something. We all live after something. We all tend to surrender to and serve what we think will give us life.

Scripture says that there are only two possible objects of our worship. At street level, no matter what your theology is, you are either worshiping the Creator, surrendering your life to him, or you are in active worship of some part of his creation. Sin reduces us all to idolaters in some way. We all put ourselves, other people, or other things in God's rightful place.

Worship of the one true and living God is the only place where life can be found, and worship of anything else is a pathway to doom.

So today, every word you say, every choice you make, and every action you take will be shaped by some kind of worship. Nothing depicts your need for the grace of Jesus better than the war of worship that will rage in your heart today.

For further study and encouragement: 1 Chronicles 16:28–34

JUNE 23

Grief is good when it mourns what God hates, but it's
dangerous when it questions God's goodness and love.

Who can't relate to the struggle of Asaph? Admit it. You've been there:

> But as for me, my feet had almost stumbled,
>   my steps had nearly slipped.
> For I was envious of the arrogant
>   when I saw the prosperity of the wicked.
> For they have no pangs until death;
>   their bodies are fat and sleek.
> They are not in trouble as others are;
>   they are not stricken like the rest of mankind. . . .
> Behold, these are the wicked;
>   always at ease, they increase in riches.
> All in vain have I kept my heart clean
>   and washed my hands in innocence.
> For all the day long I have been stricken
>   and rebuked every morning. . . .
> When my soul was embittered,
>   when I was pricked in heart,
> I was brutish and ignorant;
>   I was like a beast toward you. (Ps. 73:2–5, 12–14, 21–22)

Asaph is mourning, all right, but it's all the wrong kind of mourning. He is filled with grief, but it is a dangerous, angry, and accusatory grief. I've been there. I've felt Asaph's feelings. I've said similar words. In a fallen world, you have reasons to grieve. You should mourn your struggle with sin. You should mourn the sorry, broken condition of the fallen world that is your home address. You should mourn corruption, injustice, poverty, pollution, and disease. It is right to mourn these things, but you had better guard your mourning. Your mourning is never neutral; you are either mourning with God, who weeps for the condition of the world he made, or you're mourning against God, questioning his goodness, wisdom, and love.

It's tempting to do this because you hit moments when the contrast between what you are facing as a child of God and what the person next to you—a person who ignores God—is facing is almost too much to take. It seems that the good guys are being hammered and the bad guys have it easy. In the face of this reality, Asaph essentially says, "I've obeyed, and this is what I get?" It's an angry charge against the goodness of God. When you don't understand what's going on, run to God's goodness rather than questioning whether it exists. Say with Asaph, "My flesh and my heart may fail, but God is the strength of my heart and my portion forever" (v. 26).

For further study and encouragement: Psalm 74

JUNE 24

God is unwilling to be your means to what you call the "good life."
Your relationship with him must be your definition of the good life.

We do tend to turn God into a delivery system. We get excited about what he can do for us and what he can give us. We fall into thinking of prayer as asking God to sign the bottom of our self-composed, self-oriented, individualized wish lists. You know, what would we like God to give us that we can't give ourselves? We set our hearts on things that we think will make us happy. Perhaps it's the love of another person and our detailed picture of marital bliss. Perhaps it's a certain level of affluence and all the things we could experience and enjoy as a result. Maybe its ministry success, influence, and acclaim. Maybe it's freedom from sickness or suffering. Perhaps it's just a good week or a nerve-free job interview. Maybe it's a succulent steak, a good vacation, or children who turn out all right. Now, in a way, none of these things is inherently evil, but there's something wrong about the whole system.

So many of our ideas of what the "good life" is don't actually have God in them. We envision the "good" quite apart from the grace of his presence, promises, and provisions. It is the subtle belief that life somehow, some way can be found outside him; that the world is capable of being our savior. And because we fall into believing that life can be found outside him, God isn't central to our dreams. He's not *in* our dreams. The only way he actually touches many of our dreams is that we see him as the delivery mechanism of the good life that we dream of and ask him to produce. He is not life to us; he's the deliverer of life. He is not the end that we hunger for; he's but the means to the end we crave.

It's all a spiritual world turned upside down. In our fantasies of the good life, we are sovereign. We decide what is right, good, important, and valuable. We define what life is. We control the agenda and set the timetable. The menu of the good life is written by us. It has us at the center. It's God employed by us to do our bidding, and if he does, we will thank him and proclaim his goodness. It is self-centered religiosity that bears little resemblance to the faith of the Bible. Yet, it is so easy to set yourself up as sovereign. It's so tempting to think that you know what's best for you. It's so natural to shop horizontally for what you will only ever find vertically and to question why God failed to deliver.

Psalm 103 says that God "satisfies you with good things so that your youth is renewed like the eagle's" (v. 5). Those "good things" come in a person, and his name is Jesus. Yes, it is true—Jesus is the "good life" that you need, no matter what is on your wish list.

For further study and encouragement: John 10:1–18

JUNE 25

Discouragement focuses more on the broken glories of creation than it does on the restoring glories of God's character, presence, and promises.

They were standing on the borders of the land that God had promised them. It stretched out with beauty before their eyes. They had sent explorers into the land to check it out. The report came back that it was rich and lush, producing sweet and succulent fruit. But the children of Israel were not jumping up and down in celebration and anticipation. They were not chomping at the bit to get going. They were doing quite the opposite; they were digging in their heels and refusing to move at all. They stood there grumbling against the Lord, saying: "Because the LORD hated us he has brought us out of the land of Egypt, to give us into the hands of the Amorites, to destroy us. . . . 'The people are greater and taller than we. The cities are great and fortified up to heaven'" (Deut. 1:27–28).

The Bible says that these historical moments, significant times of spiritual evaluation and decision, have been recorded for our example and our instruction because these were people just like us. It was the most wonderful moment of grace in their lives. They were about to be given what they did not deserve and could not earn. Life, rich and full, was on the other side of that border. It was theirs for the taking because the One who had redeemed them from bondage was not just a Deliverer of freedom; he was also a Giver of life. They had earned nothing, but they were about to get it all. But they refused. They would not move. It all seemed unrealistic and impossible. It seemed like a cruel setup; the big, spiritual bait and switch. They had been promised a land of their own, but what they got was a place filled with people who didn't want them there. What in the world was God doing anyway?

Their disappointed thinking had a fatal flaw in it. What they saw as being in the way of God's plan was actually part of his plan; what caused their faith to weaken was actually God's tool to build their faith.

God knows what you too are facing. He sees well the brokenness that is all around you. He is not in a panic, wondering how he'll ever pull off his plan with all these obstacles in the way. Don't be discouraged. God has you exactly where he wants you. He knows just how he will use what makes you afraid in order to build your faith. He is not surprised by the troubles you face, and he surely has no intention of leaving you to face those things on your own. He stands with you in power, glory, goodness, wisdom, and grace. He can defeat what you can't, and he intends these troubles to be not enemies that finish you but tools of grace that transform you.

For further study and encouragement: Joshua 1

JUNE 26

*When you think you're righteous, you expect others to be righteous as well,
so you become demanding, judgmental, and constantly disappointed.*

So much of our disappointment in relationships is not because we have an unrealistic view of others, but because we have a distorted view of ourselves. When we are harsh, impatient, critical, irritated, judgmental, curt, and unkind with others, we are revealing more about what we think of ourselves than about them. Confused? Let me explain.

Late on a Thursday night, you go into your teenager's room to ask him something. You can barely open the door because of the debris that is in the way. There are dirty clothes, spoiled food items, and pieces of tech gear in a tangled pile from yesteryear. You can't believe it! You have had enough! So you explode: "I never thought one of my children would turn out to be such a slob. Don't you have an ounce of self-respect? I should take every piece of your junk and lock it away and leave you in an empty room until you put on your big-boy pants and grow up. Why, in my day, I never would have thought of treating my stuff this way." Now, unpack this statement with me. As you're going off, your teenager isn't saying to himself: "My, this is helpful. This is a truly wise person who is saying very helpful things to me. I am so thankful that this person is my parent." No, that's not what the teenager is thinking, because in that moment you're not part of what God would do in the heart and life of that kid; you're in the way of it. And why are you in the way? Well, the final part of the statement, "in my day . . . ," gives it away.

It is your self-righteousness that permits you to be angry and unkind to your child. You're not greeting his laziness with gracious parental wisdom, because you think you are essentially different from him. You're saying, "If you were as righteous as me, you wouldn't live like this." When you assign to yourself righteousness that you don't have, you expect the people around you to be as righteous as you think you are, and you greet them with judgment when they aren't. Like the Pharisees, you tie burdens on others that you are not able to bear yourself (see Matt. 23:1–12).

You deal with others with grace when you walk around with the humble realization of how deep your need for grace was and continues to be. When you enter that teenager's room with the recognition that you are more like him than unlike him, there is compassion in the way you handle his wrongs. When you admit that there are few struggles in others that don't exist in some way in your life as well, you caress them with God's grace rather than hammering them with the law. The appropriateness of my responses to others is directly related to the accuracy of my view of myself, and for that there is grace too.

For further study and encouragement: Matthew 23

JUNE 27

There is a significant difference between amazement and faith.
God doesn't just want to blow your mind; he wants to rule your heart.

It is an important distinction, one that is not made frequently enough. Faith surely does engage your brain, but it is fundamentally more than that. Faith is something that you do with your life. True biblical faith doesn't stop with thought; it radically rearranges the way that you approach everything in your life. Amazement is what you experience when you are taken beyond the categories that you carry around to explain or define things. Amazement is a step in the faith process, but there is a huge difference between amazement and faith.

Pretend you're standing next to me on a pier on the Jersey Shore. We're looking at one of those amusement park contraptions that is essentially a fifty-foot-high slingshot, into which they strap some otherwise sane human being and launch him back and forth over the Atlantic Ocean in the night. Now, that ride amazes both of us, but we're not about to strap in and let ourselves be launched into the night. Amazed? Yes, but we will not put our faith in that thing. In the same way:

- You can be amazed by the grand sweep of the redemptive story in Scripture and not be living by faith.
- You can be amazed by the labyrinthine logic of the theology of the Word of God and not be living by faith.
- You can be amazed by the great worship music you participate in every Sunday and not be living by faith.
- You can be amazed by the love of your small group and not be living by faith.
- You can be amazed by the wonderful biblical preaching and teaching that you hear and not be living by faith.
- You can be amazed by the grace of the cross of Jesus and not be living by faith.

There is a significant, yes, even profound difference between amazement and faith. God will not leave us in a state of amazement. He works by grace to craft us into people of settled, hopeful, courageous, active, celebratory, God-glorifying faith. He will settle for nothing less. He is not satisfied with the wonder of our minds. He will not relent until he has established his life-altering rule in our hearts. He works so that we really will "believe that he exists and that he rewards those who seek him" (Heb. 11:6). You can't work that faith up in yourself. It is a gift of his grace. The cross makes that gift available to you right here, right now.

For further study and encouragement: John 20:24–29

JUNE 28

If God is in control of every aspect of your world
and his grace covers all your sin,
why would you ever give way to fear?

There are many things I wish were true about me:

I wish I could say that I'm never afraid, but I can't.

I wish I could say that worry never interrupts my sleep, but I can't.

I wish I could say that I never wonder what God is doing, but I can't.

I wish I could say that I never give way to envy, but I can't.

I wish I could say that I am always aware that God is near, but I can't.

I wish I could say that I never wonder, "If only_____," but I can't.

I wish I could say that I never dread what's around the corner, but I can't.

I wish I could say that I always have peace in my heart, but I can't.

I wish I could say that all that I do is done out of faith and not fear, but I can't.

You see, I have come to be very aware that although I know the Bible and its doctrine well, the battle between fear and faith still goes on in my heart. Here's what this means at street level. It is important to understand why fear still lives in the life of a believer in the hallways, kitchens, bedrooms, family rooms, workrooms, and vans of everyday life. You could argue that he or she has every reason to be free of fear, that fear should be an artifact of a former civilization. So why the continued struggle with fear?

Fear lives and rules in the heart of a believer who has forgotten God's sovereignty and grace. If left to myself, I *should* be afraid. There are many trials, temptations, dangers, and enemies in this fallen world that are bigger and more powerful than me. I have to deal with many things that are outside my control. But the message of the gospel is that I haven't been left to myself, that Immanuel is with me in sovereign authority and powerful grace. He rules with perfect wisdom over all the circumstances and locations that would make me afraid. In grace, he blesses me with what I need to face what he has decided to put on my plate. I am never—in anything, anywhere, at any time—by myself. I never arrive on scene first. I never step into a situation that exists outside his control. I never move beyond the reach of his authority. He is never surprised by where I end up or by what I am facing. He never leaves me to the limited resources of my own wisdom, strength, and righteousness. He never grows weary with protecting and providing for me. He will never abandon me out of frustration. I do not need to be afraid. When you forget God's sovereignty and his grace, you give room in your heart for fear to do its nasty, debilitating work. Pray right now for grace to remember. Your sovereign Savior loves to hear and answer.

For further study and encouragement: Isaiah 44:1–8

JUNE 29

If you're God's child, when you sin,
you can run toward God and not away from him,
because all your sin is covered by the blood of Jesus.

There are two starkly contrasting scenes, one at the beginning of the Bible and one at the end. In the beginning scene, we see Adam and Eve quickly clothing themselves and hiding from God in the guilt and shame that is the sad result of their sin (Genesis 3). It is a disaster too horrible to be expressed with the limited words of human language. Blessed with an unimpeded relationship with the Lord, Creator, and King of the universe, blessed with a garden lush with every good thing, they really did have it all. They were made by God and made for him. Their lives were meant to have him at the center. They were hardwired to enjoy eternal fellowship with him. Love for him and worship of him were to be the two principal motivators of all they did. How could this bond be so quickly broken? How could they be afraid of God? How could they try to hide from the One who was the reason for their entire existence? It is too sad to grasp, but the answer to the questions is clear: sin, with its weight of guilt and shame, separated them from God and drove them from the garden of his presence and provision. The bond was broken; how would it ever be repaired?

The second scene is the marriage supper of the Lamb (Revelation 19). It too is a gathering of sinners, but they aren't cowering in shame. They aren't hiding in guilt. They aren't dreading his presence. They don't fear the power of his anger. No, these sinners are celebrating because the bond that was broken in the garden has been restored. They have been wed to their Savior forever. Forever they will be in his presence. Never again will they be separate from him. Never again will they hide. Never again will they be driven away. Their fellowship will never end. The sound of their celebration will never grow quiet. Their robes have been washed to purest white. They are clothed in the righteousness of another. They are accepted because of him. There is no condemnation before them. There is no sin that separates them. It is a scene of such outrageous beauty that describing it would stretch human language beyond its limits.

What made the difference between these two scenes? Not human wisdom, strength, position, or righteousness. The difference is captured in one gloriously transformational word. Other than the name of Jesus, it may be the most important word in all the Bible: *grace*. Grace in the person and work—the life, death, and resurrection—of Jesus is what made the difference. If you're God's child, stop hiding behind the trees of your shame. Step out into the light. There's a celebration in your future!

For further study and encouragement: Revelation 21

JUNE 30

If the righteousness of Christ allows me to stand before a holy God utterly unafraid, why should I be haunted by what you think of me?

So many people live with a great big gap right smack dab in the middle of their gospel, and they don't know it. I did for years. Most Christians have a basic understanding of salvation past, that is, the grace of forgiveness that they have received because of the broken body and shed blood of the Lamb, the Lord Jesus Christ. And most Christians tend to look forward with anticipation toward salvation future, that is, the grace of an endless eternity of complete peace and harmony lived in the presence of the forever glory and grace of the triune God. But, sadly, many, many Christians have little understanding of salvation present, that is, the benefits of the work of Jesus Christ right here, right now. It is vitally important that we understand the *nowism* of the gospel of the Lord Jesus Christ.

Jesus didn't die just for your past and your future. He really did shed his blood for your here and now too. He died for the tough conversation that you need to have with your spouse, your rebellious teenager, or your friend. He died for your struggle to work for that angry, constantly dissatisfied boss. He died for the tensions in your broken and dysfunctional extended family. He died for the sexual temptation that seems to get the better of you. He died for the materialism that seems to kidnap you. He died for your fear of the opinions of others. He died for the torment of your anxiety and the darkness of your depression. He died so that you would have everything you need to live as he intended between the "already" of your conversion and the "not yet" of your resurrection.

When you begin to understand the wonderful new identity and provision that is yours as his child, it really does change the way you think and the way you live. If he has granted you his full and complete acceptance, even on your worst day, then why should you seek to get your inner peace from the acceptance of a flawed human being? His present grace frees us from so much of the fear and control that distorts our relationships. If he is with you, providing in his presence and grace whatever you need to do what he has called you to do, why should you fear what's around the corner?

When you begin to understand what you have been given in his right here, right now grace, you quit asking people, places, and things to be your savior. Because you know what he thinks of you, you are free to worry less about what the person next to you thinks. That's a freedom many of us could use!

For further study and encouragement: Psalm 121

JULY 1

Does discouragement preach to you a false gospel
that causes you to forget that your future has already
been written into the pages of God's book?

It is discouraging to face:

- your struggle with sin;
- the disloyalty of a friend;
- the rebellion of your children;
- the souring of your marriage;
- the division of your church;
- the temptations that seem to be all around you;
- the injustice that lives in this fallen world;
- the pain and worry of physical sickness;
- the loss of your job;
- the hardship of old age; or
- the death of your dreams.

Yes, it's hard to face all of these things. It's easy to lose your way. It's tempting to wonder what God is doing, if he cares, and if he hears your prayers. It's hard to hold on to his promises. It's hard to stay committed to good spiritual habits. It's hard not to give in to discouragement and give way to the desire to quit.

But in the face of discouragement, there is one thing that you need to remember. It is captured in just a few powerful words from Psalm 139: "Your eyes saw my unformed substance; in your book were written, every one of them, the days that were formed for me, when as yet there were none of them" (v. 16). It is vital to remember, when trouble comes your way and discouragement begins to grip your heart, that every single day of your life was written into God's book before you lived the very first of them. None of those days and none of the things that you have faced or will face in those days are a surprise to your Lord. He carefully authored the content of every one of those days with his own hand. He controlled every twist and turn of the plot that is your story. He introduced all the characters and determined all of the locations. Nothing will happen to you that he has not written into his book. And he has already determined how your story will end.

You see, what discourages you doesn't surprise him because he authored it all with a glorious combination of wisdom and grace. Nothing is out of his control. Your Savior is sovereign. He knows what is best and will do what is best. This is where rest and courage are to be found when discouragement shakes the resolve of your heart.

For further study and encouragement: Psalm 135

JULY 2

Corporate worship is designed to turn your heart from the shadow glories of creation to the one glory that will satisfy it.

It was a warning to the children of Israel, but it is one we all need to hear and heed:

> And when the LORD your God brings you into the land that he swore to your fathers, to Abraham, to Isaac, and to Jacob, to give you—with great and good cities that you did not build, and houses full of all good things that you did not fill, and cisterns that you did not dig, and vineyards and olive trees that you did not plant—and when you eat and are full, then take care lest you forget the LORD, who brought you out of the land of Egypt, out of the house of slavery. It is the LORD your God you shall fear. Him you shall serve and by his name you shall swear. You shall not go after other gods, the gods of the peoples who are around you—for the LORD your God in your midst is a jealous God—lest the anger of the LORD your God be kindled against you, and he destroy you from off the face of the earth. (Deut. 6:10–15)

This side of eternity, material affluence is dangerous. It's not that material things are bad in and of themselves. God intentionally designed his world to be a beautiful place. It's not that it's wrong to enjoy the material world around us. God gave us the capacity to take in and enjoy this beauty. In fact, God placed a desire for beauty in our hearts. The problem with material things is not found in the material things; it's found in us. Our problem with the material world is a heart problem. This problem is captured here by God's warning to his people as they enter a land lush with physical glories. The problem is that material affluence has the power to cause us to forget God. The sight, sound, touch, taste, and splendor of these created glories tempt us to think that life is found in having these things and to think we have everything that we need because we have them. Because these things weaken our God awareness and our God hunger, we are then set up to give our hearts to the worship of what is created rather than the worship of the One who created it all. At street level, we forsake the God who created and supplied us with these physical glories, even though we continue to say that we believe in him.

The warning can be stated in a few words: *Be careful when you're full that you do not forget.* The physical world is full of many glories, but the pursuit of these glories must not rule my heart because they have no ability whatsoever to offer me the life that I so desperately need. Life is only ever found in what all those earth-bound glories point to—a God of awesome glory who is the Source and Giver of life; life that satisfies and remains forever. Because he is a God of grace, he showers glories on me so that those glories would lead me to him.

For further study and encouragement: Deuteronomy 9

JULY 3

Jesus paid it all! There are no bills due for your sin!
You are now free to simply trust and obey.

Stop trying to earn something from God. Stop trying to gain more of his acceptance. Stop trying to earn his favor. Stop trying to win his allegiance. Stop trying to do something that would pay for his blessing. Stop trying to morally buy your way out of his anger. Stop trying to reach a level where you will know lasting peace with him. Just stop trying. Just stop.

So many Christians load onto their shoulders a burden that they do not have to bear. They get up every morning and pick up the heavy load of trying somehow, some way to achieve something with God. They work hard to exercise what they do not have in hopes they can achieve what is impossible. It simply cannot work. So where does it lead? It leads either to the scary pride of self-righteousness—a culture of moralistic self-backslappers, who have no problem judging those who have not achieved the level of righteousness they think that they have—or to fear and discouragement—a culture of people who don't run to God with their sin because they're afraid of him.

Paul wipes out this distorted, debilitating "buy your way into grace" culture with a striking economy of words: "Now it is evident that no one is justified before God by the law" (Gal. 3:11). It is a statement that requires no preamble and no amendment. No one is ever accepted by God because he or she has kept the law. No one. That's it; no compromises and no deals are needed. They are not needed because, first, it is impossible to buy your way into God's favor because sin makes you a lawbreaker and, second, your bills were fully and completely paid in the single payment of the cross of Jesus Christ. Christ did not make the first payment on your moral mortgage; he paid your entire moral mortgage in one single payment so that you could live in relationship to God debt-free forever. God's law is not your payment plan because there is no payment plan when the demands of a mortgage have been satisfied once and forever in one single payment.

So stop trying to measure up to get whatever from God. Stop hiding from him when you mess up. Stop comparing yourself to other people, wondering if God loves you less because you're not as "good" as them. Stop naming the good things you do as righteousness that not only gets you closer to God, but also proves to others that you are. Just stop asking the law to do what only grace can achieve, and start resting in the fact that you don't have any moral bills due because Jesus paid them all on the cross. And when you sin, don't pretend you didn't, don't panic, and don't hide. Run to Jesus and receive mercy in your time of need, the kind of mercy he paid for you to have.

For further study and encouragement: Isaiah 53

JULY 4

When you're weary with the battle, remember that the One who is your strength never takes a break, never needs sleep, never grows weary.

Life in this fallen world is wearisome. Sometimes your marriage is just exhausting as you work to make a sinner married to a sinner coexist in love and peace. Sometimes it's just plain tiring to be a parent, particularly on those days when it seems that your children have conspired together to be corporately rebellious. Sometimes you don't feel like being nice to that neighbor who seems to be able to look at everything and find a reason to complain. Sometimes you just get exhausted with dealing with your heart—you know, those desires you shouldn't have and those thoughts you shouldn't think. Sometimes you have to drag yourself to your church service or your small group. Sometimes you'd just like to get off the Christianity treadmill and zone out, but you can't. You wake up the next day and you have to do it all over again—another temptation, another marital misunderstanding, another conflict with another friend, another resistant child, or another moment when you feel the emotional temperature change.

When you're weary and feeling weak, run to the Psalms; there's grace to be found there:

> I lift up my eyes to the hills.
>> From where does my help come?
> My help comes from the LORD,
>> who made heaven and earth.
> He will not let your foot be moved;
>> he who keeps you will not slumber.
> Behold, he who keeps Israel
>> will neither slumber nor sleep.
> The LORD is your keeper;
>> the LORD is your shade on your right hand.
> The sun shall not strike you by day,
>> nor the moon by night.
> The LORD will keep you from all evil;
>> he will keep your life.
> The LORD will keep
>> your going out and your coming in
>> from this time forth and forevermore. (Psalm 121)

This psalm confronts you and me with two truths that we must always remember. First, we are not in this battle alone. We have a Keeper, and our safety is his commitment. Second, the One who is our Keeper never, ever takes a break. His keeping care is 24/7 forever and ever. The inexhaustible Keeper is your help and strength; when weary, run to him.

For further study and encouragement: Psalm 91

JULY 5

Weakness is the window to strength. Confessing your inability produces hunger for the power that is only ever found in Jesus.

I have said it many, many times and I will say it more than once in this devotional—our problem is not our weakness; God's grace is up to the task. Our problem is our delusions of strength that keep us from seeking the grace that strengthens us in our weakness. We just don't like to be weak. We don't like to think of ourselves that way, and we don't want others to see us that way. So we act as if we know things that we don't know, and we don't ask the questions we need to ask. We act as if we can handle things that we can't handle, and we don't seek the help that's available. We act as if we've conquered things that we have not conquered, and we don't reach out for help for the battle. It is all a failed quest for the self-congratulatory glory of independence.

But we are not independent. None of us are. We were not created to be independent. We were formed to be dependent on the One who made us, and we were re-created in Jesus Christ to be dependent on his grace. God does not hold you to a standard of independent strength. God does not expect of you what you do not have. He knows who you are. He is never shocked or dismayed by your weakness. He has moved toward you in grace because you are weak and would have no hope in life and death without him. The person who is shocked and dismayed by your weakness is you. It bothers you. It embarrasses you. It makes you want to hide and cover yourself. It causes you to playact in public and to deceive yourself in private. Your weakness will drive you crazy unless you understand the gospel of Jesus.

What is that message? It is the story of a strong and able Savior who showers his powerful grace on people who are fundamentally weak and unable. He confronts you with your weakness so you will run to him for strength. He calls you to mountains too big to climb so that in your inability, you will look to him. He leads you to taste failure so that you will find your hope in him. He works to prove to you how weak you really are so that you will gladly accept his invitation to enabling grace. Perhaps it's not such a bad thing to come to the end of your rope if at the end of your rope you find a strong and willing Savior.

So don't be afraid to cry out in weakness, because when you affirm your weakness, you are teaching your heart to esteem and celebrate the grace that can make you strong. Sometime in the next week, you'll be confronted with your weakness; when you are, you'll either work to convince yourself you're strong or you'll run to the One who is.

For further study and encouragement: Exodus 15:1–18

JULY 6

The grace you've been given is not just the grace of forgiveness and acceptance; it's also the grace of empowerment. So get up and follow.

In the life of the believer, fear of weakness amounts to God-forgetfulness. Timidity is a failure to remember the promises of the gospel. Allowing yourself to be overwhelmed in the face of the call of God is forgetting the right here, right now grace of Jesus Christ. Giving way to temptation is overlooking the empowering presence of the Holy Spirit. You not only have been forgiven by the grace of the gospel and guaranteed a place in eternity with your Savior, but you also have been granted by that very same grace all that you need to be what God has called you to be and to do the things God has called you to do in the place where he has put you.

So here's how this works. God has promised to supply and empower; your job is to follow him by faith where you live every day. You don't wait for the provision before you move. God has not promised that you will see it beforehand. You don't try to figure out what God is going to do next and how he will meet your needs; you move forward in the certainty that he is with you, for you, and in you. This God of awesome power will grant you power to do what is needed. This is his sure and reliable covenant promise to you.

And what kind of power does this One to whom you're entrusting your life have? Let me refer you to one of the strangest verses in all of Scripture, one that paints a dramatic picture of the awe-inspiring power of God. It's found in Exodus 11. God is delivering his people from their captivity in Egypt, and all the firstborn of Egypt are going to die, including cattle. God says that as the result of this, there will be a great cry throughout Egypt like there has never been before. Then he says, "But not a dog shall growl against any of the people of Israel, either man or beast, that you may know that the LORD makes a distinction between Egypt and Israel" (v. 7). What kind of power does God have? He has the power to silence the growl of every dog in Egypt. But there is more. He has the power to cause the dogs to distinguish between Israelites and Egyptians. The dogs will wail against the Egyptians and be silent in the presence of Israelites, all because there is a God who rules all things. He even has the power to direct individual animals to do what he wants them to do.

Yes, your God has awesome power, distinguishing power. He knows who his people are, he knows where they are, he knows what they need, he knows when they need it, and he knows what needs to be delivered and what needs to be controlled for his will to be done. He always gives the power that his people need.

For further study and encouragement: Exodus 6:1–9

JULY 7

*As God's child, you don't sit and wait for hope. No, grace
makes it possible for you to get up and live in hope.*

Gospel hope is a mouthful. It includes so many wonderful provisions that it's hard to get it all in one bite. Yes, biblical hope gives you a lot of spiritual nutrients to chew on. Yet many believers seem to live hope-deprived lives. Perhaps one of the dirty secrets of the church is how much we do out of fear and not faith. We permit ourselves to feel small, unable, alone, unprepared, and bereft of resources. We tell ourselves that what we're facing is too big and requires too much of us. We stand at the bottom of mountains of trouble and give up before we've taken the first step of the climb. We wait for hope to come in some noticeable, seeable way, but it never seems to arrive. We pray, but it doesn't seem to do any good. We want to believe that God is there and that he really does care, but it seems that we've been left to ourselves. With each passing day, it seems harder to have hope for our marriages, for our children, for our churches, for our friendships, or just for the ability to survive all the trouble with our faith and sanity intact. We wonder, "Where is hope to be found?"

What we fail to understand is that we don't have a hope problem; we have a sight problem. Hope has come. "What?" you say. "Where?" Hope isn't a thing. Hope isn't a set of circumstances. Hope isn't first a set of ideas. Hope is a person, and his name is Jesus. He came to earth to face what you face and to defeat what defeats you so that you would have hope. Your salvation means that you are now in a personal relationship with the One who is hope. You have hope because he exists and is your Savior. You don't have a hope problem; you have been given hope that is both real and constant. The issue is whether you see it. Paul captures the problem this way in Ephesians 1:18–19: ". . . having the *eyes of your hearts* enlightened, that you may know what is the hope to which he has called you, what are the riches of his glorious inheritance in the saints, and what is the immeasurable greatness of his power toward us who believe, according to the working of his great might."

Paul prays that we will have a well-working spiritual vision system so that we will "see" the hope that we have been given in Christ. What is this hope? It is a rich inheritance. Jesus died and left us a rich inheritance of grace to be invested in facing the troubles of the here and now. It is great power that is ours in the moments when we are so weak. Hope came, and he brought with him riches and power that he gave to you. You see, you don't really have a hope problem; you have a vision problem, and for that there's enlightening grace.

For further study and encouragement: Ephesians 2:11–22

JULY 8

You always approach life with a mindset of some kind.
Scripture says there are only two possibilities: "on earth" or "above."

You think. You never stop thinking. You think much more than you are aware of. Your thinking influences you more than you know. The moment you stop thinking, you're dead. But here's what we all need to understand—our thinking is never neutral. All our thinking has deeply religious roots. All our thinking is shaped by the way we are answering the major questions of life. Everyone thinks about these questions and everyone answers them in some way.

I sat next to him on the Chinatown bus, the cheapest way to get home from New York City. I was tired and didn't really want to talk; if I could have found a completely empty seat, I would have gone for it, but the seat next to this man in his late twenties was the only one open. It wasn't long before he asked me where I was from and what I did. I told him I lived in Philly and that I was a pastor and an author. He asked me what I wrote, and I told him that I wrote about everyday life issues from the perspective of the Bible. He responded: "I don't believe in the Bible and I'm surprised that people still do. In fact, I don't think there is any such thing as truth that you can lay on someone else." I said, "But you just did—you just very confidently laid a truth on me." From there, we launched into a conversation that stretched to an hour and a half.

As I thought later about our conversation, I was struck by the utter lack of any hint of neutrality in anything he or I said. Everything we said was rooted in very deep moral commitments. Our conversation flowed out of who we thought we were, what we thought about God, what we thought about the nature of and purpose for life, and what we understood about the nature of truth and about the future.

So it is with you. Here are the practical questions: What set of values determines your schedule? What view of life determines how you make decisions? What perspective about the nature of and purpose for your existence forms your everyday street-level priorities? How does your thinking shape what you do and say every day? Paul writes: "If then you have been raised with Christ, seek the things that are above, where Christ is, seated at the right hand of God. Set your minds on things that are above, not on things that are on earth" (Col. 3:1–2). You have only two choices: an "on earth" way of thinking that is all about this right here, right now physical moment, or an "above" way of thinking that looks at life from the vantage point of the grand redemptive story and, more specifically, from the perspective of the person and work of the Lord Jesus Christ. What's your choice? Is it material reality as the only reality or material reality viewed through the lens of the radical truths of the gospel of Jesus Christ? Which is it for you, where the rubber meets the road in your daily life?

For further study and encouragement: Acts 17

JULY 9

The scary deception of sin is that, at the point
of sinning, sin doesn't look all that sinful.

We lose sight of the sinfulness of sin or the evil of evil, and when we do, we are vulnerable to the seductive lies of temptation. Perhaps this is one of the reasons why there are stories like this in the Bible:

> And when they came to the disciples, they saw a great crowd around them, and scribes arguing with them. And immediately all the crowd, when they saw him, were greatly amazed and ran up to him and greeted him. And he asked them, "What are you arguing about with them?" And someone from the crowd answered him, "Teacher, I brought my son to you, for he has a spirit that makes him mute. And whenever it seizes him, it throws him down, and he foams and grinds his teeth and becomes rigid. So I asked your disciples to cast it out, and they were not able." And he answered them, "O faithless generation, how long am I to be with you? How long am I to bear with you? Bring him to me." And they brought the boy to him. And when the spirit saw him, immediately it convulsed the boy, and he fell on the ground and rolled about, foaming at the mouth. And Jesus asked his father, "How long has this been happening to him?" And he said, "From childhood. And it has often cast him into fire and into water, to destroy him. But if you can do anything, have compassion on us and help us." And Jesus said to him, "'If you can'! All things are possible for one who believes." Immediately the father of the child cried out and said, "I believe; help my unbelief!" And when Jesus saw that a crowd came running together, he rebuked the unclean spirit, saying to it, "You mute and deaf spirit, I command you, come out of him and never enter him again." And after crying out and convulsing him terribly, it came out, and the boy was like a corpse, so that most of them said, "He is dead." But Jesus took him by the hand and lifted him up, and he arose. And when he had entered the house, his disciples asked him privately, "Why could we not cast it out?" And he said to them, "This kind cannot be driven out by anything but prayer." (Mark 9:14–29)

In stories like these, God is lovingly confronting us with two things—the shocking evil of evil and the only place where deliverance from it can be found. Examine the graphic descriptions of what evil is doing to this boy. Nothing good ever happens when evil is in control of a person's heart. Sin really is a scary, horrible thing. Evil is ugly and destructive, and must never be minimized. You just can't read this story and wonder if evil is so evil after all. This story is meant to put a holy dread in your heart. But it is meant to do more. It is meant to assure you that delivering grace is a reality. No matter how great the sinfulness of sin is, God's grace is greater. No matter how powerful the evil of evil is, God's delivering power is greater. We should fear sin in a moral sense but not in a defeatist sense, because of the powerful delivering grace of our Savior, the Lord Jesus Christ. Do you live with this balance?

For further study and encouragement: 1 Samuel 13

JULY 10

*You once desired it, but now you're persuaded that you
need it. Once you've named it a need, it has you.*

It may be the sloppiest, most all-inclusive word used in human language: *need*. We put far too many things into our "need" category. That's why Jesus reminds us that we have a heavenly Father who knows exactly what we need (see Matthew 6). Embedded in that reminder are both a comfort and a confrontation. The comfort is that there is One who once created and now controls everything that is, and who has unleashed his awesome power so that you and I may receive from his hand every good thing that we need to be what we were designed to be and to do what we have been called to do. No need has been unmet by his gracious hands. But this statement also carries with it a humbling rebuke. We need a heavenly Father who knows what we need, because we don't. We get *want* and *need* confused all the time.

Here's how need-driven addiction (spiritual slavery) develops. It all starts with *desire* ("I want . . ."). There is nothing evil about desire. God created us with the capacity to desire. Everything we say and do is the product of desire. Yet it is very hard for sinners to hold desire with an open hand. It doesn't take long for our desires to morph into *demands* ("I must . . ."). The thing that was once a desire is now taking hold of us. We're less willing to live without it. We're more and more convinced that we have to have it. Then demand morphs into *need* ("I will . . ."). Now, with great resolve and surety, we are convinced that we cannot live without it. This thing that was once an open-handed desire has been christened a need. We're now fully convinced that it would be impossible to live without it. It is now in control of our hearts. We think about it all the time. We are fearful when we're without it. We plot how to keep it in our lives.

But the cycle of slavery doesn't end there. Need forms *expectation* as to what God ought to do ("You should . . ."). You see, if you're convinced it's a need, you will think you're entitled to it, you will be convinced that you have the right to demand it, and you will judge God's love by his willingness to deliver it. Expectation then leads to *disappointment* if God doesn't deliver ("You didn't . . ."). We can't believe that God would say that he loves us yet not meet this "need." The fact is, God has been faithful to all that he's promised us, but this desire that morphed into a need is not something he's promised to give us. So disappointment leads us to some kind of *anger* ("Because you didn't, I will . . ."). Because we now judge God as unfaithful, we quit trusting him as we should and we let go of our good habits of faith. Isn't it good to know that Jesus came to free us from our idolatry?

For further study and encouragement: 1 Corinthians 10:1–13

JULY 11

God is at the center of his universe, and when you put yourself there,
it only ends in relational brokenness and personal disappointment.

There is someone at the center of all things. There is someone who rules over heaven and earth. There is someone who defines what pure love, power, wisdom, faithfulness, righteousness, and grace look like. There is someone who controls the forces of physical nature and administrates the events of human history. There is someone who authors the plot details of the story of every human being who has lived. There is someone who is worthy of honor, dominion, and power. There is someone who is deserving of the complete allegiance and unending worship of everyone. There is someone at the center, and it is not us.

It will never be about us because we have been born into a world that is, by its fundamental nature, a celebration of One greater than us. The Bible is very clear when it proclaims who is at the center:

- "In the beginning, God . . ." (Gen. 1:1).
- "You are my Son; today I have begotten you. Ask of me, and I will make the nations your heritage, and the ends of the earth your possession" (Ps. 2:7–8).
- "For to us a child is born, to us a son is given; and the government shall be upon his shoulder, and his name shall be called Wonderful Counselor, Mighty God, Everlasting Father, Prince of Peace" (Isa. 9:6).
- "He does according to his will among the host of heaven and among the inhabitants of the earth; and none can stay his hand or say to him, "What have you done?" (Dan. 4:35).
- "For from him and through him and to him are all things. To him be glory forever. Amen" (Rom. 11:36).
- "For by him all things were created, in heaven and on earth, visible and invisible, whether thrones or dominions or rulers or authorities—all things were created through him and for him. And he is before all things, and in him all thing hold together" (Col. 1:16–17).
- "Worthy are you, our Lord and God, to receive glory and honor and power, for you created all things, and by your will they existed and were created" (Rev. 4:11).

Yet the message of the garden of Eden is that sin makes us quest for God's position. We want life to work according to our will and conform to our plan. This desire to be at the center never goes anywhere good, personally or relationally. Self-centeredness is at the core of sin's dysfunction, another powerful evidence of our need for rescuing grace.

For further study and encouragement: Daniel 4:28–37

JULY 12

Life in this fallen world is hard.
That's why you need a community of love.

One of the themes that courses through the New Testament and is a repeated theme of this devotional is that your walk with God is designed by God to be a community project. Anonymous, consumerist, isolated, independent, self-sufficient, "Jesus and me" Christianity is a distant and distorted facsimile of the faith of the New Testament. You and I simply were not created ("It is not good that the man should be alone"; Gen. 2:18) or re-created in Jesus Christ ("For the body does not consist of one member but of many"; 1 Cor. 12:14) to live all by ourselves. The biblical word pictures of temple (stones joined together to be a place where God dwells) and body (each member dependent on the function of the other) decimate any idea that healthy Christianity can live outside of essential community.

Yet many, many believers live their lives with a huge separation between their public church personas and the details of their private existence. We are skilled at brief, nonpersonal conversations about the weather, sports, and politics. We are learned at giving either nonanswers or spiritually platitudinous answers to people's questions. We live in long-term networks of terminally casual relationships. No one really knows us beneath the well-crafted public display, and because they don't know us, they cannot minister to us, because no one can minister to that which he does not know.

Moreover, we think we know ourselves and we think we're okay, forgetting the blinding power of sin. That's why church is, for many of us, nothing more than a thing to attend on Sunday. Church is a formal set of activities. Church is a buffet of regularly scheduled, demographically designed religious offerings. Church is a place where music can be enjoyed and sermons can be heard. Church is what connects us to worldwide missions. Church provides wholesome activities for our children. But church isn't an interdependent, webbed-together community of personally focused love and grace for us all.

But the Bible is clear. When each part is working properly, the body of Christ grows to maturity in Christ (see Ephesians 4). We each need to live in intentionally intrusive, Christ-centered, grace-driven redemptive community. This community is meant to enlighten and protect. It is meant to motivate and encourage. It is meant to rescue and restore. It is meant to instill hope and courage. It is meant to confront and rebuke. It is meant to guide and protect. It is meant to give vision and sound warning. It is meant to incarnate the love and grace of Jesus when you feel discouraged and alone. It is meant to be a visible representation of the grace of Jesus that is your hope. It is not a luxury. It is a spiritual necessity. The question is, "Are you webbed in?"

For further study and encouragement: Romans 12

JULY 13

You don't work in the hope of getting an identity; you work in celebration of the identity that, in Christ, you have been given.

Identity
No need to search for
myself.
No need to grasp for
meaning
for my life
or purpose
for what I do.
No need to hope for
inner peace,
that sense of well-being
for which every heart
longs.
No need to hope that
someone or something
will make me
happy
or give me joy.
I no longer need any
of these things because
grace
has connected me to you
and you have named me
your child.

For further study and encouragement: Galatians 4:4–7

JULY 14

You don't get wisdom by experience or research. You get wisdom by means of relationship. Grace makes that relationship possible.

It is one of the often understated, definitively dark, and dangerous results of sin. What is it? Sin reduces all of us to fools. Sadly, we demonstrate that foolishness every day. We think we can spend what we want to satisfy our seemingly endless desires without getting into hopeless debt. We think that sex, food, and fun will satisfy the hunger of our hearts for contentment and life. We think we can rebel against authority, and it will be all right in the end. We think we can be selfish and demanding in our relationships, and our loved ones will still want to be near us. We think we can pursue the pleasures of creation at any time and in any way we want, and not get fat, addicted, and in debt. We think that we can step over God's boundaries without consequences. We think we deserve what we do not deserve and are able to do what we cannot do. Shockingly, there are more times than most of us recognize or would be willing to admit when we think we're smarter than God.

To sinners (and that includes us all), wisdom is not natural. It is one of humanity's most profoundly important quests. Perhaps there are few more significant questions than this: "Where is wisdom to be found?" It is hard for us to gain wisdom by research or experience because they are filtered and interpreted by our own foolish hearts! It is here where the Bible greets us with a radical, counterintuitive message. You can't buy wisdom. You can't get it by hard work or lots of experience. No, wisdom is the result of *rescue* and *relationship*. To be wise, you first need to be rescued from you. You need to be given a new heart, one that is needy, humble, seeking, and ready to get from above what you can't find on this earth. And then you need to be brought into a relationship with the One who *is* wisdom. Colossians 2:3 says of Jesus, "in [him] are hidden all the treasures of wisdom and knowledge." Think of this: grace has connected you to the One who is wisdom. Grace has caused wisdom to live inside you. This means that wisdom is always with you and is always available to you.

The One who is wisdom now guides you. Wisdom protects you. Wisdom convicts you. Wisdom teaches and matures you. Wisdom encourages and comforts you. Wisdom works to change your thoughts and redirect your desires. Wisdom forgives your past and holds your future in his hands. And wisdom will welcome you into an eternity where foolishness will be no more. Today you will once again demonstrate your need for wisdom's work. Don't resist. Reach out for help with a thankful heart; wisdom has come to be with you forever.

For further study and encouragement: Proverbs 2

JULY 15

You were hardwired to depend on God, so your dreams of self-reliance and self-sufficiency will prove to be more nightmares than dreams.

Why is it so hard for so many of us to ask for help? Why is it so difficult for us to admit that we don't know things? Why do we attempt to do things that we've never done before without seeking instruction? Why is it so hard for us to admit that we can't make it on our own? Why do we struggle to own our weakness and our ignorance? Why do children resist the instruction of their parent? Why do workers hate to be told what to do by their bosses? Why do we not like to ask for directions? Why do we work so hard to present ourselves as more ready, knowledgeable, and capable than we really are? Why do we often push people away when they are offering assistance? Why do we tell people that we're okay when we're not? Why do we act as if we can solve things that we don't really understand? Why do we hesitate to get the advice of the doctor, the counselor, or the wise friend? Why do we allow independence to trouble our trouble? Why?

The answer seems too straightforward and simplistic, but it is the answer nonetheless. The answer to every one of the questions above is *sin*. Self-reliance and self-sufficiency are what sin does to the heart. Hosea 10:13 captures this very powerfully: "You have plowed iniquity; you have reaped injustice; you have eaten the fruit of lies. Because you have trusted in your own way and in the multitude of your warriors." Don't miss the cause-and-effect structure of this passage. The prophet essentially asks: "Why have you experienced moral impurity? Why have you endured injustice? Why have you accepted what is not true?" There is only one possible answer to these questions, and it's not the one we want to hear. All of these things happened, the prophet says, because you wanted and trusted your own way and relied upon your own strength.

It is hard to accept, but vital to humbly admit. Bad things happen when we attempt to live as we were not created to live. Sin causes us to deny our need for God and others. Sin causes us to assign to ourselves the wisdom, strength, and righteousness we do not have. Sin causes us to dethrone God and enthrone ourselves. Sin is shockingly proud and self-assured. Sin really does cause us all to fall into the delusion that we can be like God. And because sin does this to all of us, it is dark, deceitful, and dangerous. Self-reliance and self-sufficiency as your fundamental approach to life will never lead to anything good. Sin always leads to death of some kind in some way. So we need to be rescued from our quest for independence and brought into relationship with the One who really does have everything we need. And that's exactly what the grace of Jesus does for us!

For further study and encouragement: James 3:13–16

JULY 16

Justification is the only foundation for personal transformation.
Personal transformation never results in justification.

"For the grace of God has appeared, bringing salvation for all people, training us to renounce ungodliness and worldly passions, and to live self-controlled, upright, and godly lives in the present age, waiting for our blessed hope, the appearing of the glory of our great God and Savior Jesus Christ, who gave himself up for us to redeem us from all lawlessness and to purify for himself a people for his own possession who are zealous for good works" (Titus 2:11–14).

You could not find a more confrontive, humbling, and encouraging passage. First, it confronts us with this reality—there is no way we can win acceptance with God by means of self-reformation and acts of righteousness. Our relationship with God is always the result of his initiative and not ours. He gave himself up for us. He redeemed us. He takes us as his possession. He purifies us. Why does he exercise his sovereign initiative in this way? He does it because there is no other way. Personal righteousness never precedes personal justification. If it is, in fact, God's grace that causes us to reject ungodliness, to run from worldly passions, and to live in self-controlled and upright ways, then without that grace, we're a moral mess. Justification is never God recognizing and responding to our purity and righteousness, because without his transforming grace, we don't have any. What you and I bring to our relationship with God is desperate spiritual and moral need. We come to him dirtied and burdened by our worldliness, ungodliness, and lack of self-control. We need the power of his justifying and transforming grace to wash us clean and empower us to live in the way that we were created to live.

He takes us. He justifies us. He cleanses us. He transforms us. He empowers us. He infuses us with eternal hope. He makes us his people. None of these things would happen to us if he had not willingly given himself for us, because we had no inclination or ability to do them on our own. So you and I are left with no reason to boast and every reason to give ourselves to thankful worship. And you and I have every reason to be encouraged, because this Redeemer has not acted on our behalf just once. He has acted, he is acting, and he will continue to act until we stand before him as his people, completely pure forever and ever.

You see, if you and I could have done these things for ourselves, the life, sacrifice, death, and resurrection of Jesus would not have been necessary. The most precious of things in our lives, our relationship with God, we did not earn. It is the eternal, transformative gift of his grace.

For further study and encouragement: Ephesians 1:3–14

JULY 17

Sin causes me to be all too convinced of my
righteousness and too focused on your sin.

It's a searing rebuke, hard words that capture the scary self-righteousness of sin:

> And to the angel of the church in Laodicea write: "The words of the Amen, the
> faithful and true witness, the beginning of God's creation.
>   "I know your works: you are neither cold nor hot. Would that you were ei-
> ther cold or hot! So, because you are lukewarm, and neither hot nor cold, I will
> spit you out of my mouth. For you say, I am rich, I have prospered, and I need
> nothing, not realizing that you are wretched, pitiable, poor, blind, and naked. I
> counsel you to buy from me gold refined by fire, so that you may be rich, and
> white garments so that you may clothe yourself and the shame of your naked-
> ness may not be seen, and salve to anoint your eyes, so that you may see. Those
> whom I love, I reprove and discipline, so be zealous and repent." (Rev. 3:14–19)

Here's the problem that these hard words are addressing in a warning that we
all need to hear: you and I like to think that no one has a clearer, more accurate view
of us than we do. We all tend to be way too trusting of our view of ourselves. We
do this because we do not take seriously what the Bible says about the dynamic of
spiritual blindness. If sin is deceitful (and it is), if sin blinds (and it does), then as long
as sin still lurks inside me, there will be patches of spiritual blindness. I simply will
not see myself with the accuracy that I think I do. In the language of poverty and
riches, the passage above basically says, "You look at yourself and you think you're
okay, but you're far from okay."

Not only does sin blind, but as sinners, we participate in our own blindness. We
all swindle ourselves into thinking that we are better than we are, that what we're
doing is okay when, in fact, it's not okay in the eyes of God. The spiritual reality
is that we're like naked homeless people, but we see ourselves as affluent and well-
dressed. It's an embarrassing and humbling word picture. It confronts us with how
deeply distorted and delusional our view of ourselves can be. Don't be defensive as
you read this; take in the warning.

So here's what happens. When you think that you have this righteousness thing
licked, then you quit being concerned about you and you focus your concern on the
sins of others. You really need to know that you're in spiritual trouble when you're
more concerned about the sin of the person next to you than you are with your
own. Spiritual clear-sightedness always leads to personal grief and confession, not
condemnation of your neighbor. Perhaps your eyes are more closed than you think
they are. Perhaps you don't know yourself as well as you think you do. Pray for the
sweet, loving, sight-giving, convicting ministry of the Holy Spirit. His presence in
you is a grace.

For further study and encouragement: Revelation 2–3

JULY 18

*God's grace calls you to suffer and it calls you to wait, but it never
calls you to stand in your own strength or to stand alone.*

The Bible never denies reality. The Bible never plays it safe. The Bible never offers you
a cosmetized view of the fallen world. The Bible never tricks you into thinking that
things are better than they are. The Bible is straightforward and honest but not void
of hope. While it is very candid about the hardships of life in this broken world, the
Bible is also gloriously hopeful. The honesty does not crush the hope, but neither
does the hope negate the honesty. Psalm 28 is a good example of the important
harmony of these two themes:

To you, O LORD, I call;
   my rock, be not deaf to me,
lest, if you be silent to me,
   I become like those who go down
      to the pit.
Hear the voice of my pleas for mercy,
   when I cry to you for help,
when I lift up my hands
   toward your most holy sanctuary.

Do not drag me off with the wicked,
   with the workers of evil,
who speak peace with their
      neighbors
   while evil is in their hearts.
Give to them according to their work
   and according to the evil of their
      deeds;
give to them according to the work
   of their hands;
   render them their due reward.
Because they do not regard the
   works of the LORD

or the work of his hands,
he will tear them down and build
   them up no more.

Blessed be the LORD!
   For he has heard the voice of my
      pleas for mercy.
The LORD is my strength and my
      shield;
   in him my heart trusts, and I am
      helped;
my heart exults,
   and with my song I give thanks
      to him.

The LORD is the strength of his
      people;
   he is the saving refuge of his
      anointed.
Oh, save your people and bless your
      heritage!
   Be their shepherd and carry them
      forever."

This psalm of trouble ends up being a psalm of shining hope. That's the story
of the life of every believer, because you and I are never alone in our trouble. The
"saving refuge" is always with us!

For further study and encouragement: Psalm 35

JULY 19

God puts you in hard moments when you cry out for
his comfort so that your heart becomes tender to
those near you who need the same comfort.

Sometimes we are quicker to judge than to comfort. This hit me not too long ago on the streets of Philadelphia, where I live. I walked by a young homeless person who was begging on the street, and I immediately thought, "I wonder what you did to get yourself here." Criticism came more quickly to me than compassion. Hard-heartedness is more natural for us than I think we like to admit. We're that way with our children when we yell at them as if we're shocked that they're struggling with the same things we struggled with when we were their ages. We're that way when we look down on the parents who can't seem to control their children in restaurants or on those who have trouble paying their bills. It is a function of the self-righteousness that, in some ways, still lives inside all of us. When we have named ourselves as strong, wise, capable, mature, and righteous, we tend to look down on those who have not achieved what we think we have.

So God humbles us. He puts us in situations where our weakness, foolishness, and immaturity are exposed. I remember how I struggled with the sovereignty of God in the painful days after my father's death. I had previously prided myself in how well I understood and could communicate this important doctrine, but there I was, grappling with God's plan. At street level, my dad's story made no sense to me. I wondered what in the world God was doing. It all looked chaotic and out of control. It was humbling to admit to my struggle, but doing so caused me to be much more sensitive to and patient with others who struggle with God's rule in hard moments in their lives.

Here is how Paul captures this in 2 Corinthians 1: "Blessed be the God and Father of our Lord Jesus Christ, the Father of mercies and God of all comfort, who comforts us in all our affliction, so that we may be able to comfort those who are in any affliction, with the comfort with which we ourselves are comforted by God. . . . If we are afflicted, it is for your comfort and salvation; and if we are comforted, it is for your comfort" (vv. 3–6). The hard moments are not just for your growth in grace, but for your call to be a tool of that same grace in the life of another sufferer. In difficulty, God is softening your heart and sharpening your edges so that you may be ready to make the comfort of the invisible Father visible in the life of the weary pilgrim he has placed in your pathway. God intends for you to give away the comfort you've been given. The grace that has given you hope is meant to spill over into hope for the person next to you. What a plan!

For further study and encouragement: 2 Corinthians 1:3–11

JULY 20

*Grace doesn't help you just to do different things but to become a
totally different person by changing you at the level of your heart.*

I want to refer you right now to one of the Bible's best-known prayers of confession. The problem is that it's so familiar to most of us that we've quit giving it the examination that it requires in order for us to receive from it the rescue that it offers. The confession is David's in Psalm 51:1–12:

Have mercy on me, O God,
  according to your steadfast love;
according to your abundant mercy
  blot out my transgressions.
Wash me thoroughly from my
    iniquity,
  and cleanse me from my sin!

For I know my transgressions,
  and my sin is ever before me.
Against you, you only, have I sinned
  and done what is evil in your
    sight,
so that you may be justified in your
    words
  and blameless in your judgment.
Behold, I was brought forth in
    iniquity,
  and in sin did my mother
    conceive me.
Behold, you delight in truth in the
    inward being,
  and you teach me wisdom in the
    secret heart.

Purge me with hyssop, and I shall be
    clean;
  wash me, and I shall be whiter
    than snow.
Let me hear joy and gladness;
  let the bones that you have
    broken rejoice.
Hide your face from my sins,
  and blot out all my iniquities.
Create in me a clean heart, O God,
  and renew a right spirit
    within me.
Cast me not away from your
    presence,
  and take not your Holy Spirit
    from me.
Restore to me the joy of your
    salvation,
  and uphold me with a willing
    spirit.

Look carefully at the words of David's prayer. This is not only a prayer of confession—it is also a cry for change. He admits that his problem is not environmental, but natal; he came into the world with it. He confesses that his problem is not external, but internal; it's a problem of the "inward being." So he cries out for what every sinner needs: a new heart. It is something only God can create. It is the epicenter of his work of grace. He wants more than reformed behavior; he sent his Son to die for you so that you would have a new heart, one that is constantly being renewed. If your heart is your problem, then the grace of heart change is your only hope.

For further study and encouragement: Matthew 15:10–20

JULY 21

You simply can't debate it—God's way is better than your way.
His plan is infinitely better than any plan you would have for yourself.

I was so discouraged. I was through. I had planned my exit and was pretty certain about where I would land next. The plan looked good to me, much better than what I had been going through. I was going to exit the nightmare and go live the dream. The problem was that God had a much, much better plan for me. I thought I knew better. I thought I knew exactly what was coming next. I had written the next chapter of my story. But I had forgotten that someone else was the author.

I had been chasing my ministry dream, but I didn't know it. Nothing had worked out according to my little self-oriented plan. I wasn't appreciated in the way that I thought I deserved to be appreciated, and there was much more trouble in our little church than I had ever thought I would encounter. The dream had become a nightmare, so I thought the wisest thing to do was to get out quickly and make a fresh start. But God had another plan.

At the end of the service where I announced my resignation, the oldest man in our congregation waited on the porch of the church for me. We were the last two to leave. He came up to me and asked if he could speak to me, then said: "We know you're discouraged and we know you're a bit immature, but we haven't asked you to leave. Where is the church going to get mature pastors if the immature ones leave?" God had interrupted my plan. I knew immediately that he was right. I knew immediately I was running because my dream had blown up in my face. And I knew right there, right then that I could not leave. I went home and told my wife that we couldn't leave and I called my elders and asked to rescind my resignation.

I stayed for many more years—years of growth in both grace and ministry. Nothing I have experienced since would have happened if I had left. All the blessings and trials of ministry that have enabled me to do what I now do would have been missed. I was going to jump ship and leave pastoral ministry. But thankfully I am not the author of my own personal story.

Your story isn't an autobiography either. Your story is a biography of wisdom and grace written by another. Every turn he writes into your story is right. Every twist of the plot is for the best. Every new character or unexpected event is a tool of his grace. Each new chapter advances his purpose. "Whoever is wise, let him understand these things; whoever is discerning, let him know them; for the ways of the LORD are right" (Hos. 14:9). It is almost a gross understatement to say that God's ways are better. How could they not be? He is infinite in wisdom and grace!

For further study and encouragement: Psalm 118

JULY 22

Corporate worship is designed to move the meditation of your heart from self-centered complaint to God-glorifying praise.

Every day of your life you will find reasons to complain and every day of your life you will have reasons to be thankful. These two themes, complaint and gratitude, pull at the heart of each of us. They form fundamentally different ways of viewing the world because they are rooted in fundamentally different ways of viewing yourself. What is your default language? Do you find it easier to complain than to give thanks? Is grumbling the ambient noise of your existence? Are you easily irritated and quickly impatient? Do mundane things get under your skin? Would the people who live nearest to you characterize you as a thankful person or a complaining person? Do you look at your world and find yourself blown away at the many reasons you have every day to give thanks? Do you see yourself as one who has been showered with blessings? Are you humbled by the myriad things in your life that you regularly enjoy, but that you could never argue that you deserve? How often do you whisper thanks to God or communicate thanks to those around you?

I made a provocative statement above that you may have missed. I said that the lifestyle of complaint and that of gratitude are both rooted in the way you view yourself. Complaint really is an identity issue. If you have placed yourself in the center of your world, if you have reduced your active field of concern down to the small confines of your wants, your needs, and your feelings, if it really is all about you, then you will live with an entitled, "I deserve _____" attitude, and because you do, you will have constant reason to complain. You will be constantly focused on what you want, you will have an inflated sense of what you need, and you will be all too conscious of how you feel, so you will grumble your way through life. Why? You will grumble because the reality is that you are not at the center; life is not about you. The universe doesn't operate to satisfy your desires. It is a dark and discouraging way to live. But if you humbly admit that as a sinner you deserve nothing but God's wrath, that in acts of outrageous grace he has turned his face of mercy and kindness toward you, and that every good thing in your life is an undeserved blessing, you will find reasons to be grateful everywhere you look. Feelings of need and thankfulness rather than entitlement and disappointment will fill your heart.

This is where corporate worship helps profoundly. The regular gathering of God's people for worship serves to shift your meditation from complaint to gratitude by reminding you of who you really are and confronting you with the beautiful and faithful mercy of God toward you. As the gospel puts you in your place, it also puts praise in your mouth, and that is a very good thing.

For further study and encouragement: Philippians 4:4–9

JULY 23

God will call you to do what you cannot do,
but will provide everything you need to do it.

Noah didn't have the power to get all those animals into that ark, but the Lord provided what was necessary for it to happen.

Joseph didn't have the ability to preserve his life and put himself in a position of power in Egypt, but the Lord made it happen.

Moses didn't have what it takes to free the Israelites from their slavery in Egypt, but the Lord empowered him to lead them to the Promised Land.

The Israelites didn't have the means to get across the Red Sea, but the Lord parted the waters for them.

The pilgrims in the wilderness had no means of feeding and sustaining themselves, but the Lord provided everything they needed.

The children of Israel had no means of defeating the walled city of Jericho, but the Lord gave them victory.

David had no personal power to overcome Goliath, but the Lord gave him courage and strength in the Valley of Elah.

Shadrach, Meshach, and Abednego had no ability to keep themselves from burning up in that fiery furnace, but the Lord preserved their lives.

The disciples had no means of feeding the hungry crowd that had gathered to hear Jesus, but he fed them well from a little boy's lunch.

Paul had no ability to preserve himself and those who were with him from shipwreck, but the Lord exercised his power so that none were lost.

The apostles had no ability to take the gospel of Jesus Christ to the known world, but the Lord gifted them and provided for them so that they could do so.

You and I have no natural abilities to rise and do what God calls us to do, but he refuses to leave us to our own resources. He is not so unwise, unkind, or unfaithful as to ever call us to a task without enabling us to do it. I am not able to love my wife the way Jesus loves the church, but I am not left by God to my own character and strength. I am not able to keep my heart pure, so God fills me with his empowering Spirit. You see, what 2 Peter 1:3 says is really true: we have been given everything we need for life and godliness. The God who calls us to a radical new way of living meets us with radical empowering grace. Have courage. Be active. Your Savior really is your strength.

For further study and encouragement: Nehemiah 6

JULY 24

Don't be discouraged today. No matter how alone you
feel, you've been blessed with the Father's love.

Do you feel alone today? Are there ways in which you feel alienated and unloved? Do you feel misrepresented or misunderstood? Do you feel passed by and taken for granted? Do you feel broken and in need of repair? Do you struggle to find reasons to continue? Do you wonder if it's worth it? Does it seem that there's no one to share your heart with? Do you sometimes wonder whether anyone cares? When the waves of loneliness and discouragement roll over you, where do you run, where do you hide?

I love the depiction of God's tender care in Isaiah 42:3: "A bruised reed he will not break, and a faintly burning wick he will not quench." What a beautiful word picture! Imagine walking through the bush and coming across a young tree with a bent and almost broken limb hanging at a rather grotesque angle. You spontaneously complete the job, ripping the limb completely off. Your heavenly Father would never, ever be that thoughtless. He wouldn't think of breaking you the rest of the way. He comes to you in grace to comfort, strengthen, encourage, and restore. His love toward you is tender and faithful. He is near you when it seems no one else is. He will care for you when no one else does. He will heal your wounds when no one around you seems to see how wounded you are. He will never mock or take advantage of your weakness. He will not let you go unnoticed or disregarded. If you are his child, it is impossible for you to be alone and unloved because your heavenly Father is with you and reaches out to you in tender, restoring love.

Imagine that the final little flame on the stick that is giving you light is faintly flickering and about to die. In an act of impatience and frustration, you reach out with your finger and snuff the final life out of it. Your heavenly Father would never think of doing that to you. In grace, he comes to you as a life-giver, not a life-destroyer. When your hope is fading and your faith is weak, he is not impatient and he does not grow frustrated. His beautiful mercy breathes life into your heart and vitality into your soul. He is slow to anger and abounding in mercy. He is the source of all true compassion. He really is the Father of comfort. He is a tender High Priest who is touched by our feeling of weakness and offers us just the mercy we need in our time of need. He is the ever-faithful friend. He is the Father who invites us onto his lap to be comforted by his love. Yes, life can be very hard, people can be very cruel, and there are times when you are left alone, but you are never completely alone because your Father is with you in tender restorative love.

For further study and encouragement: Hebrews 5:1–5

JULY 25

Today you'll wonder if you'll have enough, or you'll tell yourself,
"The Lord will provide" and in faith you'll move forward.

To live the way you have been called and graced to live, you have to know your address. You have to understand what it means to live where you live every day. For example, if you live in the city, you know that parking is going to be a problem. If you live in the suburbs, you know you'll have a big yard that will require maintenance. If you live in the inner city, you may need to be aware of the dangers on the streets at night. If you live in an old house, you can be sure that you'll need to hone your carpentry, electricity, and plumbing skills, because some parts of the structure are going to give way. The same is true spiritually. It is essential that you understand the implications of living where you live or you'll find yourself confused and unprepared over and over again.

You and I live between the "already" and the "not yet." Jesus has made the ultimate sacrifice. The wisdom of the Word has been placed in your hands. The Holy Spirit has come to live inside you. But the work of God in you, for you, and through you has not yet been completed. This means that sin has not yet been fully eradicated and you are not yet all that grace will transform you to be. The last enemy of God has not yet been placed under the powerful foot of the Messiah. So the moral battle still rages. The spiritual war still goes on. That means you need to understand that you live in a war zone. And you need to be very clear on this—that great spiritual war is fought on the turf of your heart and it's fought for control of your soul. Your life is lived every day in the middle of that war. It's a war of doubt and faith. It's a war of submission and rebellion. It's a war of anxiety and trust. It's a war of wisdom and foolishness. It's a war of hope and despair. It's a war of allegiance and disloyalty. It's a war.

Perhaps the epicenter of that war is this question: "Will the Lord do what he has promised?" Will the Lord provide? Can I step out in faith and courage, knowing that the Lord is with me and will provide what I need when I need it? Or do I have to worry that, when it comes to push and shove, I won't have enough? Should I be afraid or is God trustworthy?

When you hit hard times, when your weakness is exposed, be ready for the enemy to whisper in your ear, "Where is your God now?" and be ready to respond, "He is where he has been and always will be—with me in power, glory, and grace." You won't always feel his nearness, but you can rest assured he will never abandon you. He is the One who said, "Behold, I am with you always" (Matt. 28:20), and he never goes back on his word.

For further study and encouragement: Psalm 22

JULY 26

Why would you be afraid when in Christ you have been completely accepted, eternally forgiven, and richly supplied?

What are the three questions that everyone has asked and is in some way haunted by?

1. Will I be loved?
2. Will people tolerate me once they really get to know me?
3. Will I have what I need to live?

In some way, everyone fears rejection, judgment, and poverty. In some way, every person who has ever lived is on a hunt for love and scared to death that he won't find it. That's why a good love story is always so popular. In some way, everyone fears judgment. She fears the hammer will come down on her because she has failed to measure up and she will spend her life paying for her crimes. That's why mercy and forgiveness stories quickly get our attention and hit us so deeply. In some way, everyone is afraid of being poor. We're all afraid of not having the provisions we need to live. We're afraid that success will escape our grasp and we'll end up as beggars on the street. This is why we all love a "rags-to-riches story."

Isn't it amazing that each of these fundamental human fears is addressed and solved by the gospel of the Lord Jesus Christ? First, the gospel is the world's best love story. It is a story of a God of love who places his love on people who do not deserve his love. This God sends the Son of his love to make a sacrifice of love so that his children can be welcomed into his arms of love and become a community of love that takes his love to those in desperate need of that love.

The gospel of Jesus Christ is the world's most amazing forgiveness story. It is the story of One who was willing to die for crimes he did not commit so that the people who committed those crimes would be fully and completely forgiven of every wrong they had done or would ever do. It is the amazing story of a righteous God who made a way through the sacrifice of his Son to forgive rebels against his authority without compromising his holiness in any way.

The gospel of Jesus Christ is the greatest of all provision stories. It is a story of a God who created, controls, and owns everything opening his vast storehouse of provision to impoverished rebels who deserve nothing but who get everything in him. It is a story of no needed provision withheld and no necessary gift left ungiven. It is a story of a stream of supply that will never, ever run out.

If you are God's child, you don't have to be haunted by these deep questions of life. Each has been answered in the person and work of your Savior, the Lord Jesus Christ. Because of him, you are loved; because of him, you are forgiven; and because of him, you have everything that you need. Who but our God could write a story like this?

For further study and encouragement: Philippians 4:10–20

JULY 27

*Since by grace God forgives, it makes no sense to hide, excuse,
or shift the blame when you are faced with your sin.*

Here's the bottom line when it comes to moral candor—denial is rooted in fear and confession is rooted in hope. You cannot embrace the radical hope of the person and work of the Lord Jesus Christ and make sense out of our drive to present ourselves as less than needy. But that instinct is alive and well in many of us. When faced with our sin, we immediately excuse ourselves or shift the blame. When our consciences bother us, we hide the wrong that we have done like Adam and Eve hiding from God in the garden, or we try to convince ourselves that what we did was not so bad after all.

Now, because God's world is so big, there will always be places to hide, and because you live in a world that doesn't operate as God intended, there will always be people and things to blame, but it is all one big, sad, irrational lie. Why would you and I work so hard to hide or deny what has been fully, completely, and eternally forgiven? Why would we work so hard to pretend that we are something less than sinners when the message of the gospel is that Jesus loves and accepts sinners? Why would we hide in guilt when Jesus has fully borne our guilt? Why would we allow ourselves to be motivated by shame when Jesus willingly carried our shame? Why would we construct a false façade of righteousness when Jesus has given his righteousness over to our account? Why would we fear God's wrath when Jesus took the full brunt of God's anger for us on the cross? Why would we care what others will think of us if we're honest about our sin when the One who holds our destiny in his hands has accepted us as if we had never sinned? Why deny who we are and what we need when full provision has been made? Why act as if we're something that we're not when grace has met us right where we are? Why act as if no one would understand when we have been given a faithful and understanding High Priest who is sympathetic with all our weaknesses? Why act as if there is no hope for people like us when our Savior has conquered sin and death for us? Why sing the truths of the gospel on Sunday and functionally deny the gospel during the week in street-level acts of denial, excusing, and blame? Why would you defend yourself when a loved one points out a wrong or excuse yourself when you are caught? Why, in the face of wrong, would you work to soften the pain of conviction by debating the Holy Spirit's gracious prompting?

Paul encouraged the believers in Colossae to "continue in the faith, stable and steadfast, not shifting from the hope of the gospel that you heard" (Col. 1:23). Forsake excusing, denial, and all other acts of gospel irrationality that minimize your sin. That way, you will never forget the awesome hope that you have been given in Jesus.

For further study and encouragement: Philippians 3:1–11

JULY 28

Grace frees you from faking what you don't have
and boasting about what you didn't earn.

Faking is a big part of the culture of fallen humanity. Maybe you fake it when you tell a story in such a way that it makes you way more of a hero than when the incident actually happened. Perhaps you fake it when you make your job seem more important than it really is. Maybe you fake it when you finagle your way into buying a house that is way pricier than you can responsibly afford. Maybe you fake it when you try to work your way into friendships with people who are far more affluent and positioned than you'll ever be. Perhaps your fakery is best seen when you act as if you have much more theological understanding than you really have or are much more committed to ministry than you really are. Perhaps you fake it when you present your marriage as being far more mature and peaceful than it's ever been. Or maybe you're a fake when you fail to reach out for help when you are at the end of your rope as a parent. Maybe your fakery is your unwillingness to confess to the person next to you that you struggle with the same area of sin that he or she has just confessed to. Maybe your fakery is in the big boundary that you have built between your polished public persona and the messier details of your private life. Maybe you fake yourself all the time by telling yourself that you're more righteous than you are.

Here's the question that you need to wrestle with: "Is there someplace or some way in my life where I'm a fake?" Is there someplace where, to yourself or others, you pretend to be something that you're not or where you boast about something you didn't actually do? I think there are artifacts of fakery in all of our lives because there is a desire in all of our hearts to be more independently wise, righteous, and strong than we really are.

"For by grace you have been saved through faith. And this is not your own doing; it is the gift of God, not a result of works, so that no one may boast" (Eph. 2:8–9). Praise God that his grace frees all of his children from their bondage to fakery. Why is this so? God's grace offers you what you did not earn and forgives you for the wrongs you actually did. Grace radically alters your identity and your hope. Your identity is not in what you have achieved or in what the people around you think of what you have achieved. No, as a result of grace, your identity is rooted in the achievements of another. Your hope is not based on how well you are doing, but on what Jesus has done for you. Grace invites you to be real and honest. Grace allows you to live free of false hope and the faux identity of human fakery once and for all, and to rest in the honest and stable identity you have found in Jesus and his eternal work on your behalf.

For further study and encouragement: Matthew 6:1–4

JULY 29

Fish were designed to swim, the sun to shine, and you to worship God.
Grace welcomes you back to what you were designed for—worship.

If someone were to ask you what the ultimate, final goal of God's grace is, what would you answer? What is God's grace working to accomplish? God's grace can make you more financially wise. God's grace can make you a better citizen and neighbor. God's grace can cause you to be more responsible with the use of your body and more sexually pure. God's grace can help you to make better decisions in life. God's grace can assist you to communicate in a way that is less selfish and more loving toward others. God's grace can help you to think more about the future and rescue you from living just for the here and now. God's grace can make you more thankful and a better steward of what you have been given. God's grace can cause you to be a wiser and more patient parent. God's grace can help you to forge a healthier marriage. God's grace can enable you to be more honest with yourself and more forgiving in your dealings with others. God's grace can make you less anxious and more courageous. God's grace can give you a reason to get up in the morning even when things aren't going well. God's grace can pilot you through disappointment and give you joy even when you're suffering. God's grace can enable you to remember what is worth remembering and to put away what you need to forget. God's grace can make you more compassionate and less bitter. God's grace can help you to know you are loved even when you're alone and to know you have strength even when you are weak. All of these things are the beautiful harvest of grace. All of these are things for which we should be eternally thankful. But none of these good gifts is the ultimate goal of God's grace. Focus on the following words from Romans 1:18–23:

> For the wrath of God is revealed from heaven against all ungodliness and unrighteousness of men, who by their unrighteousness suppress the truth. For what can be known about God is plain to them, because God has shown it to them. For his invisible attributes, namely, his eternal power and divine nature, have been clearly perceived, ever since the creation of the world, in the things that have been made. So they are without excuse. For although they knew God, they did not honor him as God or give thanks to him, but they became futile in their thinking, and their foolish hearts were darkened. Claiming to be wise, they became fools, and exchanged the glory of the immortal God for images resembling mortal man and birds and animals and creeping things.

Here is the bottom line: sin kidnapped our worship, and grace works to restore it to its rightful owner—God. It is only when God is in his rightful place in our hearts that everything else is in its appropriate place in our lives, and only powerful grace can accomplish this.

For further study and encouragement: Deuteronomy 10:12–22

JULY 30

*What could be a greater, higher honor than to be a chosen instrument
for the most important renewal project in the universe—redemption?*

Now the eleven disciples went to Galilee, to the mountain to which Jesus had
directed them. And when they saw him they worshiped him, but some doubted.
And Jesus came and said to them, "All authority in heaven and on earth has been
given to me. Go therefore and make disciples of all nations, baptizing them in
the name of the Father and of the Son and of the Holy Spirit, teaching them to
observe all that I have commanded you. And behold, I am with you always, to
the end of the age." (Matt. 28:16–20)

Christ's commission to the disciples is his commission to the church and is his
plan for the life of every single believer. No one has been chosen to be just a recipient of the redemptive work of his kingdom. No, everyone who has been chosen to
be a recipient has also been commissioned to be an instrument of the work of that
kingdom as well. The work of evangelism, the spiritual growth work of the church
and the cause of worldwide missions, was never designed by the Redeemer to be
shouldered by a small collection of paid religious professionals. Does God set people
apart for ministry? Of course he does! But their role is not just to do ministry, but
to mobilize, train, and equip all of God's people for the great honor and privilege
of publishing his amazing grace wherever they are. It is sad that so many of God's
people spend their lives searching for some significant endeavor to give themselves to
when they have been chosen to be part of the most powerfully transformative work
in the history of the universe.

Part of our problem is that we tend to carry around with us an unbiblical definition of ministry that allows us to live comfortably as Christian consumers. We think
of ministry this way: we have our little private lives that belong to us, and we step out
of our lives into moments of ministry and then step back into our lives after those
ministry initiatives are over. The fact of the matter is that since we have been bought
with the blood of Jesus, our lives don't belong to us anymore. They are his possession for his use. This means that our life *is* ministry and ministry *is* our life. There is
no real separation between life and ministry. That means we live, work, relate, play,
and relax with a ministry mentality. It means I am always thinking about how to be
part of what God is doing in the locations where he places me. This means my connection to the work of the body of Christ is not that I'm the attender of something,
but rather that I am a participant in something along with everyone else. I am part
of God's "all of my people, all of the time" redemptive plan. The greatest honor
of my life is that I have been chosen to be both a recipient and an instrument. This
has given my life deeper meaning than anything I could have discovered on my own.
This is what grace alone can do.

For further study and encouragement: Matthew 5:13–16

JULY 31

Grace not only forgives you, but enables you to live for something hugely bigger than yourself. Why go back to your little kingdom of one?

Your spiritual life is all about inertia. It's all about inner motivations. It's all about kingdoms. It's all about warfare. It's way bigger than the surface Christianity to which it is often reduced. You could read your Bible every day and the entire Bible each year and still live for yourself. You could be faithful in your attendance at all your church's scheduled gatherings and still live for your little kingdom. You could regularly place your hard-earned money in the plate and still not live with God's kingdom in view. You could be expert in the theology of the Word of God and still shrink your life down to what you want and what you tell yourself that you need. You could participate in ministries to the poor and needy and still not live for the big kingdom. You could do all of these things, and the trajectory of your life could still be more toward the kingdom of self than the kingdom of God.

The only exhibit that is needed to demonstrate that true spirituality is about something more than public and formal acts of religion is the Pharisees. Jesus said something striking about the religion of the Pharisees: "For I tell you, unless your righteousness exceeds that of the scribes and Pharisees, you will never enter the kingdom of heaven" (Matt. 5:20). There was something deeply defective, something tragically missing in the religion of the Pharisees that caused Jesus to speak so strongly. What was wrong is captured by the following indictment:

> But woe to you, scribes and Pharisees, hypocrites! For you shut the kingdom of heaven in people's faces. For you neither enter yourselves nor allow those who would enter to go in. . . .
>
> Woe to you, scribes and Pharisees, hypocrites! For you tithe mint and dill and cumin, and have neglected the weightier matters of the law: justice and mercy and faithfulness. These you ought to have done, without neglecting the others. You blind guides, straining out a gnat and swallowing a camel!
>
> Woe to you, scribes and Pharisees, hypocrites! For you clean the outside of the cup and the plate, but inside they are full of greed and self-indulgence. You blind Pharisee! First clean the inside of the cup and the plate, that the outside also may be clean. (Matt. 23:13, 23–26)

The public religious acts of the Pharisees were not the result of deep devotion in their hearts toward God and the work of his kingdom that caused them to live the way they did. No, they did these things in the absence of that devotion. That means they did not do them for God and His kingdom at all. They did them in allegiance to the kingdom of self, for the purpose of personal power and public acclaim. They were acts of righteousness that were not righteous because they did not come from hearts of worship. True Christianity is always a matter of the submission of the heart to God, something that only rescuing grace can produce.

For further study and encouragement: Matthew 25:31–46

AUGUST 1

Hope for the believer is not a dream of what could be, but a confident expectation of a guaranteed result that shapes his life.

We constantly speak in hope language:

- "I hope my company does well."
- "I hope he isn't mad at me."
- "I hope God really does answer prayer."
- "I sure hope it doesn't rain tomorrow."
- "I hope this sickness isn't something serious."

If you are a human being, you hope. You attach your security, your sense of peace and rest to something every day. The question is not whether you hope, but what holds your hope. Take a moment to think about hope with me:

1. *You hope in something.* You could argue that the life of a human being is propelled by hope. From the little momentary hope of the young child for food or a toy to the profound hope of the young adult for meaning and purpose, we all hope. We all place our hope in someone or something, and we ask that person or that thing to deliver something to us. What are you placing your hope in right now?
2. *Hope is a lifestyle.* Your hope shapes the way you live. Your hope causes you to make the decisions that you make. A lack of hope causes you to feel stuck and de-motivated. Confident hope makes you decisive and courageous. Wobbly hope makes you timid and indecisive. Hope is not just something you do with your brain. You always live your hope in some way.
3. *Most of our hopes disappoint us.* We all do it. We place our hope in things in this fallen world that simply can't deliver. Your spouse can't make you happy. Your job won't make you content. Your possessions can't satisfy your heart. Your physical health won't give you inner peace. Your friends can't give you meaning and purpose. When our hopes disappoint us, it is a sign that we've put our hopes in the wrong things.
4. *There are only two places to look for hope.* The theology of hope is quite simple. There are only two places to put your hope. You rest the hope of your life in the hands of the Creator or you look to the creation for hope.
5. *Hope in God is sure hope.* When you hope in the Lord, you not only hope in the One who created and controls the universe, but also in One who is glorious in grace and abounding in love. Now, that's hope that is well placed and will never disappoint.

For further study and encouragement: Psalm 40

AUGUST 2

Yes, you're weak, you're often foolish, and you tend to want your own way, but God's redeeming grace is greater.

Perhaps Isaiah 53:6 is the most accurate diagnostic passage in the Bible: "All we like sheep have gone astray; we have turned—every one—to his own way; and the LORD has laid on him the iniquity of us all."

Now, what you have to see first is that this passage is divided into two parts, *diagnosis* and *cure*. You simply will not be interested in the cure if you haven't accepted the diagnosis, and you have to know that the cure is only as effective as the accuracy of the diagnosis.

The diagnosis: *All have gone astray, each turning to his own way.*

The first thing that should hit you in this diagnosis is that it is all-inclusive. There are no exceptions. It is an accurate description of the heart and life of every person who has ever lived. You and I must forsake our attempts to convince ourselves and others that we are exceptions. Whatever this passage is describing is something we all do. What is it? Well, in some way, we all wander away from the Creator's plan for us. We all find ways to step outside of his boundaries We all do things that he does not want us to do and fail to do what he has called us to do. In fact, we all, in word, thought, or deed, in moments of foolishness, weakness, or self-interest, wander away every day.

The passage says we're like sheep. That's an important element of this diagnosis; sheep wander because they're sheep. It is their nature to do so. So our wandering-away problem is deeper than moments of bad choice and behavior. Our problem is a matter of nature. There is something inside us, something with which we were born, that causes us to wander away from the good and wise will of the Great Shepherd, and the Bible names it—sin. Sin is a matter of our nature before it is ever played out in our behavior. And what does that sin do to us? It causes us to make life all about us, to want little more than our own way, and to live like little self-sovereigns.

What is the solution for people like us? Well, systems of behavior reformation won't work for us because our problem is deeper than behavior. Systems of self-help won't work because we are our own biggest problem. There is only one place to run for help. There is only one place to find a cure. It is only ever found in God's redeeming grace. The grace that placed our iniquity on the Savior, so that we could be both forgiven and delivered, is more powerful than our sinful natures. Our cure is not a system; it is a person, and his name is Jesus! Run to him, he really is all that you need.

For further study and encouragement: Ezekiel 34:11–16

AUGUST 3

The purpose of the cross is to completely decimate your loyalty to the most seductive/powerful of all idols—the idol of self.

You see it in the whines of a little boy, you see it in the entitlement of the teenager, you see it in the needless argument of the married couple over something unimportant, and you see it in the bitterness of the old man. None of us has escaped this disease. It infects all of our hearts. It is the reason for so much of the brokenness, angst, and pain of the human community. It is the foundation of so much unhappiness and generations of war. It is a personal and moral disaster, yet it seduces us all. Its power draws all of us in. We see it in others and deny it in ourselves. It makes for uncomfortable family moments, friendship disloyalty, and violence in the streets. It makes us envious and demanding. It causes discontent to be more natural than thankfulness. It ruins our vacations and holidays. It makes us spend ourselves into hopeless debt, to fall into paralyzing addiction, and to eat more than we ever should. It turns siblings on siblings and makes war-making more natural than peacemaking.

What is this thing that kidnaps us all? It is the selfishness of sin. The idol of idols really is the idol of self. We make it all about us. We put ourselves in the center of the story. We evaluate life from the vantage point of a scary and tragic "me-ism." We pull the borders of our concerns into the narrow confines of what we want, what we feel, what we dream, and what we think we need. A good day is a day that is pleasurable or easy for me. A good circumstance is one in which I get my way. A good marriage is one in which my spouse becomes a servant to my dream for my life. A good church has the worship, programs, and preaching that satisfy me. A good job is one that keeps me happy and engaged. It is a life shaped by a shrunken kingdom of one.

But the first four words of the Bible confront us with the inescapable reality that it is *not* all about us. They confront us with the truth that life comes from, is controlled by, and exists for another. We will never be at the center because God is. It will never be about us because it's about him. Our will won't be done because his will will be done. We won't rule because he rules. Our kingdom won't come because his kingdom will. Life will not submit to us because ultimately all things will submit to him. He is at center stage. He is the spotlit character. Life is not to be found in putting ourselves at the center. That only leads to dysfunction, disappointment, and brokenness. Jesus came to decimate our misplaced loyalty so that we would find freedom from our bondage to ourselves and know the peace that passes understanding. Adam and Eve's rebellion becomes our delusion, and for that there is rescuing grace!

For further study and encouragement: Amos 6:1–9

AUGUST 4

When nothing else or no one else in your life remains and
is faithful, you can rest assured that God will be both.

I love the honesty of the Bible. I love that faith in God doesn't require you and me to play monkey games with reality. I love that the Bible's description of life in this fallen world is accurate and familiar. Psalm 90 is one of the most honest and descriptive psalms. How's this for honesty? "The years of our life are seventy, or even by reason of strength eighty; yet their span is but toil and trouble; they are soon gone, and we fly away" (v. 10). Here's what the psalmist is saying: "Your life will be short and will be marked by difficulty." Not very good news is it? But it's true. You live in a fallen world that itself groans, waiting for redemption. You live with flawed people who think, say, and do wrong things. You live in a place where corruption, immorality, injustice, pollution, and disease still live and do their ugly work. You live in an environment that does not function according to God's original design. Every day is marked by little troubles, and big trouble will enter your door as well.

In all this, you are tempted to feel alone, forsaken, poor, and unable. In all this, you are tempted to wonder whether God exists, let alone if he hears or cares. In your trouble, some people around you are insensitive and unloving. They find your troubles to be too much of a burden. And the people who are sensitive and loving have little power to erase your trouble. This is why the beginning of this psalm of trouble is so important. This honest psalm doesn't begin with trouble; it begins with the most important declaration that anyone who faces trouble could ever hear: "Lord, you have been our dwelling place in all generations. Before the mountains were brought forth, or ever you had formed the earth and the world, from everlasting to everlasting you are God" (vv. 1–2).

If you are God's child, you are not alone. Glorious grace has connected you to the One whose power and love don't shift with the times. Grace has connected you and me to the One who is the ultimate dwelling place, the ultimate place to which we can run. This means that I am never left just to my own resources. I am never left to figure out and deal with life on my own. As God's child, I must never see myself as poor or forsaken. I must never buy into the lie that I have no recourse or hope. I must never think that my life is ruled by my difficulty. I must never give way to despondency or despair. Grace has opened the door of hope and refuge to me by connecting me to One who is eternal and who rules all the circumstances and relationships that would cause me to feel alone.

For further study and encouragement: Psalm 86

AUGUST 5

Today you will convince yourself that you're smarter than God and will write your own rules—or will humbly submit to his wise call.

It's often a subtle thing, going on almost unnoticed, but it has huge implications for the way we live. You and I step over God's boundaries because there are moments in our lives when we are able to convince ourselves that we are smarter than God. We tell ourselves that what he says is wrong, isn't so wrong after all. We convince ourselves that we can disobey God and it will all work out in the end. We tell ourselves that our way is better than God's way. The big lie that fuels all this is that there is life, real life to be found on the other side of the boundaries that the all-knowing, all-wise God has set for us. It is the lie that was first told, embraced, and acted upon in that terrible moment in the garden of Eden. Human beings have fallen into believing that lie ever since.

The psalmist says: "I will never forget your precepts, for by them you have given me life. . . . I have more understanding than all my teachers, for your testimonies are my meditation. . . . The unfolding of your words gives light; it imparts understanding to the simple" (Ps. 119:93, 99, 130). There it is—God's precepts give life. Yet a husband will think that he can be critical and demanding of his wife and their marriage will be okay. Or you will think that you can spend more than you make and your finances will work out in the end. Or I will come to believe that I can permit myself to lust without doing damage to my heart. In a thousand ways, we tell ourselves that somehow, some way we are, or this moment is, an exception to God's rules. It all exposes that we still have wandering hearts that are all too susceptible to the enemy's lies. Our wandering hearts don't always love what God says is good, right, true, lovely, and pure. Sometimes what God says is best doesn't look best to us, and sometimes what God says is evil doesn't appear evil to us. In those moments, we are a danger to ourselves because we have bought into what is completely impossible—that we know more and are wiser than God. It is the height of the delusion of sin. It is a dangerous and destructive moral irrationality. It leads us nowhere good. It never results in the life that we are seeking. Proverbs 16:25 captures this delusion with brief but powerful words: "There is a way that seems right to a man, but its end is the way to death."

This "I'm-smarter-than-God" temptation stands as another argument for our daily need for grace. It is yet another place where we need to be delivered from ourselves. It reminds us again that none of us has outlived our need for the rescuing mercy of an ever-present and ever-willing Redeemer. Run to that mercy once again today.

For further study and encouragement: Proverbs 6:20–23

AUGUST 6

Truth requires you to love and love requires you to be truthful.

Contrary to popular opinion, love and truth don't stand in opposition to one another. In fact, you can't really have one without the other. To love truth, you have to be committed to love, and to love love, you have to be committed to truth. The most loving person who ever lived, so loving that he died a cruel and bloody public death for crimes that others committed, was at the same time the most forthright and honest truth speaker that the world had ever known. It was not just that the love of Jesus never contradicted his candor and his candor never inhibited his love. No, there was something more profound going on. His commitment to truth speaking was propelled by his love.

The biblical call to love will never force you to trim, deny, or bend the truth, and the biblical call to truth will never ask you to abandon God's call to love your neighbor. We see this graphically displayed in a very well-known moment in the life of Jesus Christ. It is recorded in Luke 18:18–30. A rich ruler comes to Jesus to ask him about eternal life. It is a very good question that gets a very hard and honest answer. As you read the conversation, it doesn't look like Jesus is engaging in very successful evangelism by modern standards. In a moment of complete honesty, Jesus doesn't work to make the gospel attractive. Rather, he hones in on and exposes the central idolatry of this man's heart. Jesus tells this man the bad news he needs to hear if he is ever to want the good news he desperately needs. So Luke is recording something very important for us. In the face of Jesus's honesty, the man walks away, and as he does, Jesus looks at him with sadness. You see, Jesus isn't being cold and indifferent. He doesn't lack love. The hard words are motivated by love, and Jesus's sadness at the end of the conversation exposes the love that motivated the words he had said. There is no mean-spirited condemnation in the words of Christ. Those hard words are words of grace, spoken by the Savior of love, spoken to redeem.

Truth isn't mean and love isn't dishonest. They are two sides of the same righteous agenda that longs for the spiritual welfare of another. Truth not spoken in love ceases to be truth because it gets bent and twisted by other human agendas, and love that abandons the truth ceases to be love because it forsakes what is best for the person when it has been corrupted by other motives.

Today you are called to loving honesty and honest love. You will be tempted to let one or the other slip from your hands. Pray for the help of the One who remained fully committed to both, even to death. His grace is your only hope of staying true to his righteous agenda.

For further study and encouragement: 1 Corinthians 13

AUGUST 7

Mercy is what we have been given and what we are called to give.
It is my commitment to suffer with you, just as Christ suffered for me.

Perhaps it is the most normal, most frequent moral contradiction in our lives. Perhaps it is the place where we all stumble the most. Perhaps our failure here demonstrates how much we still need what we so often fail to give to others. How is it possible that we who have been blessed with eternal love far beyond anything that we ever could have hoped to earn could be so regularly unloving to those around us? How could we ever fail to respond in mercy to others when we have been given mercy that is renewed with each new morning? Why are judgment and condemnation often our more natural responses to the sin, weakness, and failure of others than offering them the same grace that we have been given? Why are we so impatient when the extent of God's patience with us stands as one of the redemptive miracles of our lives? Why do we find it so hard to forgive when we have been forgiven at the price of the suffering and death of Jesus? Why can we walk past suffering with little compassion when our lives have been rescued by the tender compassion of the Savior? Why do we resist serving one another when the Lord of all things willingly came and served us even to the point of his death? How is it that we can be so unfaithful and disloyal in the face of the unaltered faithfulness of our heavenly Father? How could we ever lie to our neighbor's harm when we have been blessed with truth that has set us free?

The answer to each of these questions is humbling. We don't always respond to others as the Savior has responded to us because we don't share his heart. Our hearts are not always ruled by what ruled his heart. Our lives are not always motivated by what motivated his. We don't always find joy in what brought him joy. So we lack the mercy that drove and shaped his life.

Our selfish hearts, often more committed to our kingdom purposes than his, want the lavish riches of grace for ourselves, but do not want to have to make sacrifices of grace for others. We see this in the self-righteous anger of a parent, in the bitter unforgiveness of a spouse, in the dysfunctional bickering between neighbors, in divisions in the body of Christ, or in our unfaithfulness in our relationships. The war of kingdoms rages in our hearts, and one of the first casualties is mercy. It is sad but true—our refusal to give grace to others reveals how much we still need grace ourselves. Our failure to forgive shows how much we still need God's moment-by-moment forgiveness. The weakness in our love demonstrates how much our hope still rests on a God who will love us even on our very worst day. Struggles to live the gospel in our relationships with others picture how much we need the rich gospel ourselves. And it all argues that we still don't deserve the favor that we are given daily and are called to give to others who are as undeserving as we are.

For further study and encouragement: James 2:1–13

AUGUST 8

For the believer, obedience is not a pain but a joy. Each act
of obedience celebrates the grace that motivates and empowers it.

I remember my brother Tedd saying it to me, but I didn't realize how right he was: "Obedience is its own reward." It is hard to overestimate the grace that motivates each act of obedience in your life and in mine:

- Sinners tend not to esteem authority.
- Sinners like to write their own rules.
- Sinners are good at convincing themselves that their wrongs are not that wrong.
- Sinners tend to believe in their own autonomy.
- Sinners tend to think they're wiser than they are.
- Sinners tend to have a moral code that is formed more by their desires than by God's law.
- Sinners tend to think that they don't need what they don't desire.
- Sinners tend to be self-focused and self-excusing.
- Sinners tend to crave what God has prohibited.
- Sinners tend to opt for short-term pleasure over long-term gain.
- Sinners tend to rebel rather than submit.

Because all of the above statements are true, it is a miracle of amazing grace that any of us ever chooses to obey God. It is even more a miracle that we can find joy in obeying someone whom we cannot see, hear, or touch. It is a wonder of transforming grace that the heart of a self-focused human being can abandon the pursuit of his own little kingdom and give itself to serve the purposes of the kingdom of another. Any time we desire, in word, thought, or action, to do what pleases God, we are being rescued, transformed, and empowered by his grace. You see, your obedience celebrates grace even in moments when you aren't consciously celebrating it yourself. Each moment of submission to the will of God celebrates this reality: "For sin will have no dominion over you, since you are not under law but under grace" (Rom. 6:14).

So smile when you obey; you are experiencing the riches of grace. Give thanks when you submit; you are being rescued by grace. Celebrate when you make the right choice; you are being transformed by grace. Sing for joy when you serve God's purposes; you have just given evidence of the presence of redeeming grace!

For further study and encouragement: 1 Corinthians 6:1–11

AUGUST 9

*Love is more than being nice to people. It's loving God above
all else so that you love people as he commands you to.*

I am more persuaded every day, as I examine my own relationships and as I observe
others in theirs, that relationships are first fixed vertically before they are ever fixed
horizontally. Paul captures this dynamic in surprising words in Galatians 5: "For the
whole law is fulfilled in one word: 'You shall love your neighbor as yourself'" (v. 14).
Now, think this through with me. If you had just written, "The entire law of God is
summarized by one command," what would you have written next? Well, I would
have written, "Love God above all else." That seems right. Is it not the greatest of
all of God's commands (Mark 12:28–30)? Is it not the command that must always
be first and foremost in our hearts? It seems that good theology would require that
this is the "one word" of which Paul is speaking. But that's not what Paul writes. He
says the entire law is fulfilled by one word, and then he says, "Love your neighbor as
yourself." What? How does that fulfill all that God has called us to as his children?

Paul is on to something very important here. He knows two things. First, he
knows that only people who love God above all else will ever love their neighbors
as themselves. It is only when God is in his rightful place in my heart that you will
be in the appropriate place in my life. This is because, if God is not in his rightful
place, guess who I insert in that place? The answer is easy: myself. In my marriage,
I have had to make this confession—my problem isn't first that I have failed to love
Luella in the way that I should. No, my deeper problem is that I have not loved God
as I should, and because I haven't, I put myself in his position. I make it all about me
and therefore do not love Luella in the way that I should.

Paul knows a second thing: that one of the ways our lack of love for God is
revealed is by the lack of active love that exists in our relationships. John says it this
way: "If anyone says, 'I love God,' and hates his brother, he is a liar; for he who does
not love his brother whom he has seen cannot love God whom he has not seen"
(1 John 4:20). Love for others really begins, continues, and is daily motivated by
love for God. When his purposes are more important than your desires, when his
glory is more valuable to you than your temporary moments of glory, and when
his agenda activates you more than your plan for you, you will be freed from your
bondage to self-love and be freed to love others. It really is true. Our relationships
need more than horizontal fixing. They need vertical rescue, and for that there is the
ever-sufficient grace of a willing and patient Savior.

For further study and encouragement: John 13:1–17

AUGUST 10

God knows everything from beyond origin to beyond destiny.
You have ____ years of sin-tainted human experience.
Why debate him? God's smarter!

It's really amazing how much I don't know:

- I don't know how children from the very same gene pool can be so different.
- I don't know how bees could ever fly.
- I don't know why I do all the things I do.
- I don't know what tomorrow will bring.
- I don't know how long my life will be.
- I don't know the motivations of my heart, let alone the hearts of others.
- I don't know so many things about art, science, and politics.
- I don't know why I wake up happy on some days and morose on others.
- I don't know many things about origins and many things about destiny.
- I don't know many things about the operation of my own body.
- I don't know many things about the function of my own brain.
- I don't know why weeds overtake flowers.
- I don't really understand what makes rain.
- I often don't understand the plan and purpose of God.
- I don't know why God brings certain things into my life.

This is just a brief, spontaneous list of some of the things I don't know. If I were to take the time, I could fill hundreds of pages with lists of things I don't know, and there would still be myriad things not on the pages simply because I don't know that I don't know them. In light of this, it is stunning to know that God knows absolutely everything. Yes, you read it right—*everything*. His knowledge is unsearchable. His grasp on what is has no beginning and no end. He is never confused. He never has to live with misunderstanding. There is nothing that ever surprises him or leaves him perplexed. He never has trouble reconciling one truth with another. He never has to deal with gaps in his knowledge. He is never in the position of wishing he could have the wisdom of another. He never has to relearn something. He never has to admit that what he thought was wrong. No one ever showed him the path of understanding or taught him knowledge (Isa. 40:14). So run from any thought that you are smarter. Consume his wisdom and be thankful for the grace that rescues you from your own foolishness and connects you to One who defines what is wise.

For further study and encouragement: Isaiah 40

AUGUST 11

You disobey not because you lack the God-given grace to obey, but because you love something more than the God who's given you that grace.

Your disobedience is never God's fault. Maybe you're thinking: "Of course it's not, Paul. You don't really think that I think that, do you?" As much as we know theologically that God is not responsible for our behavior, we have subtle ways of shifting the blame to him. We say:

- "If only my pastor was more available in times of need, then I would've . . ."
- "If only I had had a better job at the time, I wouldn't have . . ."
- "If only my parents had been better models for me, I could've . . ."
- "If only I had come to Christ earlier in my life, I'm sure I would've . . ."
- "If only I hadn't gotten sick, there would've . . ."
- "If only my husband had been more romantic, I wouldn't have . . ."
- "If only my children weren't so rebellious, I wouldn't be . . ."
- "If only there weren't so much pornography on the Internet, I wouldn't have been tempted to . . ."
- "If only I weren't so busy, I could take more time to . . ."

If God is present with you everywhere you go (and he is), and if he is sovereign over every situation, relationship, and location of your life (and he is), then when you blame other people for your circumstances or for the wrongs that you do, you are, in fact, blaming God. You are saying that God didn't give you what you needed to be what he has called you to be and to do what he has called you to do. You are essentially saying: "My problem isn't a heart problem; my problem is a *poverty of grace* problem. If only God had given me _____, I wouldn't have had to do what I did." This is the final argument of a self-excusing lifestyle. This argument was first made in the garden of Eden after the rebellion of Adam and Eve. Adam: "The woman you gave me made me do it." Eve: "The Devil made me do it." It is the age-old self-defensive lie of a person who doesn't want to face the ugliness of the sin that still resides in his or her heart.

It is hard for us to accept that our words and behavior are not caused by what's outside us, but by what's inside us (see Luke 6:43–45). But the Scriptures are clear that every wrong you and I do flows out of the thoughts and desires of our hearts. It is only when you admit and confess this that you begin to feel the need for and get excited about God's grace. If you have convinced yourself that you're not your problem, but people and situations are, you are not excited about God's provision of powerful forgiving and transforming grace, because, frankly, you don't think you need it. For many of us, subtle patterns of blaming God are in the way of receiving the grace that we need at the very moment we are working to convince ourselves that we don't need it.

For further study and encouragement: Deuteronomy 30

AUGUST 12

Remember, what is out of your control exists under the careful control of the One who is all-knowing, all-wise, all-good.

Too much of our emotional energy is sapped by worry. Too many of us are captured by discouragement. Too many of us are too often motivated by fear. Too many of us regularly lose sleep because of worry. Too many of us feel our lives are out of control. Too many of us wish that we had power that we will never have. Too many of us are paralyzed by regret. Too many of us wonder where God is and what he is doing. Too many of us feel alone and misunderstood. Too many of us envy the lives of others. Too many of us think that it's us against the world. Too many of us, when we are assessing our lives, leave out the ultimate explanatory fact—the existence, character, and plan of God.

I am convinced that many of us need to take in or return to the worldview that is presented to us in the book of Daniel. Daniel's world is a world of trouble. It's a world of injustice, oppression, idolatry, danger, political corruption, war, and various other kinds of trouble, but it is not a world that is out of control. In fact, in the face of all the trouble, Daniel presents to us the very opposite of what we would tend to think if we were to assess his world. Daniel presents to us a world that, in every way and at every point, is under the control of One who is powerful and wise, and who holds the events of human history in the palms of his hands. Events happen according to his plan. History moves according to his will. Individuals' lives are shaped by his purpose. It is a world under rule. Consider these words: "He is the living God, enduring forever; his kingdom shall never be destroyed, and his dominion shall be to the end. He delivers and rescues; he works signs and wonders in heaven and on earth" (Dan. 6:26–27).

Many things in your life are out of your control. You face many things that make you feel unprepared, small, or weak. But you must not give way to thinking that your life is out of control. You need to remind yourself of the truths that Daniel confronts us all with—that over all the trouble that confounds and dismays us is a God of glorious wisdom, power, and grace who rules every moment of every situation. No, you will not always see his hand. You often won't understand what he is doing. There will be points when life won't make sense to you. At times, you will wish that life could be different. There will be moments when you will feel unprepared for what is on your plate. In these moments, look up and remember that above it all there is a throne, and on it sits a God of unimaginable majesty, ruling all for his glory and for your good.

For further study and encouragement: Daniel 6

AUGUST 13

Self-righteousness is being more concerned for, and motivated
by, the knowledge of the sin of others than your own.

It's a spiritual rendition of the old question, "Which came first, the chicken or the egg?" Is self-righteousness the reason for personal spiritual blindness or is personal spiritual blindness the root of self-righteousness? Whatever the case, they motivate and strengthen each other, and because they do, they present a grave danger to anyone who still has sin living inside him or her (that's all of us).

I've seen this operate so powerfully in married couples that it locks their marriages in a permanent state of paralysis that precludes any hope of real lasting change. The husband comes to counseling with a long list of his wife's sins, weaknesses, and failures, but with little awareness or concern for his own, and his wife comes armed with a detailed list of her husband's wrongs, but with little reference to her own. When I ask the husband what is wrong with his marriage, he doesn't talk about himself, he talks about his wife, and when I ask the wife what is wrong, she doesn't talk about herself, she talks about her husband. How is it possible to have two utterly righteous people and a marriage that is broken and dysfunctional?

Be honest right here, right now as you are reading this devotion. Whose sin bugs you more: your own or that of someone near you? Who are you desperate to see change: you or someone else in your life?

The self-righteousness/spiritual blindness/judging of others dynamic that causes so much spiritual and relational damage between the "already" and the "not yet" is directly addressed by Christ in Matthew 7:1–5:

> Judge not, that you be not judged. For with the judgment you pronounce you will be judged, and with the measure you use it will be measured to you. Why do you see the speck that is in your brother's eye, but do not notice the log that is in your own eye? Or how can you say to your brother, "Let me take the speck out of your eye," when there is the log in your own eye? You hypocrite, first take the log out of your own eye, and then you will see clearly to take the speck out of your brother's eye.

Self-righteousness means you don't see yourself or the other person with accuracy. It means you see his or her speck as a log and your log as a speck. So you are condemning of him or her and excusing of yourself. You treat the other person with judgment while you respond to yourself with patience. This troubling dynamic is another powerful argument for our desperate need for rescuing grace. Only this grace, as it comes to us in the insight-giving and convicting ministry of the Holy Spirit, can help us to see ourselves with accuracy and others with clarity. You see, it takes grace for you to realize how much you still need grace.

For further study and encouragement: Matthew 18:21–33

AUGUST 14

Could there be a greater consolation known to man than these six hope-giving words: "His mercies are new every morning"?

Post those six words on the mirror that you look into each morning. Affix them on the door of your refrigerator. Tape them to the dashboard of your car. Glue them on the inside of your glasses. Put them somewhere where you will see them every day. Don't allow yourself to have a view of yourself, of others, of circumstances, of daily joys and struggles, of God, of meaning and purpose, and of what life is all about that is devoid of this gorgeous redemptive reality: mercy.

Mercy is the theme of God's story. Mercy is the thread that runs through all of Scripture. Mercy is the reason for Jesus's coming. Mercy is what your desperate heart needs. Mercy is the healer your relationships need. Mercy is what gives you comfort in weakness and hope in times of trial. Mercy can do what the law is powerless to do. Mercy not only meets you in your struggle, but guarantees that someday your struggle will end. Mercy is what this sin-broken world groans for. Mercy triumphs where justice can't. If God offered us only justice, no one would run to him. It is the knowledge of his mercy that makes us honestly face ourselves and gladly run to him. And it is mercy that we will sing about and celebrate a million years into eternity.

I love the words of Lamentations 3:22–23: "The steadfast love of the LORD never ceases; his mercies never come to an end; they are new every morning; great is your faithfulness." Let these amazing words sink in. If you are God's child, they describe your identity and your hope. They give you reason to get up in the morning and to continue. They enable you to face and admit how messed up you really are. They allow you to extend mercy to the failing people around you. And they allow you to be comforted by God's presence rather than be terrified at the thought that he is near.

Not only does God lavish on you love that will never cease and grace that will never end, and not only is he great in faithfulness, but the mercy he extends to you and to me is renewed each new morning. It is not tired, stale, irrelevant, worn out, ill-fitting, yesterday mercy. No, God's mercy is *new morning mercy*. It is formfitted for the needs of your day. It is sculpted to the shape of the weaknesses, circumstances, and struggles of each and every one of his children. Yes, we all get the same mercy, but it doesn't come to all of us in the same size and shape. God knows who you are, where you are, and what you're facing, and in the majestic combination of divine knowledge, power, and compassion, he meets you with just the right mercies for the moment. Stop allowing yourself to assess your life in a way that is devoid of new morning mercies. Any scan of your life that doesn't include those mercies is tragically lacking in truth.

For further study and encouragement: Daniel 9:4–19

AUGUST 15

Don't complain to someone else, cry out to God.
He'll never turn a deaf ear to the cries of his people.

Your life really is shaped by whom you cry to. If your cry is a complaint, you will find yourself with other complainers because misery loves company, and your heart will grow more discouraged and hardened. If you cry to people instead of God, you will ask those people to do what only God can do. They will feel overwhelmed and unable, and you will grow more desperate. If you silence your cries, crying only to yourself, you will feel increasingly alone and without anyone who cares and understands, and you'll feel more and more helpless. The good news of the gospel is that you don't have to muffle your cries. You don't have to be ashamed that you have reason to cry, and you surely don't have to feel that God is too grand, too far off, or too busy with more important things than to listen to your measly little cries for help.

I think one of the reasons for the Psalms in the Bible is to give us courage to cry and to teach us when to cry:

- "O, LORD, how many are my foes! Many are rising up against me; many are saying of my soul, there is no salvation for him in God" (Ps. 3:1–2).
- "Answer me when I call, O God of my righteousness! You have given me relief when I was in distress. Be gracious to me and hear my prayer!" (Ps. 4:1).
- "Why, O LORD, do you stand far away? Why do you hide yourself in times of trouble?" (Ps. 10:1).
- "How long, O LORD? Will you forget me forever? How long will you hide your face from me?" (Ps. 13:1).
- "My God, my God, why have you forsaken me? Why are you so far from saving me, from the words of my groaning?" (Ps. 22:1).
- "Contend, O LORD, with those who contend with me; fight against those who fight against me" (Ps. 35:1).
- "My tears have been my food day and night, while they say to me all the day long, 'Where is your God?'" (Ps. 42:3).
- "O God, you have rejected us, broken our defenses; you have been angry; oh, restore us" (Ps. 60:1).

There are many more passages like these in the Psalms. They are there to encourage you to cry to the One who will never turn a deaf ear to your cries and who has the power and willingness to meet you in your need.

For further study and encouragement: Psalm 46

AUGUST 16

Somehow, some way, your little kingdom will look very
attractive to you today, but it is the very kingdom from
which grace works unrelentingly to rescue you.

The Bible really is a story of kingdoms in conflict, and that battle rages on the field of your heart. It rages for control of your soul. The two kingdoms in conflict cannot live in peace with one another. There will never be a truce. There is no safe demilitarized zone where you can live. Each kingdom demands your loyalty and your worship. Each kingdom promises you life. One kingdom leads you to the King of kings and the other sets you up as king. The big kingdom works to dethrone you and decimate your little kingdom of one, while the little kingdom seduces you with promises it cannot deliver. The big kingdom of glory and grace is gorgeous from every perspective, but it doesn't always look that way to you. The little kingdom is deceptive and dark, but at points it appears to you as beautiful and life giving. You either pray that God's kingdom will come and that his will be done or you work to make sure that your will and your way win the day.

So it makes sense that Jesus came to earth as a King to establish his kingdom. Like a hero Monarch, he died so his kingdom would last eternally. But he did not come as an earthly king to set up a physical, political kingdom. He came to set up a much better, much greater, much more expansive kingdom than one that locates itself in a certain place and time. He came to dethrone all other rule and set up his grace-infused, life-giving reign in your heart. He came to free you and me from our bondage to our own self-serving kingdom purposes. He came to help us understand that his grace is not given to make our little kingdom purposes work but to invite us to a much, much better kingdom.

So tell yourself again today that there is a King but he is not you. Tell yourself that there is a kingdom that will protect and satisfy your heart but it is not yours. As Jesus said, there is a kingdom that you should seek, but you will never, ever be its monarch. Quite apart from anything you could have done, achieved, earned, or deserved, you have been given a kingdom. The price of that gift was the suffering and death of the King. But he conquered death so that by grace he could establish his rule in your heart. Right now he reigns on your behalf (see 1 Corinthians 15), and he will continue to do so until the last enemy of your soul and of his kingdom has been defeated. Then he will invite you into the final kingdom, where peace and righteousness will reign forever and ever. This is the story of your faith. The story of this Savior King is now your biography. Why would you ever want to go back to the delusional hopes of your kingdom of one?

For further study and encouragement: Exodus 32

AUGUST 17

One of the most basic sins in relationships is inattention;
we make greater commitments to our gardens
than to the people we say we love.

It really is true that the number one reason that relationships of all kinds go bad is neglect. Here is the structure of every relationship this side of eternity: it is a flawed person in relationship to a flawed person, in a fallen world, but with a faithful God. Since it is a flawed person in relationship to a flawed person, if you are in a relationship, you simply cannot let that relationship coast and expect that it will be okay. It's like planting a garden. You clear the land, you break up the soil, and you plant, water, and nurture your flowers, but at that point, you do not have the liberty of walking away. Your work has not ended; in fact, it has just begun, because you have planted your flowers in impure soil and in a less-than-perfect environment. Weeds will immediately begin to grow, and if you don't attend to them, they will soon dominate the turf and choke the vitality out of your beautiful flowers.

So it is with relationships. Once a relationship is planted, weeds quickly sprout. Weeds of conflict, control, bitterness, unforgiveness, anger, selfishness, pride, greed, jealously, impatience, unkindness, and self-righteousness grow and choke the life out of the relationship. Daily attention is needed, because every person in a relationship brings something dangerous and destructive into that relationship; something that is antisocial at its core. The Bible names this thing *sin*. As long as sin lives in us, it has the power to wreak havoc on our relationships, so we cannot neglect the daily nurture that they need. A good relationship is a good relationship because the people in the relationship never quit working on the relationship.

Does this sound dark to you? Does it make you want to run away from relationships? Well, you need not be afraid, because if you're God's child, you bring something else into your relationships that should give you hope. Peter reminds married couples in 1 Peter 3:7 that they are joint heirs of the *grace of life*. There is hope for your relationships; there are resources for the struggle, because you have inherited big, expansive, powerful, rescuing, and transforming grace. This grace is so huge and powerful that there is no way to wrap human words around it. This grace motivates and empowers the hard work that every relationship requires. In times of trouble, you move toward the other person, knowing the inheritance that you have been given for such a time as this. Day after day, knowing the grace you have been given, you rid your relationships of the weeds of selfishness and sin so that flowers of peace and love may grow. And in the end, you don't celebrate how good you are at relationships. No, you celebrate the Giver of that grace. This grace daily rescues you from your bondage to you and gives you the resources to be a person who truly loves others.

For further study and encouragement: Ephesians 5:22–6:9

AUGUST 18

*If you're God's child, the gospel isn't an aspect of your life,
it is your life; that is, it is the window through which
you look at everything.*

It has been a theme of my ministry, a sad recognition that has motivated me to speak the things I speak and to write the things that I write. Thousands and thousands of sincere believers have a huge hole right smack dab in the middle of their gospel. They tend to see the gospel as a thing of the past and a thing of the future; an entrance thing and an exit thing. Sure, they celebrate the forgiveness they have been given and their welcome into God's family, and they look with hope to the future, when they will be with the Lord forever, but they don't understand the radical, mind-changing, and life-altering *nowism* of the gospel of the Lord Jesus Christ. They don't grasp that when they came to Christ, it wasn't just their past and future that changed; no, everything in their lives right here, right now changed.

For a believer, nothing in his or her life is unchanged by the gospel. If you look at life from the vantage point of the present benefits of the person, work, presence, and promises of the Lord Jesus Christ, nothing in your life looks the same. The apostle Peter encourages people to live in a radical new way because they have been given "all things that pertain to life and godliness" (2 Pet. 1:3). So you and I aren't left to our own maturity, character, ingenuity, righteousness, wisdom, or power. Not only that, but the gospel redefines how we understand our whole story, how we think about the meaning of life, how we understand the human struggle, where we get our identity, where we look for peace and security, what we consider in life to be dangerous, what we see as successful living, and so on. It is true that when Jesus takes up residence in us, everything in life changes. Nothing remains the same.

Now, if you don't know this, you celebrate your salvation, but for help with your marriage, parenting, sex, money, friendships, fear, addictions, decisions, and such, you don't look to the gospel. You log on to Amazon.com and scan for the latest self-help book that addresses your topic of concern. You do this because you're a functional gospel amnesiac. You've forgotten who you are as a child of God. You've forgotten the glorious warehouse of spiritual wisdom that you have been given. You think you are poor when really you are rich. You think you need wisdom when you have been united by grace to the One who is wisdom. You think that there is something you need that you haven't yet found, when in fact you have already been given every single thing you need to be what you're supposed to be and to do what you're supposed to do in the place where the Savior has positioned you. The gospel gives you everything and changes everything in your life. Are you living as if you actually believe that?

For further study and encouragement: 1 Corinthians 2:1–5

AUGUST 19

*God's care comes in many forms. Fellowship is God caring enough
to put people in your life to encourage, rebuke, and comfort you.*

Read the following passage carefully, and when you've finished reading it, read it again:

> Put on then, as God's chosen ones, holy and beloved, compassionate hearts, kindness, humility, meekness, and patience, bearing with one another and, if one has a complaint against another, forgiving each other; as the Lord has forgiven you, so you also must forgive. And above all these put on love, which binds everything together in perfect harmony. (Col. 3:12–14)

This passage immediately confronts us with the fact that our relationships don't belong to us. They belong to God for his use for his purpose. We cannot allow ourselves to have an owner's view of our relationships, as if they exist for the sole purpose of our happiness. Something big, important, and transformational is being said here about us and our relationships, something that we need to know, understand, and live out. This passage is a statement of need, identity, and calling for every believer.

First, this passage defines our *need*. We were not wired by creation or re-creation to live on our own. Independent, self-focused living never goes anywhere good. We must all come to understand and accept the truth that our walks with God are community projects. We were not designed to live the Christian life on our own. The reason God calls us to this high quality of relationships is because relationships are an irreplaceable tool in his redemptive hands.

Second, this passage defines our *identity*. Think with me; where did Paul get this character list? The answer is that these are traits of Christ. Paul is figuratively telling us to put on Christ, and in telling us to put on Christ, he is defining what our identity is in the right here, right now work of God. The best word for that identity is *ambassador*. Every believer is called to be an ambassador of the Savior King. Now, you know that the only thing an ambassador does is represent the king who sent him. This means that Jesus makes his invisible presence visible through his people, who represent him in one another's lives. You are the look on Christ's face. You are the tones of his voice. You are the touch of his hands. You are the physical representative of his grace. This is your mission in every relationship of your life—to make the grace of the invisible King visible.

Third, this defines our *calling*—to ask again and again, "What of the person and work of Jesus does this person need to see in this particular moment of his or her life?" Now, none of us is up to this task, so the Redeemer who sent us also comes with us so that we will have the grace we need to represent him well.

For further study and encouragement: Ephesians 4:1–16

AUGUST 20

*Corporate worship is meant to so enthrall you with God's grace that
you want to be an instrument of that grace in the lives of others.*

Life in a fallen world is hard. Ministry to fallen people is hard. Together they leave
you exhausted, discouraged, and tempted to be a tad cynical. You simply cannot live
with sinners and not be sinned against. You cannot live with people without seeing
their true hearts revealed.

I understand why people, after experiencing the hurt and disappointment that so
often mars our relationships, decide to live in isolation or in a comfortable collection
of terminally casual relationships. I understand why people say to themselves, "I've
been taken once and I won't be taken again." I understand why married couples
choose to live in long-term cold-war relationships that lack intimate friendship and
unity. I understand why ministry people often choose to live in functional isolation
from the body of Christ. I understand why adult children choose to live a great distance away from their parents. I understand why many people dread the extended
family gatherings that accompany the holidays. I understand why people hide their
hurt and refuse to talk about painful topics with one another. I understand why
people don't want to ask for help or give help when asked. I understand that none
of us have ever lived in one single relationship that hasn't disappointed us in some
way. I understand that relationships are hard.

But there is one other thing that I understand. It is that, for the believer, relationships are not a lifestyle option. No, they are an essential piece of God's calling
between your salvation and your final resurrection. Biblical faith is fundamentally
relational. It is shaped and driven by two primary communities. First and foremost
is the community with God that is the whole reason for our existence. Life is found
in community with the Creator. Then there is God's call not only to live in self-
sacrificing love of your neighbor, but also to be a tool of God's work in your neighbor's heart and life. You and I just don't have the choice of opting out. We are
relational beings who have been called to lifelong community with God and others.

We need help to face the often overwhelming call to relationships, following
God's high standards and not giving way to the desire to run. Part of God's purpose
in corporate worship is to correct your vision about those relationships. If you're
not looking at your relationships through the lens of God's amazing grace, you're
not seeing those relationships accurately. So gathering after gathering is intended to
so enthrall you with the grandeur of God's grace that you can't think of anything
better than being a tool of that grace in the lives of others.

For further study and encouragement: Romans 13:8–14

AUGUST 21

You're not called to work for God's acceptance; you're called to trust the One who completed that work on your behalf.

We keep trying it, even though we've been told again and again that it's impossible. It causes us to be either delusionally proud or irrationally fearful. It causes us to hide in guilt and shame, fearing the only One who can help us. In fear, we work for what we have already been given. In weakening hope, we seek what we already have. In redemptive delusion, some of us boast about what we did not earn or achieve on our own. In our misunderstanding, we envy what we think others have and we wish we could achieve what they have accomplished. We spend our lives feeling not only that we haven't measured up, but also that we'll never measure up. We wonder what God really thinks of us, and the thought of his presence produces more fear than comfort in our hearts. It all gets to the very heart of the message of the gospel.

Jesus lived the perfect life you and I never, ever could have lived, and now his righteousness is credited to our account. He died the death that we should have died. His death satisfied the Father's anger with our sin. He rose again, conquering sin and death so that we would know life eternal too. All of this was done so that the chasm between us and God would be bridged, so that we would be fully and eternally accepted into his family, never again to face his rejection, never again to pay the penalty for our sins, and free from having to measure up to his standard in order to garner his love. What needed to be done, Jesus did. The work is complete.

Now, having said that, it is true that you have been called to work. You have been called to give yourself to the work of God's kingdom and to daily obey the commands of the King. You've been called to recognize that your life is no longer your own because you were bought with a price. But the work you do is never to be done in order to earn something. The work you're called to do is to be done in celebration of something. You don't work to earn God's favor; rather, your work is a hymn of thanks for the favor that Christ achieved on your behalf. You don't have to wonder if you've worked enough. You don't have to fear that you'll mess up and get booted out of the family. You don't have to fear seeing the back of God's head. You don't have to be haunted by the question of whether you've done enough for long enough. The bridge of impossibility has been walked by Christ. The job is done. Your relationship with God is eternally secure. Now, in thankfulness, go out and do his work.

For further study and encouragement: Luke 1:67–79

AUGUST 22

Don't be satisfied with anything less than all God's powerful
grace is able to produce in you and through you.

I know it's my problem and I suspect it's yours too—we're just too easily satisfied. It's not that we want too much from God. No, the reality is that often we are willing to settle for too little. We are content with a little bit of change, a little bit of growth, or a little bit of maturity. We settle for a little bit of biblical understanding and a little bit of theological knowledge. We say we love redemption and that we are thankful for God's grace, yet we become spiritually satisfied long before that grace has completed its work.

If our parenting seems to be working, if our marriages are livable, if our jobs aren't terrible, if our finances aren't a disaster, and if we have nice houses, good churches, and good health, most of us are satisfied. But God is not satisfied. He knows that we will continue to need his transforming grace until sin is no more. We will continue to need his intervention until we have been completely formed into the likeness of Jesus. We will continue to need the forgiving, enabling, transforming power of his grace until every thought and desire of our hearts is pleasing in his sight. We will continue to need his deliverance and protection as long as we are still susceptible to the seductive voices of temptation that are all around us in this fallen world. Our Savior loves us enough to continue to be dissatisfied even in those moments when we are all too satisfied. He will not abandon the work of his hands. He will not turn from his grace. He will not forsake his saving zeal. He will not relent until his grace has done everything it can do in each one of his children.

So you'll find yourself in situations you do not like. You'll find yourself having to deal with things you didn't plan. You'll find yourself dealing with trouble you never thought would enter your door. You'll face the unplanned, the unexpected, and the unwanted. The reason you will is because your Lord will be using all these hard and uncomfortable moments to wrench you out of your satisfaction, to cause you to esteem his redemption and to create heart-and-life change that will not be created any other way. Your Lord pries open your hands and takes away your crutches and distractions. He exposes your weaknesses so that you will cry out for what he knows you need, but what you have been willing to live without.

So be thankful for all that grace has done for you, but be dissatisfied. Don't quit before grace has completed its work. Cry out for more rescue, transformation, and deliverance. And be grateful that your Savior continues to work even in those moments when you don't value the work that you so desperately need.

For further study and encouragement: Philippians 1:3–11

AUGUST 23

Don't waste your time in envy. You always have what you need
because God's faithfulness is never tainted by partiality.

In a world of
justice gone bad,
where disloyalty brings
daily pain,
where government is
corrupt,
and even faithful friends
come up short;
where the haves get more
and the have-nots wonder why;
and where it is very
tempting
to look over the fence
at someone else's life
and wonder why
so much good
has fallen on him,
it is so good to know that you
never play favorites.
You lavish riches of grace
on each and every one
of your children.
You meet every child's
every need,
and you do it with unbroken
faithfulness.
So I will quit keeping score.
I will not judge your goodness.
No, I will rest in the bounty of your
mercy.

For further study and encouragement: Psalm 84

AUGUST 24

Yes, you live in a world where evil still exists, but the One who conquered sin and death is still with you.

It is the disastrous duo—the evil outside us and the evil that still remains inside us. It is not just that we live in a world where evil still exists. If that were our only problem, life would be much easier and simpler. No, the danger of the external evil that we all face every day is made incredibly greater by the evil that lives inside us. You see, it is only ever the evil inside you that magnetizes you to the evil outside you. Sin is only ever attractive to a sinner. It really is true, "To the pure, all things are pure" (Titus 1:15). The problem is that none of us are yet completely pure. Yes, by the operation of powerful grace, we are purer than we once were. But here is our dilemma: our purification from sin—that work that will not end until every last microbe of sin is eradicated from every single cell of every heart of every believer—is a lifelong process and not a single event. The process of heart purification is taking place in the environment of a dramatically broken world that is not functioning as God intended and where evil lurks around every corner. And there is not a day in our lives when internal and external evil do not intersect somehow, some way.

Are you discouraged as you read this? Does it seem to you that God's will is both irrational and impossible, as if life in the fallen world is the ultimate nasty trick? Well, you must remember that you have not been sent out into this world on your own. You have not been asked to do the impossible in your own strength. You have not been asked to journey through this dark world all by yourself. And you surely haven't been asked to comfort yourself by denying the presence and power of the internal and external evil that you deal with every day. As Jesus was sending his disciples out into this dark world to bring the message of the gospel to those enshrouded by evil external and controlled by evil internal, he said something that really changes everything: "And behold, I am with you always, to the end of the age" (Matt. 28:20).

Jesus doesn't send us out with a pack of principles and promises. He doesn't just guide our travels with a set of rules. No, he does so much more. He comes with us! He knows that we'll never make it unless he is with us in every moment of every situation, location, and relationship. He is not a rescue squad that leaps into action in our moment of trouble. He's there with us in trouble because he's been there with us all along. In our struggle with evil, he gives us the only gift that will help us—he gives us himself, because he knows that in him we really do find everything we need until our journey has ended. *He* is the best gift of his grace.

For further study and encouragement: Isaiah 7:10–17 and Matthew 1:23

AUGUST 25

*Real faith never calls you to swindle yourself
into thinking that things are better than they are.
Biblical faith is shockingly honest and hopeful.*

Biblical faith is not about wearing a saccharine smile while living in a constant state of religious denial. It's not about covering the stark and dark realities of a fallen world with overused pseudobiblical clichés. It's not about praying in King James English because somehow that makes you feel more spiritual. It's not about priding yourself on your ability to keep God's rules or thinking you're more sanctified because you're on pace to read through the whole Bible again this year. It's not about cleaning yourself up on Sunday so your public persona hides the real details of your private spiritual life. It's not about keeping score of how many years you've gone through without missing a worship service. It's not about polishing your righteousness so you look better to you and to others. It's not about saying you're okay when you give daily empirical evidence that you are anything but okay. If you are doing, saying, or thinking religious things that are meant to protect you from reality, you are not living biblical Christianity. You may feel better, but your heart has not been quieted by biblical faith. The faith of the Bible will never call you to deny reality in any way. The faith of the Bible is so in awe of the grandeur and glory of God that it is able to look at the darkest of realities in life and not be afraid.

Abraham did not need to deny reality in order to leave his home without knowing for sure where God was taking him. Noah did not need to deny reality in order to spend 120 years building that ark. The children of Israel did not need to deny reality in order to walk around Jericho for seven days. David did not need to deny reality in order to face Goliath in battle. Shadrach, Meshach, and Abednego did not need to deny reality in order to step into that white-hot furnace. Peter didn't need to deny reality in order to stand before the Sanhedrin and refuse to quit preaching the gospel. You see, it wasn't the naïveté of faith that propelled these people. No, it was the clarity of faith that caused them to do what they did.

It is only when you look at this dark world through the lens of the existence, power, authority, wisdom, faithfulness, love, and grace of the King of kings and Lord of lords that you see reality with clarity. You cannot ever assess and understand what you are facing if you omit the fact of facts—the existence of God. In fact, that's how the writer of Hebrews defines faith: "And without faith it is impossible to please him, for whoever would draw near to God must *believe that he exists* and that he rewards those who seek him" (11:6).

Are you lacking faith? Run to the One who freely gives it as his gift of grace to you.

For further study and encouragement: Daniel 3:8–30

AUGUST 26

Why fear when God has already given you, in Christ,
everything you need to be what you're supposed to
be and to do what you're called to do?

I think it's one of the dirty secrets of the church of Jesus Christ that many of the things we do are done out of fear and not faith. Fear happens when I look at myself, assess my resources, and conclude that I do not have what it takes to do what God is calling me to do or to face what I have to face. Fear in a believer is a function of forgetfulness. To the degree that you forget who God is, who you are as his child, and what you have been given by his grace, fear is your default emotion. I am deeply persuaded that the only solution to fear is fear. In other words, fear is defeated only by a bigger, greater fear. Here's what I mean. When the fear of God overwhelms and controls your heart, it protects you from the paralyzing and debilitating fear of other things. It's only when God looms hugely larger than anything you could ever face in this fallen world that your heart is able to experience peace even when you don't understand what is happening (and you don't have the power to solve it if you did).

Meditate on these passages:

- "Even though I walk through the valley of the shadow of death, I will fear no evil, for you are with me" (Ps. 23:4).
- "The LORD is my light and my salvation; whom shall I fear?" (Ps. 27:1).
- "The fear of the LORD leads to life, and whoever has it rests satisfied" (Prov. 19:23).
- "Fear not, for I am with you; be not dismayed, for I am your God; I will strengthen you, I will help you, I will uphold you with my righteous right hand" (Isa. 41:10).
- "I sought the LORD, and he answered me and delivered me from all my fears" (Ps. 34:4).
- "Blessed is the one who fears the LORD always" (Prov. 28:14).

So how can you enter the experience of vertical fear (fear of God) overwhelming and quieting horizontal fear (fear of anything else)? Well, first run to God and pray that he will grace you with the eyes to see and the heart to remember his awesome glory. Then require yourself to quit meditating on your problems and instead meditate on the glory of the God who has become your Father and who is always with you. No, you should not deny your problems, but if you let them be the subject of your meditation, they will loom larger and larger, and you will grow more and more afraid. Today, face reality, but meditate on God's glory.

For further study and encouragement: Psalm 111

AUGUST 27

God calls you to live a wise and righteous life, then he connects you to the One who is wisdom and righteousness, the Lord Jesus Christ.

Who do you think you are? I'm serious. What is the identity (or identities) that you assign to yourself that defines who you are and what you're supposed to be doing? Even more important, who do you tell yourself that God is, and how does that shape the way you think about and respond to the opportunities, responsibilities, and temptations of everyday life? There's a real way in which the gospel of Jesus Christ is one big massive identity story.

The Bible was written to pull back the curtains and reveal to us the One who sits at the center of all things. The Bible doesn't just reveal his position, his power, and his plan. The Bible reveals to us his character as well. The Bible tells us that God is the Creator, Controller, and King over all things. It tells us that God is boundless in authority, wisdom, and power. However, the Bible also tells us that this high and mighty One is slow to anger and plenteous in love; that he is merciful, tender, kind, and forgiving. It tells us that he is the longsuffering Giver of amazing grace.

But the Bible also reveals your identity. It tells you that not only are you the creation of this awesome God, but that because of sin you are a fallen creation. You were created by God to be dependent on him, but sin makes you rebellious. Sin makes you quest for independence and self-sufficiency. Sin makes you love what is foolish while thinking that you're wise. Sin makes you think you're capable of what you cannot do. Sin makes you think you're righteous when really your heart is corrupt. Sin convinces you that you are okay when actually you're heading for disaster. The Bible lovingly confronts you with everything you are not. It does so in order that you would run after everything you could be. The Bible forces you to face your foolishness and failure so you would run to One who *is* wisdom and righteousness, and find your hope in him.

Yes, the Bible does call you to do what you cannot do, but it doesn't leave you there. It introduces you to the One who gives you absolutely everything that you need. This is what the gospel is about. The cross makes a way for the One who is everything that you're not to become for you and in you everything that you need. "You are in Christ Jesus, who became to us wisdom from God, righteousness and sanctification and redemption" (1 Cor. 1:30).

For further study and encouragement: John 15:1–8

AUGUST 28

*God's grace calls you to submit. But it offers you true
freedom like you've never known before.*

I think we misunderstand both true freedom and debilitating bondage. Freedom
that fills and satisfies your heart is never found in setting yourself up as your own
authority. True freedom is not found in doing whatever you want to do whenever
you want to do it. True freedom is never found in putting yourself in the middle of
your world and making it all about you. True freedom is not found in resisting the
call to submit to any authority but your own. True freedom is never found in writing
your own moral code. True freedom is not the result of finally getting your own way.
When you attempt to do these things, you never enjoy freedom; you only end up in
another form of bondage.

Why is this true? It's true because you and I were born into a world of authority.
First, there is the overarching authority of God. There is nothing that exists that
does not sit under his sovereign and unshakable rule. If God created this world (and
he did) and if he owns what he created (and he does), then you and I do not have
autonomy (independence from his rule). This means that as his creatures, we were
created to live in willing submission to his will for us. Hence, freedom is not found
in spinning free of his authority. No, freedom is found in the willing submission of
our hearts to his authority. Then there are all the levels of human authority that God
put on earth to make his invisible authority visible. Personal freedom is not found in
resisting human authority either. Freedom and authority are not enemies.

Here is the point: you and I always exist under some kind of authority. We either
willingly submit to God's rule and the authorities that he has placed in our lives or
we set ourselves up as our own authorities and rule our lives as we see fit. But none
of us is wise enough, strong enough, faithful enough, or righteous enough to rule
ourselves well. We are no more hardwired to rule our own lives than a beagle is
hardwired to live in a water-filled aquarium. Self-rule never leads anywhere good.

So the goal of grace is not to produce in you the ability to live independently.
The agenda of grace is to transform you into a person who humbly recognizes your
need for authority and celebrates the holy, loving, and benevolent authority of God.
"But now that you have been set free from sin and have become slaves of God, the
fruit you get leads to sanctification and its end, eternal life" (Rom. 6:22). It is sin
that makes me want to rule me and it is grace that draws me into the best slavery
ever—the slavery that gives life, slavery to the Creator, the Savior King who knows
what is best and gives what is best always.

For further study and encouragement: Romans 13:1–7

AUGUST 29

The transformative power of grace will be one of the divine wonders
that we will celebrate forever when eternity is our final home.

The Bible is not a collection of stories of human heroes. No, the Bible is the story of a hero Redeemer who transforms weak and ordinary people by his powerful grace. Think with me of the characters who walk across the pages of Scripture:

- Moses wasn't a natural-born leader. He begged God to send someone else to Egypt, yet by transforming grace, there was no prophet in all of Israel like him.
- Joshua was scared to death of what God was calling him to do, but by divine power, he led the Israelites into the Promised Land.
- Gideon was convinced God had the wrong address, that he didn't really mean to call Gideon to lead the Israelite army against the Midianites, but when Gideon did it, he witnessed the awesome power of the God who had called him.
- Samson forsook his calling for the love of a deceitful woman, but he brought down the temple of Dagon by the power of God.
- David was the least likely son of Jesse to rise to the throne of Israel, but God's grace gave him a heart of courage.
- Elijah, when left to himself in a moment of discouragement, asked God to take his life, but he did great things by God's power.
- Peter was so fearful that he denied that he knew Jesus, but he became the man who stood before the Sanhedrin and essentially said, "You can threaten to kill me, but I will not stop preaching the gospel" (see Acts 4:19–20).
- Paul was the least likely of the apostles. He had murderous hatred for the followers of Jesus, yet by grace he became the most eloquent spokesman of the gospel.

The Bible does not celebrate the steely spirit of a bunch of heroic characters. No, the Bible puts before us people who were just like you and me. They were weak and fearful. They were easily deceived and disloyal. They doubted God as much as they trusted him. They sometimes followed God's way and at other times demanded their own way. These were not natural-born heroes. These were not individuals to be celebrated. Yet, they all accomplished great things, things that were crucial for the advancement of God's purpose. What made the difference? You can answer the question with one word: grace. Grace transformed their hearts, giving them the desire, power, and wisdom to do what they would not have been able to do on their own. Grace means that when God calls you, he goes with you, supplying what you need for the task at hand. They weren't naturals; no, they were transformed!

For further study and encouragement: Revelation 19
(Listen to what the voices on the other side celebrate.)

AUGUST 30

Grace smashes your pride, but it gives you more reason
for confidence than you have ever had before.

It is a statement of complete assurance and confidence, spoken by a man whose pride had just been smashed.

Nebuchadnezzar was the arrogant king of the conquering nation of Babylon. He not only had devastated Judah and taken its people as his captive servants, but he had taken implements from the temple to be used as tools of idol worship, which he commanded everyone in his kingdom to render or face death. The extent of his pride is captured by these words: "Is not this great Babylon, which I have built by my mighty power as a royal residence and for the glory of my majesty?" (Dan. 4:30). But while the words were still in his mouth, he was dramatically humiliated by the One who alone has true glory and majesty. By the power of God, Nebuchadnezzar was "driven from among men and ate grass like an ox, and his body was wet with the dew of heaven till his hair grew as long as eagles' feathers, and his nails were like birds' claws" (v. 33).

The pride of the king had been destroyed by the finger of God. We don't know for sure how long Nebuchadnezzar was in that humiliated, animalistic state, but we do know that when he rose out of it and his senses returned, his choking arrogance had been replaced with confidence. Are you confused at the distinction? Well, read these words and compare them to what Nebuchadnezzar had said before:

> At the same time my reason returned to me, and for the glory of my kingdom, my majesty and splendor returned to me. My counselors and my lords sought me, and I was established in my kingdom, and still more greatness was added to me. Now I, Nebuchadnezzar, praise and extol and honor the king of heaven, for all his works are right and his ways are just; and those who walk in pride he is able to humble. (Dan. 4:36–37)

Nebuchadnezzar was confident in the position and power he had been given, but the old pride had been broken. You can see this in the fact that what he once took credit for building, he now praised God for establishing. Nebuchadnezzar did not minimize or deny the power and splendor of his reign, but he did not say as he once would have said, "This is from me, about me, and for me." You see, pride takes credit for what it could not achieve on its own, while confidence stands strong because it recognizes the power and presence of One greater. Only divine grace can lead you from one to the other.

For further study and encouragement: Ephesians 3:7–8

AUGUST 31

If you're God's child, you are blessed with the convicting ministry of the Holy Spirit. The question is, are you listening?

It is possible to be a believer in the Lord Jesus Christ, saved by his blood, and still have a hard heart. So the warning of Hebrews 3:12–13 is much needed by all of us: "Take care, brothers, lest there be in any of you an evil, unbelieving heart, leading you to fall away from the living God. But exhort one another every day, as long as it is called 'today,' that none of you may be hardened by the deceitfulness of sin."

It is tempting to not listen to the protective promptings of the Holy Spirit because you think you have a more accurate view of yourself than you ever really have. Since sin is deceitful and since sin still remains in us all, there are places in our lives where we are deceived into thinking that we're better off spiritually than we actually are.

It is tempting to resist the convicting ministry of the Holy Spirit because few of us actually believe that we need the sight-giving ministry of others in our lives. Because we do not believe this, we have not opened ourselves up to the gospel community that is one of the primary tools of conviction that the Holy Spirit employs.

It is tempting to harden your heart against the ministry conviction of the Holy Spirit by arguing for your righteousness when a sin, weakness, or failure is revealed.

It is tempting to refuse to listen to the convicting voice of the Spirit by comparing yourself to other believers and arguing that you are surely more righteous than they are.

It is tempting to resist the personal insight-giving ministry of the Holy Spirit by confusing biblical literacy and theological knowledge with the evidence of a transformed and God-pleasing life.

It is tempting to run from the Spirit's restoring and protective work by rewriting your history, swindling yourself into believing that your wrongs are not so wrong after all.

It is tempting to resist the Spirit's loving work of conviction by confusing ministry skill, experience, and success with personal spiritual maturity.

It is tempting to resist the convicting ministry of the Holy Spirit when he uses an instrument who you think is unqualified or less mature than you.

But be comforted. You serve a dissatisfied Redeemer who will not turn from his work of grace even when you fail to esteem it and work to resist it. With patient grace, once more he calls you to listen. Do you?

For further study and encouragement: John 16:1–15

SEPTEMBER 1

*Don't be disheartened because you feel weak. By grace your
Savior lives inside you, and he is your strength.*

Where do you run when you're discouraged? Where do you tend to turn when you're
faced with your weakness? What do you say to yourself when you're confronted with
failure? What do you do when you feel unable to do what God has called you to do?
I run to Romans 8:1–11. When weakness has become evident in my life, this passage
has been my friend and comforter again and again:

> There is therefore now no condemnation for those who are in Christ Jesus. For
> the law of the Spirit of life has set you free in Christ Jesus from the law of sin
> and death. For God has done what the law, weakened by the flesh, could not do.
> By sending his own Son in the likeness of sinful flesh and for sin, he condemned
> sin in the flesh, in order that the righteous requirement of the law might be
> fulfilled in us, who walk not according to the flesh but according to the Spirit.
> (Rom. 8:1–4)

First, this passage comforts us with the radical redemptive reality that we will
never again face condemnation for our sin. Jesus bore every aspect of our penalty.
Even on days of evident weakness and repeated failure, we will not be punished for
our sin. This means that in those moments, we don't have to hide or run *from* the
Lord, but we can run *to* his presence for his help and forgiveness. But that is not all.

> You, however, are not in the flesh but in the Spirit, if in fact the Spirit of God
> dwells in you. Anyone who does not have the Spirit of Christ does not belong to
> him. But if Christ is in you, although the body is dead because of sin, the Spirit is
> life because of righteousness. If the Spirit of him who raised Jesus from the dead
> dwells in you, he who raised Christ Jesus from the dead will also give life to your
> mortal bodies through his Spirit who dwells in you. (Rom. 8:9–11)

Not only does God, in grace, deal with the guilt of our sin; he deals with its
power as well. Sin does leave us weak, lame, and unable. It makes it impossible for us
to keep God's law. It wasn't enough for God to forgive us, although that forgiveness
is a glorious thing. God comes to live inside us by his Spirit, animating us with new
life and empowering us to desire and do what we would be unable to do without his
indwelling presence. This means that you do not have to fear or deny your weakness.
You do not need to swindle yourself into thinking that you are strong. You can face
your weakness with joy because you know that you have been given grace for that
weakness; grace that is not a thing, but a person—the Holy Spirit, who makes you
the place where he dwells in power.

For further study and encouragement: Ephesians 3:14–20

SEPTEMBER 2

Grace causes us to be alive to God and causes our eyes to be
open to spiritual realities we once had no capacity to see.

Yet among the mature we do impart wisdom, although it is not a wisdom of this age or of the rulers of this age, who are doomed to pass away. But we impart a secret and hidden wisdom of God, which God decreed before the ages for our glory. None of the rulers of this age understood this, for if they had, they would not have crucified the Lord of glory. But, as it is written,

> "What no eye has seen, nor ear heard,
>   nor the heart of man imagined,
> what God has prepared for those who love him"—

these things God has revealed to us through the Spirit. For the Spirit searches everything, even the depths of God. For who knows a person's thoughts except the spirit of that person, which is in him? So also no one comprehends the thoughts of God except the Spirit of God. Now we have received not the spirit of the world, but the Spirit who is from God, that we might understand the things freely given us by God. And we impart this in words not taught by human wisdom but taught by the Spirit, interpreting spiritual truths to those who are spiritual. The natural person does not accept the things of the Spirit of God, for they are folly to him, and he is not able to understand them because they are spiritually discerned. The spiritual person judges all things, but is himself to be judged by no one. "For who has understood the mind of the Lord so as to instruct him?" But we have the mind of Christ. (1 Cor. 2:6–16)

This really is one of those "That says it all" passages. It confronts us with our inability to see and understand the things of God, things that are critical not only for knowing God, but also for living life as he designed it to be lived. You and I simply cannot know all that we need to know in order to be what we're supposed to be and to do what we're supposed to do by means of personal experience and collective research. There is a body of wisdom that comes to us only by means of revelation. God first reveals this wisdom to us in his grand redemptive book, the Bible, and then he opens our eyes and our hearts so that we can receive and understand what he has revealed. Without this ministry of illumining grace, these things would be at worst completely concealed from us and at best a whole lot of foolishness to us. We need Christ to come to us by his Spirit to reveal his mind to us so that we can think his thoughts after him.

All of this is vitally important because one of the things that sin does is turn us all into fools. Sin brings with it a functional insanity from which we all need to be delivered. So here is delivering grace that opens the eyes and understanding of our hearts so that we may know God, know his grace, and seek and receive the life that only he can give.

For further study and encouragement: John 14:15–31

SEPTEMBER 3

*Hope is more than wishing things will work out. It is resting in
the God who holds all things in his wise and powerful hands.*

We use the word *hope* in a variety of ways. Sometimes it connotes a wish about
something over which we have no control at all. We say, "I sure hope the train comes
soon," or, "I hope it doesn't rain on the day of the picnic." These are wishes for
things, but we wouldn't bank on them. The word *hope* also depicts what we think
should happen. We say, "I hope he will choose to be honest this time," or, "I hope the
judge brings down a guilty verdict." Here hope reveals an internal sense of morality
or justice. We also use *hope* in a motivational sense. We say, "I did this in the hope
that it would pay off in the end," or, "I got married in the hope that he would treat
me in marriage the way he treated me in courtship." All of this is to say that because
the word *hope* is used in a variety of ways, it is important for us to understand how
this word is used in Scripture or in its gospel sense.

Biblical hope is foundationally more than a faint wish for something. Biblical
hope is deeper than moral expectation, although it includes that. Biblical hope is
more than a motivation for a choice or action, although it is that as well. So what is
biblical hope? It is *a confident expectation of a guaranteed result that changes the
way you live.* Let's pull this definition apart.

First, biblical hope is *confident.* It is confident because it is not based on your
wisdom, faithfulness, or power, but on the awesome power, love, faithfulness, grace,
patience, and wisdom of God. Because God is who he is and will never, ever change,
hope in him is hope well placed and secure.

Hope is also an *expectation of a guaranteed result.* It is being sure that God will
do all that he has planned and promised to do. You see, his promises are only as
good as the extent of his rule, but since he rules everything everywhere, I know that
resting in the promises of his grace will never leave me empty and embarrassed. I
may not understand what is happening and I may not know what is coming around
the corner, but I know that God does and that he controls it all. So even when I am
confused, I can have hope, because my hope does not rest on my understanding, but
on God's goodness and his rule.

Finally, true hope *changes the way you live.* When you have hope that is guaranteed, you live with confidence and courage that you would otherwise not have. That
confidence and courage cause you to make choices of faith that would seem foolish
to someone who does not have your hope. If you're God's child, you never have to
live hopelessly, because hope has invaded your life by grace, and his name is Jesus!

For further study and encouragement: Psalm 20

SEPTEMBER 4

Sin is more than bad behavior. It's a heart condition that results in
bad behavior. That's why we can't independently defeat sin.

In his teaching that we call "The Sermon on the Mount" (Matthew 5–7) Jesus power-fully makes the point that sin is a heart problem. Yet we still find it difficult to accept and believe. We want to hold on to two operational falsehoods. The first is that sin is simply a matter of bad behavior. Maybe we want to hold on to this idea because sin seems less sinful if it isn't some dark defect in our character. Or perhaps, if sin is just behavior, it seems that we have more independent power to free ourselves from it. All we need to do is give ourselves with discipline to systems of behavior reformation and we can free ourselves from sinful acts. But sin is not just a matter of behavior.

The second operational falsehood that we all tend to want to believe is that our sin is caused more by what is outside us than what is inside us. If you ask the little boy on the playground at school why he hit the little girl, he probably won't talk about himself. He will point to someone or something outside himself as the cause of his behavior. We don't want to face the fact that sin is caused by what's inside us. We all tend to want to think that we are more righteous than we actually are.

So Jesus confronts our misperceptions about what sin is and what causes us to sin with these words:

> You have heard that it was said to those of old, "You shall not murder; and who-ever murders will be liable to judgment." But I say to you that everyone who is angry with his brother will be liable to judgment. (Matt. 5:21–22)

> You have heard that it was said, "You shall not commit adultery." But I say to you that everyone who looks at a woman with lustful intent has already committed adultery with her in his heart. (Matt. 5:27–28)

What is Christ doing with these words? No, he is not redefining the law; he's ex-plaining to us the law's original intent. God's law is meant to address and expose the heart because sin is always a matter of the heart before it is an action of the body. It's hatred within my heart that causes me to use the members of my body to do harm to the body of another. It is the lustful desires of my heart that lead me to sexual sin. This is why the delivering grace of Christ is essential. You can escape many things, but you cannot escape your heart. In gorgeous mercy, God delivers you from you.

For further study and encouragement: Romans 3:9–20

SEPTEMBER 5

God's care is sure, but will you run to him in your time
of need or look elsewhere for hope and comfort?

By his promises, God invites us to run to him:

- "[Cast] all your anxieties on him, because he cares for you" (1 Pet. 5:7).
- "He has said, 'I will never leave you nor forsake you'" (Heb. 13:5).
- "Come to me, all who labor and are heavy laden, and I will give you rest. Take my yoke upon you, and learn from me, for I am gentle and lowly in heart, and you will find rest for your souls. For my yoke is easy, and my burden is light" (Matt. 11:28–30).
- "The LORD is my light and my salvation; whom shall I fear? The LORD is the stronghold of my life; of whom shall I be afraid?" (Ps. 27:1).
- "He gives power to the faint, and to him who has no might he increases strength. Even youths shall faint and be weary, and young men shall fall exhausted; but they who wait for the LORD shall renew their strength; they shall mount up with wings like eagles; they shall run and not be weary; they shall walk and not faint" (Isa. 40:29–31).
- "And my God will supply every need of yours according to his riches in glory in Christ Jesus" (Phil. 4:19).
- "Cast your burden on the LORD, and he will sustain you; he will never permit the righteous to be moved" (Ps. 55:22).

These are just a small representation of God's words of invitation and welcome. He really is the "Father of mercies and God of all comfort" (2 Cor. 1:3). He can do for you what no one else can do. He has power that no one else possesses. He is able and willing to meet you in your moments of need, even when that need is self-inflicted. He will never mock you in your weakness. He will not stand idly by and sarcastically say, "I told you so." He finds no joy in your suffering. He is full of compassion. He abounds in mercy. He will never walk away disgusted. He will never use your weakness against you. He has no favorites and shows no partiality. He never grows tired. He never becomes impatient. He will never quit because he's had enough. He will never refuse to give you what he's promised because you've messed up so badly. He is just as faithful to all of his promises on your very worst day as he is on your very best day. He doesn't ask you to earn his compassion or to do things to gain his mercy. He knows how weak and fickle your heart is, yet he continues to move toward you with unrelenting and empowering grace. He delights in meeting your needs. He finds joy in bringing peace to your heart. He really is everything that you need. Why would you run anywhere else in your time of weakness or trouble?

For further study and encouragement: Isaiah 12

SEPTEMBER 6

What kind of Jesus do you want? Do you want the Prozac Jesus, who will make you feel better? He will be only your sovereign Savior King.

What do you define as blessing? What do you identify as a sign of God's faithfulness and care? What fills your picture of the "good life"? When you say, "If only I had _____, then I'd be content," what goes in the blank? When you are tempted to envy the life of someone else, what are you envying? What causes you to question God's goodness and love? What tempts you to be disappointed with your life? Be honest—what do you want from God? Or maybe this is a more provocative way of saying it—what kind of Messiah do you want Jesus to be?

I think many of us are just not on Jesus's agenda page. What we dream of and hope for is not the same as what he has promised us and works by zealous grace to deliver to us. Perhaps many of us struggle with disappointment with God because, at street level in our daily lives, we don't esteem what God values. Could it be that many of us don't treasure what God has harnessed the forces of nature and controlled the events of human history to deliver to us? Maybe many of us *do* want nothing more than Prozac Jesus, who will make us feel better and make our lives easier, for which we would give him thanks and name him as faithful.

Perhaps many of us want *control* more than we want redemption. We wish we had more control over the people and circumstances of our lives. That would be the good life for us.

Perhaps many of us crave *success* more than we crave redemption. We are willing to do almost anything to be successful; meanwhile, we neglect the things that God says have eternal value.

Perhaps many of us esteem *acceptance* more than we esteem redemption. We find more joy in the acceptance of the people around us than we do in the abounding love of God.

Perhaps many of us desire *comfort and pleasure* more than we desire redemption. If our lives could just be easier and more predictable, we would be satisfied.

Perhaps many of us want *material things* more than we want redemption. We tend to judge the quality of our lives by the size of the piles of stuff we have acquired.

Now, none of these things is inherently evil. It is not wrong to desire any of them. The question is this: "What set of desires rules my heart?" This is important because the desires that rule your heart determine how you evaluate your life, how you make small and large decisions, and, most importantly, how you think about the goodness and faithfulness of God. Your Messiah is ever faithful; maybe your struggle of faith comes from the fact that you don't really value what he's working to produce in your heart and life. He is much, much more than Prozac Jesus; he is your sovereign Savior King.

For further study and encouragement: Luke 12:13–21

SEPTEMBER 7

Do you want the Vacation Planner Jesus, who'll take you to a place where life is more pleasurable? He will be only your sovereign Savior King.

If you judge God's goodness by the amount of suffering in your life, you will end up concluding that he is not good. If you judge God's love by the degree to which your life is difficult, you will end up thinking that God does not love you. If you judge the faithfulness of God by how much disappointment and grief you have had to deal with, you will end up questioning his faithfulness. Here is the bottom line: *you will suffer because your suffering is an essential part of God's good plan for you.*

The moments when life doesn't seem to be working as it should, the moments when you are bitterly disappointed, the moments when you have experienced loss, or the moments when unexpected trials have entered your door are not indications of the failure of God's plan. These moments do not depict that he has forgotten you. These moments do not reveal that he is unfaithful to his promises. They do not show you that God has favorites. These moments do not demonstrate that sometimes God doesn't answer your prayers. Here's what you and I need to understand and live in light of: these difficult moments of life are not the failure of God's plan or in the way of God's plan; these moments are part of his plan. They are placed in our lives as tools of his ongoing work of rescuing, transforming, and delivering grace. They are in our lives because the God we serve esteems holiness more than he esteems our temporal definition of happiness. He is not working to give us that temporary situational emotional high; he is working to produce something much better—eternal joy.

The reality is that God has little allegiance to my selfish little wish list. He has not signed on by his grace to deliver to me that catalog of things that I think will make me happy. He has not committed to meet everything I have christened as a need. He is not working to make my journey between the "already" and the "not yet" as easy as it could possibly be. God is never caught up short when one of his children is enduring difficulty, as if something strange were happening. No, walking with Jesus is not the grand vacation, a life free of responsibility and trial. Walking with Jesus is not like that because our right here, right now life with him is not a destination (as a vacation would be). He is not Vacation Planner Jesus; he is our sovereign Savior King. Thus, this present life is meant by God to be a time of preparation for the final glorious destination that will be our eternal home. So our right-now life is not a paradise. Right now, God in grace is working to prepare us through the difficulties of life in this fallen world for what is guaranteed to each and every one of his children.

For further study and encouragement: Acts 20:17–24

SEPTEMBER 8

Maybe you want the Suggestion Box Jesus, whose law is more advice than command. He will be nothing less than the sovereign Savior King.

Consider how these passages portray God's law:

The law of the LORD is perfect,
    reviving the soul;
the testimony of the LORD is sure,
    making wise the simple;
the precepts of the LORD are right,
    rejoicing the heart;
the commandment of the LORD is pure,
    enlightening the eyes;
the fear of the LORD is clean,
    enduring forever;
the rules of the LORD are true,
    and righteous altogether.
More to be desired are they than gold,
    even much fine gold;
sweeter also than honey
    and drippings of the honeycomb.
Moreover, by them is your servant warned;
    in keeping them there is great reward. (Ps. 19:7–11)

Oh how I love your law!
    It is my meditation all the day.
Your commandment makes me wiser than my enemies,
    for it is ever with me.
I have more understanding than all my teachers,
    for your testimonies are my meditation. (Ps. 119:97–99)

God's law is not a curse; it is a grace. God's law is not a burden; it is a gift of his love. Immediately after redeeming his children from the slavery of Egypt, he took them to Mount Sinai to give them his law. He did this because they were the children of his love, the objects of his redemptive glory. As your Creator, he knows you, he knows the world you live in, and he knows the plans he has for you. Because he knows all of these things, he is infinitely more qualified to set the boundaries of your living than you are. He is your sovereign Savior King, not the Suggestion Box Jesus.

One of the sad and destructive desires of the sinful nature is the desire for self-rule. One of the dark delusions of sin is that it causes us at points to buy into the insane thought that we might be smarter than God. His grace works in your heart of submission, that is, a heart that esteems his authority and finds joy in his law.

For further study and encouragement: 2 Kings 22:3–23:25

SEPTEMBER 9

Maybe today you want the District Attorney Jesus, who'll get all those people who've made your life hard. He will be only your sovereign Savior King.

Who of us has not desired vengeance at some point in our lives? God has placed a desire for justice in each of our hearts. So when we face injustice, it is very tempting to want to take justice into our own hands. We see it in the little child, who, when hit, immediately hits back. We see it in the teenager who has been publically embarrassed by a friend; he not only cuts that friend out of his life, but looks for a way to heap embarrassment on him as well. We see it in a marriage, when one of the spouses curses the other with the silent treatment for a couple of days because he or she has been hurt. We really do find it easier to make war than to make peace, and we often wish that God would make war with others on our behalf.

Consider how Paul approaches this topic in Romans 12:14–21:

> Bless those who persecute you; bless and do not curse them. Rejoice with those who rejoice, weep with those who weep. Live in harmony with one another. Do not be haughty, but associate with the lowly. Never be wise in your own sight. Repay no one evil for evil, but give thought to do what is honorable in the sight of all. If possible, so far as it depends on you, live peaceably with all. Beloved, never avenge yourselves, but leave it to the wrath of God, for it is written, "Vengeance is mine, I will repay, says the Lord." To the contrary, "if your enemy is hungry, feed him; if he is thirsty, give him something to drink; for by so doing you will heap burning coals on his head." Do not be overcome by evil, but overcome evil with good.

The foundation of this passage is God's promise that he will exercise his righteous justice and mete out vengeance. This doesn't mean that Jesus is your district attorney. God does not promise that he will do it at such a place or in such a way that you will know it or see it. He does not promise that he will do it according to your schedule. He does not promise that he will abandon his mercy for his justice. But he does promise to repay. When Paul says, "Leave it to the wrath of God," he is essentially saying, "Stop trying to do God's job, and trust him to do what he has promised he will do." You can trust him because he is your sovereign Savior King.

Where does that leaves us? With these simple and practical directives:

1. Never repay evil for evil.
2. Work to live in peace with everyone.
3. Overcome evil with good.

None of us has the strength of character to live this way. Even the evil that is done to us exposes the depth of our need for God's grace. Thankfully, that grace is yours for the taking!

For further study and encouragement: Matthew 5:38–48

SEPTEMBER 10

Perhaps today you long for the Match.com Jesus,
who will give you someone to love. He will be to you
what you need, your sovereign Savior King.

We were designed to be social beings, to live in vertical community with God and horizontal community with others. But we can know the true joys of human love only if love for God first rules our hearts. It is only when he is in his rightful place in our hearts that people can be in their appropriate places in our lives. If love for God isn't the place where you find your rest, you need human relationships too much and you are asking people to do for you what only your Savior can do. You are looking to find your identity and deepest sense of well-being in the acceptance and love of people. This never works because there are no perfect people in your life. In some way, all the people around you will fail you. In some way, every relationship in your life will disappoint you. In some way and at some point, you will be sinned against. No mere human being is qualified to be your personal messiah!

You see, if God is not in his rightful place in my heart and life, guess who I insert in his place? The answer, of course, is me. I make my relationships all about me. Rather than love for God shaping my relationships and motivating me to say and do the things I do, love of self drives me. Rather than being a patient servant in those relationships, I live in them as a demanding king. And because God is not at the center of my thoughts and desires, I expect to get from people in my life what only God can deliver. This always leads to disappointment and acrimony in my relationships. So I pray harder and work harder to make those relationships what they will never be. I look for help to Match.com Jesus, but what I am actually asking God to do is to replace himself with other messiahs in my life—messiahs I can see, hear, and touch. This is the source of so much relational dysfunction and heartache.

But this picture is also a primary argument for our need for grace. Sin does make us focus on us too much. Sin does cause us to live in our relationships more like monarchs than servants. Sin does cause us to forget God and elevate people in our lives to the role of savior. Sin does cause us to question the goodness of God because he hasn't placed these perfect little messiahs in our lives. Sin does cause us to crave the love of people more than we celebrate the eternal love of God. Only when we are progressively freed from our bondage to ourselves do we come to love God as we should; and as we love God as we should, we love people in the way that God has designed. For this struggle, there is amazing, perseverant grace. God bestows on us his eternal transforming love so that by means of that love we will become people who find our rest in his love, and because we do, we are then able to love others well.

For further study and encouragement: Mark 12:28–34

SEPTEMBER 11

Maybe today you want the Neiman Marcus Jesus,
who will deliver all your golden dreams.
He will be nothing less than your sovereign Savior King.

Life is all about to whom and where you look for satisfaction of heart. The shape and direction of your life are determined by what you tell yourself will make you content. Everyone in some way says, "If only I had this, I would be content and able to stop looking for the next thing." What sits on the other side of your "If-only"?

We are all dreamers. We all chase a vision of what we would like life to be. We all wish we were sovereign over our lives so our dreams would come true. We all fantasize and imagine. Now, this ability is not evil in and of itself, but combine it with the selfishness of sin, and it will surely get you and me into trouble.

Here's what happens: it's not just that you have a dream, but that your heart gets captured by your dream. It becomes your definition of "life." You no longer hold your dream with open hands. What was once a desire has morphed into a demand, and it won't be long before you view that demand as a need. This thing that you once wished that you had becomes your nonnegotiable, the thing that you are unwilling to live without. Soon you're unhappy, not because life has been hard or God has been unfaithful, but because this thing that is effectively and functionally ruling your heart lies beyond your grasp. You are despondent and discouraged. You envy people who seem to have captured their dreams. You wonder why you've been singled out. You wonder why God has forgotten you. Dream? Yes, but when your dream becomes a ruling thing, it wreaks havoc on your spiritual life.

Pay attention also to what happens to your relationship with God as your dreams gobble up more of the turf of your heart. God is no longer the thing that motivates you and gives you courage and hope. God is no longer your source of sturdy joy. The glory of God is no longer the thing that you're living for. Awe of God is no longer the reason you do everything you do. Sadly, God has been reduced to a delivery system; your Savior has become Neiman Marcus Jesus. If he delivers, you'll worship and serve him, but if he fails to deliver, you will question his goodness and love, and you'll have little motivation to offer your life to him.

I think there are thousands of Christians in this sad position. Perhaps this is what the Bible is picturing when it talks of those who have "abandoned the love you had at first" (Rev. 2:4). However, there is grace for this struggle—grace that battles for your heart, grace that is more powerful than the draw of any dream. Own the dangerous dreams of your fickle heart and run to the grace that is yours in Jesus.

For further study and encouragement: Matthew 6:19–24

SEPTEMBER 12

Grace means you can never say that it's too hard,
that you've been left on your own,
or that you simply don't have enough.

You did it a hundred times yesterday, you'll do it a hundred times today, and you'll do it a hundred times tomorrow. Most of the time, you are completely unaware that you're doing it. It is a major part of what it means to be a rational human being. You never leave your life alone. You are constantly trying to make sense out of the situations and experiences of your life. We are all theologians and philosophers, no matter what our normal jobs in life may be. Every one of us is an archaeologist; we dig through the mounds of our own little lives to make sense of the "civilization" that has shaped us. Because we all have this inner drive for life to make sense, we are all in a constant conversation with ourselves. You really do talk to you a hundred times a day. Most of us have learned that it's best not to move our lips or people will think that we're crazy. But we all do it.

The things you say to you about yourself, about God, and about life are very, very important because they are formative of the way you act and react to the things that God places in your life. In those silent and private conversations that you have with you, you are remembering God's grace or you're not. When you remember God's grace, you tell yourself that you're not alone, that you're not left to the small batch of your own resources, and that you have been graced with all that you need right here, right now to be what God has called you to be and to do what God has chosen for you to do. When you remember God's grace, you are also reminded of his presence and his promises. Ultimately, human rest is not found in measuring the size of your righteousness, strength, and wisdom against the size of what you're facing. No, rest is found when you compare the size of what you're facing to the person, presence, character, power, and grace of the One who is with you wherever you go.

What is God's best gift of grace? The answer is easy—himself. God knew that our need would be so great that the only gift that would meet our need would not be an it or a thing. No, grace means that he meets our deepest need with the greatest, most transformative of gifts—he willingly gives us himself. Today, as you're having that conversation with yourself one more time, remind yourself of that gift, and as you do, rest in the fact that because you have been given the gift of gifts, you are never alone and never without the resources that you need.

For further study and encouragement: Psalm 23

SEPTEMBER 13

*Prayer is abandoning all other objects of worship and
giving myself to the daily worship of God alone.*

I shouldn't have to say this, but I think it is necessary—prayer is an act of worship.
It is profoundly more than bringing to God our grocery lists of self-defined wants
and needs. Here are seven ways in which prayer is rooted in worship:

1. *Prayer acknowledges God's existence.* This is the bottom line of all true prayer.
   It begins and ends with the recognition that there is something more ultimate in
   the universe than you. Prayer places emphasis firmly on the first four words of
   the Bible: "In the beginning, God . . ." So prayer is an acknowledgment of God
   as Creator and Sovereign. It is rooted in assent to his power, wisdom, and rule. It
   would make no sense to pray if you thought that God was your equal.
2. *Prayer bows to God's glory.* This is the constant requirement of prayer. You cannot pray properly without recognizing that there is a greater glory in this universe
   than your own glory or the variegated glories of the physical created world.
   Prayer is recognition that no created glory can or will ever satisfy the heart of
   the one who prays. It flows from the understanding that it is only when you live
   for the glory of God that your heart can rest content.
3. *Prayer submits to God's plan.* Prayer is not asking God to endorse and resource
   your plan for your life. Prayer is recognition that the One who made the world,
   including you, knows what is best for you. As the psalmist says, "the rules of the
   Lord are true, and righteous altogether" (Ps. 19:9). Prayer is not bringing your
   list and asking God to sign on the bottom. Prayer is handing God a blank sheet
   that you have already signed and trusting him to fill it out as he sees fit.
4. *Prayer confesses allegiance to God's kingdom.* Prayer is recognition that on this
   side of eternity there is a war between the kingdom of God and the kingdom of
   self. In prayer, you don't ask God to endorse the self-focused little dreams of your
   claustrophobic kingdom of one; rather, you commit your heart to the plans and
   purposes of God's kingdom and seek the grace to be part of what God is doing
   and not in the way of it.
5. *Prayer rests in God's provision.* True prayer isn't spoken in a panic, but in a spirit
   of trust and rest. You know that the One to whom you pray is near, faithful, and
   willing to meet your every need.
6. *Prayer celebrates God's grace.* True prayer arises when you are blown away by
   grace, for it is grace that gives you the desire to pray, the welcome of God to pray,
   and the promise that he will answer.
7. *Prayer commits to God's work.* Finally, prayer is an acknowledgment that between the "already" and the "not yet," there is work of God to be done, and you
   need wisdom and strength for that work.

Prayer is laying down your idols and kneeling before God in humble and joyful
worship.

For further study and encouragement: Psalm 77

SEPTEMBER 14

The disappointments of relationships are many,
but his grace is sufficient—in fact,
it is made perfect in your weakness.

It is a fact that we all have to face—none of us has ever had a relationship in our lives, not even one, that has been free of disappointment. None of us has realized our relational dreams. So we have to ask: Why are our relationships such a struggle? Why do we have to strive to live in peace and harmony with those whom we say we love? Why are our relationships marked by so much conflict? Why do we experience so much irritation, hurt, and impatience? Why?

The answer to these questions is both clear and hard to accept. Our relationships are a struggle because we all carry something into our relationships that is destructive to them. The Bible names it: sin. Sin causes us to be self-absorbed and self-focused because it causes us to live for ourselves (see 2 Cor. 5:15). Sin causes each of us to be selfish in the real sense of what this word means. It makes us more demanding than serving, more accusing than forgiving, more defensive than approachable, and more critical than understanding and patient. You and I shouldn't be surprised that our relationships are marked by problems. Given the presence and power of the sin that we drag into our relationships, what should surprise us is that our relationships survive at all!

Does the harsh reality of sin make you want to give up and quit? Does it make you long for that mythical island in the sea where you can live in peace all by yourself? You don't need to panic, you don't need to fear, and you surely don't need to consider abandoning hope for the relationships you are in right now. Why? Because there is grace for this struggle. The hope for your relationships is not to be found in you or in the others in those relationships. Hope is found in a third person who has invaded your relationships by his grace. You are never alone in your relationships. He is with you. He is in you. He is for you. He offers you grace that is up to the task even when you're not.

James 4 begins with one of the New Testament's most honest discussions of conflict in our relationships. This passage is honest and direct about what we all face and why we face it, but the passage doesn't leave us there. In the middle of this passage is this little phrase that changes everything: "But he gives more grace" (v. 6). There is grace for every hurtful moment. There is grace for every time you sin or are sinned against. And the grace that you are given for your relationships will never, ever run out. There is always more of that grace for what is coming around the corner. You can give yourself to love, to forgive, to confess, to confront, to trust, and to persevere even when things are hard, because "he gives more grace."

For further study and encouragement: James 4:1–10

SEPTEMBER 15

You will face loss, trouble, and disappointment, but nothing has the power to separate you from your Redeemer's unrelenting love.

As I've said before, I really do love the honesty of the Bible. I don't need vacuous religious platitudes that delude me into thinking that life is better than it really is. I don't need a form of faith that requires that I deny pieces of reality in order to have peace of heart. I don't want to be in the position of having to close my eyes to things and make believe that they are not there. If it is anything, the Bible is honest. The blood, guts, and dirt of the fallen world stain its every page. Filled with brutally honest stories of flawed people and marked with stinging analyses of the brokenness of the world, the Bible requires us all to be honest as well.

John 13–17 recounts Jesus's last hours with his disciples before his crucifixion. He is preparing them for life without his physical presence. He is warning them of the things they will face in this broken world. This passage is way more than "Good-bye, I love you." It is honest to the point of being scary. Jesus says, "If they persecuted me, they will also persecute you" (15:20). He says, "The hour is coming when whoever kills you will think he is offering service to God" (16:2). He says, "Behold, the hour is coming . . . when you will be scattered" (16:31). It's not a very bright picture of the disciples' future. His words are probably enough to make the disciples panic, but this is not all Jesus says. This passage is also dyed with amazing grace. This grace is formfitted for everything the disciples will face (and everything we will face too). Again and again he reminds the disciples of his presence and power. He assures them that he will not leave them like a bunch of orphans (14:18). He comforts them with the promise of the ongoing ministry of the Holy Spirit (14:25ff.).

The disciples' reason for hope in the trials they will face (and ours for the ones we face daily) is captured by the final words of John 16: "I have said these things to you, that in me you may have peace. In the world you will have tribulation. But take heart; I have overcome the world" (v. 33). This world can be a tough address. Yes, there will be times when you feel that you simply don't have what it takes to deal with what you're facing. Yes, you will be tempted to think that you have been singled out to endure particular difficulty. Yes, you will have moments when you look back with regret and moments when you look forward with fear. But in all of this there is real reason for peace and hope. It's not the peace that comes when life seems to be working well, when the people around you seem to appreciate you, or when your health and finances are good; there is a sturdier peace to be found. It is found in knowing that your heavenly Father is not afraid of, or will not be defeated by, what makes you afraid or has the power to defeat you. Peace comes when you rest in the fact that grace has connected you to the One who has overcome everything that could cause your heart to be troubled, and nothing can sever that connection.

For further study and encouragement: Romans 8:31–39

SEPTEMBER 16

Every time you work to make a wrong you've done look right,
you deny the gospel of the grace of the Lord Jesus Christ.

It is so tempting to do. Perhaps we all do it more than we are aware of. If what we say we believe is true, it makes no sense whatsoever. Yet for many of us, it's our first instinct when confronted with a wrong. We do it instinctively and thoughtlessly, without recognition of the danger we are to ourselves when this becomes a pattern.

When you are confronted with a wrong, caught in a wrong, or feel internally uncomfortable with a wrong that you have done and you rise to your own defense—when you refuse to see that what you have done is wrong and then turn and work to make yourself comfortable with the wrong that you have done—you aren't just rewriting your own history, you aren't just being self-righteous, and you aren't just deceiving yourself. You are fighting God, in the person of the Holy Spirit, who at that moment is gracing you with insight, conviction, protection, and rescue. In grace, he is blowing through your walls of spiritual blindness and self-righteousness to help you to see yourself as you actually are and, in seeing yourself accurately, to seek the grace that is yours in Christ Jesus.

These moments of painful internal discomfort are not bad things; they are very good things. They are evidences of the tender, patient care of your Savior. He works again and again to give sight to your eyes and tenderness to your heart so that you will be progressively freed from the hold of sin on your thoughts, desires, attitudes, and actions. These moments of personal conviction are always moments of beautiful grace in action. But you and I don't always see them as grace. We tend to hate being confronted. We tend to have a hard time admitting when we are wrong. We tend not to be thankful when we are in the position of needing to confess sin. We tend to want to avoid looking at how much we are still in need of grace. So we give ourselves to that which, in light of the gospel, makes no sense at all. We deny our wrongs and argue for our righteousness, seemingly afraid of where humble confession will lead us.

The fact is that we do not need to fear facing our sin and spiritual need. There really is nothing that we will ever need to admit to and to honestly face that hasn't been fully addressed by the grace that is ours because of the life, death, and resurrection of Jesus. There is nothing that we could ever do that is outside that grace. There is nothing that we could ever do that would cause God to turn his back on us. There is no reason for us to deny and defend when every sin has been carried to the cross by Jesus. Open your heart to the Spirit's work. To defend yourself against his painful promptings never takes you anywhere good.

For further study and encouragement: 1 John 1

SEPTEMBER 17

This isn't paradise. You can't make it into paradise.
Paradise is coming, and your place was secured
for you on the cross of Jesus Christ.

We all do it because the longing has been hardwired into us by God. We all try to turn this present world into the paradise we dream of. Why do we all attempt this impossible task? Because deep in the heart of every human being who has ever lived has been the longing for paradise. Somehow, some way, we all desire for things to be the way the Creator intended them to be. We are all dissatisfied with the world the way it is, each in our own way. We all feel the pain of living in a world gone bad. We all career from disappointment to disappointment because reality never seems to rise to the level of our dreams. We all face things in our lives that we wish we could change. We all examine things and hope that somehow they will get better. Each of us tries to turn this moment into the paradise it will never be, and each of us faces the frustration that results from our failed attempts.

The cry of an infant who is dealing with a pain he doesn't understand is a cry for paradise. The tears of a little boy who has been mocked on the playground are tears for paradise. The anger of a teenager whose iPad has been stolen is a cry for paradise. The frustration of a young professional with a boss who never seems to be satisfied is a cry for paradise. The grief of a young wife who misses her estranged husband is a cry for paradise. The grumpiness of an old man whose body doesn't work as it once did is a cry for paradise. We all groan, and those groanings are cries for a better world.

But here's what you have to face. God, for your good and his glory, has chosen to keep you for a while in this broken-down world. He has chosen to employ the hardships of this world to complete the work that he has begun in you. He does not leave you alone. He does not leave you without resources. He blesses you with his new morning mercies. But he has you right where he wants you. This means your marriage, your job, your church, your family, and your friendships will never be the paradise that you want them to be in this world.

But more needs to be said. In his grace, God has granted you a place in paradise. If you're God's child, the final chapter of your story will take place in an eternal paradise beyond your wildest dreams. Listen to the words of Jesus: "In my Father's house are many rooms. If it were not so, would I have told that I go to prepare a place for you?" (John 14:2). As you face the hardships of today, remember that grace has purchased you a ticket for the paradise that is to come.

For further study and encouragement: John 14:1–14

SEPTEMBER 18

Today, remember that this moment isn't intended to be a destination,
but it is what God's using to prepare you for your final destination.

If you live with a destination mentality, you are going to be regularly disappointed. If you live with a destination mentality, you will have unrealistic expectations and you will not guard yourself against temptation as you should. If you live with a destination mentality, you will struggle to believe that God is loving, good, faithful, and kind. If you live with a destination mentality, it will be easier for you to complain than to be content. If you live with a destination mentality, you will be tempted to envy the life of someone else. If you live with a destination mentality, you will tend to hook your happiness to the degree of ease and comfort that you experience in your present situations and relationships. If you live with a destination mentality, you simply won't be on God's agenda page at all.

Living with a destination mentality means that you load all your hopes and dreams, your search for a definition of the good life, and your inner sense of well-being into this present moment. It means that no matter what your theology says about eternity, you live as if this is all there is. And because you are living as if this is all there is, you try to turn this present moment in this fallen world into the paradise that it will never be. Yes, if you are God's child, you have been promised a paradise beyond your ability to conceive, but you must understand that this is not it. This sin-broken world, populated by sin-scarred people, will never be the paradise that you and I tend to long for it to be.

You see, a sound biblical doctrine of the future is the only way to arrive at a sound biblical understanding of the present. If there is a final glorious destination for all God's children, then this time is not a destination, but a preparation for a final destination. There is meaning and purpose in everything we are going through. In a real way, God is using all the difficulties of life in this fallen world to change and mature us, making us ready for the world that is to come.

But there is more for you and me to understand. It's not just that this is a time of preparation; the fact that we are guaranteed a place in the life that is to come tells us who we are and what we have been given in the here and now. Who are we? We are pilgrims on a journey with a glorious destination assured. What have we been given? Well, the guarantee of the future grace of eternity assures us that we will have all the grace we need in the present or we would never have what we need to finish the journey. So don't try to turn today into paradise, but thank God that you are being prepared by grace for the paradise that will be your forever home.

For further study and encouragement: 2 Corinthians 5:1–10

SEPTEMBER 19

Corporate worship is designed to make you thankful, not just for possessions and accomplishments, but for what you've been given in Christ.

I carried all the seductions and attractions of life in a fallen world into worship that morning. I needed to have my values reoriented and my celebration recalibrated. I needed to become, once again, a thankful man. More specifically, I needed to be not just thankful for the ease, comforts, and accomplishments of life, but thankful for things of eternal value. I needed to see, understand, cry out for, and celebrate grace once again. It was the second song of the worship service that gave the sadness of sin and the joy of grace back to my heart:

No list of sins I have not done, no list of virtues I pursue,
no list of those I am not like can earn myself a place with you.
O God! Be merciful to me. I am a sinner through and through.
My only hope of righteousness is not in me, but only you.

No humble dress, no fervent prayer, no lifted hands, no tearful song,
no recitation of the truth, can justify a single wrong.
My righteousness is Jesus' life. My debt was paid by Jesus' death.
My weary load was borne by Him, and He alone can give me rest.

No separation from the world, no work I do, no gift I give
can cleanse my conscience, cleanse my hands, I cannot cause my soul to live.
But Jesus died and rose again. The pow'r of death is overthrown!
My God is merciful to me and merciful in Christ alone.

My righteousness is Jesus' life. My debt was paid by Jesus' death.
My weary load was borne by him, and He alone can give me rest.
And He alone can give me rest.

As I listened to my brothers and sisters sing and as I took in each phrase, I began to remember the impossibility of my sin and the totality of the solution that is found only in Jesus Christ. My heart was torn between weeping and laughing; sadness crashed into celebration as the grace of remembrance flooded my heart.

Forgetfulness seems like a minor thing. We forget little things every day. We get frustrated for a moment, then remember what we forgot, laugh it off, and go on our way. But forgetfulness is not a minor thing when it comes to grace. It robs you of worship, identity, humility, courage, and hope. Thank God he ordained for us to gather and remember.

For further study and encouragement: Colossians 1

SEPTEMBER 20

Hopelessness is the doorway to hope. You have to give up on yourself before you will be excited about the hope that is yours in Christ Jesus.

We tend to give ourselves far too much credit:

- We tend to attribute too much righteousness to ourselves.
- We tend to think we have more wisdom than we do.
- We tend to pride ourselves on having the "right" character.
- We tend to think of ourselves as being more patient than we are.
- We tend to regard ourselves as perseverant.
- We tend to think we are submissive and obedient.
- We tend to believe we are more committed to the kingdom of God than we are.
- We simply tend to see ourselves as more godly than we are.

Here's the problem with this tendency: when you name yourself as righteous, when you attribute to yourself more maturity than you actually have, you don't seek the grace that is your only hope. We don't think we devalue grace, but that's exactly what many of us do. Because we look at ourselves and conclude that we're spiritually okay, we don't tend to have a deep esteem and appreciation for the grace that is our only hope in life and in death. You see, only people who acknowledge how deep their need is and who admit that they have no ability whatsoever to meet that need on their own get excited about the grace that meets every one of their spiritual needs.

On the other hand, we don't like to think of ourselves as needy, so we tend to minimize our sin. Sadly, many of us are far more concerned about the sin of others than our own. We pay far more attention to the spiritual needs of others than our own. Because we minimize our sin, seeing ourselves as righteous, we don't cry out for and run after the rescuing and transforming grace that is ours as the children of God. As long as we still have hope in us—that is, hope in our ability to be righteous on our own—we won't run after the grace that is offered us in Christ Jesus. It's only when we are willing to give up on us that we seek the rescue that God offers us.

Yes, it really is true that hopelessness is the doorway to hope. Seeing yourself as hopeless and helpless if left to yourself initiates and ignites your pursuit of God's grace. The fact is that we all give daily evidence of our continuing need for grace. Simply put, we have no ability to make it on our own. We still stand in desperate need of divine help. Are you willing to admit that and run to where grace can be found?

For further study and encouragement: Hebrews 4:14–16

SEPTEMBER 21

Good is not good enough; complete conformity to
Christ's image is the plan of grace.

Most of us are just too easily satisfied. It's not that we ask too much from our Savior. We have the polar opposite problem—we are willing to settle for far too little. Our personal goals, wishes, and dreams fall far short of God's plans and purposes for us. God will settle for nothing less than each of us being completely conformed to the likeness of his Son. He will finally and completely defeat sin and death. He will not abandon his purpose for any reason at any time. Our problem is that often we don't share his mind or buy into his purpose. Other mentalities capture us:

1. *The Consumer Mentality.* Here we're like religious shoppers. We really don't have functional loyalty to the plan of God. We're looking for a religious experience that is comfortable and meets our felt needs, and we have no problem in moving when we're dissatisfied.
2. *The "Good Is Good Enough" Mentality.* Here we're thankful for the changes that grace has brought into our lives, but we get satisfied too easily. We're satisfied with a little bit of biblical literacy or theological knowledge, a slightly better marriage, a little personal spiritual growth, and so on. We quit seeking, but God is far from being finished with transforming.
3. *The "This Bad Thing Can Work" Mentality.* Here we work to make the best out of what God says is not good. So, for example, a married couple is satisfied with marital détente; they learn to negotiate one another's idolatries rather than working toward a truly godly marriage.
4. *The Personal Comfort vs. Personal Holiness Mentality.* Here what captures our hearts is the craving for a life that is comfortable, pleasurable, predictable, and problem free. We tend to judge God's goodness based on how well life is working for us rather than on his zeal to make good on his redemptive promises to us.
5. *The Event vs. Process Mentality.* Here we are just impatient. We sort of want God to do the good things he has promised us, but we don't want to have to persevere through a lifelong process. We want God's work to be an event rather than a process, and when it's not, our commitment begins to lag.

Ask yourself today, "What do I really want from God?" Have you made the purposes of his grace your life purpose? Do you want what he wants or are you simply too easily satisfied?

For further study and encouragement: Philippians 2:1–18

SEPTEMBER 22

There is no need to be paralyzed by the opinions of another.
God gives you the ultimate tool of self-assessment,
the mirror of his Word.

It was twelve pages long, the kind of letter no one really wants to get. I didn't want to read it, but I knew I had to. She took me apart like a coroner doing an autopsy. Each paragraph was like a knife cutting into a different organ, searching for disease. The judgment was harsh and unrelenting. The examples of my failures in her eyes were many. There was little grace to be found in those twelve pages. When I got to the end of the letter, I felt that there was nothing left of me. I sat at my desk stunned. I was her pastor, but she had no respect for me whatsoever. I couldn't believe what I had read and I was paralyzed by the thought that others felt the same way. I felt glued to the seat, unable to move, without strength to continue. The next morning was worse. I woke up with a knot in the pit of my stomach. I wanted to run, to quit.

Now, no opinions of people should have that power, but often they do. Without knowing it, we put our identity and inner peace in the hands of the people around us. We look to them for what no flawed human being will ever be able to deliver. We ride the roller coaster of their views of us. We begin to do things not because they are right, but because we know they will please those whose opinion of us and acceptance of us mean more than they should. I think fear of man is a bigger motivation for many of us than we tend to admit.

The gospel of Jesus Christ frees us from this. First and foremost, it presents to us the only reliable standard of self-evaluation—the perfect mirror of the Word of God. Then it frees me from seeking my identity horizontally because I am given an eternal identity in Christ. It also frees me from being worried about being known or exposed because I know that nothing could ever be exposed about me that hasn't already been covered by the precious blood of Jesus. Further, it allows me to be approachable when people bring things to me that I need to hear and evaluate. I can do this because I know I'm a sinner and I know that the grace that has been given to me is greater than all of my sin. Finally, I am not worried about or haunted by what you think of me because I don't look to you for my inner sense of well-being. No matter how little I am appreciated by those around me, no matter how little I am understood, no matter how little I am loved, and no matter how little respect comes my way, I can go to bed in peace knowing that the one person who counts knows me thoroughly, but he will never turns his back on me even in light of his complete knowledge of my sin, weaknesses, and failures. Now, that's a reality that can free you from your bondage to the opinion of others.

For further study and encouragement: John 16:32

SEPTEMBER 23

God's care comes in many forms. In his patience,
God cares enough to give ample time for his
grace to do its transforming work.

When was the last time you reflected on the amazing patience of your heavenly Father? When was the last time you thanked him for his willingness to wait? Do you know that without God's incredibly patient heart, you and I would have no hope? God's patience is what gives time for his grace to do its work.

When I read through the Old Testament, I am blown away by the extent of God's patience. I have often thought that if I were on the joystick, given the degree of my impatience, Adam and Eve would've fallen in the morning, and Jesus would've come in the afternoon and then died and risen again that evening. But God's ways are not like my ways. Year laps upon year, decade upon decade, century upon century until literally thousands of years pass before Jesus comes to deal with the disaster of the fall. Yet Scripture says that Jesus comes at just the right moment (Rom. 5:6). This means that for all those years, God is preparing the world for the coming of the Savior.

I am also impressed by God's patience with Israel. We are hit with this when we read through the prophets. God doesn't just send one prophet to give one warning. No, in an amazing display of divine patience, he sends prophet after prophet, giving his children opportunity after opportunity to respond to his mercy.

I am also convicted by the patience of Jesus with his disciples. They never seem to get it quite right. Even as he is ascending, they are asking the wrong questions. But Jesus doesn't give up on them. He doesn't tell them that he has had it and that he is going to go out and pick new disciples. He gives time for his grace to transform this group of arrogant and confused men.

How can you and I not be grateful for God's patience with us? He doesn't demand of us instant maturity. He doesn't require that we get it right quickly. He doesn't teach us a lesson just once. He comes to us in situation after situation, each controlled by his sovereign grace, each designed to be a tool of transformation, and he works on the same things again and again. I don't like to have to repeat myself. I tend to want the people around me to understand quickly. I am grieved that my heart is still not like that of my Savior.

So God's care cannot be detached from his patience. It is his tender willingness to wait that allows his powerful grace to finish its transforming work. Thank God today for that patience. It is your hope. And as you are thanking him, pray that he will make you more like him—willing to give time for his mercy to do its work.

For further study and encouragement: 2 Peter 3:8–9

SEPTEMBER 24

We wander. God pursues and reconciles. We stumble and fall.
God forgives and restores. We grow tired and weary.
God empowers us by his grace.

It is a humbling and yet vital thing to acknowledge—you and I simply don't have much in our relationship with God and our growth in grace for which we can take credit. The fact of the matter is that we give daily proof of our ongoing need for that grace. The reality is that if we followed Jesus for a thousand years, we would need his grace as much for the next day as we did the first day that we believed.

He is the sun that gives us light. He is the refuge where we can hide. He is the water that nourishes us and the bread that feeds us. He is the solid rock on which we stand. He is the Captain who defends us against the enemy. He is wisdom, blessing us with the insight of truth. He is the Lamb that bore the penalty for our sin. He is the High Priest who daily brings our case to the Father. He is the faithful friend who will not forsake us even in our worst moments. He is the Giver who blesses us with spiritual riches that we could never earn. He is the One who makes us aware of our sin and brings conviction to our hearts. He is the Shepherd who seeks us when we have wandered and are lost, and brings us back to the fold of his care. None of these actions is a luxury for us. They are all necessary ingredients of our spiritual lives, yet they are not things that we could ever provide for ourselves. We are like babies, unable to meet our own needs and completely dependent on the love of our Father for life, sustenance, and health.

Thoughts of independent righteousness are a grand delusion. Taking credit for what only grace can produce is the height of spiritual arrogance. Thinking that the grace you once needed is no longer essential is a recipe for disaster. Without the patience, forgiveness, rescue, provision, transformation, and deliverance of his grace, we would have no spiritual hope whatsoever. We are not spiritually independent in any way. The opposite is true. Just as in the first moment we believed, we are always completely dependent on the grace of the Savior for every spiritual need. We cannot go it on our own. We have not produced fruit by our own righteousness and strength. There really is no good thing that we have that we have not received from God's gracious hand.

So there is no reason to boast. There is nothing for which we can take credit. All praise, honor, worship, and service go to God and God alone. He sought us. He birthed us. He sustains us. He matures us. He protects us. And he will finally deliver us. To him be the glory. Amen.

For further study and encouragement: Luke 15:11–32

SEPTEMBER 25

*Discouragement focuses more on the broken glories of
creation than on the restoring glories of God's
character, presence, and promises.*

What captures your mind controls your thoughts and dominates the desires of your
heart. Outside of intentional moments of public or private worship, what occupies
your private meditation? That which dominates your meditation shapes the way you
view yourself, life, and God, and your view of those things shapes the choices you
make and the actions you take.

Is your meditation kidnapped by:

- the disloyalty of that good friend?
- the sorry state of your finances?
- disappointment with your church?
- the dysfunction of your extended family?
- problems in your marriage?
- the daily struggles of parenting?
- your frenetic and demanding schedule?
- physical sickness?
- the daily hardships of life in this fallen world?

Now, you may be thinking: "Paul, what do I do with this stuff? How am I supposed to respond?" Well, one of the themes of this devotional is that biblical faith—
that is, true faith in the existence, presence, promises, and provisions of God—never
requires you to deny reality in any way. It is not biblical faith to try to convince
yourself that things are better than they actually are. It is not biblical faith to work
to make yourself feel good about what is not good. Biblical faith looks reality in the
face and does not flinch.

On the other hand, there is a crucial difference between facing hard realities
and allowing those realities to dominate the meditation of your heart (see God's
counsel to Joshua, Josh. 1:1–9). Here's what biblical faith does: it examines reality,
but it makes the Lord its meditation. It is only when you look at life through the
window of the glory of the One who has been the source of your meditation that
you see reality accurately. The more you meditate on your problems, the bigger and
more insurmountable they seem to be. Meditating on God in the midst of your
trouble reminds you once again that the God to whom grace has connected you is
magnificent in his grandeur and glory. He is infinitely greater than any problem you
could ever experience. Then your responses are shaped by his glory and not by the
seeming size of your problems.

For further study and encouragement: Psalm 143

SEPTEMBER 26

True faith lives on the basis of two unshakable realities—
that God really does exist and that he always
rewards those who seek him.

Grace has positioned me
on two foundation stones
that have redefined
my identity,
redirected my purpose,
reshaped my desires,
rescued my thoughts,
and reformed my living.
I have new reason
to get up in the morning
and face my day
with courage,
hope
joy,
confidence,
and rest.
Your grace has changed
everything,
for it has made me
sure
that you exist
and that
you reward
those who seek you (Heb. 11:6).

For further study and encouragement: Hebrews 11

SEPTEMBER 27

No need to fear what God will ask of you, because in the asking is always the promise of grace to empower your heart and hands.

Consider God's call to Moses to lead the Israelites out of their cruel captivity in Egypt. In Moses's reply, we see a reflection of our frequent response when God asks something of us:

> Then the LORD said, "I have surely seen the affliction of my people who are in Egypt and have heard their cry because of their taskmasters. I know their sufferings, and I have come down to deliver them out of the hand of the Egyptians and to bring them up out of that land to a good and broad land, a land flowing with milk and honey, to the place of the Canaanites, the Hittites, the Amorites, the Perizzites, the Hivites, and the Jebusites. And now, behold, the cry of the people of Israel has come to me, and I have also seen the oppression with which the Egyptians oppress them. Come, I will send you to Pharaoh that you may bring my people, the children of Israel, out of Egypt." But Moses said to God, "Who am I that I should go to Pharaoh and bring the children of Israel out of Egypt?" He said, "But I will be with you, and this shall be the sign for you, that I have sent you: when you have brought the people out of Egypt, you shall serve God on this mountain." . . .
>
> But Moses said to the LORD, "Oh, my Lord, I am not eloquent, either in the past or since you have spoken to your servant, but I am slow of speech and of tongue." Then the LORD said to him, "Who has made man's mouth? Who makes him mute, or deaf, or seeing, or blind? Is it not I, the LORD? Now therefore go, and I will be with your mouth and teach you what you shall speak." But he said, "Oh, my Lord, please send someone else." (Ex. 3:7–12; 4:10–13)

Throughout this amazing encounter with the Lord, Moses does what we often do as we evaluate what God has put on our plates and how he has called us to respond. Moses omits the ultimate fact that changes everything about the way we think and should respond to God's call. That fact is not the difficulty of the calling or your perceived ability to answer that call. It is not the size of the situation or the size of your wisdom and strength. This life-changing fact is that the God of glory and grace, who calls his people to do his will on earth, always goes with them as they obey his calling. He never sends without going too. When he sends you, he doesn't give you a bunch of stuff to help you along the way. He always gives you himself because *he* is what you need and he alone can give you what is required.

When Moses finally says, "Oh, my Lord, please send someone else," it is clear that he does not understand the present power of his identity as a child of God. Because he is God's chosen child, he is never, ever alone. Because he is God's child, God will never send him on a task by himself. Hope for Moses's success is not to be found in his personal strength and wisdom, but in the expansive glory of the One who sent him. Remember today that when God sends, he goes too!

For further study and encouragement: Deuteronomy 31:1–8

SEPTEMBER 28

Laziness is rooted in self-love. It's taking ourselves off the hook,
opting for the comfortable instead of the best. Grace isn't lazy.

It's hard to hear. We want to think it applies to others and not us. It's bad news that we need, but don't really want to consider. Here it is—as long as sin lives inside us, laziness will be an issue for us all. Before you quit reading and skip to the next devotion, let me explain.

Second Corinthians 5:15 says that Jesus came so that "those who live might no longer live for themselves." Embedded in this phrase is a diagnostic that applies to every person who has ever lived. Paul is arguing here that the coming of and sacrifice of Jesus were necessary because the DNA of sin is selfishness. Sin causes me to ignore God's existence and his rightful claim on every area of my life. Because God is not in his rightful place in my living, that is, in the center of it all, I then insert myself in that place. My life becomes all about me. The borders of my concern go little further than my concerns for me. I reduce my focus down to the small space of my wants, my needs, and my feelings. In ways that really do shape my living, I make it all about me. The desires of my heart are gobbled up by my ease, my comfort, my pleasure, and my success. I want what I want, and when I get what I want, I am happy.

Now, because as a sinner I tend to make life all about me, I work to avoid anything that is hard or uncomfortable to do. I tend to curse hard work, the need to serve others, the call to persevere, the inescapable reality of suffering, the requirement of daily labor, the call to engage myself in the work of a bigger kingdom than my own, or the moral requirement to use my gifts for the glory of someone other than myself.

There are ways in which sin makes us all work avoiders. It tends to make us all think that the good life is the life free of the need for labor. But the fact of the matter is that we were created to work, and not just for the good of our own lives, but in willing and joyful submission to the One who created us. Work is not a curse; it is our created identity. One of the reasons we were put on earth is to care for the physical world that God made. It is true that the work that we are called to do in submission to the One who made us has been made more difficult because we now labor in a seriously broken world; but before the fall of the world, Adam and Eve were instructed to work. So laziness is another one of those ever-present arguments for our need for grace. Until grace has completed its work, we will tend to find work more of a burden than a calling and a joy. Grace and grace alone is able to make otherwise lazy people industrious workers to the glory of God.

For further study and encouragement: Genesis 1–3

SEPTEMBER 29

God calls you to grow in your faith and then feeds you with
the growth-producing nutrients of his grace and truth.

Are you growing in your faith? Do you care if you're not? Have you become satisfied with a little bit of Bible knowledge and a little bit of doctrinal understanding? Have you stopped feeding on the spiritual food of God's grace even though that grace has not yet come anywhere near to finishing its work in you? Do you hunger for the grace you've been given to continue to do its transforming work in the places where there's evidence that there's more work to be done? Are you satisfied with being a little more religious or a little more spiritual? Could it be that you claim to be a believer, but are satisfied to have parts of your life shaped by other values? Does your relationship with God really shape the way you think about and act in your marriage, in your friendships, in your parenting, in your job, in your finances, as a citizen or neighbor, in your private pursuits, or in your secret thoughts and desires? As you examine yourself, are you able to be satisfied in places where God is not? Are you pursuing the grace that you've been given because you know that you regularly demonstrate that you are not yet a grace graduate?

When I think on this topic, my mind immediately runs to two passages:

So put away all malice and all deceit and hypocrisy and envy and all slander. Like newborn infants, long for the pure spiritual milk, that by it you may grow up into salvation—if indeed you have tasted that the Lord is good.

As you come to him, a living stone rejected by men but in the sight of God chosen and precious, you yourselves like living stones are being built up as a spiritual house, to be a holy priesthood, to offer spiritual sacrifices acceptable to God through Jesus Christ. (1 Pet. 2:1–5)

About this we have much to say, and it is hard to explain, since you have become dull of hearing. For though by this time you ought to be teachers, you need someone to teach you again the basic principles of the oracles of God. You need milk, not solid food, for everyone who lives on milk is unskilled in the word of righteousness, since he is a child. But solid food is for the mature, for those who have their powers of discernment trained by constant practice to distinguish good from evil. (Heb. 5:11–14)

Be honest today—which passage best describes you? Are you that ravenous baby who can't get enough of his mother's milk or the person who should be mature enough to digest solid food, but isn't ready? Remember, you don't have to defend yourself or deny the evidence; the grace of Jesus has freed you from that. The cross of Jesus welcomes you to be honest because all the places where you need to be honest have been covered by the blood of Jesus. And remember too that it takes grace to admit how much you still need grace. That grace is yours in Jesus.

For further study and encouragement: Hebrews 5:11–6:12

SEPTEMBER 30

The life we couldn't live, he lived for us. The death we should have died, he died for us. The new life we need, he gives to us.

Only the amazing grace of God has the power to transport us from death to life. There is just no human effort that could accomplish this. Salvation is simply beyond our grasp. A relationship with God stands outside our reach. Moral perfection is a mountain too high for us to climb. Living to God's glory exceeds our finest motivation. Righteousness and wisdom fall outside the scope of our natural abilities. If left to ourselves, there is no way that we would ever be what we were created to be or would do the things we were made to do. We all fall short of God's standard and are all deserving of his penalty.

If you don't understand and accept the gravity of your condition and your inability to alter it, the Bible, and particularly the work of Christ, will make no sense to you at all. Why did God go to the history-shaping extent of sending his Son to earth? Why was it necessary for Jesus to live a completely perfect life for thirty-three years? Why was it important for him to walk in our shoes and experience the full range of the temptations that we face? Why was it vital for him to suffer and die? Why did there absolutely have to be a resurrection? Why? The answers to these questions can be found by tracing a thread that runs throughout the Bible. God went to this radical extent because there was no other way. We were not only hopelessly ensnared by sin and tragically guilty before God, but we were also completely unable to help ourselves. We were dead in our sin—about as able to help ourselves out of our condition as a corpse would be able to help itself out of its casket.

There had to be a Savior because we have no ability whatsoever to save ourselves. We can escape situations, locations, and relationships, but we cannot escape ourselves. We cannot run from who we are, what we have done, and what we deserve. The only hope is that God in redeeming love and glorious grace will move toward us, doing for us what we cannot do for ourselves.

So God sent his Son to be the second Adam. He would face the temptations that Adam faced, but he would not fall. He would obey perfectly where Adam disobeyed and he would willingly take on himself Adam's punishment. The second Adam would die in Adam's and his descendants' place. He would meet God's moral requirement and satisfy his anger, and in so doing, he would open the way again for us to have an eternal relationship with God. Everything Jesus did, he did as a substitute. Everything he did, he did for you.

For further study and encouragement: Romans 5:12–21

OCTOBER 1

Because he is zealous to rescue you from you, God's care can be violent.
He rips you from what is dangerous to give you what is better.

When you think of God's care, what picture comes into your mind? When you consider God's grace, what mental images does the term *grace* conjure up? Could it be that there are times in your life when you are crying out for the grace of God even though you're getting it? God's grace does not always come in the form of comfort and encouragement. His care doesn't always mean relief and release. Could it be that the "care" that we often cry out for is not the care that we really need?

There was a cycle in the life of the children of Israel that is very instructive. Remember that they were people just like us, and the accounts about them were written for our example and instruction, so that we would not fall into the same errors. In grace, God recorded for us their struggles with grace so that we would esteem and run toward the grace we've been given. Carefully examine the description that follows:

> And the people of Israel did what was evil in the sight of the LORD and served the Baals. And they abandoned the LORD, the God of their fathers, who had brought them out of the land of Egypt. They went after other gods, from among the gods of the peoples who were around them, and bowed down to them. And they provoked the LORD to anger. . . . So the anger of the LORD was kindled against Israel, and he gave them over to plunderers, who plundered them. And he sold them into the hand of their surrounding enemies, so that they could no longer withstand their enemies. . . .
>
> Then the LORD raised up judges, who saved them out of the hand of those who plundered them. Yet they did not listen to their judges, for they whored after other gods and bowed down to them. They soon turned aside from the way in which their fathers had walked, who had obeyed the commandments of the LORD, and they did not do so. Whenever the LORD raised up judges for them, the LORD was with the judge, and he saved them from the hand of their enemies all the days of the judge. For the LORD was moved to pity by their groaning because of those who afflicted and oppressed them. But whenever the judge died, they turned back and were more corrupt than their fathers, going after other gods, serving them and bowing down to them. They did not drop any of their practices or their stubborn ways. (Judg. 2:11–19)

The children of Israel were not on God's care agenda page. God sent the violent care of trouble in order to rescue their hearts from idolatry, but all that his children wanted was the situational care of freedom from their enemies, and when they got it, they turned back to their sinful ways. Today, what kind of care do you long for from the hands of your Messiah of grace?

For further study and encouragement: Judges 2–3

OCTOBER 2

You simply must not underestimate sin
and you simply cannot overestimate grace.

Think for a moment: whose sin do you tend to minimize? Your friends'? Your spouse's? Your children's? Your neighbors'? Your extended family members'? Your father's or mother's? Your boss's? For most of us, the problem is not that we underestimate the sin of others. No, we tend to do the opposite. We're typically all too focused on the failure of others. We find it all too easy to point out their flaws. We're all tempted to keep a running record of the specific sins of the people around us. If we were honest, most of us would have to humbly confess that we tend to be far more concerned about the sin of the people around us than our own. We tend to be hyperaware of the weaknesses of those living near us while we appear to be functionally blind to our own. For this reason, we begin to forget that we are more like them than unlike them, that there are few things that we can see in the lives of others that are not present in our own lives in some way.

Now, this outward concern/inward denial dynamic is not okay. Blindness to your own sin is a denial of the presence of personal spiritual need. Such a denial always leads to a devaluing of and a resistance to God's grace. Denying your need for grace and underestimating the power of what that grace can do never, ever leads to anything good.

Here's the problem—this side of forever, we are all very good at doing both. We're all very good at looking at our sin and naming it less than sin, and we all tend to degrade the glory of what grace has done, is doing, and will do. People who deny sin tend to not progressively conquer it, and people who devalue grace tend not to run to it for help. What we're talking about here are the two sides of a healthy Christian life. You confess that although you are in Christ, the presence of sin is still within you. However, it is being progressively defeated, and you humbly embrace the fact that you have been given glorious grace that can do for you what you could never do for yourself.

The admission of sin doesn't lead you somewhere dark and depressing, because you know you've been given grace that is greater than your sin, and your celebration of grace is real and heartfelt because it's done in the context of your confession of the very sin that grace addresses. Confession of sin without the celebration of grace leads to guilt, self-loathing, timidity, and spiritual paralysis. Embracing grace without the admission of sin leads to confident theological "always rightism," but does not result in change in your heart and life. So today, refuse to minimize sin, reject the temptation to devalue grace, and run to Jesus weeping and celebrating at the same time.

For further study and encouragement: 1 John 2:1–17

OCTOBER 3

You don't have to understand everything in your life,
because your Lord of wisdom and grace understands it all.

It is a paradox that many of us don't handle well. We were created by God to be rational human beings and we carry around with us a desire to know and understand, but we must not forget that we will never experience inner peace simply because all our questions have been answered. Biblical faith is not irrational, but it takes us beyond our ability to reason. As believers in our identity as God's image-bearers and the truthfulness of his Word, we do recognize that it is important to study, to learn, to examine, to evaluate, and to know. But we are not rationalists. We do not trust our reason more than we trust God. We do not reject what God says is true when it doesn't make sense to us, and we know that God's secret will leaves us with mysteries in our lives; mysteries that, even with the best of our theology, we won't be able to solve. Biblical literacy does not dispel all confusion and mystery from your life because while God reveals his will for you in the Bible, he does not reveal all the things he will do in your life for your good and his glory. God surprises you.

So you ask, "Where is peace to be found?" This question is answered clearly and powerfully in Isaiah 26:

> You keep him in perfect peace
>   whose mind is stayed on you,
>   because he trusts in you.
> Trust in the LORD forever,
>   for the LORD GOD is an everlasting rock. (vv. 3–4)

This passage tells us where peace is to be found. It is never found in trying to figure out the secret will of God. It's not to be found in personal planning or attempts to control the circumstances and people in your life. Peace is found in trusting the person who controls all the things that you don't understand and who knows no mystery because he has planned it all. How do you experience this remarkable peace—the kind of peace that doesn't fade away when disappointments come, when people are difficult, or when circumstances are hard? You experience it by keeping your mind stayed on the Lord. The more you meditate on his glory, his power, his wisdom, his grace, his faithfulness, his righteousness, his patience, his zeal to redeem, and his commitment to his eternal promises to you, the more you can deal with mystery in your life. Why? Because you know the One behind the mystery is gloriously good, worthy not only of your trust but also the worship of your heart. It really is true that peace in times of trouble is not found in figuring out your life, but in worship of the One who has everything figured out already.

For further study and encouragement: Psalm 139

OCTOBER 4

Our struggle with sin is so deep that it was not enough for God to forgive us, so he also unzipped us and got inside of us by his Spirit.

Perhaps all good theology is meant to be both humbling and comforting at the same time. Why is this? God did not intend the theology of the Bible to be an end in itself, as if theological knowledge were the goal of grace. No, every part of the Bible's teaching is designed to be a means to an end, and the end is a radically transformed life. Having said this, the theology of the Holy Spirit in the New Testament is particularly humbling.

Why doesn't God just save me in the beginning, welcome me into his presence in the end, and leave me to myself in between? Why is the indwelling presence of the Holy Spirit presented as an absolute gift of necessity for every believer? The answer is because of the utter gravity of my condition as a sinner. You see, justification deals with the guilt of sin and final glorification with the ultimate defeat of sin, but the presence and power of the sin that remains in between must be addressed or the work of grace will not be complete.

Sin does not leave us merely *guilty*; it renders us *unable*. It robs us of the ability to live in a way that pleases God. Sin kidnaps our desires and distorts our thoughts. It controls our tongues and rules our behavior. It saps our resolve and weakens our knees. It leaves us lame, weak, and unable. We don't just need forgiveness and ultimate deliverance; we also desperately need present help—help so that we will have the will to desire and the power to do what is good in the sight of God. Our struggle with sin is so deep that only God living inside us can give us the power to please him with our living. So God doesn't just forgive us, call us to do what is right, and promise us a final home with him; he comes to us in between. He gets inside us, working within us, because there is no possibility that we will desire and do what is right without the inner working of his power.

How humbling! Not only can we not take credit for our salvation, because it is all the result of God's justifying grace, but we also cannot take credit for any aspect or any instance of our obedience, because apart from the Spirit's presence, we would have neither the motivation nor the power to obey. Yes, we are new creatures in Christ, and yes, we are alive in him, but without the Spirit, we would have no power to defeat sin.

Where's the comfort in this? Here it is: if you're God's child, you already have the Holy Spirit inside you. You don't have to hope and pray that he will be there for you. He has come, and his convicting and enabling grace is his moment-by-moment gift to you.

For further study and encouragement: Philippians 2:1–13

OCTOBER 5

Faith in God is more than believing the right things.
It's living the right way because you believe the right things.

Hebrews 11:1–7 is a say-it-all description of what faith is and what faith does:

> Now faith is the assurance of things hoped for, the conviction of things not seen. For by it the people of old received their commendation. By faith we understand that the universe was created by the word of God, so that what is seen was not made out of things that are visible.
>
> By faith Abel offered to God a more acceptable sacrifice than Cain, through which he was commended as righteous, God commending him by accepting his gifts. And through his faith, though he died, he still speaks. By faith Enoch was taken up so that he should not see death, and he was not found, because God had taken him. Now before he was taken he was commended as having pleased God. And without faith it is impossible to please him, for whoever would draw near to God must believe that he exists and that he rewards those who seek him. By faith Noah, being warned by God concerning events as yet unseen, in reverent fear constructed an ark for the saving of his household. By this he condemned the world and became an heir of the righteousness that comes by faith.

The belief of the heart and mind is an essential ingredient of faith, but it does not summarize all that faith is. True biblical faith is always something that you live. If your faith does not reshape your life, it is not true faith. Faith is not just intellectual assent to a body of truth. I'm afraid that's what faith looks like in evangelical academic circles. But real faith radically rearranges your life. This is why Hebrews 11 focuses more on what people did with their lives than it does on the details of their theology. Faith *is* deeply theological, but it is much, much more than that.

As the writer of Hebrews defines faith, he immediately gives three examples of how real faith in God transforms the way that you live. First, faith redirects and recaptures the *worship* of your heart (Abel). Second, it produces in you a heart of *obedience* (Enoch). Third, faith causes you to submit to the *calling* of God (Noah). Now think about it: everyone's life is shaped by what he worships, by the rules that she obeys, and by the life calling that he gives himself to. True, living, biblical faith causes you to submit all three of these shaping influences to God. He becomes the object of the worship of your heart. His rules define the moral boundaries of your life. And his kingdom work becomes your joyful calling. It's radical to believe that God really does exist and rewards those who seek him, and that radical belief does radical things to your living. Remember, you can't conjure up this life-shaping faith. No, it is a gift of his grace.

For further study and encouragement: Genesis 6–9

OCTOBER 6

*Without eternity in the center of our thinking, our picture
of life is like a jigsaw puzzle missing a central piece.*

One of the themes of this devotional is that all human beings have a theological bent, whether they consider themselves religious or not. Everyone wants life to make sense. Everyone is a committed interpreter. No one leaves his or her life alone. We all pick our lives apart, trying to make sense of them. We all develop our own systems of theology, biblical or otherwise. We all develop particular philosophies of life. We all carry around with us worldviews that shape the way we think, the things that we desire, the choices that we make, the words that we say, and the actions that we take. None of us is passive. We all shape the way life looks to ourselves.

So God, knowing who we are and knowing that we are hardwired to make sense of our lives, has given us his Word. In it, he reveals who he is, he defines who we are, he explains the meaning and purpose of life, he unfolds the greatest of humanity's problems—sin—and he points us to the hope of his amazing grace. He doesn't tell us everything, because we would not be able to understand everything or deal with it in our daily lives, but he does give us all the necessary pieces of an "origin-to-destiny worldview" so we can live as we were created to live.

Essential to this biblical worldview is eternity. The Bible confronts us with the reality that this is not all there is. It tells us that this world is marching toward a final conclusion. You and I are eternal beings who will spend eternity somewhere. It will either be in the presence of God forever and ever or separated from him in a place of eternal punishment forever and ever.

The reality of eternity infuses the here and now with seriousness and hope. The way you live is important because there is an eternity to follow. The choices you make are important because there is a forever. The things you believe are important because the world is moving toward eternity. The things you surrender your heart to are important because there is an eternal tomorrow. You simply cannot hold to an "all that's important is the pleasures of the moment" view of life and believe in eternity at the same time. In light of eternity, it makes no sense to forget God and live for yourself. In the face of eternity, it is irrational to write your own rules and demand your own way. Eternity requires you to take life seriously.

But eternity also fills this moment with hope. Because I know that this is not all there is, I also know that the sin, trials, and sufferings of the present will not last forever. For God's children, eternity promises that sin will die, suffering will end, our trials will be no more, and we will live with God in perfect peace forever and ever and ever. You just can't make proper sense of life without viewing it from the perspective of eternity.

For further study and encouragement: John 5:19–29

OCTOBER 7

A thing I can't live without, such that I doubt God's love when it is absent, becomes a functional God-replacement, directing my heart more than he does.

Be honest right here, right now—what do you tell yourself that you don't have? What have you become convinced that you can't live without? What are the "if-onlys" that you carry around with you that shape the way you think about yourself, about life, and about the goodness of God? In the absence of what are you tempted to doubt the faithfulness of God? When you look back with joy at how things have gone in a certain situation or relationship, what gives you that joy?

Here's where all these questions are going: What things of this earth tend to capture your heart and, in so doing, control your thoughts, words, and behavior? The apostle Paul captures the struggle that we're examining here with these words: "If then you have been raised with Christ, seek the things that are above, where Christ is, seated at the right hand of God. Set your mind on things that are above, not on things that are on earth" (Col. 3:1–2). Immediately after writing a beautiful depiction of the gospel of Jesus Christ, why does Paul lay out the call of this passage? The answer is that he knows his audience. He knows that even though they are God's children, the spiritual war is not over for them yet. There is a constant struggle for the rulership of their hearts. From a big-picture perspective, the heart can be captured or ruled by only two things. I'll use Paul's terms. Your heart is always living under the rule of "things that are above" or "things that are on earth."

At street level, you and I are either worshiping and serving the creation or the Creator. The spiritual struggle is that we all tend to vacillate between the two. There are times when we get it right, and the deepest motivation and joy of our hearts is to live in a way that pleases God. But there are other times when we tell ourselves that there is some created thing that we have to have, and we functionally forget God and give ourselves to getting this thing that has captured our thoughts and shapes our desires.

This "above" or "earth" struggle is the great spiritual war between your conversion and your final homegoing. It really is fought in all of the situations, locations, and relationships of your daily life. It is not wrong to celebrate created glories. It is not wrong to want them in your life. It is not wrong to work to get them. But they must not be allowed to rule your heart and, in ruling your heart, to become your functional God-replacement. Not only is this struggle the big battle of the Christian life, it is also a principal argument for our ongoing need of grace—grace that can free us from our bondage to things that will never give us what God alone can give: life.

For further study and encouragement: 1 Timothy 6:17–19

OCTOBER 8

Corporate worship reminds you that hope is not a situation, location, idea, or thing. Hope is a person, and his name is Jesus.

But when the goodness and loving kindness of God our Savior appeared, he saved us, not because of works done by us in righteousness, but according to his own mercy, by the washing of regeneration and renewal of the Holy Spirit, whom he poured out on us richly through Jesus Christ our Savior, so that being justified by his grace we might become heirs according to the hope of eternal life. The saying is trustworthy, and I want you to insist on these things, so that those who have believed in God may be careful to devote themselves to good works. These things are excellent and profitable for people. (Titus 3:4–8)

Everyone wants it. It's the thing that fuels what we do. It's the thing that stimulates courage and perseverance. It's what gets you through the tough times and keeps you from quitting. It's hard to be happy and hard to get up and continue when you don't have any of it. What is it? Hope, of course. Everyone craves hope.

Now, the radical message of the Bible, captured well by the Titus passage, is that sturdy hope, hope that won't ever fail you or leave you embarrassed, is only found vertically. The horizontal situations, locations, experiences, and relationships of everyday life are dangerous places to look for hope. Why? They all fail you. First, everywhere you could look horizontally has been affected by the fall in some way. There are simply no perfectly ideal situations, no paradise locations, no completely satisfying experiences, and surely no perfect people this side of eternity. Add to this the fact that all these things are fleeting. None of them lasts. Every horizontal thing, this side of eternity, is in the process of decay. So hope that addresses your deepest needs, that gives you reason to continue no matter how hard life is, and that promises you eternal good is only ever found vertically.

Perhaps it's not enough to say that hope is found in God and his covenant promises. That surely is true, but more needs to be said. Hope really does rest on the shoulders of the One who is the fulfillment of all those covenant promises. It's not enough to say that reliable hope is hope in Jesus. The message of the Bible is more powerful and pointed than even that. Reliable hope *is* Jesus! In his life, death, and resurrection, your life is infused with hope. The grace of the cross is not just grace that forgives and accepts, but grace that also supplies you with everything you need until you are needy no more. And what does this hope produce, according to the Titus passage? It produces a brand-new way of living. Because the One who is hope has infused my life with hope, I do not have to search for hope any longer and can now give myself to a life of good works. Do you know this hope? If not, a good first step toward finding it would be to gather with other believers this Lord's Day to worship the One who is your hope. To find hope, find Him.

For further study and encouragement: Romans 5:1–11

OCTOBER 9

Today you are called to abandon the purposes of your kingdom and give yourself to the will of a greater King. Grace makes it possible.

It is the view of life between the "already" and the "not yet" that every Christian needs to have. It's captured powerfully by the apostle Paul in Ephesians 6:10–18:

> Finally, be strong in the Lord and in the strength of his might. Put on the whole armor of God, that you may be able to stand against the schemes of the devil. For we do not wrestle against flesh and blood, but against the rulers, against the authorities, against the cosmic powers over this present darkness, against the spiritual forces of evil in the heavenly places. Therefore take up the whole armor of God, that you may be able to withstand in the evil day, and having done all, to stand firm. Stand therefore, having fastened on the belt of truth, and having put on the breastplate of righteousness, and, as shoes for your feet, having put on the readiness given by the gospel of peace. In all circumstances take up the shield of faith, with which you can extinguish all the flaming darts of the evil one; and take the helmet of salvation, and the sword of the Spirit, which is the word of God, praying at all times in the Spirit, with all prayer and supplication. To that end keep alert with all perseverance, making supplication for all the saints.

Why does Paul end his letter to the Ephesians this way? He does so because he understands that on this side of forever, life *is* war. When he tells his readers to put on gospel armor and get ready for war, Paul is not introducing a new topic; no, he's summarizing everything he's said so far. Every directive he has given—that is, every application of what it means to live in light of the gospel of Jesus Christ—must be lived out in the context of a great spiritual battle. What is this war about? It is the great war for the rulership of our hearts. With sin still living inside of us, we are still torn between our love for the claustrophobic little kingdom of self and the grand and glorious purposes of the kingdom of God. We still are tempted to want our own way and to write our own rules. We still tend to value comfort and pleasure more than we love redemption. We are tempted to have more excitement in the things of this world than we do with the reality that we have become the children of God. We still complain when sanctifying trials come our way and we still tend to credit God with faithfulness only when things in our lives seem to be working.

This great spiritual war is not the rare, exotic experience of demons dancing on the table that we often think it is. No, it is the constant battle for our hearts that will rage between God and a seductive and deceptive enemy until that enemy is under the foot of Jesus. Ephesians 6:10–18 reminds you that you have been given ample grace for this battle.

For further study and encouragement: 1 John 2:15–17

OCTOBER 10

If you're God's child, you've been called to forsake your "my life"
mentality and daily live with a moment-by-moment ministry mentality.

What do you want for your life? What are you really living for? If you could have the
"good life," what would it look like? If you were to say, "If only I had _____, then my
life would be _____," how would you fill in the blanks? Could it be that even though
you are God's child, you still think of your life as belonging to you? When you think
of your life this way, then ministry is about stepping out of your life, giving God a
little bit of your time, energy, and money, and then stepping back into your life. In
this way of thinking, ministry is something separate from your daily life. It tends to
be structured and scheduled by the leaders of your church, and you support it for
a while with your own efforts. But behind this view of ministry is the thought that
your life still belongs to you, and you give moments of it to the Lord for his work.

The view of ministry in the New Testament is radically different (see Eph.
4:1–16; 1 Corinthians 12; Col. 3:12–17). The New Testament is quite clear in its call
to us to understand that our lives no longer belong to us. We don't own our physicality. We don't own our emotionality. We don't own our spirituality. We don't own our
mentality. We don't own our psychology. We don't own our communicative abilities.
We don't own our relationships. We don't own our gifts or our experiences. We don't
even own our possessions in the deepest sense of what ownership means. Paul gets
at this when he says at the end of a discussion of sexuality in 1 Corinthians 6, "You
are not your own, for you were bought with a price" (v. 19). You begin to get close
to what God has designed your life to be as one of his children when you understand
that nothing that makes up you and your life belongs to you. You and all that makes
up you were bought with a price, so you are owned by the One who paid that price.

But there is a second thing that the New Testament makes very clear. It is that
God has called all his children not to be mere recipients of his kingdom work of
grace, but to be instruments of that work as well. It is what I call the "total involvement paradigm," that is, all God's people all of the time. Every one of God's children
has been given a call to ministry, and every one must think of himself that way.

Finally, the New Testament does not teach a separation between life and ministry.
Every dimension of your life is a forum for ministry. Marriage is ministry. Friendship
is ministry. Parenting is ministry. Being a neighbor is ministry. The workplace is a
place of ministry.

You have been called to represent a glorious Savior, who has graced you with
everything you need to live with a ministry mentality.

For further study and encouragement: Luke 17:7–10

OCTOBER 11

God is not satisfied with you being a witness to his work of grace.
He's called you to be an instrument of that grace to others.

The position God has chosen for us in the work of his kingdom is an amazing thing. All of his children have a mind-boggling calling. Sadly, many of them don't understand their position, and because they don't, they are quite comfortable being consumers and quite timid when it comes to being instruments.

So many people who attend evangelical churches on Sunday have little life commitment to the work of those churches. Most pastors would be thrilled if the vast majority of their people were every-Sunday attenders and committed to financially supporting the work of the churches. But all this sadly falls far below God's wise design for his church. Think about it: you will simply never be able to hire enough professional ministry people to cover all the ministry needs in a given week, no matter what size your church is. It is no wonder people reach outside the body of Christ for help. It is no wonder problems are left to grow until they reach intense levels of complication.

All God's children have been called to the same position. We've all been called to be his ambassadors. Remember, the only thing an ambassador does is represent. God's plan is to make his invisible presence and his invisible grace visible through his people, who incarnate his presence and carry that grace to others. That's God's call to every one of his children. There are to be no self-satisfied recipients, no consumers. The body of Christ is designed by God to be an organic, constantly ministering community.

If the church is ever going to be this, then God's people need three things. First, we need *vision*. We need to be reminded again and again of our place in the work of the Redeemer. Next, we need *commitment*. We need to be encouraged to make specific and concrete decisions to better position ourselves for the work to which God has called us. Last, we need *training*. We need to understand what it really looks like to represent the grace of the Redeemer in the lives of the people whom he puts in our paths. We need to be trained not to see those relationships as belonging to us for our happiness, but rather as workrooms in which the Lord can do his transforming work of grace.

What an amazing way to live! We have been chosen by God to be part of the most important work of the universe. We have been chosen to carry the life-changing message of the grace of the Savior King with us wherever we go. And we have been given the same grace to enable us to be the ambassadors that we have been chosen to be.

For further study and encouragement: 1 Chronicles 16:8–27

OCTOBER 12

Prayer is abandoning a life of demand and complaint, recognizing undeserved blessing, and giving myself to a life of thankfulness.

When you think of prayer, what comes to mind? When you pray, what is it that you want from God? What requests dominate your life of prayer?

True prayer happens at the intersection of *surrender* and *celebration*. Prayer is profoundly more than handing a wish list to God and letting him know that you're thankful that he exists and has the power to deliver. This kind of prayer puts you at the center and, in a real way, reduces God down to the divine waiter. It's not him that you want. It's not his wisdom that you see yourself as needing. It's not his grace that your heart craves. Wish-list prayer essentially says, "I know what's best for my life and I'd appreciate it, God, if you would use your might to make it happen." You pray like this when you forget that God, as Creator and Savior, knows infinitely more than you do about what you really need. But even more than that, this kind of prayer makes life all about your wants, your needs, and your feelings. This is not really prayer after all. In true prayer, you surrender your claim on your life to the greater and wiser plans and purposes of God. You submit your will to his will. It's not God signing your list, it's you surrendering your life to him.

Then prayer is celebration. In prayer, you bask in the wonder of what it means that you actually do have a heavenly Father. You find joy in the reality that he has chosen to give you his kingdom. You are blown away by the fact that he unleashes his almighty power to meet your needs. You celebrate forgiving, rescuing, transforming, enabling, and delivering grace. You find joy in your inclusion in his work of redemption. You find hope in the glorious future that is to come. You are amazed by the fact that because Immanuel has invaded your life by his grace, you are never, ever alone. You find peace in the fact that grace means you are never left to the small resources of your own wisdom, righteousness, and strength. You meditate on God's glory and goodness, then celebrate. You rejoice in the fact that you no longer have to look for life in the people, situations, and locations around you, but you've been given life—life that is eternal.

Does true prayer include making requests of God? Sure it does. God encourages us to cast our cares on him, because he really does care for us. But the requests of true prayer are always in the context of surrender and celebration. It is surrender and celebration that keep those requests from being selfish demands or bitter complaints. This kind of prayer is a tool of God's grace in your life. As you put God in his proper place and celebrate your place as his child, prayer becomes a tool God uses to free you from your bondage to you. Now, that's grace!

For further study and encouragement: Matthew 6:5–15

OCTOBER 13

You can't hear him, but he's wiser; you can't see him, but he's more faithful; you can't touch him, but he's nearer than whatever else you'd trust.

It is one of the most amazing statements of what only grace can do. On the surface, it doesn't make any sense. If it were not rooted in the most important fact of the universe that you could ever consider, you would call the people involved "crazy." It marks the fundamental dividing line of all human beings. The apostle Peter is talking about believers living between the "already" and the "not yet" when he says of their relationship to Jesus Christ: "Though you have not seen him, you love him. Though you do not now see him, you believe in him and rejoice with joy that is inexpressible and filled with glory, obtaining the outcome of your faith, the salvation of your souls" (1 Pet. 1:8–9).

Now, allow yourself to consider the radical nature of what this passage says about the deepest motivations of the hearts of God's people. They have connected their deepest love, belief, joy, and faith to someone they have never seen, heard, or touched. They have staked the hopes and dreams of their lives to this invisible One. Their relationship to him is one of life-altering love. When they think of him, they experience joy, joy so deep that it cannot be expressed.

If it were not for the fact that the ultimate fact of human existence—the fact that gives meaning to every other fact—is the existence, character, and plan of God, none of this would make any sense at all. You would stand back, look at these "believers," and conclude that they were delusional, crazy. But they are not crazy. They are the blessed ones, the enlightened ones, the ones whose hearts have been opened to the most important thing that your heart could embrace.

This is what grace does. It rescues us from our spiritual blindness. It releases us from our bondage to our rationalism and materialism. Grace gives us the faith to be utterly assured of what we cannot see. It frees us from refusing to believe in anything we cannot experience with our physical senses. But grace does more. It connects us to the invisible One in an eternal love relationship that fills us with joy we have never known before and gives us rest of heart that we would have thought impossible.

And that grace is still rescuing us, because we still tend to forget what is important, real, and true. We still tend to look to the physical world for our comfort. We still fail to remember in given moments that we really do have a heavenly Father. Grace has done a wonderful thing for us and continues to do more and more.

For further study and encouragement: 1 Peter 1:1–12

OCTOBER 14

The battles of sanctification are many, but God's mercies
are new morning after morning after morning.

The battle for your heart still goes on. Temptations exist all around you. The enemy lurks as a roaring lion. Falsehood battles with truth. The people of God live as an often misunderstood minority. Sickness and suffering enter your door. You need to grow in grace. In weakness, you give way to what you should resist. You are sinned against by others. Hopes, dreams, and plans fail. You experience corruption and injustice. There are times when you are tempted to wonder if it's all worth it. But in all this, God is still at work, molding you into the likeness of his Son. It is, in many ways, a multifaceted life of hardship—the hardships of life in this fallen world intersecting with the restorative hardships of grace.

Maybe you're reading and thinking, "Boy, Paul, this has been *very* encouraging so far." Well, let me ask you to reflect on something that is incredibly encouraging in the midst of the hardships that will not end until we are on the other side. It is captured by these words: "The steadfast love of the LORD never ceases; his mercies never come to an end; they are new every morning; great is your faithfulness" (Lam. 3:22–23).

Consider what this passage says about who you are and what you have been given as a child of God. God's steadfast, faithful, and never-failing love has been placed on you even though you never could have done anything to earn or deserve it. But there's more to say about this love. It never ceases. God will never give up on you. He will never walk away in disgust. He will never regret that he placed his love on you. He will love you just as much on your worst day as he does on your best day. This gift of love is yours forever.

But the passage says more. It announces that as God's child, you have been blessed with eternal mercies that are new every morning. Consider what this means. There are fresh mercies for you today, formfitted for all the things you will face, both those that you know about and may worry about, and those that you don't know about yet. God's mercy isn't generic. It is personal grace, situational care, and concrete help. It meets you right where you are and gives you just what you need. You get it as you need it and are given as much as you need. You don't have to wonder about the supply of God's mercy. It flows from a renewable font of grace that will never end. Yes, life this side of forever can be hard, but you're not alone; you've been given sturdy love and new morning mercies—just what you need right here, right now.

For further study and encouragement: Lamentations 3:22–27

OCTOBER 15

Today, a war of love will be fought on the turf of your heart.
Will you be ruled by love for God or for some other lover?

It's easy to give the right spiritual answer to the question above: "No doubt about it, my heart will be controlled by love for God above all else." The problem is that at street level, there is still a war of love in our hearts. We do lose our way. Love of the world and the things that are in the world still kidnaps our hearts. We forget God and tell ourselves that we must have _____. Love for God competes in our hearts with love of self. Love for God battles with our craving for the love of others. Material things and physical experiences command our affections and our motivations. Yes, the battle still rages.

I wish I could say this is not true of me, but it is. Sometimes I want my comfort too much, and I become an irritable and grumbling man because I'm not getting what I think I deserve. Sometimes I want to be right too much, and I become aggressive and argumentative. Sometimes I want the respect and affection of others too much, and because I do, I am all too controlled by their opinions. Sometimes I set my heart on a particular thing too much, and I feel bereft until I am able to cobble together a way to get it. Sometimes I want control too much, and I become more demanding than serving. Sometimes I esteem personal pleasure too much, and I invest far too much time in pursuit of it. Sometimes I crave the edible glories of creation too much, and I ingest more than I should.

I find that most of the things that lay claim to my heart and battle for the position that only love for God should have are not evil in and of themselves. The desire to be right, to be respected, to own possessions, to have some control, to experience pleasure, or to eat delicious things is not inherently evil. But here's the thing that you and I need to remember, what the battle for the love of our hearts is all about: a desire for a good thing becomes a bad thing when that desire becomes a ruling thing. When good things become controlling, they command the affection of our hearts and then shape our words and behavior. When this happens, they take the place in our hearts that only God should have.

You see, we are always placing the love of our hearts on something, and it is important to remember that there are only two places where we can invest that life-shaping love—on the Creator or on the creation. It's not wrong to love God's glorious creation, but it's a spiritual disaster to be ruled by that love. So here is yet another argument for our need for the grace we have been given. We are all in possession of fickle hearts. We all still need protecting and rescuing grace. Thank God that grace has been given!

For further study and encouragement: 2 Timothy 2:22–26

OCTOBER 16

The difficulties of your life are not in the way of God's plan;
they are a tool of it. They're crafted to advance his work of grace.

Perhaps the two most important questions you could ask between your conversion and your final resurrection are:

1. What in the world is God doing right here, right now?
2. How in the world should I respond to what God is doing?

The way that you answer these questions determines, in a real way, the character of your faith and the direction of your life. Consider how James answers these questions in the very first part of his letter:

> Count it all joy, my brothers, when you meet trials of various kinds, for you know that the testing of your faith produces steadfastness. And let steadfastness have its full effect, that you may be perfect and complete, lacking in nothing.
>
> If any of you lacks wisdom, let him ask God, who gives generously to all without reproach, and it will be given him. But let him ask in faith, with no doubting, for the one who doubts is like a wave of the sea that is driven and tossed by the wind. For that person must not suppose that he will receive anything from the Lord; he is a double-minded man, unstable in all his ways.
>
> Let the lowly brother boast in his exaltation, and the rich in his humiliation, because like a flower of the grass he will pass away. For the sun rises with its scorching heat and withers the grass; its flower falls, and its beauty perishes. So also will the rich man fade away in the midst of his pursuits.
>
> Blessed is the man who remains steadfast under trial, for when he has stood the test he will receive the crown of life, which God has promised to those who love him. (1:2–12)

What is God doing in the here and now? He is employing the difficulties of life as tools of grace to produce character in you that would not grow any other way. So your trials are not a sign that God has forgotten you or is being unfaithful to his promises. Rather, they stand as a reminder that he is committed to his grace and will not forsake it—it *will* complete its work. No, he's not exercising his power to make your life easy. No, he's not at work trying to deliver your particular definition of happiness. He's giving you much more than that—eternally faithful, forgiving, and transforming grace.

And what should your response be? James says, "remain steadfast under trial." Don't become discouraged and give up. Don't listen to the lies of the enemy. Don't forsake your good habits of faith. Don't question God's goodness. Look at your trials and see grace. Behind those difficulties is an ever-present Redeemer who is completing his work.

For further study and encouragement: Hebrews 12:3–11

OCTOBER 17

Idolatry occurs when anything created to point you to God
replaces God in the thoughts and desires of your heart.

This struggle goes all the way back to the beginning in the garden of Eden and has marked humanity ever since. What was designed to point us to God replaces God in our hearts. It is the sad tragedy of sin. Sin is fundamentally idolatrous. Because of it, we love something more than God. We look to what God made to do what only God can do. We surrender control to what was made rather than surrendering it to the One who made all. We celebrate the physical while forgetting the One who created every physical thing. We worship the gift and neglect the Giver.

Consider how the disobedience of Adam and Eve is described: "So when the woman saw that the tree was good for food, and that it was a delight to the eyes, and that the tree was to be desired to make one wise, she took of its fruit and ate, and she also gave some to her husband who was with her, and he ate" (Gen. 3:6). Eve knew the boundaries that God had set. Yes, the garden was a gorgeous place. It was a place of beautiful sounds, smells, sights, and tastes. It's hard to imagine what created perfection looks like in the world of nature; Adam and Eve were blessed to live in that perfection. But every wondrous physical thing that God created was intended to point to him. Every tree, flower, bird, stream, piece of fruit, and animal was meant to remind Adam and Eve of God's existence, presence, love, and authority. God had embedded reminders in everything he had made so that Adam and Eve would remember who he was, who they were, and what life was all about.

When Eve ate the fruit and Adam after her, they weren't experiencing boundary confusion. It wasn't that they were uncertain about what God had commanded them to do and not to do in the garden. They knew that the tree was off limits, but at the moment of eating, they didn't care. By the time they had sunk their teeth into the succulent fruit, they had already given away the love and allegiance of their hearts. Love for God should have given them the motivation and ability to say no to temptation and run away from the tree. But what ruled their hearts in that moment was love for something else. Their hearts, created for love of the Creator, had been kidnapped by love for the creation. It was the beginning of sin's disastrous exchange—worship and service of the Creator exchanged for worship and service of the created thing (Rom. 1:25). Sadly, that exchange has taken place millions and millions of times since the garden. It is humanity's great spiritual dysfunction; we allow the creation to replace the Creator in our hearts. No wonder Jesus had to come. No wonder his grace is so essential. No wonder God knew that he could not leave us to ourselves, that he had to send a rescuing Redeemer.

For further study and encouragement: 1 Corinthians 10:14–31

OCTOBER 18

Don't give way to discouragement, feelings of futility, or waves of fear,
because the Father has graciously chosen to give you the kingdom!

There are so many reasons to be discouraged in this fallen world, it's a wonder that anyone is happy. It's discouraging to watch your marriage turn cold and distant. It's disheartening to be betrayed by a dear friend. It's disappointing to lose the job you worked at with such commitment. It's depressing to face a sickness that you're not sure you'll ever lick. It's hard to face the rebellion and rejection of one of your children. It's discouraging to hear so often about corruption in politics and government. It's disheartening to have to be concerned about crime and injustice. It's tough to deal with the weaknesses of old age. It's hard to be mocked and rejected for your faith. It's sad to see your church become more a place of controversy than gospel healing. It can seem as if everything in your life is in the process of decaying or in danger of going bad. People die, dreams die, flowers die, and marriages, churches, jobs, and friendships go bad. If you look around, this old world that God created isn't doing very well. In many ways, it's a hard, discouraging place to live. The downward spiral of the fallen world can get to you. It seems that everything is impermanent or in the process of falling apart.

But that's not all that is discouraging. It often seems as if you're powerless to make much of a change. You do everything you can to restore your marriage, but it just seems stuck. You know you don't have the power to change other people and you have limited power to change situations. It so often seems that you're a witness to or affected by things you have little ability to alter.

So where is encouragement to be found? It's found in grace, as depicted by these beautiful words: "Fear not, little flock, for it is your Father's good pleasure to give you the kingdom" (Luke 12:32). With these words, everything changes. These words tell you that it's not you against a world gone bad. Yes, you are a citizen of this world and you are touched by its brokenness, but as you are, you must remind yourself that you are the citizen of another kingdom. Your King rules over everything that would discourage and disappoint you, and he rules for your good and his glory. What is out of your control is under his rule. What you don't understand is under his careful administration. But there is more. While everything around you seems impermanent, this kingdom will have no end. Long after the kingdoms of this world have been destroyed, you will reign with your King in his kingdom forever and ever and ever.

For further study and encouragement: Luke 12:22–34

OCTOBER 19

By calling you to die daily, the gospel welcomes you to live eternally.
Contrary to popular opinion, death really is the portal to life.

It is one of the principal paradoxes of grace. From a distance, it seems to make no sense at all, but you cannot understand God's work of grace in your life if you don't face this paradox. It's clearly presented in these words of Jesus Christ:

> And he said to all, "If anyone would come after me, let him deny himself and take up his cross daily and follow me. For whoever would save his life will lose it, but whoever loses his life for my sake will save it. For what does it profit a man if he gains the whole world and loses or forfeits himself? For whoever is ashamed of me and of my words, of him will the Son of Man be ashamed when he comes in his glory and the glory of the Father and of the holy angels. But I tell you truly, there are some standing here who will not taste death until they see the kingdom of God." (Luke 9:23–27)

Death leads to life—something seems not right about this, but it is right. It makes perfect sense when you face the reality that you and I cannot live for ourselves and God at the same time. We cannot live for his kingdom and our kingdoms. We cannot write our own rules and submit to his rules. We cannot pride ourselves on our independent righteousness and cast ourselves on his righteousness at the same time. We cannot live for our glory and his glory. We cannot love the world in our hearts and love him above all else at the same time. We cannot insert ourselves in the center of our worlds and have him at the center too.

You see, coming to Jesus is not a negotiation. Coming to Jesus is not an agreement. Coming to Jesus is not a contract. Coming to Jesus is a death—your death. He died so that you may live. Now he asks you to lose your life so that you may find life in him.

Here's what you need to understand: in asking you to die, Jesus is giving you eternal life the only way it can be given. He has to call you to die because you are in the way of you having life. It is our pride, our rebellion, our independence, our foolishness, and our denial that stand in the way of his offer of life. We tell ourselves that we are okay. We act as if we're smarter than God. We like our little kingdoms more than we love his. We think our rules are better than his. We tell ourselves that present pleasure is better than eternal gain. If someone doesn't rescue us from our delusions about our lives, we will lose our lives. Yes, we must die if we are ever going to live. So grace is out to kill us. But in presiding over our deaths, grace gives us life—real, abundant, and eternal life. Don't fight the death of your old life; instead, celebrate the new life that is yours by grace and grace alone. And remember that your Savior will continue to call you to die; it is the way of life.

For further study and encouragement: John 12:23–26

OCTOBER 20

Naming Jesus as Lord is the start of a theological commitment. Living as though he is Lord demands day-by-day forgiving, rescuing, and transforming grace.

I love the theology of Scripture. I wouldn't know how to think without it. In my early seminary days, I would take the subway home, run up the stairs to our third-floor apartment, and say to Luella: "I'm learning to think. I'm learning to think." It was more than dusty, esoteric theological academia. It was much, much more than gathering together the elements of a system of theology. It was profoundly more than getting to know my faith better. I was receiving more than advanced biblical literacy. I was being given a way to think about everything, and the whole system stood on four radical words, the first four words of the Bible: "In the beginning, God . . ."

I wasn't simply being educated. I wasn't just collecting a boatload of theological information. No, something deeper was happening. I was going through a process of heart and life transformation that was deeper and more formative than I understood at that moment. I was changing, and the whole direction of my life, my thoughts about my identity, my definition of meaning and purpose, and where I would look for my inner sense of well-being were changing as well. Everything that I have written has been written out of the life-altering perspectives I was helped to see from the Word of God in those early and exciting days. I can still see myself in the back row of my theology class, saying to myself, "I think my mind is melting." All this gave shape and direction to my life. It provided the context in which all my decisions would be made. It gave me a reason to get up in the morning and it confronted me with how huge my need for grace was.

This is what the theology of Scripture is meant to do. The purpose of the doctrine that is revealed in the Word of God is not to produce generation after generation of what I call "theo-geeks." You know what I mean: egghead biblical academics, who think about things no one else does, who talk in a language no one else understands, and who don't do many people much good. Here's the thing we need to be reminded of again and again: the theology of the Word of God was never intended to be an end in itself, but a means to an end, and that end is a radically transformed life. The purpose of theology is not knowledge but holiness.

Now, think about what the Bible actually is. It's a grand story of redemption. Maybe it would be better to say that it is a theologically annotated story. It's a story with God's essential notes. It is the story of Jesus, who came to offer the one thing you desperately need—grace. Theology that isn't zealous to promote forgiving and transforming grace, the kind of grace that changes your life, is simply bad theology.

For further study and encouragement: 2 Timothy 3:10–17

OCTOBER 21

Corporate worship is designed to remind you of your identity in Christ
so that you won't waste your time looking for identity elsewhere.

It's so easy to be an *identity amnesiac*. It's so easy to forget who you are in Christ and what you have been given as his child. It's so easy to shop horizontally for what you have already been given vertically. It's so easy to give in to fear, to give way to shame, or to allow yourself to be weakened by guilt because you forget the present benefits of Jesus's finished work. It's so easy, in the hardships of life, to forget that nothing is powerful enough to separate you from God's love. When you are struggling, it's so easy to forget that if God gave you his Son, he will also give you everything else you need. It's so easy to fail to live in light of the fact that Jesus didn't die just for your past forgiveness (praise God that he did) or your future resurrection (what hope!), but also for everything you are facing in the here and now.

It's so easy to forget that every trial sent your way is sent by a Savior of grace as a tool of grace to advance the work of grace in your heart and life. It's so easy to forget that because your life has been invaded by the grace of the One who is the "I Am," it is impossible for you to ever be in any situation, relationship, or location by yourself. It's so easy to forget that God really does live inside you in the powerful convicting, protecting, and enabling presence of the Holy Spirit. It's so easy to forget that God loves and accepts you no less on your worst day than he does on your best day. It's so easy to fail to remember that because of the grace of the life, death, and resurrection of Jesus, you are never left to the limited resources of your own wisdom, righteousness, and strength. It's so easy to fall into fearing what grace has already defeated on your behalf.

It's so easy to feel weak in the face of temptation and give way to what grace has given you the power to resist. It's so easy to wonder if God is near and if he hears. It's so easy to question the goodness of God in times of trouble. It's so easy to ask yourself if God has forgotten you when you compare the trouble of your life to the seeming ease in the life of the person next to you. It's so easy to think that life can be found somewhere outside of the Messiah. When life seems out of control, it's so easy to forget that Jesus Christ rules over all things for his glory and for your good. It's so easy to forget who you are and look for identity elsewhere,

So God has ordained that we should gather again and again to remember again and again who we are and what we have been given. His church is a tool of grace, a vehicle for remembering, so that we may celebrate and grow.

For further study and encouragement: Hebrews 10:19–25

OCTOBER 22

We disobey. God convicts and restores. We doubt. God works to make us people of faith. We hunger. God feeds us with the bounty of his grace.

Plenteous grace
is what we're given;
grace that is
deeper,
fuller,
richer,
and greater
than our sin.
This grace does not
suspend operations
in the face of our
disobedience.
It will not
turn its back
in the face of our
doubt.
It will not stand
idly by
in the face of our
hunger.
No, this is
rich grace,
perseverant grace
tender grace,
powerful grace.
There really is nothing
like it,
because it comes from the hand
of Jesus.

For further study and encouragement: 1 Timothy 1:12–17

OCTOBER 23

We panic. God stays true to his sovereign plan. We wonder. God knows the end from the beginning. We pray. God answers with wisdom and grace.

There simply is no panic in heaven. God is never anxious. There is no confusion in the Trinity. God never wrings his hands and wishes he had made a better choice. God never worries about what is going to happen next or stresses over how things are going to turn out. God is never surprised or caught up short. He is never in a situation that overwhelms him. God never feels needy or unprepared. God never regrets that he did not do better. God never fails at a task. He never makes promises that he cannot keep. He never forgets what he said or what he wants to do next. God never contradicts himself or fails to be exactly who he said he was. He is all-powerful, absolutely perfect in every way, faithful to every word, sovereign over all that is, the definition of love, and he is righteous, just, tender, and patient all at the same time. He is not dismayed or distracted by our panic and our questions. No, the sovereign move of his grace marches on!

> Blessed be the God and Father of our Lord Jesus Christ, who has blessed us in Christ with every spiritual blessing in the heavenly places, even as he chose us in him before the foundation of the world, that we should be holy and blameless before him. In love he predestined us for adoption as sons through Jesus Christ, according to the purpose of his will, to the praise of his glorious grace, with which he has blessed us in the Beloved. In him we have redemption through his blood, the forgiveness of our trespasses, according to the riches of his grace, which he lavished upon us, in all wisdom and insight making known to us the mystery of his will, according to his purpose, which he set forth in Christ as a plan for the fullness of time, to unite all things in him, things in heaven and things on earth.
>
> In him we have obtained an inheritance, having been predestined according to the purpose of him who works all things according to the counsel of his will, so that we who were the first to hope in Christ might be to the praise of his glory. (Eph. 1:3–12)

So God is not discouraged in the face of our weakness and wondering. His plan is not thwarted by our spiritual vacillation. He doesn't look at us and ask whether it's worth it. No, in the face of our ongoing struggles, his plan marches on. Why? It marches on because it is not based on our character, but on his. Redemption does not rest on our resolve, but on his. Salvation doesn't hang on our strength, but on his. We have hope because it all comes from him and rests on him. It is humbling to admit, but it is the only place of hope. Nothing of our salvation depends on us. It all rests on his sovereign grace. Here is the bottom line: he is able, he is willing, and he is faithful. Grace supplies everything we need. Grace will win!

For further study and encouragement: Philippians 4:19–20

OCTOBER 24

*We are fearful. God's presence gives courage. We are alienated. His
love draws us near. We are doubtful. His promises give us hope.*

God meets us where we are. This is the beautiful, hope-giving reality of grace. If
God asked us to meet him where he is, we would all be damned. There is no better
example of this than Jesus's response to Peter after Peter's denial:

> When they had finished breakfast, Jesus said to Simon Peter, "Simon, son of
> John, do you love me more than these?" He said to him, "Yes, Lord; you know
> that I love you." He said to him, "Feed my lambs." He said to him a second time,
> "Simon, son of John, do you love me?" He said to him, "Yes, Lord; you know
> that I love you." He said to him, "Tend my sheep." He said to him the third
> time, "Simon, son of John, do you love me?" Peter was grieved because he said
> to him the third time, "Do you love me?" and he said to him, "Lord, you know
> everything; you know that I love you." Jesus said to him, "Feed my sheep. Truly,
> truly, I say to you, when you were young, you used to dress yourself and walk
> wherever you wanted, but when you are old, you will stretch out your hands, and
> another will dress you and carry you where you do not want to go." (This he said
> to show by what kind of death he was to glorify God.) And after saying this he
> said to him, "Follow me." (John 21:15–19)

If there's someone on whom you would expect Jesus to turn his back forever,
it would be Peter. How could he deny Jesus, even after being warned? Wasn't that
unforgivable? No! What Peter did was not a picture of the defeat of the cross. The
opposite is true. Peter's denial is a shockingly concrete picture of the essentiality of
the cross of Jesus Christ. The life, death, and resurrection of Jesus were necessary
because we are people like Peter. We have no power in ourselves to be faithful, wise,
good, and righteous. We cannot save ourselves. We are people in need of rescue.
Without the rescue of grace, we are a danger to ourselves and to others, without
hope and without God.

So in amazing condescending grace, God meets us where we are, just as he did
with Peter. He comes to us in our fear. He draws near to us when we are separated.
He meets us in our doubt. He pursues us when we wander. When we sin, he comes
to us with conviction and forgiveness. He empowers us when we're weak. He restores
us when we are unfaithful. When we deny him, he does not deny us. He comes to us
at the moment of our salvation, and he comes to us again and again as we journey
from the "already" to the "not yet." He sits down with us, assuring us again of his
love, drawing out from us love for him, and sending us on our way to do the work
he has chosen us to do. He does not wait for us to come to him; he comes to us. It
is the way of grace.

For further study and encouragement: John 18:15–18

OCTOBER 25

God's agenda is change. Your need is change.
The promise of grace is change.
The hope of eternity is the completion of the work of change.

We all tend to share in a big, bad personal problem. It's one that doesn't get much press or pulpit time. Yet this problem is a huge interrupter of our personal spiritual development. If you have this problem, you won't be concerned that you have this problem precisely because you have this problem! I confess that I think this is a big deal for me as well. The problem is *personal spiritual self-satisfaction.* The more I travel from church to church, the more I engage with leaders, and the more I have opportunities to interview people in the seats, the more I grow convinced that the true crisis in the modern evangelical church is not dissatisfaction; it's the opposite. We're all too satisfied. We're all too satisfied with who we are, where we are, and what we're doing. We're satisfied with a little bit of biblical literacy. We're satisfied with occasional moments of ministry. We're satisfied with manageable debt that allows us to put a few coins in the plate. We're satisfied that we've been married for a while and it doesn't look as if we'll break up soon. We're satisfied with a bit of a grasp on the theology of Scripture. We're satisfied with faithful attendance at the weekend services of our churches. We're satisfied with quick morning devotions. We're satisfied with a little ministry experience. We're satisfied that we don't act out most of our lust and we don't communicate most of our envy. We're satisfied that in our disappointment with God, we don't walk away. We're satisfied that we can harness a good bit of our fear of man. We're satisfied to use most of our material resources to make and keep ourselves comfortable. We're satisfied to be mere consumers of the work of the church rather than committed participants in it. We're satisfied with hearts that occasionally wander and with thoughts that contradict what the Bible says is good and true. We're satisfied with the amount of conflict we have in our lives. We're satisfied.

None of us is yet a grace graduate, but we're satisfied. We all give evidence that we still need to grow, but we're satisfied. And because we are satisfied, we are resistant to the grace that is our only hope. If you are able to convince yourself that you are healthy, even though there may be indicators that you are not, you are probably not going to go to the doctor asking for his diagnostic and curative skill.

But here's what you and I need to remember: we serve a dissatisfied Redeemer. He knows we still need the transforming work of his powerful grace. Isn't it wonderful that, in gracious dissatisfaction, he will not relent until every microbe of sin is removed from every cell of every one of the hearts of his children?

For further study and encouragement: 1 Peter 2:1–12

OCTOBER 26

God justifies the ungodly. This means there really is hope for people like us.

I wish I could say that all my actions are godly, but they're not. I wish I could say that I always live with God's kingdom in view, but I don't. I wish I could say that all my responses to the people in my life are motivated by love for God and for them, but they're not. I wish awe of God was the principal motivation for all I do, but often it isn't. I wish I could say that I love God's glory more than my own, but there are still moments when I live as a glory thief. I wish I could say that selfishness and greed are in my rearview mirror, but there's evidence that they're not. I wish I could say that I have a heart of pure submission, but, sadly, there are times when I want my own way. I wish I could say that I always exhibit the fruit of the Spirit, but there are times when I don't. I wish I could say that I always live inside the wisdom boundaries of God's Word, but there are times when I foolishly think I'm smarter than God.

I wish I could say that materialism doesn't kidnap my heart anymore, but there are still times when it does. I wish I could say that I always rest in God's control, but there are times when I want to be in charge. I wish I could say that there are never times when I am irritated or impatient, but I still struggle with both on occasion. I wish I could say that the worship of God rules my heart unchallenged, but the truth is that idolatry still nips at me. I wish I could say that I always rest in the righteousness of Christ, but there are still times when I give way to the pride of parading my so-called righteousness before others. I wish I could say that the great spiritual battle is over for me, but there is clear and regular evidence that it is not.

All this means that I value justifying grace. I celebrate that, in Christ, God found a way to be "just and the justifier" (Rom. 3:26) of the ungodly. I am daily thankful for the perfect life of Jesus. I am thankful that he subjected himself to the temptations of this fallen world. I am thankful that on the cross he took my stripes and carried my guilt and shame. I am thankful that he took the father's rejection. I am thankful that he burst out of that tomb, conquering death. I am thankful that his righteousness is attributed to my account. I am thankful that he fulfilled the law and satisfied the Father's anger. I still celebrate the fact that I have been granted full, complete, and unending acceptance.

I celebrate justifying grace because I am still unable to stand before God based on my own righteousness. I still fall short of his glory. So I am so very thankful that justifying grace ensures that I will forever be accepted as one of his righteous ones, even though I still don't measure up. Yes, today I have reason again to be thankful for justifying grace.

For further study and encouragement: Galatians 5:4–5

OCTOBER 27

Belief is not simply a function of the brain. No, it's an investment of the heart that fundamentally changes the way that you live.

It was an academic illusion, an intellectual replacement for the real thing, but I didn't know it. Because I had filled my brain during seminary with the details of the theology of the Word of God so that I could hold my own in almost any theological debate, I thought of myself as a man of faith. Because I had a high level of biblical literacy, having committed many passages of Scripture to memory, I looked at myself as spiritually mature. Because I had ministry gifts and a ministry calling, I thought I was living a life of faith. But my faith was like a luxury car with no engine. It was beautiful on the outside, but it lacked the power necessary to do what it was meant to do. If you had questioned my faith, I would have been highly offended. If you had confronted me as being immature, I would have quickly risen to my defense. But this house of spiritual cards was about to come down.

Here's the good news: God is faithful and will do what is necessary to craft real faith in us. Faith isn't natural for us. It's not natural for us to rest our entire past, present, and future on someone we cannot hear, see, or touch. Doubt is natural. Envy is natural. Fear is natural. Worry is natural. Trying to figure out what's coming next is natural. Trusting our own strength and wisdom is natural, but faith is not natural for us. So God works in sanctifying grace to turn baby believers into mature people of faith. He will not relent until that work is complete. Nothing can stop the move of his transforming grace. Here's what you need to understand: your faith is not your hope; his zealous grace is the only source of hope for fickle-faith sinners.

So God used marriage and ministry to expose my weak, shallow, and immature faith. Oh, I worked hard to deny the evidence that marriage and ministry produced. I pointed to my acts of righteousness to pump air into my delusion. But God would not turn away. I was a very angry man, but I denied that anger and its roots in my heart. I was a very proud man, but I refused to see it. I was a self-sovereign controller, but I said it was just me using my God-given leadership gifts. But things didn't get better, they got worse. My wife, Luella, confronted me again and again about my anger. People in our congregation confronted me about my pride. I once preached what I thought was the ultimate sermon on pride. It was really a case study of the same. God used ministry and family brokenness to begin to craft in me mature faith. I am a very different man today, but the Craftsman is still at work, maturing the faith that only his grace can produce.

For further study and encouragement: 1 John 3:1–10

OCTOBER 28

Will your responses today be shaped more by fear of your inability or by celebration of Christ's sufficiency?

No one just lives life. No one acts or reacts neutrally. No one is objective. No one is passive. You and I always bring an interpretive grid to our view of ourselves, our behavior, others, God, and life. Our reactions are not shaped by the facts of our experience, but by the way we interpret those facts. The gospel of the person and work of Jesus is intended to be the life-altering interpretive grid of the believer. This is what Paul means when he says "let the word of Christ dwell in you richly" (Col. 3:16).

Why does he say "word of Christ"? What Paul means is the gospel. The overarching message of the Bible is the gospel of Jesus Christ. The Bible is a not a series of stories or a compendium of wisdom statements. The Bible is not a textbook of systematic theology. The Bible is the grand biography of the Lord Jesus Christ. Perhaps it is more accurate to say that the Bible is the annotated story of the Lord Jesus Christ, that is, his story with God's essential explanatory and applicatory notes. You do violence to the Word of God when you reduce it to a book of theology, principles, and rules. You simply cannot make sense of Scripture without the person and work—the grace—of the Lord Jesus Christ.

So where does all of this lead us? You have two ways of looking at life. You can look at all your internal and external challenges from the perspective of your track record and present catalog of abilities, or you can look at them from the vantage point of the sufficiency of the work of Jesus on your behalf. The Bible was given not only to radically alter your identity and potential, but to radically alter the way you think about and interpret life. You are not left to your own resources. Because you are "in Christ," your potential is greater than the sum of your parts. You are never in any situation or location all by yourself. There is one who fights against sin for you even when you don't have sense enough to fight for yourself.

The gospel of Jesus Christ must not be just an aspect of your theology. It must not be relegated to the "religious" dimension of your life. Your relationship with God through Jesus Christ *is* your life. It touches and alters every aspect of your existence; it redefines your identity. It infuses your life with new meaning and purpose, and it completely reshapes your destiny. So the work of Jesus on your behalf must be the window through which you look at everything in your life. Don't give way to the fear of inability when the work of Jesus has supplied you with everything you need.

For further study and encouragement: 2 Peter 1:1–11

OCTOBER 29

If you trust only when you understand, you'll live with lots of doubt.
God's wisdom is bigger than anything your mind can conceive.

It's humbling to admit, but important nonetheless. You will never reach true, sturdy, and lasting peace and rest of heart by means of understanding. "Why?" you may ask. Because there will always be things in your life that you do not understand. God reveals in his Word all the things that you need to know, but he does not tell you all the things that could be known. He reveals his plan for all his people in his Word, but he does not tell you his individualized sovereign plan for you. You and I simply are not able to contain in our limited brains all of God's plans for us and all of the reasons for those plans.

Now, here's the rub: God created you to be a rational human being. He designed you to think, that is, to strive to make sense out of your life and your world. That is not a bad thing in itself. In fact, it is a very good thing. Your ability to think, interpret, examine, define, explain, and understand is meant to drive you to God. Your mentality is meant to lead you to him and to enable you to understand his revelation to you. So biblical faith is not irrational, but you must face this: it will take you beyond your ability to reason. You and I never could have started at the fall of Adam and Eve and used reason to predict the coming of Jesus and his death on the cross. Old Testament believers knew that God was going to deal with sin and give new life to his people because God told them that this was what he was going to do. But they did not know that the death of the Son of God would be the means by which this would happen.

In the same way, as we stand between the "already" and the "not yet," we can be assured of all that God has told us in his Word, but we can also be sure that there is much that he has not told us about what is to come, personally and collectively. So there will be mysteries and surprises in our lives. If you and I suspend belief at every encounter with mystery, we will spend large portions of our lives not believing. If we question God's goodness and love every time he acts in a way that is unexpected, we will end up concluding that he is not good. If we refuse to rest when we don't understand, we will end up living lives of distress.

So where is peace and rest of heart to be found? You rest in the fact that in his Word God has told you all the things you absolutely need to know, and then you rest in the complete perfection of his wisdom and character. You rest not because you know, but because the One who knows it all is the definition of what is wise and what is good.

For further study and encouragement: 1 Corinthians 1:18–31

OCTOBER 30

*People make good friends and loved ones, but they make
bad messiahs. Life is only ever found in Jesus.*

We do tend to put people in the place of God and ask them to do for us what only he can do. We do look to people, who suffer from the same condition of sin, weakness, and failure as we do, as if they were the fourth member of the Trinity. We ask our loved ones to give us identity. We ask them to heal our hurts. We ask them to cause us to be happy. But they cannot give us those things. They simply never, ever will rise to the level of our expectations. In our relationships, we often try to drink from a dry well, and then we wonder why we come up thirsty. No human being can be your personal Savior. The following passage confronts you with this truth and then directs you to where real life in the here and now and for all eternity can be found:

> In the beginning was the Word, and the Word was with God, and the Word was God. He was in the beginning with God. All things were made through him, and without him was not any thing made that was made. In him was life, and the life was the light of men. The light shines in the darkness, and the darkness has not overcome it.
>
> There was a man sent from God, whose name was John. He came as a witness, to bear witness about the light, that all might believe through him. He was not the light, but came to bear witness about the light.
>
> The true light, which gives light to everyone, was coming into the world. He was in the world, and the world was made through him, yet the world did not know him. He came to his own, and his own people did not receive him. But to all who did receive him, who believed in his name, he gave the right to become children of God, who were born, not of blood nor of the will of the flesh nor of the will of man, but of God.
>
> And the Word became flesh and dwelt among us, and we have seen his glory, glory as of the only Son from the Father, full of grace and truth. For from his fullness we have all received, grace upon grace. For the law was given through Moses; grace and truth came through Jesus Christ. No one has ever seen God; the only God, who is at the Father's side, he has made him known. (John 1:1–18)

Here is the bottom line, so powerfully captured by this passage: *Jesus is life*. As Creator, he gave physical life to our bodies. As eternal God, he is the source of the life of everything that lives. But there is more. As Savior, he is the One who alone gives spiritual life to our dead hearts. The passage says we are not born again by human blood, by human flesh, or by human will, but by God. It is his fullness that we receive; life-giving grace upon life-giving grace. Don't put the burden of life on the person next to you. It will only crush that person and disappoint you. Besides, you don't need him or her to give you life, because you've already been given life in the person and work of Jesus.

For further study and encouragement: John 20:30–31

OCTOBER 31

Be aware that the kingdom of self is a costume kingdom. It does a perversely brilliant job of masquerading as the kingdom of God.

Spiritual fakery is one of the chief tools of the enemy. It is one of the key ingredients of spiritual blindness. This is why we read the warning in Matthew 7:15: "Beware of false prophets, who come to you in sheep's clothing but inwardly are ravenous wolves." The kingdom of self is very skilled at wearing the clothing of the kingdom of God. So:

- A focus on material things can masquerade as good stewardship of your possessions.
- Loving personal control can masquerade as using God-given leadership gifts.
- Anger can masquerade as having a heart for what is right.
- Self-righteous legalism can masquerade as loving God's law.
- Building your own ministry empire can masquerade as a commitment to the expansion of God's kingdom.
- Fear of man can masquerade as a sensitive heart toward the needs of others.
- Selfish attention-seeking can masquerade as being candid about your needs.
- Judgment and criticism can masquerade as a commitment to honesty.
- Theological pride can masquerade as a commitment to God's truth.
- A craving to be known and respected can masquerade as a commitment to ministry.
- Bondage to the opinions of others can masquerade as a commitment to community.
- Lust can masquerade as a celebration of the beauty of God's creation.
- Gossip can masquerade as a prayerful concern for others.

It really is true—the kingdom of self is a costume kingdom. This is because one of the enemy's most useful tools is the ability of wrong to imitate right. Couple this with our natural propensity to spiritual blindness and you end up with personal spiritual confusion. It is scary to think of the number of times we think we are serving God when we're actually serving ourselves, or the number of times we think we are worshiping God when we're actually giving worship and service to some aspect of the creation.

The masquerading nature of sin plays to the fickleness of our idolatrous hearts. So what is often is not what we think it is, and the masquerading idol has no power at all to deliver to our hungry hearts what Jesus alone can give us. Only God can give us insight into our hearts and free us from our bondage to the little costume kingdom of one.

For further study and encouragement: Jeremiah 10:1–16

NOVEMBER 1

Yes, God disciplines his children, but rest assured, the full penalty for your sin has been borne by Christ and won't again be borne by you.

I'm a parent of four children, and I can honestly say that there weren't many moments in my children's lives when they seemed genuinely thankful for the faithful discipline of their parents. They tended to see discipline as vengeful, harsh, punitive, and unloving. (Sadly, human discipline often is like this.) Our children didn't seem to understand that our discipline wasn't a suspension of our love, but a result of it. They didn't seem to get the fact that we disciplined them not because we were surprised that they did or said bad things, but in order to be part of God's gracious work to transform them into people who delighted in doing good things. We didn't discipline them because we were upset because we were stuck with them in our family, but because they were unshakably part of the family. We didn't discipline them in order to remind them that they hadn't quite yet been good enough to earn our love, but rather because they were the objects of our love.

I think we have the same difficulty with the loving disciplinary zeal of our heavenly Father. He disciplines us not to teach us how far we have to go to earn the right to be his children, but because we *are* his children. In his discipline, he is not making us pay the penalty for our sins, but delivering us from the sins for which Christ has already paid the penalty. His discipline, therefore, is never the result of his rejection, but the fruit of his acceptance. Since our penalty was fully and completely paid by Jesus on the cross, it needn't be paid by us ever again!

Think with me for a moment. It is only when you understand the completeness of your *justification* (that your penalty has been paid and you have been made eternally right with God by the life and death of Jesus) that you are able to rest in the ongoing discipline of your *sanctification*. That discipline is not to make you right with God, but an expression of the fact that you have been made right with God, and because you have, you are now the object of his fatherly love. You can expect his discipline, but you do not have to fear his anger. You will experience his correction, but you will never face his rejection. He disciplines all his children in order to produce a harvest of righteousness, but he will never punish you for your sin. "For Christ also suffered *once* for sins, the righteous for the unrighteous, that he might bring us to God, being put to death in the flesh but made alive in the spirit" (1 Pet. 3:18). Amen and amen!

For further study and encouragement: Psalm 106

NOVEMBER 2

The cross of Jesus Christ stands as a beacon of hope in a world gone bad. Life, hope, forgiveness, and change really are possible!

The cross doesn't stand stained with the death blood of the Messiah in the darkness of moral defeat. It is not the sad symbol of a plan gone wrong. It doesn't preach that the good gets smashed at evil's hand. It doesn't suck salvation hope out of those who would believe. The cross isn't the grand symbol of redemption's embarrassment. The cross shouldn't make you ashamed. No, it should stand at the epicenter of your boasting. Hear the words of the apostle Paul: "But far be it from me to boast except in the cross of our Lord Jesus Christ, by which the world has been crucified to me, and I to the world" (Gal. 6:14). In a sin-scarred world, there really aren't many things worth boasting about. As sinners, rescued from ourselves by powerful grace, we don't have many valid reasons for puffing out our chests. We're all more case studies of mercy than heroes. The world around us groans under the weight of its fallenness. The history of humanity would be a sick and dreary story if it weren't for the rough-hewn tree of death on the hill of Golgotha. It was an unlikely place for a scene of history-changing triumph. The place where they executed criminals seems to be the last place to go to find hope. The scene where they killed the world's only innocent man doesn't seem to be a place that excites celebration. But such is the paradox of grace. Death is the doorway to life. Hopelessness is the entrance to hope. Weakness is the place to find strength. Injustice is where mercy flows. Life comes to those who deserve death. Defeat is actually a victory. The end is really a beginning. Out of sorrow comes eternal celebration. The tomb is the place where new life begins.

The impossible paradoxes of redemption become the regular moves of transforming grace. Hope is sung to suffering's tune. Life is played on death's instruments. Grace doesn't play by the law's score. God composes hope from tragedy's notes. So we look at Calvary and we don't sing a dirge—we sing a song of triumph and celebration, of hope and salvation. Satan's players have not been able to drown out salvation's song. The songs of hope by the company of the redeemed will never end. They grow in volume, celebration, and glory. The cross is the subject of those songs, and its life-giving mercy is the chorus.

It is the cross of Jesus Christ that gives you reason to hope, sing, celebrate, and live. It was never the interruption of God's saving plan, but the essential means of it. It was never a defeat. It was always a victory.

For further study and encouragement: Revelation 5

NOVEMBER 3

How do you measure your capability—by your previous successes and failures or by the boundless resource of grace that's yours in Christ?

It is something every human being does many times a day; most of the time, we do it unconsciously. The way we do it says a lot about who we think we are and what we think we are facing. The young child learning to walk does it, and so does the elderly woman facing serious sickness. What you conclude after doing it determines how you respond to the struggles in your life. What am I talking about? Measuring your capability. We are always assessing what we bring to the table to deal with what is currently on our plates.

Now, it is not stupid or irrational to measure your potential by examining your track record. How have you done so far? What are the things that tend to trip you up? What are the weaknesses that have been exposed? What have you learned that will help you do better the next time? These are all good questions as far as they go, but they lack something that is dramatically important. They lack the gospel of Jesus Christ. You see, the message of the infusion of God's grace is that you haven't been left to your track record. You aren't restricted to your limited collection of personal spiritual resources. Rather, in Christ, you have been given both a new identity and new potential. How could this new potential be more radically and powerfully stated than in the apostle Paul's words: "It is no longer I who live, but Christ who lives in me" (Gal. 2:20)?

God knew exactly what you would face as you journeyed through this fallen world. He knew that temptation would greet you every day. He knew the sin still within you would rear its ugly head. He knew that sorrow and suffering would get you down. He knew all the things that you would have to deal with at the address where he ordained you to live. So he gave you exactly what you need so that you can be what you're supposed to be and do what he has called you to do even in the broken surroundings where you live. What did he give you? He gave you himself! His grace isn't a set of insights. It isn't a change of location. It isn't the altering of situations. His grace is more fundamental and glorious than that. His grace goes far beyond anything we would dare to ask or reach out for with our imaginations. Here is the best way to say it: *he is the grace that he gives.* God's best gift of grace is himself. He comes to us. He makes us the place where he lives. This means that divine power resides inside us. Our potential as God's children is much more than our natural gifts and track records predict, because Immanuel, the Lamb, the Savior, the Lord almighty, the sovereign King has made us his residence. A new identity and a wildly new potential are ours in Christ. Now go out and live as if you really believe it.

For further study and encouragement: Galatians 2:15–21

NOVEMBER 4

*If you're God's child, don't ever tell yourself that you are
alone—for you, "alone" is a redemptive impossibility.*

Walking away from the funeral of a loved one, you can feel very alone. Dealing with long-term sickness is a very lonely experience. Facing financial difficulties that you have no means to solve can make you feel very weak and alone. It's a lonely experience to deal with the personal rejection of a loved one. Standing for what is right in a culture that mocks the morals you hold dear can make you feel fearful and alone. Assessing that you don't have what it takes to face what you cannot escape can make you feel unprepared and alone. Loneliness of some kind is the universal experience of people living this side of eternity. Sin brought alienation and separation into the world. It first broke the fellowship between God and man, and because it did, it also shattered the fellowship between people and their family members, friends, and neighbors. This aloneness is spiritual, emotional, relational, and cultural. It's nearly impossible to escape.

The drama of human aloneness is captured by the apostle Paul, but there is more. He also captures how the grace of Jesus Christ reconciles us to God and, in so doing, reconciles us to one another so that we will never again be alone:

> Therefore remember that at one time you Gentiles in the flesh, called "the uncircumcision" by what is called the circumcision, which is made in the flesh by hands—remember that you were at that time separated from Christ, alienated from the commonwealth of Israel and strangers to the covenants of promise, having no hope and without God in the world. But now in Christ Jesus you who once were far off have been brought near by the blood of Christ. For he himself is our peace, who has made us both one and has broken down in his flesh the dividing wall of hostility by abolishing the law of commandments expressed in ordinances, that he might create in himself one new man in place of the two, so making peace, and might reconcile us both to God in one body through the cross, thereby killing the hostility. And he came and preached peace to you who were far off and peace to those who were near. For through him we both have access in one Spirit to the Father. So then you are no longer strangers and aliens, but you are fellow citizens with the saints and members of the household of God, built on the foundation of the apostles and prophets, Christ Jesus himself being the cornerstone, in whom the whole structure, being joined together, grows into a holy temple in the Lord. In him you also are being built together into a dwelling place for God by the Spirit. (Eph. 2:11–22)

Let the words sink in: from "having no hope and without God in the world" to "reconcile[d] . . . to God" and "being built together into a dwelling place for God by the Spirit." What is the movement of grace? We have gone from being hopeless and alone to being reconciled and inhabited by God, and therefore never alone again! Don't forget to remind yourself again today that as God's child you simply cannot be alone, no matter what you feel.

For further study and encouragement: Genesis 3 contrasted with Ephesians 2

NOVEMBER 5

You will never turn any created thing into your personal messiah.
There is one true Messiah, and life can be found only in him.

I wish I could say that I never look for life where it can't be found, but the temptation to do this still haunts me. As much as we all know that there is only one true God, we still hunt for God-replacements. We all still tend to look horizontally for what we will only ever find vertically. There are times when we ask creation to be our Savior:

- We attach our identity to the respect of another.
- We draw too much of our sense of well-being from our physical appearance.
- We think material possessions have the power to make us happy.
- We attach our meaning and purpose to our achievements.
- We ask our jobs to make us content.
- We try to base our identity on our children.
- We attach our sense of spiritual well-being to the "perfect" church.
- We base our identity on our education.
- We ask our spouses to make us happy.
- We look to food and drink to satisfy and calm us.
- We continually say, "If only I had _____, then my life would be _____."
- We attach our identity to the luxury of our cars or the affluence of our neighborhoods.

The list is really endless. There is nothing in creation that you can't try to turn into your personal messiah, but it never, ever works. The creation can never, ever give you what the Creator alone can. It makes no sense at all to desperately look for what you have already been given by your Savior.

All the good and glorious created things that God puts in our lives are things he has designed and placed there to point us to the only place where life can ever be found—in him. All created things are signs that point us to what can be found in him. You know how this works from driving around or from taking a trip: a sign points you to a thing, but the sign is not the thing. Creation points us to the Creator, but it can never give us what the Creator can give. All the good situations, locations, possessions, relationships, achievements, and natural beauties of this physical world are wonderful blessings from the hand of God, but they have no ability to give you the one thing that your heart desperately desires—life. Jesus said it this way: "I am the way, and the truth, and the life" (John 14:6). With these words, he ends our need to search. He is life, so there is no need to look for it anywhere else.

For further study and encouragement: Psalm 115

NOVEMBER 6

*God loves too much to be willing to forsake his glorious kingdom
of grace for your self-absorbed little kingdom of one.*

On this side of our final destination, the great spiritual battle is all about kingdoms in conflict. Sin causes us all to anoint ourselves as kings and to live our lives with kingdom purposes. We all set ourselves up as sovereigns over our kingdoms of one. We all want our will to be done. We all know what we want, when we want it, how we want it, where we want it, and who we want to deliver it. So God gives us his grace. Is his grace given to give you what you need to be your own king? Is his grace bestowed on you so your little kingdom purposes will happen? No, God's grace dethrones you from your little kingdom and welcomes you to a much better kingdom than you could ever want for yourself. But in this kingdom, you will never be at the center, it will never be all about you, and you will never rule, because in this kingdom, all things are for God and God alone.

The dynamic of kingdoms in conflict is powerfully demonstrated in one poignant moment in Jesus's interactions with his disciples:

> They went on from there and passed through Galilee. And he did not want anyone to know, for he was teaching his disciples, saying to them, "The Son of Man is going to be delivered into the hands of men, and they will kill him. And when he is killed, after three days he will rise." But they did not understand the saying, and were afraid to ask him.
>
> And they came to Capernaum. And when he was in the house he asked them, "What were you discussing on the way?" But they kept silent, for on the way they had argued with one another about who was the greatest. And he sat down and called the twelve. And he said to them, "If anyone would be first, he must be last of all and servant of all." And he took a child and put him in the midst of them, and taking him in his arms, he said to them, "Whoever receives one such child in my name receives me, and whoever receives me, receives not me but him who sent me." (Mark 9:30–37)

The juxtaposition of the two parts of this vignette is really quite stunning. In the most pointed and poignant way yet, Jesus talks to the disciples about his coming death. Clearly the disciples do not fully grasp what he is saying, but they ask no questions. There is no display of grief or even concern on their part. No, they quickly move on to the topic that is really important to them and which reveals the true desires of their hearts. After Christ's announcement of the violent death that is to come for him, they immediately begin to argue about who is the greatest. In this moment, their claustrophobic kingdoms of one collide with God's kingdom of glory and grace. These kingdoms collide today as well. Only grace can make us love God's kingdom more than our own.

For further study and encouragement: Luke 11:1–13

NOVEMBER 7

God calls you to deny yourself and then blesses you with the
indwelling Holy Spirit so you have the power to say no.

You have called me to say
no.
Not no to you
or no to others,
but no to myself.
I must say no to
selfish desires,
wrong thoughts, and
dangerous emotions.
I must say no to
the world's values,
sin's temptations, and
my desire to control
what only God can rule.
But left to myself,
I have
little desire
or power
to say
no.
So you have given me
exactly what I need.
It's the only thing
that will solve my
problem.
You have given me
your Spirit.
So, when necessary,
I am able
to say
no.

For further study and encouragement: Matthew 16:24–28

NOVEMBER 8

Today you can give way to fear-producing "what-ifs" or rest in the sovereign care of your wise and gracious Savior King.

Here's the bottom line: if you're God's child, your life is never, ever out of control. It's not spinning wildly in who knows what direction with no intelligent administration. It's not controlled by the hopeless inertia of impersonal determination or abstract luck. Yes, vast pieces of your existence are out of your control, beyond your power to alter. But you must not conclude that your life is out of control.

There are two reasons for this. First, the story that is your life has been included, by grace, in the greater story of redemption. This story is about God's age-old commitment to call a people to himself, to fix everything that sin has broken, to conquer sin and death, to establish a new heaven and a new earth, and to invite all his children to live there in communion with him forever. This huge story was set in motion before the earth was created, it is unstoppable, and it will never have an end. Your inclusion in this story took place before you breathed your first breath; in fact, it took place before anyone breathed his or her first breath. Because your story is woven into the fabric of the redemption story, there is meaning, purpose, and direction to every part of it. The inertia of redemption carries your story along. The goal of redemption guarantees your destiny. The future grace of eternity secures for you all the grace you will ever need in between. No, you won't understand all that you face, and yes, God's will will confuse you at points, but your story has been infused with meaning and purpose because it's been included in God's story of redemption and restoration.

But the fact that your life is under control is even more personal than that. God has appointed his Son, the Lord Jesus Christ, to be "head over all things to the church" (Eph. 1:22). Right now, Jesus is ruling over all things. That means that every situation, relationship, and location of your life is ruled by King Christ. You cannot be in a place that is not under his rule. Paul says elsewhere that he will continue to reign in this way "until he has put all his enemies under his feet" (1 Cor. 15:25). The phrase "to the church" is better translated "for the church." This means that not only is everything under the careful rule of the risen Lord Jesus and not only does he sit in rule at the right hand of the Father on high, but he expedites his rule for his people. In other words, he rules over all things for your help and benefit. He rules over all things so that his grace can finish its work in you unabated. You see, the promises of his grace are only as secure as the extent of his rule. His story is unstoppable. His rule is benevolent. There is grand and gracious control over every aspect of your life.

For further study and encouragement: Isaiah 43:1–13

NOVEMBER 9

While sin is still a sad and ever-present reality in each of our lives,
it is simply no match for the grace of the Lord Jesus Christ.

One of the themes of this devotional is that biblical faith never requires that you deny reality. If you have to turn your back on what is real and true in order to have some temporary personal peace, you may feel better, but what you're exercising is not the faith of the Bible. This realism applies to the sin that still remains in you and is being progressively eradicated by God's powerful grace. There is a great temptation to deny or at least to minimize our sin. However, you are never moving in a productive spiritual direction when, by self-atoning arguments, you make your sin look less like sin. You don't protect the message of the gospel by denying your own spiritual struggles, and God surely doesn't need you to defend his reputation by faking it.

This is not to say you should make your sin the focus of your meditation. It is simply a denial of the amazing grace of the gospel of Jesus Christ to treat yourself as an unworthy, impure, and incapable spiritual worm. You must not meditate on the judgment of God. You must not squirm at the thought of his presence. You must not allow yourself to wonder if he loves you. You must not see yourself as unworthy of his care. You must not work to measure up in his sight. You must not think that he acts more favorably to you when you are obedient than when you sin. You must not beat yourself up when you fail. You must not give yourself to acts of payment and penance after you have messed up in God's eyes. You must not envy the worthiness of the person next to you, as if he or she is more accepted by God because he or she is more spiritually mature than you. You must never run from God in fear as you think of the empirical evidence of remaining sin that you give every day.

What you and I must meditate on every day is the absolute perfection and completeness of the work of the Lord Jesus Christ. He was perfect in his life, perfect in his death, and perfect in his resurrection. There is nothing we could ever think, desire, say, or do that could in any way add to the forgiveness and acceptance that we have received from God based on Christ's work. You are perfect in the eyes of God because the perfect righteousness of Jesus has been attributed to your spiritual account. You are righteous before God even in those moments when what you are doing is not righteous. You measure up in his eyes even on those days when you don't measure up, because Jesus measured up on your behalf. Yes, you should acknowledge the sad reality of remaining sin, but you must not make that sin your meditation. Meditate on and celebrate the amazing grace that has completely changed your identity, potential, and destiny.

For further study and encouragement: Galatians 3

NOVEMBER 10

God is not satisfied with informing you about the work of his kingdom.
He transforms you to participate in the work of his kingdom.

God has not revealed his truth to you so that you can be the audience, a viewer of his work of redemption. God has called all his children to participate in the work of his kingdom. Everyone who has been brought into a relationship with God through Jesus Christ has also been drafted into the ministry of the Lord Jesus Christ. He really does mean to employ all his children in his work of redemption. Yes, you read that right—all his children. The *total involvement paradigm* is his normal plan for the church.

Now, those biblical passages that say that the body of Christ grows as every part does its part (Eph. 4:11–16) or that every one of God's children should be prepared to teach and admonish (Col. 3:12–17) seem very radical to us, but they were not radical in the context in which they were given. Paul doesn't introduce them by announcing that radical material is coming. They are an explanation of God's normal plan for his people and his church. They appear radical to us because we have drifted so far from God's norm for his church. Many, many Christians' church attendance is the spiritual edition of going to a concert. They regularly go to experience the religious performance of ministry professionals, but they have little commitment to the health of the church or to its work in the world. Their relationship to the church is self-focused ("Here's the kind of church I want to attend") and passive ("I'm so thankful for the good work our church staff does").

But God's plan for his church is very different. He has called all his children to be his ambassadors, that is, to represent his message and his character in whatever environment he has placed them. Here's the plan: a God of grace makes his invisible grace visible by sending his people of grace to reflect his grace to people who need grace. You have been called to be the look on his face, the tone of his voice, and the touch of his hand. You are to represent his presence and his love. You are placed where you are to make his mercy and faithfulness visible and concrete.

This all means that your life doesn't belong to you anymore. You have been bought with a price. Your mentality, your personality, your emotionality, your physicality, your possessions, and all your relationships belong to you from the Lord for his using. So God's people of grace are driven to the throne of grace so that they can reflect his grace in the place where he calls them. You and I have no ability to represent God well. His ambassadorial call drives us to him to receive the grace we need to represent his grace in the lives of others. What a plan!

For further study and encouragement: Mark 16:14–18

NOVEMBER 11

You don't wait for grace and then do what God has told
you to do. You get enabling grace in motion.

Moses didn't understand this. Gideon didn't understand this. The fearful army of
Israel didn't understand this. The disciples in hiding after the death of Jesus didn't
understand this. Many of us panic today because we don't understand this. God's
grace provides everything you require. God's grace is formfitted for your moment of
need. God's grace is multifaceted and expansive, but also focused and personal. God,
in grace, doesn't just forgive you, he also empowers you to do what he called you to
do. But he gives you his grace as you follow him and at the moment when you need it.

It has always been hard for the people of God to rest in the reality of *grace in
motion*. There is no better example of this than when the children of Israel found
themselves at the Red Sea with the angry army of Egypt bearing down on them:

> When Pharaoh drew near, the people of Israel lifted up their eyes, and behold,
> the Egyptians were marching after them, and they feared greatly. And the people
> of Israel cried out to the LORD. They said to Moses, "Is it because there are no
> graves in Egypt that you have taken us away to die in the wilderness? What have
> you done to us in bringing us out of Egypt? Is not this what we said to you in
> Egypt: 'Leave us alone that we may serve the Egyptians'? For it would have been
> better for us to serve the Egyptians than to die in the wilderness." And Moses
> said to the people, "Fear not, stand firm, and see the salvation of the LORD, which
> he will work for you today. For the Egyptians whom you see today, you shall never
> see again. The LORD will fight for you, and you have only to be silent."
>
> The LORD said to Moses, "Why do you cry to me? Tell the people of Israel to
> go forward. Lift up your staff, and stretch out your hand over the sea and divide
> it, that the people of Israel may go through the sea on dry ground. And I will
> harden the hearts of the Egyptians so that they shall go in after them, and I will
> get glory over Pharaoh and all his host, his chariots, and his horsemen. And the
> Egyptians shall know that I am the LORD, when I have gotten glory over Pharaoh,
> his chariots, and his horsemen." (Ex. 14:10–18)

Even though they have just experienced God's miracles that secured their escape
from the slavery of Egypt, the children of Israel, stuck between the Red Sea and the
Egyptian army, with no means of altering their circumstances, are in a complete
panic. They are convinced that Moses has dragged them out into the wilderness to
die. But God knows exactly what he is doing. He has manufactured this whole situation to demonstrate his glory to his people and to defeat the Egyptian army, and if it
is necessary to part the waters of the Red Sea, he will do that for his children. What
he does not do is tell them what is going to happen beforehand. Why? Because he is
working in them, as he works in us, to craft them into people of robust and sturdy
faith. He calls them to follow, and he willingly unleashes his grace as they do so.

For further study and encouragement: Psalm 136

NOVEMBER 12

You will never find fulfillment of heart on the far side of rebellion.
True rest of heart is always found in submission to the Savior.

Today is my birthday. I mention this not because I hope you will log on to Amazon.com and rush me a gift (although Amazon's delivery system is quite efficient, if you're so inclined). I have walked with the Lord and studied his Word for many, many years; longer than I would like to admit. Over the years, I have gained a high level of biblical literacy and a solid understanding of the theology of the Word of God. I have surely grown in my faith. I have an understanding of the glories of redeeming grace that I did not have for many of my years as God's child. I have been involved in many ministry enterprises in many locations. What God has called me to do has taken me to almost every continent to fellowship and serve with God's people there. I have a library filled with grace-filled books. I love to worship and I love to sit under Christ-centered, grace-filled preaching. I'm married to a godly wife who encourages my faith. This birthday, like many others, stimulates me to count my blessings, and they really are many. But there is one thing today that confronts me as it did the year before: I am not a grace graduate.

I am still tempted to think that my way is better. No, not in big, grand, public sins, but in the more acceptable sins of pride, impatience, failure to be gentle, loving myself more than my neighbor, and loving pieces of the creation more than I should. It is embarrassing to admit that all of this is fueled by a grand delusion that I thought I had conquered long ago. It is a delusion that I have expounded much in my writing and my speaking. It is the lie of lies, the lie that was first told in the garden and that has been repeated a billion times since. Believing this lie not only turns you into a fool, but it also makes you a rebel against your heavenly Father. What is this lie? It is the lie that life can be found outside of the Creator.

We all want lasting rest and sturdy peace of heart. We want to be able to quit searching and have hearts that are satisfied. But we forget that real rest of heart is never found on the other side of the Creator's boundaries. Peace and rest are always found when we give our hearts in submission to the Savior. Rest is found in these words: "Your kingdom come, your will be done, on earth as it is in heaven" (Matt. 6:10). We say to God: "May your kingdom come in all that I think, desire, and say. May your kingdom come in my marriage and in my family. May your kingdom come in my work. May your kingdom come in my leisure. May your kingdom so rule my heart that stepping over your boundaries would no longer be attractive to me." That is my prayer for myself and for all who read this devotion.

For further study and encouragement: Mark 8:34–38

NOVEMBER 13

Prayer is abandoning my righteousness, admitting my need for
forgiveness, and resting in the grace of the cross of Jesus Christ.

He also told this parable to some who trusted in themselves that they were righteous, and treated others with contempt: "Two men went up into the temple to pray, one a Pharisee and the other a tax collector. The Pharisee, standing by himself, prayed thus: 'God, I thank you that I am not like other men, extortioners, unjust, adulterers, or even like this tax collector. I fast twice a week; I give tithes of all that I get.' But the tax collector, standing far off, would not even lift up his eyes to heaven, but beat his breast, saying, 'God, be merciful to me, a sinner!' I tell you, this man went down to his house justified, rather than the other. For everyone who exalts himself will be humbled, but the one who humbles himself will be exalted." (Luke 18:9–14)

It is a shocking prayer that the Pharisee speaks in Christ's confrontational parable. It isn't shocking just because he compares himself to sinners worse than him. We are all tempted to do the same, to ease our consciences by pointing to someone whom we assess to be more unrighteous than we are. It isn't shocking just because he lists his good works in his prayer. We all make ourselves feel better about our spiritual state by cataloging the good things we have done. It's shocking because he is saying these things to God, who knows us all even to the deepest recesses of our hearts. He feels quite comfortable in God's presence because he is deeply convinced that, as a righteous man, he deserves to be there.

What's shocking about this prayer is that it is not a prayer at all. There is nothing prayerlike about what this man is doing. What he says is not prayerlike in posture, attitude, or content. In shocking self-confidence, he essentially looks God in the face and says: "I don't need you. I don't need your compassion. I don't need your forgiveness. I don't need your strengthening. I don't need your wisdom. I don't need your help. I'm doing quite well on my own." If you pray a prayer in which you essentially tell God that you don't need him, it may be a pseudo-religious pronouncement, but it is not a prayer.

Real prayer is prayed in an attitude of what the Puritans called *importunity*, which is the condition of being troublesome or persistent because of a deep sense of urgency. It means being frightened into crying out for help. It is a condition of heart that is there only as the result of grace. It's grace that causes you to acknowledge your sin. It's grace that causes you to be frightened by where that sin can lead you. It's grace that opens your heart to the help that only God can give. Real prayer is motivated by that grace and acknowledges your need for that grace. Prayer isn't an announcement of personal righteousness, but a cry for help that rests in the righteousness of another. Have you prayed today?

For further study and encouragement: Luke 18:1–14

NOVEMBER 14

We dream of having perfect relationships, but in reality,
relationships are messy. God has mercy for that mess.

I have been married for many years. I have a wonderful wife (I have hoped for years that she won't realize what a bad deal she got!). From a distance, you would conclude that we basically have a problem-free marriage. But our relationship is still messy. We typically spend Mondays together. We love these days and enjoy the ability to spend them with one another. But somewhere in the middle of one recent Monday, a misunderstanding erupted between us. We both got a bit defensive. The tension was obvious. Too much silence followed until we asked one another's forgiveness. "Too minor to worry about," you say, but these are the moments we live in.

I tell people all the time that we don't just live in big, important moments. We make only a few grand decisions in our entire lives. Most of us won't have a biography written about us. After we die, most of our personal history will die with us, forgotten. We live in little moments, so the character of our relationships is not set in three or four big moments, but in ten thousand little moments of life. What do the little moments of your relationships look like? How are you dealing with the messiness that lives there?

The reality is that you and I have never had a relationship in our lives that hasn't disappointed us in some way. Why is this so universally true? It is true because we all carry into each of our relationships something that is destructive to them. It is something that produces antisocial instincts in all of us. It's something that can make us impatient, self-serving, irritable, proud, critical, and demanding. This relationally destructive thing is sin. Second Corinthians 5:15 tells us that Jesus came so that "those who live might no longer live for themselves." Yes, it is true—the DNA of sin is selfishness. It causes us all to be far too self-focused and self-absorbed. It reduces the field of our normal concern down to our wants, our needs, and our feelings. It makes us all too entitled and all too demanding. It causes us to be quicker to mete out judgment than to extend mercy. It makes us unwilling to overlook minor offenses. It makes us hold onto what we should have long since forgiven. It makes us self-righteously defensive instead of being ready to confess. The mess of relationships is the mess of sin.

Admitting that the mess of relationships is the mess of sin is a major step toward hope. It is the very "me-ism" of sin from which Jesus came to deliver us by his life, death, and resurrection. This means there is grace for every messy moment. You enter into that grace by admitting just how much you need it.

For further study and encouragement: Ephesians 4:17–32

NOVEMBER 15

Today you have hope, not because people like you or because situations are easy, but because God has placed his unshakable love on you.

Looking to the fallen world to give you hope to continue just doesn't work very well. Think about the address where you live:

- You live with fallen people who inevitably disappoint you in some way.
- You live in a broken world where corruption and injustice are commonplace.
- You face temptation somehow, some way every day.
- Your physical body is growing older and can be infected with disease.
- Storms and pollution complicate your life.
- Satan prowls, doing his evil work.
- The physical creation groans, waiting for redemption.
- War and strife pit nation against nation.
- Partiality and prejudice divide us.

Sin creates constant instability and unpredictability around us because the world that we live in simply does not function the way the One who created it intended. There are times when life works well and seems easy, but there are many other times when sickness, a betrayal, an injustice, a financial loss, the corruption of an official, a crime against you, or the death of a loved one makes life very hard.

It is so good to know that you don't have to frantically look for sturdy hope horizontally, where it just can't be found. No, you are freed from this search because powerful grace has connected you to hope. You see, hope is not a situation, a location, a feeling, or a relationship. Hope is a person, and his name is Jesus. He died so that you can know life, real life. He is present with you so that you are guaranteed to have everything you need. He forgives you of all your sins and empowers you to do much better. He never leaves you or turns his back on you. He always responds to you in tender compassion and righteous justice. He never mocks your weaknesses or throws your sin in your face. He never gets tired of you or gives up on his relationship with you. He doesn't ask you to earn what you can never deserve, and he never makes you feel guilty for needing his good gifts. His love isn't conditional and his grace is never temporary. Jesus is your hope as you live in a world where hope is a precious and rare commodity. And remember, you are connected to him forever. This means there will be a day when you won't have to hope anymore, because the paradise you have hoped for will be the eternal reality in which you live.

For further study and encouragement: Psalm 42

NOVEMBER 16

If you're God's child, you are loved today even if, in your human relationships, you are completely alone.

So what do you do, where do you run, what do you tell yourself, or how do you respond when, in this broken world, you are left alone? In some way, it happens to us all. Made to live in community with God and with one another, we find ourselves alienated and alone. Such aloneness cuts deep and hurts a lot precisely because we were designed to be social beings. We were made to live in self-sacrificing love and peace with one another. Harsh words, disloyal acts, slanderous intentions, and violent moments were never supposed to infect and destroy the community for which we were made. But immediately after Adam and Eve disobeyed God, tension and accusation erupted in their relationship, and then it became really bad really fast. Cain, the son of Adam and Eve, murdered his brother in a fit of sibling jealousy.

Since sin has infected our world, wrong infects our relationships. It shatters the community God intended us to live in and leaves many of us alone. This aloneness takes many forms:

- Friends turn their backs on friends.
- Husbands and wives divorce.
- Neighbors move away.
- Employees get fired.
- Children reject their parents.
- Churches divide.
- Problems of life carve a gulf between us.
- Friends and relatives lose contact.
- Old age leaves us lonely.
- Death takes dear ones from us.

Yes, somewhere in your life, you will be left alone. But it is in this experience of aloneness that you must remember the gospel of Jesus Christ. Jesus captured the relational beauty of this in his own life when, as he faced death, he said to his disciples: "Behold, the hour is coming, indeed it has come, when you will be scattered, each to his own home, and will leave me alone. Yet I am not alone, for the Father is with me" (John 16:32). Yes, people and circumstances leave you alone. Yet, it is impossible for one of God's children to be completely alone, because we have a Father in heaven who is always with us and who will not leave us, no matter what. Remind yourself today that, as God's child, no matter how many people have walked out of your life, fundamental aloneness is a thing of your past.

For further study and encouragement: Psalm 94

NOVEMBER 17

Since sin is deeper than bad behavior, trying to do better isn't a solution. Only grace that changes the heart can rescue us.

There is a difference between a person in whom disappointment leads to self-reformation and someone in whom grief leads to heartfelt confession. I think that we often confuse the two. The first person believes in personal strength and the possibility of self-rescue, while the second has given up on his own righteousness and cries out for the help of another. One gets up in the morning and tells himself that he'll do better today, but the other starts the day with a plea for grace. One targets a change in behavior, and the other confesses to a wandering heart. One assesses that he has the power for personal change, while the other knows that he needs to be given strength for the battle. One has to hold on to the possibility of personal reformation, but the other has abandoned that hope and therefore runs to God for help.

Self-reliant personal reformation and the penance that follows is the polar opposite of heartfelt confession with the repentance that follows. People who acknowledge that what they've done is wrong and then immediately lay out plans to do better unwittingly deny what the gospel of Jesus Christ says about them, how real change takes place, and where help can be found. What they have omitted or neglected is confession. When you confess your sins to God, you don't just admit that you have sinned; no, you also confess that you have no power to deliver yourself from the sin you have just confessed. True confession always combines an admission of wrong with a plea for help. The heart then, encouraged by the forgiveness and presence of Jesus, longs to live in a new, better way (repentance).

A person who manifests a self-reliant recognition of wrong assigns to himself the power to do better and then gives himself to spiritual-looking acts of penance that make him feel good about himself and his potential ability to do better. But while he is acknowledging sin, there is no verticality to what he is doing. By that I mean that there is no Godward confession, no recognition of his desperate need for rescue, and no repentance that is motivated by a heart filled with gratitude for and worship of God. It is an "I can save myself" way of dealing with sin, and it is far more prevalent in the church of Jesus Christ than we would think. It never results in lasting change. It never produces a protective and preventative humility of heart. It never stimulates further worship and service of the Savior. It simply does not work. If you had the power to change yourself without God's help, Jesus wouldn't have had to come. The whole story of the gospel in Scripture is a story of people who are desperately trapped in sin and have no hope except the rescuing grace of the Redeemer. When your sin is revealed today, which of these two pathways will you take?

For further study and encouragement: Luke 15:1–10

NOVEMBER 18

God is holy, but we're not. Jesus became our righteousness
so that we can stand before God, holy in him.

Sin left us in a desperate condition—unrighteous in every way. The comprehensive nature of our unrighteousness grieved the heart of God. This is powerfully captured in Genesis 6:5–8:

> The LORD saw that the wickedness of man was great in the earth, and that every intention of the thoughts of his heart was only evil continually. And the LORD regretted that he had made man on the earth, and it grieved him to his heart. So the LORD said, "I will blot out man whom I have created from the face of the land, man and animals and creeping things and birds of the heavens, for I am sorry that I have made them." But Noah found favor in the eyes of the LORD.

This is a shocking statement of the sorry state of things as the result of sin. We tend to want to think that sin is not so sinful; that our unrighteous attitudes and actions are not really that unrighteous. But one little phrase in this passage says it all. It forcefully declares why our only hope is the righteousness of the Lord Jesus Christ. This phrase is powerful and sobering because it is the assessment of the human heart by the One who is the Creator and knower of our hearts. Here it is: "every intention of the thoughts of his heart was only evil continually."

God wasn't grieved because the people he had made occasionally did wrong things or once in a while had bad thoughts. He wasn't grieved because their responses were sometimes colored with bad intentions. This would have been bad enough, but things were fundamentally worse. The effect of sin on people was total. It distorted everything people desired and thought, and consequently everything they said and did. It is humbling to grasp, but sin leaves us in the one condition none of us want to believe that we're in. The result of sin is that there is nothing righteous about us. There is nothing that is naturally commendable. There is nothing that we can hold before God as a reason to quiet his grief and engender his acceptance. Nothing.

But this passage tells us more. It lays out the pattern by which God would deal with sin—judgment and redemption. He would wipe out people from the face of the earth in an act of righteous judgment, but he would redeem one man and his family, and renew his covenant promises to them. The redemption of Noah was to be a finger that pointed to another redemption, one following the same pattern. God would send his Son, the Lord Jesus Christ. Jesus would be righteous in every way, yet judgment would fall on him. He would experience the full weight of God's anger over sin, even to death, so that we wouldn't have to. His death would satisfy God's anger. His righteousness would be attributed to us. His resurrection would guarantee us life. His righteousness is our only hope, because sin renders us all deeply unrighteous.

For further study and encouragement: Romans 3:21–31

NOVEMBER 19

*You must never let your enthusiasm for the gift replace
your worship of and service for the Giver.*

God asks a stinging question of the children of Israel at the beginning of the book
of Jeremiah, a question that should cause all of us to search our own hearts:

> Has a nation changed its gods,
>   even though they are no gods?
> But my people have changed their glory
>   for that which does not profit.
> Be appalled, O heavens, at this;
>   be shocked, be utterly desolate,
>   declares the LORD,
> for my people have committed two evils:
> they have forsaken me,
>   the fountain of living waters,
> and hewed out cisterns for themselves,
>   broken cisterns that can hold no water. (Jer. 2:11–13)

It is a significant spiritual dynamic to consider. It was at the root of the spiritual
failures of Israel. It poses a spiritual threat to us all. What we celebrate as a blessing
from God can become an idol that rules and directs our hearts. It happens too easily
and so subtly. The genuine obedience that was the fruit of grace morphs into self-
righteous pride that I parade before other people. The house that I once viewed as
an undeserved gift of God becomes an idol that gobbles up the thoughts and desires
of my heart. That relationship that I once saw as a blessing from God's good hand
replaces him as the source of my identity. The theological knowledge that is the gift
of the illumining ministry of the Holy Spirit becomes the reason why I look down
on those who don't know what I know.

Not only have I replaced God as the center of my spiritual hope, but I look for
spiritual hope to things that are empty and cannot and will not ever deliver. I have
replaced the fountain of living water with wells that are completely dry, and I may
not even know that I've done it. Here is the biblical principle—it's not that I desire
only evil things. No, the struggle is more subtle than that. It's that good things can
replace the Giver of those things in my heart. A desire for a good thing becomes a
bad thing when that desire becomes a ruling thing. It's not wrong to desire theological knowledge, personal comfort, or the respect of others, but these things must not
rule our hearts. Here is another argument for the depth of our need for grace. We all
still have wandering hearts. We are all still tempted to put the gift in the place that
the Giver alone should occupy.

For further study and encouragement: Jeremiah 2

NOVEMBER 20

No need to deny, rationalize, or otherwise excuse away evidence of your sin. God wouldn't have sent his Son if your sin were not real.

- "I think you misunderstood me."
- "I wasn't angry, just emphasizing an important point."
- "It wasn't lust; I'm just a man who enjoys beauty."
- "I wasn't feeling well."
- "I just have a strong personality."
- "I think you're being too judgmental."
- "No harm, no foul."
- "It wasn't a lie, just another way of looking at things."
- "Sometimes you have to choose the better of two evils."
- "I was planning on giving it back."
- "It wasn't gossip. I was just asking them to pray."
- "I'm not proud, just exercising God-given leadership gifts."
- "I had to defend myself."

The list could go on and on. We're all so good at doing it. We're all so skilled at convincing ourselves that our sin is less than sin and that we are more righteous than we actually are. In the end, it's all a big insult to the God who controlled every situation, location, and person in every moment of human history so that at the perfect time his Son could come for the express purpose of forgiving us for and delivering us from the very thing that we are minimizing. It is a scandal of self-righteous unbelief, a refusal to take God at his word when he says that we are in a bad condition apart from his grace. It is destructive pride rearing its ugly head. Why destructive pride? It's destructive because it is only when you humbly admit the depth of your unrighteousness and the impossibility of independently altering that condition that you begin to cry out for and get excited about redeeming grace.

Now, all you really need to convince yourself of the depth and seriousness of your sin is the cross of Jesus Christ. That God would go to the extent that he did to sacrifice his one and only Son ought to be demonstration enough that the moral tragedy of sin is real. It is so real that God's real Son had to come in a real birth, live a real life of perfection, die a real death, and walk away from a real tomb so that you could have real forgiveness and real hope in the face of your real sin. When sin is real, real grace is the only hope!

For further study and encouragement: Psalm 32

NOVEMBER 21

Corporate worship is designed to keep you humble by reminding you of your need and thankful by reminding you of God's gift.

To the unbelieving world, it's just a bunch of foolishness. "Sin? Who cares? Grace? Who needs it? Moral law? I'll make up my own rules, thank you. Heaven? Hell? Nobody believes that stuff anymore. Right and wrong? Who knows? True and false? Who has the right to decide? Just be happy and don't hurt anyone else." You and I live in a world that tells us it's all foolishness. That's why we need to be reminded again and again. There's no way I could say it better than the apostle Paul:

> For the word of the cross is folly to those who are perishing, but to us who are being saved it is the power of God. For it is written,
>
> > "I will destroy the wisdom of the wise,
> > and the discernment of the discerning I will thwart."
>
> Where is the one who is wise? Where is the scribe? Where is the debater of this age? Has not God made foolish the wisdom of the world? For since, in the wisdom of God, the world did not know God through wisdom, it pleased God through the folly of what we preach to save those who believe. For Jews demand signs and Greeks seek wisdom, but we preach Christ crucified, a stumbling block to Jews and folly to Gentiles, but to those who are called, both Jews and Greeks, Christ the power of God and the wisdom of God. For the foolishness of God is wiser than men, and the weakness of God is stronger than men.
>
> For consider your calling, brothers: not many of you were wise according to worldly standards, not many were powerful, not many were of noble birth. But God chose what is foolish in the world to shame the wise; God chose what is weak in the world to shame the strong; God chose what is low and despised in the world, even things that are not, to bring to nothing things that are, so that no human being might boast in the presence of God.
>
> And I, when I came to you, brothers, did not come proclaiming to you the testimony of God with lofty speech or wisdom. For I decided to know nothing among you except Jesus Christ and him crucified. And I was with you in weakness and in fear and much trembling, and my speech and my message were not in plausible words of wisdom, but in demonstration of the Spirit and of power, so that your faith might not rest in the wisdom of men but in the power of God. (1 Cor. 1:18–2:5)

Isn't it good that God devised a plan so that we would regularly gather and remember what the world around us ignores or mocks? As we remember, our hearts fill once again with gratitude and are moved once again to worship. We leave with a fresh knowledge that grace isn't foolishness; no, it's the foundation of our hope.

For further study and encouragement: 1 Corinthians 2:6–16

NOVEMBER 22

How could you not have all that you need when your Savior
has promised not to withhold any good thing from you?

Need—it's a very interesting word. It's one of the most frequently used words in human culture and one of the words used most sloppily. We use it to refer to a vast and ever-expanding category that includes all the things that we become convinced that we just can't live without. Most of us think of ourselves as needy in some way, and most of us worry that our needs will never be met. And we all have those moments when we wonder if God really does know what we need and really is committed to providing it. It's tempting to look over the fences at the lives of others and conclude that their needs have been met, which leads us to wonder why ours haven't. Yes, *need* is an interesting and troubling word.

The problem is that, if *need* means "essential for life," most of the things we load into our need category aren't really needs. They are actually desires that have become so precious and important to us that we have come to the point that we cannot conceive of being happy without them. At this point, they capture our thoughts, direct our desires, shape the way we think about our lives, and ultimately define how we think about God.

Here are three things that happen when you name something a need:

1. If you are convinced that something is a need, you feel *entitled* to it. This means you are sure it is your right to have it in your life.
2. If you are convinced something is a need, you think that it's your right to *demand* it. You do not feel uncomfortable about asking for it again and again.
3. If you are convinced that something is a need, you *judge* the love of God by his willingness to deliver it.

This is the scary pathway down which this concept of "need" leads you. If you're convinced something is a need and God does not deliver it, you begin to question his goodness. What is deadly about questioning God's goodness is that you tend not to run for help to someone you doubt. Misnamed "needs" can be devastating to your communion with God. I am persuaded that many people struggle with doubts about the goodness and faithfulness of God for this very reason. They cannot believe that God would fail to deliver a thing that seems impossible for them to live without. God hasn't promised to deliver what you desire, but he has committed himself to meet every one of your needs. That's why it's so comforting to know that you have a heavenly Father who knows exactly what you need and is actively delivering.

For further study and encouragement: Psalm 84:11 and Matthew 6:25–32

NOVEMBER 23

Obedience is an act of thankful worship, not a fearful
means of trying to gain favor with God.

There is simply nothing you can do to gain God's favor. You have to accept this and remember it. You will never be righteous enough for long enough to satisfy God's holy requirements. Your thoughts will never be pure enough. Your desires will never be holy enough. Your words will never be clean enough. Your choices and actions will never be God-honoring enough. The bar is too high for you and me to ever reach. There are no exceptions. We all live under the same weight of the law and the same inability of sin. We're all better rebels than submissives. We're all more naturally proud than humble. We're all more given to idolatry than the worship of God. We do better at making war with our neighbors than loving them. We all find envy more natural than contentment. We're all thieves in one way or another. We all covet what others have. We more naturally bend the truth than protect it. We condemn with our words rather than giving grace. We lay down evidence every day that we will never independently reach God's standard.

Here is your "That says it all" statement: "For by the works of the law no human being will be justified in his sight" (Rom. 3:20). And why is this true? It's true because "all have sinned and fall short of the glory of God" (Rom. 3:23). The language is all-inclusive. It leaves no room whatsoever for exceptions. It is the devastatingly humbling news that all people need to accept into their hearts and into their sense of their identity. But this hard-to-accept news is the doorway not to depressive self-loathing, but to eternal hope and joy. It's only when you accept who you are and what you are unable to do that you begin to understand the necessity of God's gift. Let's put the bad news and the good news together, as Paul does in Romans 3. He writes, "all have sinned and fall short of the glory of God," but that is not the end of the story. He goes on to say that we "are justified by his grace as a gift, through the redemption that is in Christ Jesus, whom God put forward as a propitiation by his blood. to be received by faith" (vv. 23–25).

A propitiation is an atoning sacrifice. The sacrifice of Jesus appeased the wrath of God and created a reconciliation between God and all who place their faith in him. Since God hates sin, the only way we sinners could have a relationship with him is by Christ giving his life to pay the penalty for our sin. You don't need to obey to gain God's favor. Christ has gained God's favor on your behalf. So your obedience is never a fearful payment, but a hymn of gratitude to a God who met you where you were and did for you what you could not have done for yourself.

For further study and encouragement: Hebrews 3

*It is dangerous to live without your heart being captured by awe
of God, because awe of God is quickly replaced by awe of you.*

It is a daily battle,
one that is free of
physical weapons,
political parties,
and national boundaries.
It is a battle that has been raging
since the garden
and will not stop until the war
is finally won.
This battle is not fought
between people,
it is fought
within people.
It is a much greater danger
to each of us
than war between nations
will ever be.
It is a battle of awe.
We were created to live in
a real,
heart-gripping,
agenda-setting,
behavior-forming
awe of God.
But other awes kidnap our hearts.
Awe of creation,
awe of other people,
and awe of ourselves
shove the awe of God
out of our hearts.
So we need grace to see again,
to tremble again,
and to bow down again
at the feet of the One who deserves
our awe.

For further study and encouragement: Exodus 19

NOVEMBER 25

The question is not whether you will worship, but rather what you will worship—your glorious Creator or something he created.

I disappointed myself yesterday. I failed to live up to my standards. It hit me later that if I cannot live up to my standards, how can I ever hope to keep God's law? Let me unpack this moment for you.

I was doing some of the reading that I have to do in order to do what God has called me to do. I was enjoying my peace and comfort. As I was reading, Luella interrupted me to ask me a question. Immediately I snapped at her that I was busy and didn't need to be disturbed. She walked away quietly, only to come back a few moments later to ask, "Can you explain to me why you responded to me as you did?" The minute she said this, I was crushed, filled with grief. I had done it again. I had been the husband that I don't want to be. I had treated a person that I say I love with irritation and impatience.

Now, why did this happen? It is humbling to admit, but my problem wasn't a relationship problem, it wasn't a schedule problem, and it wasn't just a misunderstanding; No, I did what I did because I still have a worship problem. You see, all our hearts live and respond under the rulership of something, and there are only two options: God or something he created. Let me say it this way—it is only when God is in his rightful place of rule in our hearts that people are in their appropriate place in our lives. You and I can keep the second greatest commandment ("You shall love your neighbor as yourself," Mark 12:31) only if we keep the Great Commandment ("You shall love the Lord your God," v. 30). If God is not in his rightful place, guess who we insert in his place. In that regretful moment with Luella, I gave way to the most seductive, addictive, and deceptive of all idols—the idol of self.

The idolatry that defeats us is usually not the worship of formal religious idols, but of a whole catalog of God-replacements, the chief of which is the self. So I am in desperate need of a Redeemer who not only can protect me from external idols, but who can rescue me again and again from me.

No, you cannot divide people into those who worship and those who don't. The most irreligious person on earth worships, because worship is first a human identity before it is a human activity. Everything we do and say is rooted in worship. Every choice or decision flows from worship. Worship is the inescapable occupation of every human being. The question is not *if* we worship, but *what* we give our hearts to worship.

Because we worship things other than God, we fail to keep God's law. So Jesus came to defeat the sin that causes us to worship everything but God. The purpose of the cross of Christ was not only to forgive us for our idolatry, but to reclaim us for the one thing that every human being was created to do—worship of God. The grace to worship what we are meant to worship is the grace that we all need.

For further study and encouragement: Romans 1

NOVEMBER 26

Can you tell the story of redemption in one sentence? Sin has driven us out of the garden, but grace drives us right into the Father's arms.

It is the most amazing turnaround in human history. It is the unexpected plot twist. You wouldn't have predicted it. The announcement foretells everything else that is going to happen in this story of stories. What am I talking about? God's announcement of how he would deal with the outrageous sin of Adam and Eve, and the evil that had flooded into the world as a result.

Adam and Eve had it all: they were perfect people living in a perfect world and enjoying a perfect relationship with God. There was no tension between them and no separation between them and God. There was no pollution or disease, no injustice or corruption, and no hatred or violence. They lived in a world that was in a constant state of "*shalom.*" *Shalom* means more than "peace." It refers to things being in the state that God intended them to be in; in other words, *shalom* is the way things were meant to be. It was the world as we have never experienced it—untainted and unharmed. Life for Adam and Eve was complete in every way.

But it wasn't enough for them. They wanted more. So they stepped over the one boundary God set for them. They ate the fruit that God had forbidden. It was an in-your-face act of self-centered rebellion. It was a quest for autonomy, revealing a desire for self-rule. It was evil and ugly. God had every right to judge them, and he did, but shockingly, that judgment would not be the end of the story. If the story of Adam and Eve were a movie, we would expect God's judgment, their removal from the garden, and then fade to black, but the God writing the script is a God of glorious grace.

Grace leads the biblical story in a very different direction than we would anticipate. God announced immediately after the rebellion of Adam and Eve that he was not only going to judge sin, he was going to defeat it forever. He said to the Serpent: "I will put enmity between you and the woman, and between your offspring and her offspring; he shall bruise your head, and you shall bruise his heel" (Gen. 3:15). Who is the offspring that God was talking about? It is the son of Mary, the son of David, the Son of Man, the Son of God, Jesus of Nazareth, the Messiah. Where did this bruising take place? It took place on that hill called Golgotha, outside the walls of Jerusalem. On the cross, Jesus was bruised, but the enemy was defeated forever. Yes, Jesus died, but the grave could not hold him, and with resurrection power he now reigns until the final enemy is under his feet. It is a story of astounding mercy granted to rebels, of amazing grace bestowed upon fools. It is a radical, unexpected story of hope and help for every sinner. It is the story that gets me up in the morning, and I hope it does the same for you.

For further study and encouragement: Acts 2:22–41

NOVEMBER 27

*Today you'll envy the blessings of another or you'll bask in
the wonder of the amazing grace you have been given.*

I wish I could say that I am always content. I wish I could say that I never complain. I wish I could say that I never want what others have. I wish I could say that I have never envied the life of another. I wish I could say that I have never thought that God gave something to someone else that he meant for me. I wish I could say that I am better at counting my blessings than I am at assessing what I don't have. I wish I could say that my appetite for things wasn't so large. I wish my heart would finally be satisfied. These are all wishes because they are not yet completely true of me. Envy still lurks in my heart. It is one of the dark results of the sin that still resides there.

Why does the Bible speak so strongly against envy? Here it is: when envy rules your heart, the love of God doesn't. Let's think about what envy does. It assumes that you deserve blessings that you don't deserve. When your heart is ruled by envy, the attitude of "I am blessed" gets replaced with the attitude of "I deserve." Envy is selfish to the core. Envy always puts you in the center of the world. It makes everything all about you. It causes you to examine life from the sole perspective of your wants, needs, and feelings.

Sadly, envy causes you to question the goodness, faithfulness, and wisdom of God. Envy accuses God of not knowing what he's doing or of not being faithful to what he's promised to do. When you are convinced that a blessing that another person has ought to belong to you, you don't just have a problem with that person, you have a problem with God. When you begin to question God's goodness, you quit going to him for help. Why? Because you don't seek the help of someone you've come to doubt.

Envy does something else that is spiritually deadly. It assumes understanding that no one has. Envy not only assumes that you know more about that other person's life than you could ever know, it assumes that you have a clearer understanding of what is best than God does. Furthermore, envy causes you to forget God's amazing rescuing, transforming, empowering, and delivering grace. You become so occupied with accounting for what you do not have that the enormous blessings of God's grace—blessings that we could not have earned, achieved, or deserved—go unrecognized and uncelebrated. And because envy focuses more on what you want than it does on the life that God has called you to, it keeps you from paying attention to God's commands and warnings, and therefore leaves you in moral danger.

The only solution to envy is God's rescuing grace—grace that turns self-centered sinners into joyful and contented worshipers of God.

For further study and encouragement: 1 Samuel 12

NOVEMBER 28

The person next to you doesn't need the gospel more than you do;
he just needs it differently than you do. All people sin and fall short.

The indictment of Romans 3 puts us all in the same boat:

What then? Are we Jews any better off? No, not at all. For we have already charged that all, both Jews and Greeks, are under sin, as it is written:

"None is righteous, no, not one;
    no one understands;
    no one seeks for God.
All have turned aside; together they have become worthless;
    no one does good,
    not even one."
"Their throat is an open grave;
    they use their tongues to deceive."
"The venom of asps is under their lips."
    "Their mouth is full of curses and bitterness."
"Their feet are swift to shed blood;
    in their paths are ruin and misery,
and the way of peace they have not known."
    "There is no fear of God before their eyes." (Rom. 3:9–18)

Yes, we are all sinners. We are all in the same desperate condition. None of us is better off than any other. None of us is more righteous. None of us is more deserving. None of us has anything to point to that would commend us to God. We all need to be rescued from the dark rebellion of our own hearts. There is only one hope for us all—the amazing, forgiving, rescuing, transforming, and delivering grace of Jesus. The problem is that we often don't see it that way.

Part of the blindness of sin is our tendency to be more irritated by and more concerned about the sin of the people next to us than our own. Because we are blind to our own sin and our eyes are open to theirs, we tend to see our neighbors as bigger sinners than we are. And when you fall into comparing yourself to another person, you almost always conclude that you are more righteous than he is, and when you conclude that you are more righteous than he is, you begin to minimize you own need for grace. In this way, false spiritual comparisons put you in spiritual danger. They make you think that you're better off than you are and weaken your resolve to seek and celebrate redeeming grace. We must cry out for grace to deliver us from this tendency.

Yes, we all stand before God deserving of his anger. How grateful we ought to be that Christ bore our penalty so that we could bask in God's grace.

For further study and encouragement: Ephesians 4:17–24

NOVEMBER 29

Your world is dramatically broken and you are still riddled with flaws, but Jesus is present, gracious, and faithful.

You and I have two big problems. First, we live in a dramatically broken world that does not function the way God intended. You will not live in this fallen world without suffering in some way. Perhaps it will be a situation of heart-breaking injustice. Maybe you'll be the victim of an act of violence. Perhaps you'll suffer a divorce or the betrayal of a friend. Maybe you'll be robbed or mugged. Perhaps, like many, you'll suffer under the weight of corrupt government. Maybe a disease will infect and weaken your body. But even if none of these things comes your way, you'll suffer the hardship and toil of living in a world where things simply don't work in the way that God designed. But that's not all. You'll also be required to deal with the endless temptations that wait for you around every corner. What God says is ugly will be presented to you as beautiful. Seductive voices will whisper untruths in your ears. You'll be tempted to desire things that are outside God's plan for you. If you don't take the fallenness of your world seriously, you'll live with unrealistic expectations and be naive to temptation.

But we have a second and even more fundamental problem. It is far more troublesome than the evil that is outside us. It's the evil inside us. If you're God's child, the power of sin has been broken in God's justifying grace, but the presence of sin still remains and is being progressively eradicated by sanctifying grace. This means sin still lives inside you. Your trouble is never just environmental, it is always also internal. If you were completely pure in heart, life in this fallen world would be infinitely easier. But if you embrace the theology of the heart that is in Scripture, you know that sin is first a heart problem before it is ever a behavior problem.

Here's what you and I need to understand and never forget: it is only ever the evil inside us that hooks us to the evil outside us. Sin makes me susceptible to the lure of temptation. Temptation plays to the evil desires and idolatrous cravings that still live in my heart. Temptation appeals to my selfishness and greed. Temptation targets my laziness and impatience. Temptation hooks my materialism and discontent. Temptation goes after my desire to have my own way and write my own rules.

But in his grace, Jesus is present to help us overcome both of these problems: "Where sin increased, grace abounded all the more" (Rom. 5:20). Isn't it good to know that "as sin reigned in death, grace also might reign through righteousness leading to eternal life through Jesus Christ our Lord" (v. 21)?

For further study and encouragement: Romans 8:1–17

NOVEMBER 30

You were created to be dependent. God welcomes your dependency with his grace, so why would you want to go it on your own?

Wrapped into the devious temptation of the Serpent in the garden were two foundational lies. These lies have been believed somehow, some way by every person who has ever lived. If you're a parent, you've seen the acceptance of them in your children from a very early age.

The first lie is the lie of *autonomy*. This lie tells you that you are an independent human, that your life belongs to you, and that you have the right to live your life as you please. It is an attractive and seductive lie. Believing this lie makes a little child protest when he's told to go to bed or to eat his peas. However, the doctrine of creation destroys the lie of autonomy. Think with me. Creation depicts ownership. I am a painter by avocation. Once I have composed, painted, and completed a painting, it belongs to me because I made it. You can buy it from me or I can gift it to you, but until I relinquish it, it is mine because I created it. Since God created you and me, we belong to him. We don't own our mentality, our spirituality, our emotionality, our psychology, our personality, or our physicality. We are not independent beings and we do not have a natural right to do with our physical and spiritual selves whatever we desire to do. Autonomy is a life-destroying lie.

The second lie is the lie of *self-sufficiency*. This lie tells you that you have everything within yourself to be what you're supposed to be and to do what you're supposed to do. This lie explains why a little child struggling to tie his shoelaces will slap his mom's hand away when she tries to help, even though he has no idea how to make a bow. However, the doctrine of creation destroys this lie as well. Creation depicts dependency. The flower you plant in your garden is not self-sufficient. If it is not weeded and not watered, it will not grow. You and I were created to be dependent, first on God and second on others in interdependent relationships. Immediately after creating Adam and Eve, God began to talk to them because he knew they had no capacity to figure life out on their own. The lie of self-sufficiency is also life-destroying because it causes us to resist the help of our Creator—the very help we were designed to need and he is willing to give.

Going it on your own simply does not work. The self-made man is always poorly made. Here is an argument for how much we need grace. It takes an act of grace to release us from our bondage to these lies so that we will confess our need for grace and then seek the grace that is our only hope in life and death. It really does take grace to know how much you need grace.

For further study and encouragement: John 15:1–17

DECEMBER 1

You have one place of hope, security, and rest.
It is found in these words: "God is love."

It is something every human being does. It separates us from the rest of creation. It causes us much anxiety and much joy. It shapes the decisions and investments that we make. It calms our fears or leaves us scared and feeling alone. It turns all of us into theologians and philosophers. Where we land in this pursuit shapes the way we look at life and interpret the things that happen to us. It proves that we don't live by instinct or by impersonal determinative forces. It exposes the fact that we are deeply spiritual beings. It is one of our most foundational quests. As different as we are one from another, in this way we are all the same. We all are looking for something in which to place our hope. We're all in search of security.

I don't know if you've thought about this, but there are only two places to look for hope. You can search for it horizontally, thinking that something in creation will give you the security, peace, and inner sense of well-being that you seek, or you can seek it vertically, entrusting your life into the loving hands of your Creator. People put their hope in the creation all the time. They seek satisfaction of heart in the love of other human beings or in the success of their careers. They think their hearts will be satisfied by a certain set of achievements or by a certain catalog of possessions. But none of these things has the power to satisfy your heart. They are all meant to point you to the one place where you heart will find secure rest. You and I need to face this reality—creation will never be our savior!

So where is hope to be found, hope that will never disappoint or shame you? It really is found in three of the most glorious words ever penned in human language. These words have the power to transform you and everything about you. These words can end your frantic search and give your weary heart rest. These words describe the One who alone is capable of carrying your hope: "God is love" (1 John 4:16). Because he is love and because he has placed his love on you, you have security and hope even in those scary moments when it feels as if you have neither. The One who is love sent his Son of love to be a sacrifice of love so you and I could be rescued by his love and rest in that love forever and ever.

For further study and encouragement: 1 John 1:1–4

DECEMBER 2

If you are not fully formed into the image of Jesus, your Redeemer
is neither satisfied nor finished, and neither should you be.

We don't talk about it much. It doesn't find its way into our theological outlines. It's not the typical way we think about our Redeemer. Yet it is an observation that not only gives you hope, but defines for you what your Lord is doing right here, right now. Here it is—you serve a dissatisfied Redeemer. You ought to be very thankful that your Lord isn't easily satisfied. He does not do his work poorly or incompletely. He does not walk away from what he has begun until it is perfectly finished. He does not grow bored, tired, discouraged, or distracted. He does not have a short attention span. He does not suffer from redemptive attention deficit disorder. He never grows impatient. He isn't irritated by how long his work is taking. He never wishes that he hadn't begun in the first place. He never tries to rush what takes time. He never uses his power to turn what must be a process into an event. He never wonders if it's worth it and contemplates calling it all off.

Your Redeemer is zealous for one goal—the final renewal of all things. Ultimate salvation from all that sin is and all that sin has broken is his unrelenting pursuit. He will continue to unleash his power to accomplish redemption and he will not be satisfied until the last enemy is under his feet and the final kingdom has come. Yes, there is great and eternal hope for you in the dissatisfaction of your Redeemer.

Our problem is that we are all too easily satisfied. We're satisfied with a little bit of theological knowledge, a degree of biblical literacy, occasional moments of ministry, and a measure of personal spiritual growth. We're sadly satisfied with being a little bit better when God's goal is that we be completely remolded into his image. In fact, it is even worse than that. Not only are we too easily satisfied, willing to stop before the Redeemer's work is fully accomplished in us, we are all very easily distracted. We get distracted by the temporary glories of the created world, and we actually begin to think that we can find our satisfaction there. So we quit pressing on because our Redeemer is pressing on. While he, in glorious dissatisfaction, still works to redeem us from us, we are out chasing other lovers. We begin to believe that they can do for us what he alone can do. We begin to invest our time, energy, and hope in things that can never deliver.

Hope is not found in the places where our hearts look for satisfaction, but in the dissatisfaction of our Redeemer. He will complete his work even in those moments when we don't care that he does.

For further study and encouragement: 1 Thessalonians 5:23–24

DECEMBER 3

Corporate worship is a regular, gracious reminder that it's not about you. You've been born into a life that is a celebration of another.

Corporate worship is a celebration that serves as a very important reminder for us all. We gather together to celebrate the One who created, controls, and sits at the center of all things. Every biblical worship service is guided and shaped by the words of Romans 11:33–36:

> Oh, the depths of the riches and wisdom and knowledge of God! How unsearchable are his judgments and how inscrutable his ways!
>
> "For who has known the mind of the Lord,
>   or who has been his counselor?"
> "Or who has given a gift to him
>   that he might be repaid?"
>
> For from him and through him and to him are all things. To him be glory forever. Amen.

The final verse says it all. It is not only a prescription for every worship service, but also a powerful statement about what life is all about. Life is not about us. It is not about our wants, our needs, or our feelings. It is not about our comfort, pleasure, and ease. It is not about us getting our personal definition of happiness. It's not about our satisfaction and contentment. It's not about how many of our dreams we actually get to experience. It's not about our successes and achievements. It's not about how successfully we avoid difficulty and suffering. It's not about how well our relationships are working.

It's not wrong to desire personal happiness, peace, a healthy body, and healthy relationships. The issue is this—these things must not rule our hearts, because when they do, they place us at the center of our world and make it all about us. It is sad that many people, even professing Christians, live in a way that is God-forgetting and God-replacing. We put ourselves in the center, we decide for ourselves what we want life to be like, and we reduce God to little more than the delivery system for our catalog of self-oriented dreams.

So corporate worship calls us back again and again to remember and to celebrate. It calls us to remember that all that exists, including us, is from God, exists through him, and points to him. He is the beginning, the center, and the end of all things. His will is preeminent and will be done. His kingdom will come. Grace decimates our lordship and causes us to bow to the one true Lord. It is only by grace that we celebrate a lordship other than our own. Corporate worship points us to our need for and the availability of that grace.

For further study and encouragement: Romans 11

DECEMBER 4

You were designed for it. You have missed the point without it.
What is it? Living every day for the glory of the Father.

I have written about it much and I will continue to write about it as long as I am able. It is a theme that cannot be repeated too much. It is a practical concern that touches everything that we think, desire, say, and do. It reaches to the deepest levels of human motivation. It sits at the epicenter of our spiritual struggles. It is one of the underlying causes of the most important battles of the heart. It exposes the deepest wishes of our souls. It is at the heart of why we were created. It expresses God's will for everyone who has ever taken a breath. It is the great moral dividing line. And it is the reason Jesus had to come.

Life is all about glory. Sin is all about glory. Grace is all about glory. Spirituality is all about glory. Heaven and hell are all about glory. Submission and rebellion are all about glory. Love and hatred are all about glory. A life of demand and a life of service are both propelled by glory. Contentment and craving are both motivated by glory. Every word you speak and every action you take is directed by glory. Glory causes you to want some things and despise others. Glory makes you arrogant and causes you to be humble. Glory reduces you to a thief or motivates you to give. Glory makes your heart glad or causes it to be eaten with envy. Glory makes you constantly thankful for a Savior or causes you to forget he exists.

We human beings were hardwired for glory. Glory orientation was woven into the fabric of our hearts. We were designed this way so that we would be able to take in all the glories of creation and so that those glories would point us to the one glory that is truly glorious and alone able to satisfy our hearts, the glory of God. This means that we are always living in pursuit of some kind of glory. Either our hearts have been captured by the temporary glories of the created world or by grace they have been captured by the eternally satisfying glory of God. We are working for our own glory, pursuing some created glory, or living for God's glory. But we are always living for glory.

Jesus came to liberate us from our addiction to glories that will never satisfy our hearts. He came to free us from our bondage to our own glory and our obsession with the shadow glories of the created world. He willingly died for glory thieves (us) so that we would find our satisfaction in and live in service of the glory of God. Jesus not only revealed God's glory on earth; he died so that that glory would be the final resting place of our hearts.

For further study and encouragement: Psalm 145

DECEMBER 5

You can't live to meet all your needs and live to serve Christ at the same time. Live as his disciple; he's got your true needs covered.

We place many things in our "I just can't live without" category, but the reality is that many of them are not things we actually require for life. These things may be wonderful to enjoy and sweet blessings from a tender and loving Father, but they are not needs and must not be named as such. When we call them needs, we tell ourselves that we have to have them, that we cannot live without them, and that we have a right to demand them. So we end up evaluating the love of God on the basis of how many of the things that we have christened as needs he has delivered to us. As we do this, our lives get shaped by a needs focus, and we spend so much time thinking about and working toward acquiring our needs that we have little personal time left for the larger pursuits of the kingdom of God.

Because of this, Philippians 4:10–20 is very instructive for us:

> I rejoiced in the Lord greatly that now at length you have revived your concern for me. You were indeed concerned for me, but you had no opportunity. Not that I am speaking of being in need, for I have learned in whatever situation I am to be content. I know how to be brought low, and I know how to abound. In any and every circumstance, I have learned the secret of facing plenty and hunger, abundance and need. I can do all things through him who strengthens me.
>
> Yet it was kind of you to share my trouble. And you Philippians yourselves know that in the beginning of the gospel, when I left Macedonia, no church entered into partnership with me in giving and receiving, except you only. Even in Thessalonica you sent me help for my needs once and again. Not that I seek the gift, but I seek the fruit that increases to your credit. I have received full payment, and more. I am well supplied, having received from Epaphroditus the gifts you sent, a fragrant offering, a sacrifice acceptable and pleasing to God. And my God will supply every need of yours according to his riches in glory in Christ Jesus. To our God and Father be glory forever and ever. Amen.

You quit worrying about your catalog of "I must haves" and therefore are freed to give yourself to the work of God's kingdom when:

1. you are convinced that God will give you the strength you need to face whatever he has ordained you to face ("I can do all things through him who strengthens me") and
2. you really do believe that God is actively committed to meeting every one of your true needs ("And my God will supply every need of yours according to his riches in glory in Christ Jesus").

When grace causes your heart to rest in these truths, you no longer live a need-obsessed life and are free to give yourself to the worship and service of God.

For further study and encouragement: Psalm 63

DECEMBER 6

Every day you need it. You simply can't live without it.
What is it? The heart-convicting ministry of the Holy Spirit.

I love the hymn, "Come, Thou Fount of Every Blessing." I especially appreciate the honest admission and plea of the third verse:

O to grace how great a debtor
daily I'm constrained to be!
Let thy goodness, like a fetter,
bind my wandering heart to thee.
Prone to wander, Lord, I feel it,
prone to leave the God I love;
here's my heart, O take and seal it,
seal it for thy courts above.

Here is an honest, excuse-free expression of the spiritual struggle we experience between the grace of conversion and the grace of eternity. It is what we all deal with every day. It's what causes us to lose our way. It's what leads us to live in a way that is contradictory to what we profess to believe. It's what makes us susceptible to temptation. We are all still in possession of wandering hearts. We would like to think that our hearts are perfectly faithful and true, but they are not. We would like to think that nothing could lure us away from our loyalty to our Lord. We would like to think that our moral commitments are unshakable. We would like to think that what God says is wrong would not be attractive to us. We would like to think that we always think God's thoughts after him and that our desires are always in the right place. We would like to think all of these things. But the problem is that we still have fickle hearts.

You see, our biggest problem is not that we live with flawed people who bring trouble our way. Our great difficulty is not that we live in a fallen world where temptation tends to greet us around every corner. The big issue for us is not that we live in a world that isn't operating the way God intended, as a result of which we face difficulty, disease, suffering, loss, and grief. No, our big difficulty is that sin still resides in our hearts. It still distorts our thoughts and redirects our desires. The less-than-perfect people, the temptations around us, and the broken world in which we live are problems for us because we have this problem in our hearts. It is humbling, but it is important to remember that it is only ever the sin inside us that hooks us to the sin outside of us. So what we need most is not a change of location or relationship, but a fundamental rescue of heart, and that is exactly what God's grace in the person of the Holy Spirit provides for us.

For further study and encouragement: Mark 7:14–23

DECEMBER 7

No one knows you more deeply and fully than your Savior, so no one offers you help formfitted for your deepest needs like he does.

It is one of the most comforting passages in all of the New Testament. It is one that you and I should meditate on again and again:

> Since then we have a great high priest who has passed through the heavens, Jesus, the Son of God, let us hold fast our confession. For we do not have a high priest who is unable to sympathize with our weaknesses, but one who in every respect has been tempted as we are, yet without sin. Let us then with confidence draw near to the throne of grace, that we may receive mercy and find grace to help in time of need. (Heb. 4:14–16)

This passage is a call to live with hope, encouragement, courage, and confidence. Why? Not only because you have a High Priest who has passed through the heavens and now sits at the right hand of the Father on high, but also because he is sympathetic to your weaknesses. But there is more. He is sympathetic to your weaknesses because he hears and answers you from the vantage point of an experiential basis of knowledge of exactly what you are going through. He came to earth and, from the time he was an infant until he ascended after his resurrection, he faced the full range of the sufferings and temptations that we face. He knows what it is like to be homeless, hungry, and rejected. He is acquainted with disease and physical pain. He knows the power of accusation and injustice. He faced the siren voice of temptation. He knows what it is like to be forsaken by loved ones. He understands suffering and death. He stared evil in the face. He knows us and has a firsthand understanding of what we deal with day in and day out.

The word translated as "weaknesses" in this passage is profound. It's almost untranslatable. It is used in many ways. It's probably best understood as "the human condition." Our High Priest understands what it is like to be a human being in this fallen world because, in an act of shocking, condescending love, he took on human flesh and lived with us as a man. Now, as the resurrected and ascended man, he sits next to the Father as our High Priest. This means that our struggles and prayers are not greeted with harshness, condemnation, or impatience, but with understanding and sympathy.

All of this means that we can rest assured that we will receive from his hand mercy that is formfitted for the particular needs in which we find ourselves. We can be confident that he hears us with the sympathy of shared experience and, because he does, he will provide for us exactly what we need. Now, that's amazing grace!

For further study and encouragement: Hebrews 2:14–18

DECEMBER 8

*If Christ is your life, you are free from the desperate quest
to find life in situations, locations, and relationships.*

It is a wonderful freedom that we just don't think about and discuss enough. It liberates you from the stress, fear, and anxiety that so many people live with every day. It is a sweet gift of grace that is given to you right here, right now. You never could have found it on your own. You never could have earned or achieved it. You still can't stand before God and say that you deserve it. It is a gift that is not to be ignored or misunderstood.

You have been given Christ, and in being given Christ, you have been given life. You don't need to search for meaning and purpose. You don't need to search for identity. You don't need to look for something to give you the inner sense of well-being that every person wants. You don't have to wonder if you'll ever be loved. You don't have to worry that your life and work will result in nothing. You don't have to wonder if you'll have what you need to face what will be on your plate today. You don't have to worry about your future. You will never be left to the limited range of your own resources. You will never, ever be left alone. There is always someone who understands you and offers you the help that you need. You don't have to worry about whether your wrongs will be forgiven and your weaknesses greeted with patience and grace. You don't have to worry, because you have a Savior who has invaded your life with his grace and has made you the place where he dwells.

So you have been freed from the endless quest for life that consumes so many people. So many look for life where it cannot be found. They hope their marriages will give them the happiness they have not yet found. They look to their jobs to give them identity. They look to people and possessions to give them peace. They don't know it, but they are asking the situations, locations, and relationships of everyday life to be their saviors. Sadly, they're drinking from wells that are dry and eating bread that will never satisfy. The situations, locations, and relationships of daily life are wonderful to enjoy, but we must understand that they will never, ever satisfy our hearts. For that, we have been given a true Savior, the Lord Jesus Christ.

So instead of wasting time on that endless quest for life, you have been invited to enter into God's rest for the rest of your life. Rest in your identity as his child. Rest in his eternal love. Rest in his powerful grace. Rest in his constant presence and faithful provision. Rest in his patience and forgiveness. Rest.

For further study and encouragement: Hebrews 4:1–13

DECEMBER 9

*God harnessed the forces of nature and controlled the events of history
to redeem you. Will he abandon you now in your moment of need?*

The Bible isn't a series of stories. It isn't a catalog of interesting characters. It isn't a manual of theology. It isn't a book of interesting wisdom principles. One story, with one hero, forms the cord that holds the whole Bible together. The Bible is essentially the story of redemption. This grand redemptive story, with God's essential explanatory notes, is the main content of the Word of God.

The Bible displays for us the extent to which God has gone in order to provide salvation for us. He really controlled every event in human history, and he really harnessed the forces of nature so that at a certain time his Son would come and live, suffer, die, and rise again to provide salvation for us. It is a stunning story that should provide the interpretive grid for everything you face in your life in this broken world.

If God went to such lengths as to control the events of the world and to sacrifice his one and only Son, would it make any sense at all for him to abandon you between the "already" of your justification and the "not yet" of your final glorification? Would it make any sense for him to turn his back on you now? Would it make any sense for him to ignore you in your hour of need? Would you expend a great amount of personal effort and sacrifice to secure something of value and then not work to keep, maintain, and protect it?

The fact that you are precious in God's sight is clear because he purchased you at a great price. No higher price could be paid than the death of the Messiah. But that's exactly the price that God paid to redeem you and me. Since he paid such a price, we can rest assured he will expend his divine power and grace to protect, mature, provide for, and keep us until we are with him in a place where the dangers of sin and death are no more. Paul says it this way: "If he freely gave us Jesus, doesn't it make sense that he will also give us everything that we need?" (see Rom. 8:31–33).

So don't let any evil enemy whisper lies into your ear. Don't let him tell you that you are alone, that you're left to your own resources, or that God doesn't hear or care. Don't let yourself doubt God's presence and his goodness. Don't let yourself wonder if you'll make it through. God unleashed his power to make you his own, and he will continue to unleash his power to keep and protect you until you are with him forever in that place where you will need his protection no more because the final enemy will be under his feet.

For further study and encouragement: 2 Kings 6:8–17

DECEMBER 10

It is a grace to be willing to listen to and consider criticism.
It takes grace to quiet the mind and settle the heart to hear.

We are not naturally open to criticism. Most of us don't like to be confronted. It is natural for us to rise to our own defenses when we are questioned. It is natural for us to work to convince ourselves and others that we are righteous. When questioned, it is natural for us to get out our catalogs of righteousness as evidence to convince others that they must have misjudged or misunderstood us. It is natural for us to be more focused on and concerned about the sin of others than our own. It is natural for us to confront others with things that we excuse in ourselves. It is natural for us to see our wrongs as less than wrong. It is natural for us to swindle ourselves into believing that we are far more righteous than we really are. For sinners, self-righteousness is more natural than humility.

In short, it is more natural for us to have hard hearts that are resistant to change than hearts that are open, humble, and crying out for change. So if you are open to loving confrontation, if you are ready to admit your sin, if you are thankful for those who have loved you enough to help you see what you would not see on your own, and if you are ready to confess and seek forgiveness, you know that you have been visited by the grace of Jesus, because none of these attitudes is natural for us apart from divine intervention.

It takes powerful redeeming grace to remove the hearts of stone from us and re-place them with hearts of flesh—hearts that are sensitive to sin, sensitive to the grace of conviction, sensitive to the need for change, and resting in the forgiveness that is found only in Jesus. It takes grace that guarantees that the blood of Jesus has covered everything about us that could ever be known or exposed to give us the courage to look at ourselves in the searching mirror of the Word of God. It takes grace for us to let go of excuses, rationalizations, self-atoning arguments, and our tendency to shift the blame to others. It takes grace for us to be able to stand as sinners before a holy God and admit that there are ways in which we are still rebels against his lord-ship and his commands.

Confession is not intuitive for sinners. Humility is not our natural first response. Love of God more than love of self is not a first instinct. The glory of God isn't naturally the core motivator of what we do and say. So if you are willing to say, "God, show me my heart," and willing to speak these words, "Please forgive me," you know that you have been showered with amazing grace—grace that has already changed your heart and grace that promises more change to come.

For further study and encouragement: Psalm 51

DECEMBER 11

If obedience is a personal act of worship, then disobedience is personal too. Every sin is a violation of a relationship—a sin against God.

I think that we often misunderstand what sin is about, and in so doing, we minimize how horrible it really is. If you unwittingly devalue the heinous nature of sin, you will also devalue the grace that alone is able to rescue you from it.

The first way we devalue sin is to think that sin is about behavior and behavior alone. But that is not what the Bible teaches. Sin is first and foremost a matter of the heart (see Jesus's teaching in the Sermon on the Mount, Matthew 5–7). Since you live out of the heart (see Luke 6:43–45), sin always originates there. Sin is always a matter of the thoughts, desires, motives, and choices of the heart. Sin is a matter of the heart that expresses itself in the behavior of the body—your body physically goes where your heart has already gone. This is precisely why we need rescuing grace. We can run from a certain situation, location, or relationship, but we have no ability whatsoever to escape our hearts; for that, we need rescuing grace.

Second, we tend to think of sin as the breaking of a set of abstract rules. But sin is much more than that. Sin is the breaking of a relationship that results in breaking God's rules. Remember, the Ten Commandments begin with a call to worship God above all else. You see, it is only when God is in his rightful place in my heart that I desire to live in a way that pleases him. If God is not in his rightful place, I insert myself in his place, write my own laws, and give myself to doing what pleases me. So every sin is against God. Every sin is an assault on God's rightful place. Every sin is a betrayal of him. Every sin steals glory from him. Every sin denies his existence and his authority. Every sin replaces him with something else. Every sin quests for his power and his glory. Every sin is after his throne.

Sin is personal and relational, even if you are not conscious of it at the moment when you are sinning. That is why it is right for David, who has just committed adultery and murder, to say, "Against you, you only, have I sinned and done what is evil in your sight" (Ps. 51:4). David is not minimizing the horrible wrongs he did against Bathsheba, Uriah, and the people of Israel. What he's doing is confessing the core of what sin is about. Sin questions God's goodness, wisdom, faithfulness, and love. Sin challenges God's personal rule. Sin says that you know better than God. Sin is personal, and that is why Jesus suffered and died so that you and I would receive forgiving grace.

For further study and encouragement: 1 Samuel 15

DECEMBER 12

No matter how people treat you today, if you're God's child, you're being loved right now by an ever-present, ever-loving Redeemer.

Who has believed what he has heard
    from us?
    And to whom has the arm of the
        LORD been revealed?
For he grew up before him like a
    young plant,
    and like a root out of dry
        ground;
he had no form or majesty that we
    should look at him,
    and no beauty that we should
        desire him.
He was despised and rejected by
    men;
    a man of sorrows, and
        acquainted with grief;
and as one from whom men hide
    their faces
    he was despised, and we
        esteemed him not.

Surely he has borne our griefs
    and carried our sorrows;
yet we esteemed him stricken,
    smitten by God, and afflicted. . . .

He was oppressed, and he was
    afflicted,
    yet he opened not his mouth;
like a lamb that is led to the
    slaughter,
    and like a sheep that before its
        shearers is silent,
    so he opened not his mouth.
By oppression and judgment he was
    taken away;
    and as for his generation, who
        considered
that he was cut off out of the land of
    the living,
    stricken for the transgression of
        my people?
And they made his grave with the
    wicked
    and with a rich man in his death,
although he had done no violence,
    and there was no deceit in his
        mouth.
(Isa. 53:1–4, 7–9)

It is incredibly encouraging to think about as you and I make our way through a world that is marked by hatred, violence, injustice, racism, betrayal, disloyalty, selfishness, abuse, and many other forms of relational sin and brokenness. It is something that needs to be remembered in those moments when you have been sinned against in some way. Read carefully what I am going to write next: Jesus was willing to be despised. He was willing to face rejection. He was willing to subject himself to hatred and violence. He was even willing to have the Father turn his back on him. Why was he willing to do all this? He did it willingly so that, as his children, you and I would be able to live in the hope and peace of knowing that no matter what we face in the human community, we are perfectly and eternally loved by him. He endured rejection so that we would know God's accepting love forever and ever and ever. How amazing is this grace!

For further study and encouragement: Mark 15:33–39

DECEMBER 13

Don't buy the false gospel of self-reliance. If you could make it without help, Jesus would not have needed to come.

It is a seductive lie. It's told again and again. There is nothing new in its message. It was told first in the garden of Eden and hasn't ceased to be told since. It is told in many forms:

- "No one knows you better than you know yourself."
- "You really don't need the ministry of others in your life."
- "You used to struggle with sin, but not anymore."
- "Since you know the Bible so well, you're probably okay."
- "Look at your track record; you've come a long way."
- "Your little sins aren't really that sinful."
- "You're way beyond the level where you need to be taught by others."
- "You're on your own; you just have to get up and do what you've been called to do."

The voices of self-reliance are many and deceptive. In some way, they greet you every day. Their deceptive whispers started in the garden and continue with the sole devious purpose of convincing you to rely on yourself and not on God. The lie of self-sufficiency is attractive to us all because we don't like to think of ourselves as weak and needy. We don't like to think of ourselves as dependent. We don't like to think of ourselves as fools who need to be rescued from ourselves. We like the story of the self-made man; you know, the person who pulled himself out of the mire and made it on his own with no one to thank but himself.

But the message of the gospel is devastatingly humbling. It tells me that I am in a hopeless, impossible, and irreversible state apart from divine intervention. Even Adam and Eve could not make it on their own. Even though they were perfect people living in a perfect world and in a perfect relationship with God, they did not have the ability to go it on their own. So immediately after creating them, God began to give them his revelation, because he knew they would not figure life out on their own. They were dependent on the words of God in order to make proper sense out of life. They could not be what they were supposed to be and do what they were supposed to do without God's counsel and his help. Now, that was the state of people before sin entered the world and did its internal and external damage. How much more is it true of us!

Self-reliance is a lie that leads you nowhere good. You do not have what you need inside yourself to live as you were created to live. So a God of tender grace comes to you in the person of his Son and offers you everything you need for life and godliness. In grace, he is ever with you because he knows you'll never make it on your own.

For further study and encouragement: John 6:60–65

DECEMBER 14

What does it mean to be an ambassador of the King?
It means reflecting his message, his methods,
and his character wherever he's placed us.

It really is a very different way of looking at life. It's a very different basis for making decisions. It's a very different template for deciding how you should act, react, and respond. It's a very different way of thinking about who you are and what you're supposed to be doing. It is a radical way of living, quite different from the worldview that is preached all around us.

The common cultural worldview has you at the very center. It says that life is all about your pursuit of happiness. When someone or something makes you unhappy, it says that the world is not operating the way it is supposed to operate. It really does pull the walls of your motivation and concern to the tight confines of your wants, your needs, and your feelings. But the Bible presents a polar opposite worldview that is to form the identity and lifestyle of every believer. Scripture asserts that you were bought with a price (the life and death of Jesus), so you don't belong to you anymore (actually, because of creation, you never did belong to you). Take time to look at 1 Corinthians 6:12–20, which applies this truth to something as personal as your sexual life.

God has a purpose for you. It is that you would live as one of his representatives; that is, that you would live representatively. And what are you representing? You are called to represent your Savior King. And what does that practically look like? Representing the King means you represent his *message*, his *methods*, and his *character*. Representing the King's message means that you look at every situation and relationship in life through the lens of the truth of Scripture—the center of which is the gospel of Jesus Christ—and determine to help others look at life that way too. Representing his methods means that you seek to be a tool of the kind of change he intends to make in people and in the world around you. And representing his character simply means asking yourself again and again, "What of the person, work, and character of the Lord Jesus Christ does this person need to see in the situation that he or she is now in?"

There is no better word for this bigger-purpose-than-my-happiness way of living that God has called each of us to than the word *ambassador*. It reminds us that there is a King and that we are not him. It moves us to remember once again that our lives do not belong to us. And it puts practical legs on what it means to represent the Savior King in practical ways every day. God's grace has not only rescued you, but has included you in much bigger and more beautiful purposes for your life than you would have ever chosen on your own.

For further study and encouragement: 2 Corinthians 5:11–21

DECEMBER 15

*As God's child, live today with the surety, hope,
and courage that come from knowing that
your standing before God is secure.*

You want to be sure. You want to be secure. You want to have hope. You want to live with courage. You don't want to be weakened by fear, paralyzed by doubt, or filled with the anxiety of wondering what's next. You want to know that your life means something. You want to know that your labors are worth something. You want to know that you're not alone. You want to know that you'll have the resources to face whatever is coming next. You want to have inner peace. You want to have motivation to continue. You don't want to feel unprepared, weak, or unable. You don't ever want to think that it's all been for naught. Yes, you want to stand on the firm foundation of surety, and you will look to something to give it to you.

The fact of the matter is that in a world where things break, die, get corrupted, or otherwise fade away, surety is found only vertically. If you're God's child, your standing before him is sure, and because it is, you have surety in life right here, right now; in death; and in eternity:

- You have the surety of knowing that you don't have to hide or playact, because every one of your sins and weaknesses has been covered by Jesus's blood.
- You don't have to fear that you will not have what it takes, because your Savior gives you all that you need to do what he's called you to do.
- You don't have to worry that you'll be left alone, because your Savior has made you the place where he dwells.
- You don't have to live with regret, because all your past sins have been forgiven by his grace.
- You don't have to search for identity, meaning, or purpose, because he has made you his child and called you to his purpose.
- You don't have to worry about the future, because all the mysteries of what is to come are held in his sovereign hands.
- You don't have to fear trouble, difficulty, or suffering, because your Savior uses all these things for your good and his glory.
- You don't have to hope that your labors are worth something, because the work you do in his name is never in vain.
- You don't have to fear being punished, because your Savior took your punishment and satisfied God's anger.

Yes, you stand before God sure and secure, and because you do, your life right now is blessed with every kind of security you could ever want.

For further study and encouragement: Ephesians 1

DECEMBER 16

It's futile to try to establish your own sovereignty.
People don't want you as their king,
and God won't forsake his holy throne.

I often give way to the fantasy
that I have the
wisdom,
power,
and character
to control
people,
places,
and things in my life
that seem to be out of control.
I insert myself in
the center
and make it all about me.
But I don't have the
right,
power,
or need to control
because you have
every situation,
every location,
and every person
under your wise control.
You rule over all things
for my sake
and for your glory.
So once again you call me
to surrender control
and rest
in your sovereign care.

For further study and encouragement: Daniel 2:20–23

DECEMBER 17

Every time you desire to do and choose to do what is right in God's eyes, you celebrate the grace that is yours in Christ Jesus.

It's hard to admit, but doing what is right isn't natural for us. Sin turns us all into self-appointed sovereigns over our own little kingdoms. Sin makes us all self-absorbed and self-focused. Sin causes us all to name ourselves righteous. Sin seduces us into thinking we are somehow, some way smarter than God. Sin causes us all to trust in our own wisdom. Sin makes us all want to write our own rules. Sin makes us resistant to criticism and change. Sin makes our eyes and our hearts wander. Sin causes us to crave material things more than spiritual provision. Sin causes us to want and esteem pleasure more than character. In our quest to be God, sin causes us to forget God. It reduces us all to glory thieves, taking for ourselves the glory that belongs to him. All of this means that sin causes us to step over God's wise boundaries in thought, desire, word, and action again and again. This is what's natural for a sinner.

So when you have a hunger to know what is right in God's eyes, when you care about his glory, when you willingly submit to his will, when you forsake your plan for his plan, and when you find joy in surrendering to his lordship, you know that you have been visited by rescuing grace. Notice how Paul talks about our submission to the will of the Father: "Therefore, my beloved, as you have always obeyed, so now, not only as in my presence but much more in my absence, work out your own salvation with fear and trembling, for it is God who works in you, both to will and to work for his good pleasure" (Phil. 2:12–13).

Here is a call to a faith-filled life of submission and obedience. It is a call to be serious about the life that grace has made possible for you. The passage is a call to follow the example of the Lord Jesus Christ. But then Paul reminds you that if you follow, if you obey, and if you do what is right in the eyes of your Savior, you can take no credit whatsoever. This is because your right desires and your right actions exist only because of his indwelling presence and ever-active grace. Paul is saying that we do the right that we do because grace is at that moment rescuing us from ourselves. Grace is protecting us from the self-righteousness and self-sovereignty that would make us all too independent and all too rebellious.

Every moment of our obedience is an evidence of and a celebration of the grace that not only forgives but rescues, and not only rescues but transforms. We live in God's sight not in our own strength, but only by grace.

For further study and encouragement: Romans 6

DECEMBER 18

Don't be discouraged as you face your problems. You have more than strength and wisdom. You have the empowering grace of Jesus.

Here are some of Jesus's final words to his disciples before facing his death on the cross: "Behold, the hour is coming, indeed it has come, when you will be scattered, each to his own home, and will leave me alone. Yet I am not alone, for the Father is with me. I have said these things to you, that in me you may have peace. In the world you will have tribulation. But take heart; I have overcome the world" (John 16:32–33).

Here's what this passage tells you:

1. *In your troubles, you don't have to act as though things are okay when they're not okay.* This passage, like so many others, welcomes us to honesty. We aren't called to pretend. We're not forced to act as if things are okay when they're not okay. Biblical faith never asks us to deny the harsh realities of life in this fallen world. God invites our cries and welcomes us to run to him in our grief. This passage is a compassionate and honest warning about the inescapable troubles that we all face between the "already" and the "not yet."

2. *In your troubles, you need to remember that what you're experiencing is part of God's plan.* Jesus is announcing something to his disciples that is discouraging and encouraging at the same time. He is telling his disciples that it is the plan of God for his glory and their good to keep them in a world that is terribly broken and therefore does not function in the way that God intended. You and I should never think that the troubles that we face are an indication of the failure of God's plan and his promises. No, this present suffering exists under his rule and according to his wise and loving plan.

3. *In your troubles, you are invited to remember that you are never alone.* Here Jesus speaks personally. Even when forsaken by all of his followers, he says it is impossible for him to be alone because his Father is with him. In the same way, as God's children, you and I are never left alone in our troublesome circumstances. God, in power, wisdom, and grace, is always with us. This means that in times of trouble, we are never left with the ministry resources of our own power.

4. *In your troubles, you need to know that your troubles may overcome you, but they cannot overcome the Savior who protects and keeps you.* You may be discouraged and stymied in your troubles, but your Lord never is. This means your troubles don't determine your destiny; he does!

For further study and encouragement: Matthew 10:16–33

DECEMBER 19

I know that, like me, you want the present to be a more comfortable destination, but it isn't that. It's an uncomfortable preparation for a comfortable destination.

I would drag myself out of bed each morning and get dressed with feelings of dread. I knew what was facing me because I had been through it before. I would arrive at the locker room, where the lingering smell of yesterday's sweat mixed with that of the ointment we were rubbing on yesterday's bruises. As we slowly put on our equipment, our desire to be there mixed with our knowledge of the hardship that was before us. On the field, under the blazing sun and after a series of grueling drills, you wanted to vomit, to have just a moment to breathe, or to walk off the field and quit altogether. Night was taken up with ingesting a huge amount of food, taking a scalding-hot bath, receiving a rubdown, and getting to bed early. Morning came quickly and the routine started all over again.

This was the daily routine of the two-a-day summer football practices. It was a grueling but amazingly efficient way of preparing us for the season to come. It really did separate the men from the boys. It taught us to work through pain. It taught us the importance of getting each play right. It taught us how to work together and the importance of following the commands of the coach. And most of all, it whipped our bodies into shape. At the end of the summer, you weren't as breathless as before and you couldn't remember the last time you wanted to vomit in the middle of practice. Those two-a-day practices were hard, but they were for our good. And they weren't our destination, but a preparation for the destination of the football season that was to come.

Yes, your life is hard right now. You are being called to do difficult things under the heat of the sun of this fallen world. You are called to say no to feelings of discouragement and the desire to quit. You are called to persevere, doing the same good things over and over again until they become second nature to you. You are called to work with others who are going through the same hardship and you are called to submit to the wise commands of your Savior King. You will face hardship tomorrow and the day to follow, but your hardship will not last forever. Yes, there will be moments of comfort along the way—times of rest, healing, and retreat—but they will be followed by more hardship. You must face these repeated hardships because the place where you are is not your destination. No, it is a place of preparation for the final destination that is to come. Preparation is hard, but you and I aren't ready, so we need to be made ready for the final place that will be our home.

Today, thank God that he has a home waiting for you and that he loves you enough to use hardship to make you ready for your welcome to your final home. Your preparation won't last forever, but your destination will have no end.

For further study and encouragement: Isaiah 48:1–11

DECEMBER 20

*God calls you to make war with sin every day, and then he fights on
your behalf with divine power even when you don't have the sense to.*

I wish I could say that sin always appears horribly ugly and destructive to me, but it
doesn't. I wish I could say that all the time and in every way I hate what God hates,
but I don't. I wish I could say that I always love to do what is right, but I don't. I
wish I could say that I never think that my way is better than God's way, but I can't. I
wish my heart were forever settled with staying inside God's boundaries, but it isn't.
I wish I could say that my war with sin is over, but it's not.

Here's the danger for me and for you: sin doesn't always look *sinful* to us. It's
hard to admit it, but sometimes sin actually looks beautiful to us. The man lusting
after the woman in the mall doesn't actually see something ugly and dangerous. No,
he sees beauty. The guy who is cheating on his taxes doesn't see the moral danger of
deception. He sees the excitement of having additional money to satisfy his desires.
The woman gossiping on the phone doesn't see the destructiveness of what she's
doing because she is taken up with the buzz of passing a tale. The child who is rebel-
ling against the will of her parents doesn't see the danger that she's placing herself
in because she is captivated by the thrill of her temporary independence. Part of the
deceptive power of sin in my heart is its ability to look beautiful when it is actually
terribly ugly.

So we need help, and God in grace has met us with that help. This help doesn't
come to us first in a theology or a set of commands or principles; it comes to us in
a person. God knew that my struggle with sin would be so great that it would not
be enough to forgive me. That forgiveness is a wonderful thing, but I need more. So
God not only forgives, but he also gets inside me by his Spirit. The Spirit that now
lives inside me is a Warrior Spirit, who by grace does battle with my sin even in moments when I don't care to. His redemptive zeal is unstoppable. Think of Peter, who
denied any knowledge of Christ. Was it the end of his story? No, but not because
Peter had the sense to pursue Jesus; it was because Jesus, in unrelenting, forgiving
grace, pursued Peter (see John 18:12–14, 25–27; 21:15–19).

In our battle with sin, are we called to wrestle, run, fight, and pray? Yes, we are,
but our hope is not in our ability to do these things, but in the God of grace, who
will war with sin until sin is no more. He never grows tired, never gets frustrated,
and never gives up. Now, that's hope!

For further study and encouragement: Titus 2:11–14

DECEMBER 21

Jesus willingly lived without an earthly home so that by grace we would be guaranteed a place in the Father's home forever.

It is an amazing story, one that becomes no less amazing with every retelling. The King of kings and Lord of lords leaves the splendor of glory to come to a shattered earth to suffer and die for self-oriented rebels. The Messiah is not born in a palace, but in a stable. He lives his life as a pilgrim, denied a small luxury even animals enjoy—a home (Matt. 8:20). He is despised and rejected, then subjected to a bloody and painful public crucifixion. And he does it all intentionally and willingly so that those rebels will be forgiven, so that those separated from God will have a home with him forever, and so that grace will be supplied to people in desperate need of it.

The words of the wonderful old Christmas hymn "Thou Didst Leave Thy Throne" capture so well the stunning contrast between Jesus's suffering and our resultant blessing:

> Thou didst leave Thy throne and Thy kingly crown,
> When Thou camest to earth for me;
> But in Bethlehem's home was there found no room
> For Thy holy nativity.

> Heaven's arches rang when the angels sang,
> Proclaiming Thy royal degree;
> But of lowly birth didst Thou come to earth,
> And in great humility.

> The foxes found rest, and the birds their nest
> In the shade of the forest tree;
> But Thy couch was the sod, O Thou Son of God,
> In the deserts of Galilee.

> Thou camest, O Lord, with the living Word,
> That should set Thy people free;
> But with mocking scorn and with crown of thorn,
> They bore Thee to Calvary.

> When the heav'ns shall ring, and her choirs shall sing,
> At Thy coming to victory,
> Let Thy voice call me home, saying "Yet there is room,
> There is room at My side for thee."

This Christmas, remember that you have an eternal home, because in amazing grace Jesus was willing to leave his home and have no home.

For further study and encouragement: Luke 9:57–62

DECEMBER 22

Jesus faced separation from his Father in the here and now so that we would know the Father's acceptance now and for all eternity.

Jesus knew what he was facing. He knew the price that needed to be paid. He knew what it would mean to stand in our place. He was quite aware of the spiritual math: suffering for a moment = acceptance for all of eternity. And he was willing.

A great moral tragedy was being played out every day in the lives of every person born into this sin-shattered world. Unlike anything else, God had created human beings in his image and for intimate, loving, and worshipful community with him. A relationship with him was to be the deepest, most influential motivation in their lives. It was meant to shape every thought, every desire, every word, and every action. And this community between God and people was meant to be unbroken forever and ever. But it had been broken in an outrageous act of rebellion and sedition. Not only had Adam and Eve stepped over God's clear boundaries, but also they had quested for his position. So in the saddest moment in human history, they had been driven out of the garden and away from God's presence.

From the vantage point of creation, it was all very unthinkable. People living separate from God? This was like fish without water, honey that is not sweet, or a sun that provides no heat. Not only did it defy the logic and design of creation, it could not work. Human beings were not hardwired to live independently. We were not made to function on our own and to live based on our own wisdom. We were not created to live by our own limited resources. We were made to live in a constant, life-giving connection to God. People's separation from God was a functional and moral disaster.

So this disaster had to be addressed. The tragic gap between God and man had to be bridged, and there was only one way. Jesus would have to come to earth as the second Adam and live a perfect life in our place. He would have to bear the punishment for our rebellion and endure the unthinkable—the Father's rejection. It happened at that horrible ninth hour on the day of his crucifixion, when, in a loud voice, he cried, "Eloi, Eloi, lema sabachthani?" ("My God, my God, why have you forsaken me?") (Mark 15:34). This was Jesus's most painful moment of anguish as he took on himself the tragedy of our separation from God.

This moment really was the epicenter of the Christmas story. It was why Jesus came. It was why the angels rejoiced at his coming. He came to be the temporarily separated Son so that we can be the eternally accepted children of God. Now, that's a story worth celebrating!

For further study and encouragement: John 12:27–36

DECEMBER 23

*Jesus endured human injustice in the here and now so that
we would be blessed with divine mercy for all eternity.*

Is it possible that the celebration of grace could collide more directly with the horror
of sin than at the birth of the baby Jesus?

> Now when [the wise men] had departed, behold, an angel of the Lord appeared
> to Joseph in a dream and said, "Rise, take the child and his mother, and flee
> to Egypt, and remain there until I tell you, for Herod is about to search for the
> child, to destroy him." And he rose and took the child and his mother by night
> and departed to Egypt and remained there until the death of Herod. This was to
> fulfill what the Lord had spoken by the prophet, "Out of Egypt I called my son."
>
> Then Herod, when he saw that he had been tricked by the wise men, be-
> came furious, and he sent and killed all the male children in Bethlehem and in
> all that region who were two years old or under, according to the time that he
> had ascertained from the wise men. Then was fulfilled what was spoken by the
> prophet Jeremiah:
>
> "A voice was heard in Ramah,
>   weeping and loud lamentation,
> Rachel weeping for her children;
>   she refused to be comforted, because they are no more."
>   (Matt. 2:13–18)

The Christmas story is this—that babe in the manger was the Son of the Most
High God. He willingly came to a place where such unthinkable violence and injustice exists. The wrath of the ruler would eventually fall on him. He would die a
violent death at the hands of evil men. Followers would weep that the Messiah was
dead, but he would rise again and complete the work that he came to earth to do.

As we sit beneath a beautifully decorated tree and eat the rich food of celebration, we must not let ourselves forget the horror and violence at the beginning and
end of the Christmas story. This story begins with a horrible slaughter of children
and ends with the violent murder of the Son of God. The slaughter depicts how
much the earth needs grace. The murder is the moment when that grace is given.

Look into that manger and see the One who came to die. Hear the angels' song
and remember that death would be the only way that peace would be given. Look
at your tree and remember another tree—one not decorated with shining orna-
ments, but stained with the blood of the Son of God. As you celebrate, remember
that the pathway to your celebration was the death of the One you celebrate, and
be thankful.

For further study and encouragement: 1 Peter 2:23–25

DECEMBER 24

*Jesus willingly entered the darkness so that we could
live in the light of his presence forever.*

In the beginning was the Word, and the Word was with God, and the Word was
God. He was in the beginning with God. All things were made through him,
and without him was not any thing made that was made. In him was life, and
the life was the light of men. The light shines in the darkness, and the darkness
has not overcome it.

There was a man sent from God, whose name was John. He came as a witness, to bear witness about the light, that all might believe through him. He was
not the light, but came to bear witness about the light.

The true light, which gives light to everyone, was coming into the world. He
was in the world, and the world was made through him, yet the world did not
know him. He came to his own, and his own people did not receive him. But to
all who did receive him, who believed in his name, he gave the right to become
children of God, who were born, not of blood nor of the will of the flesh nor of
the will of man, but of God.

And the Word became flesh and dwelt among us, and we have seen his glory,
glory as of the only Son from the Father, full of grace and truth. (John bore
witness about him, and cried out, "This was he of whom I said, 'He who comes
after me ranks before me, because he was before me.'") For from his fullness we
have all received, grace upon grace. For the law was given through Moses; grace
and truth came through Jesus Christ. No one has ever seen God; the only God,
who is at the Father's side, he has made him known. (John 1:1–18)

The Christmas story really is a light story. No, not the lights that decorate the
city where you live, the lights that you have carefully hung on the tree in your living
room, or the candles that you have placed in your windows. No, this story is about
the light coming into a world that had been sadly cast into darkness. Under the
burden of the shroud of rebellion and sin, the world had become a dark place. In
the darkness of immorality, injustice, violence, greed, self-righteousness, thievery,
racism, and a host of other ills, the world was desperate for light. Everyone was part
of the problem and everyone suffered from the problem, but no one could solve the
problem.

God's solution was the only way. He sent the One who is light to be the light
that would light the world by his grace. He came into the darkness so that we could
know light and life forever. Here is the Christmas story—only light can defeat the
darkness, and light has come!

For further study and encouragement: Isaiah 9

DECEMBER 25

*Jesus was despised and rejected in the here and now so that
you would have the Father's love and acceptance forever.*

The words you are about to read should be included in every celebration of Christmas. They express the glorious result of the coming of the Christ child to earth. He experienced the manger, the flight to Egypt, the daily suffering of hunger and homelessness, the rejection of the religious authorities, the disloyalty of the disciples, the unjust trial, the cruel death, and the tomb so that you would have what these words express. He came and endured all these things for you and me so that we would have forever what we never could have earned, deserved, or achieved on our own:

> What then shall we say to these things? If God is for us, who can be against us? He who did not spare his own Son but gave him up for us all, how will he not also with him graciously give us all things? Who shall bring any charge against God's elect? It is God who justifies. Who is to condemn? Christ Jesus is the one who died—more than that, who was raised—who is at the right hand of God, who indeed is interceding for us. Who shall separate us from the love of Christ? Shall tribulation, or distress, or persecution, or famine, or nakedness, or danger, or sword? As it is written,

> > "For your sake we are being killed all the day long;
> > we are regarded as sheep to be slaughtered."

> No, in all these things we are more than conquerors through him who loved us. For I am sure that neither death nor life, nor angels nor rulers, nor things present nor things to come, nor powers, nor height nor depth, nor anything else in all creation, will be able to separate us from the love of God in Christ Jesus our Lord. (Rom. 8:31–39)

Sit in front of your Christmas tree and read these words out loud to your loved ones so that you all will remember what the Christmas story is all about. Remember that Jesus willingly endured constant rejection and life-ending injustice so that you and I would experience the unalterable, unshakable, undefeatable love of God forever. Remember that he readily went unloved so that we would know constant love. Remember that he deserved to be loved, but was rejected so that we who deserve to be rejected would be eternally loved. Remember that he was willing to subject himself to the fickle and failing love of his followers so that we would know the faithful and unfailing love of the Father. Remember that he endured separation so that nothing could ever separate us from the Father's love.

As you remember these things, remember this: if God was willing to give up his Son so that we would know his love, doesn't it make sense that he will also with him give us everything else that we need? The promise of the Christmas story is unshakable love and every need met. Now, that's worth celebrating!

For further study and encouragement: John 10:1–18

DECEMBER 26

*Jesus endured suffering in the here and now so that
you and I could escape suffering for eternity.*

It didn't start with the cross; from the very first breath he took until he ascended, Jesus suffered:

- He suffered an uncomfortable and unsanitary birth in a stable.
- He suffered the terror of fleeing for his life as an infant.
- He suffered the trials of growing and learning as a boy.
- He suffered powerful temptation.
- He suffered exposure to disease.
- He suffered homelessness.
- He suffered hunger.
- He suffered sadness and grief.
- He suffered disloyalty and betrayal.
- He suffered physical pain.
- He suffered disrespect and mockery.
- He suffered misunderstanding and misrepresentation.
- He suffered the emotional pain of the rejection of his Father.
- He suffered punishment for the sins of others.
- He suffered injustice.
- He suffered violence.
- He suffered death.
- He suffered the full range of the hardships of life in this fallen world.

His calling, his mission, was to suffer, and suffer he did. His suffering was wide-ranging and constant. For the Messiah, suffering was an everyday thing, even a moment-by-moment thing. And every act of his suffering was substitutional. He suffered in our place. He suffered in every way we do so that he could be a Savior to us in our suffering and put an end to our suffering. He suffered every day so that there would be a time when all suffering would end and so that we could live with him in a world where suffering is no more.

He did not come to earth in regal splendor. He did not come to earth to live in a palace and be given homage as King. Although he was the King of kings, he came as a suffering servant who, in his suffering, would save us from ourselves and finally from our suffering. His suffering is our salvation. His suffering is our hope.

For further study and encouragement: Psalm 22

DECEMBER 27

Why give way to fear when, in Christ, it is impossible for you to ever be alone because you are now the temple in which God dwells?

It is far more than a "too good to be true" story. It is so amazing that it defies all normal human logic and intuition. It is the spiritual miracle of miracles that becomes the normal identity of all of God's blood-bought children by grace.

It is amazing enough that we are forgiven and accepted by God by grace and grace alone. There is nothing natural about this. We naturally think that we have to work our way into God's favor and earn our way into his presence, but the biblical story is anything but natural. It's the story of rebels who not only don't desire a relationship with God, but who could not possibly earn it even if they did. This is a story of divine intervention, of divine substitution, of divine sacrifice, and of divine grace. It is a story of God sending his Son to live as we were meant to live, to die the death that each of us deserves, to satisfy God's righteous requirement and placate his anger, and to rise out of the grave, conquering sin and death. It is a story of incredible patience, tenderness, compassion, love, mercy, and grace—forgiveness granted, acceptance secured, and righteousness given to those who could not have merited them on their own.

But as amazing as the grace of forgiveness and the acceptance of God are, there is still more amazing grace to this story. God knew that the dilemma of our sin was such a deep personal moral disaster that it was not enough to forgive us. That forgiveness should never be minimized, but God knew we needed more. He knew that after our forgiveness and acceptance, we would need daily help. He knew we would need rescue, strength, wisdom, and deliverance. So he didn't just forgive us. He didn't just accept us. He came to us and made us the place where he dwells. Paul says it well: "It is no longer I who live, but Christ lives in me" (Gal. 2:20). I don't think that we talk about this enough. I don't think that we celebrate this reality enough. I don't think we let our hearts consider the wonder of this identity enough. By grace, we are the temple of the Most High God. By grace, he lives in us. By grace, his power is at our disposal. By grace, he fights on our behalf even if we don't have the sense to do so. By grace, he works within us to complete the labor of grace that he has begun. By grace, he animates us to desire and do what is right. By grace, he exposes us and convicts us. We are able to choose and do what is right only because he lives in us and gives us the power to do so by his grace. He hasn't just forgiven us, he's taken up residence in us, and in that there is real hope.

For further study and encouragement: Ephesians 2:11–22

DECEMBER 28

Even pleasure preaches grace. Every day we all experience a symphony of pleasures we never could've earned the right to enjoy.

These are some of God's pleasant gifts to us:

- the sound of the birds in the spring
- the delicate beauty of a rose
- the multihued display of a sunset
- the pristine blanket of new-fallen snow
- the tenderness of a kiss
- the smell of flowers in bloom
- the wide variety of tastes and textures of food
- the glory of a wonderful piece of music
- the bright colors of leaves in the fall
- the enjoyment of a great drama
- the wonder of a master's painting
- the sweet voice of a child
- the stunning grandeur of a mountain

God created for us a world of amazing beauty where pleasures exist all around us. He created us with pleasure gates (eyes, ears, mouths, noses, hands, brains, and so on) so that we could take in the pleasure. He blesses us with these good and beautiful things every day. That means that on your very worst day and on your very best day, you are blessed with pleasures that come right from the hand of God. That tells you that you don't get these pleasures because you've earned or deserved them, but because he is a God of grace. He graces you with good things because he is good, not because you are.

Perhaps it's just a really good sandwich at lunch. You don't deserve the pleasure of that sandwich. You don't deserve a tongue that can take in its tastes and textures. You don't deserve a brain that can make sense of the whole experience. It is just another gift from the hands of God, who daily bestows on you what you do not deserve because he loves you. Maybe you look out your window and see that the leaves on your tree have turned fire red. The sight takes your breath away. Stop and be thankful that the God of amazing grace created that tree and your ability to see, understand, and enjoy it. He chose you to experience its pleasure at that moment because he is the God of tender, patient grace: "For he makes his sun rise on the evil and on the good, and sends rain on the just and on the unjust" (Matt. 5:45).

For further study and encouragement: Psalm 104

DECEMBER 29

Yes, change is possible, not because you have wisdom and strength, but because you've been blessed with the grace of Jesus.

You're not stuck. You're not encased in concrete. Your life is not a dead end. The possibility of change has not slipped through your fingers. Change is possible for you and me even in the places where change seems most hopeless. Why? Because the Giver of transformative grace has made you and me the place where he dwells!

If you were to ask what God is doing, what he is working on between the "already" of your justification and the "not yet" of your sanctification, the answer could be given in one word: *change.*

First, there is that work of personal growth and change the theologians call progressive sanctification. It is God's lifelong commitment to actually make me what he declared me to be in justification—righteous. In every situation, location, and relationship of my life, God is employing people, places, and things as his tools of transformative grace. He is not resting. He does not leave the work of his hands. He takes no breaks; he is relentlessly working to change me into all that his grace makes it possible for me to be. He will not be content for me to be a little bit better. He will work by grace until I am finally and totally free of sin, that is, molded into the image of his perfectly righteous Son.

This zealous Savior is also a dissatisfied Creator. He is not content to leave this world in its present sin-scarred condition. So there will come a day when he will make all things new. He will return his world to the condition it was in before sin left it so damaged. Change really is the zeal of your Redeemer. Personal change (Titus 2:11–14) and environmental change (Rev. 21:1–5) are his holy zeal. When you are disappointed in yourself, grieved at the sin in your relationships, or upset with the condition of your world and you cry out for change, you are crying for something that hits right at the center of the zeal of your Savior's grace.

Change doesn't mean that you'll get your wish list of things that you think will give you the good life. Change doesn't mean that God will turn the people around you into the people you'd like them to be. And change surely doesn't mean that God will exercise his power to make life easier and more pleasurable according to your definition. But you can rest assured that where real change is needed, there is a God of grace who knows just where that change needs to take place and offers you everything you need so that it can happen.

For further study and encouragement: Colossians 3:1–17

DECEMBER 30

One of the themes of this devotional is hope. Every human being is hardwired for and concerned about hope. We're all in a constant search for hope that delivers and lasts. We're all a bit discouraged and paralyzed when our hopes are dashed. When one hope dies, we grab hold of another hope as fast as we can.

The Bible is a hope story. It is about hope misplaced and hope found. It's about hope that cannot deliver and hope that gives you everything that you need. It's about where not to look for hope and the only place where true hope can be found. The great hope drama of the Bible is summarized by a few very important words that are buried in the middle of the apostle Paul's letter to the Romans:

> Therefore, since we have been justified by faith, we have peace with God through our Lord Jesus Christ. Through him we have also obtained access by faith into this grace in which we stand, and we rejoice in hope of the glory of God. Not only that, but we rejoice in our sufferings, knowing that suffering produces endurance, and endurance produces character, and character produces hope, and hope does not put us to shame, because God's love has been poured into our hearts through the Holy Spirit who has been given to us. (Rom. 5:1–5)

Notice what Paul does here:

- *He connects our hope to our justification.* We have hope because, by grace, we have been forgiven and accepted by the One who holds everything we need.
- *He connects our hope to the glory of God.* Our hope is that God will complete his work, getting the glory that is his due. His glory is our good.
- *He connects our hope to our sufferings.* There is even hope in suffering because in that suffering the God who is our hope is doing good things in us and for us.
- *He says that our vertical hope (hope in God) will never put us to shame.* This means that all other forms of hope fail us in some way. Hope in created things never delivers what hope in the Creator can.
- *He connects our hope to the Holy Spirit who lives inside us.* Here is the ultimate reason that you and I have hope—God has made us the address where he lives. This means that the One who can do more than we are able to conceive of is constantly with us and constantly working on our behalf.

Now, that's hope! As you worship God with other believers and hear the truths of his Word proclaimed, your hope will be rekindled.

For further study and encouragement: Hebrews 6:9–20

DECEMBER 31

God's work in you is a process, not an event. It progresses not in three or four huge moments, but in ten thousand little moments of change.

Well, it's that season once again. It's the fodder for blogs, newspaper articles, TV magazine shows, and far too many Twitter posts. It is the time for the annual ritual of dramatic New Year's resolutions fueled by the hope of immediate and significant personal life change.

But the reality is that few smokers have actually quit because of a single moment of resolve. Few obese people have become slim and healthy because of one dramatic moment of commitment. Few people who were deeply in debt have changed their financial lifestyles because they resolved to do so as the old year gave way to the new. And few marriages have been changed by means of one dramatic resolution.

Is change important? Yes, it is important for all of us in some way. Is commitment essential? Of course! In various ways, all our lives are shaped by the commitments we make. But growth in grace—which has the gospel of Jesus Christ at its heart—simply doesn't rest its hope on big, dramatic moments of change.

The fact of the matter is that the transforming work of grace is more of a mundane process than a series of a few dramatic events. Personal heart and life change is always a process. And where does that process take place? It takes place where you and I live every day. And where do we live? Well, we all have the same address. Our lives don't lurch from big moment to big moment. No, we all live in the utterly mundane.

Most of us won't be written up in history books. Most of us will make only three or four momentous decisions in our lives, and several decades after we die, the people we leave behind will struggle to remember the things we did. You and I live in little moments, and if God doesn't rule our little moments and doesn't work to re-create us in the middle of them, then there is no hope for us.

The little moments of life are profoundly important precisely because they are the little moments that we live in and that form us. This is where I think "Big Drama Christianity" gets us into trouble. It can cause us to devalue the significance of the little moments of life and the "small-change" grace that meets us there. And because we devalue the little moments in which we live, we tend not to notice the sin that gets exposed there. We fail to seek the grace that is offered to us. You see, the character of a life is not set in two or three dramatic moments, but in ten thousand little moments. The character that is formed in those little moments shapes how we respond to the big moments of life. And what makes all of this character change possible? Relentless, transforming, little-moment grace. So we wake up each day committed to live in the small moments of our daily lives with open eyes and humble, expectant hearts.

For further study and encouragement: John 1:16

SCRIPTURE INDEX

PERSONAL NOTES

PERSONAL NOTES

_____

_____

_____

_____

_____

_____

_____

_____

_____

_____

_____

_____

_____

_____

_____

_____

_____

_____

_____

_____

_____

_____

_____

_____

_____

PERSONAL NOTES

PERSONAL NOTES

PERSONAL NOTES

PERSONAL NOTES

PERSONAL NOTES

PERSONAL NOTES

PERSONAL NOTES

PERSONAL NOTES

PERSONAL NOTES

PERSONAL NOTES

PERSONAL NOTES

PERSONAL NOTES

PERSONAL NOTES

PERSONAL NOTES

PERSONAL NOTES

PERSONAL NOTES

PERSONAL NOTES